ADVANCE PRAISE FOR
MUSEUM EDUCATION FOR TODAY'S AUDIENCE:
MEETING EXPECTATIONS WITH NEW MODELS

"Jason L. Porter and Mary Kay Cunningham and their authors have done the impossible—they've captured the fast-changing museum education landscape AND projected to the future. This book's case studies demonstrate how sophisticated museum teaching has become, drawing upon audience research and learning theory without sacrificing creativity or joy. Through highly readable prose, the authors address challenges, issues, and opportunities that museums face today, offering ideas, models, and solutions to practitioners. The chapters can be read in any order; it's easy to choose because each starts with an abstract. Many end with reflections about 'what we've learned,' making reading feel like a conversation with friends." —**Cynthia Robinson**, editor-in-chief, *Journal of Museum Education*, and Tufts University Museum Studies Program Director

"An astutely curated collection of essays by a selection of profound thought leaders across the field. Filled with kernels (and entire cornfields) of wisdom and timely provocations. This is an important anthology for practitioners and leaders at all levels who seek to uplift equitable and artful informal educational practices." —**Ben Garcia**, deputy executive director and chief learning officer, Ohio History Connection

"*Museum Education for Today's Audience* is an incredible tool that goes beyond program ideas to provide insight on lessons learned by practitioners that are decentering systemic exclusion. More importantly, this book provides the spark for reflective practice to support continued innovation to meet the needs of all learners and increased self-awareness for museum educators." —**Dr. Chris Taylor**, chief inclusion officer, State of Minnesota

"Amidst an intense moment of crisis and upheaval, this practical and hope-filled collection of writings can guide museum educators—and the entire museum field—into a new future. All of the contributors to this important book make clear the vital role of museum education in leading the transformation needed right now within our institutions." —**Mike Murawski**, consultant and author of *Museums as Agents of Change: A Guide to Becoming a Changemaker*

"*Museum Education for Today's Audiences* is equal parts manifesto on the power and potential of museums who center community needs and interests, and handbook for the education staff who have championed and led this work for decades." —**Kelly McKinley**, CEO, Bay Area Discovery Museum

Museum Education
for Today's Audiences

AMERICAN ALLIANCE OF MUSEUMS

The American Alliance of Museums has been bringing museums together since 1906, helping to develop standards and best practices, gathering and sharing knowledge, and providing advocacy on issues of concern to the entire museum community. Representing more than 35,000 individual museum professionals and volunteers, institutions, and corporate partners serving the museum field, the Alliance stands for the broad scope of the museum community.

The American Alliance of Museums' mission is to champion museums and nurture excellence in partnership with its members and allies.

Books published by AAM further the Alliance's mission to make standards and best practices for the broad museum community widely available.

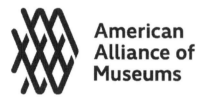

Museum Education for Today's Audiences

MEETING EXPECTATIONS WITH NEW MODELS

EDITED BY

Jason L. Porter and Mary Kay Cunningham

ROWMAN & LITTLEFIELD
Lanham • Boulder • New York • London

Published by Rowman & Littlefield
A wholly owned subsidiary of The Rowman & Littlefield Publishing Group, Inc.
4501 Forbes Boulevard, Suite 200, Lanham, Maryland 20706
www.rowman.com

86-90 Paul Street, London EC2A 4NE

British Library Cataloguing in Publication Information Available

Library of Congress Cataloging-in-Publication Data

Names: Porter, Jason L., editor. | Cunninham, Mary Kay, editor. | American Alliance of Museums.
Title: Museum education for today's audiences : meeting expectations with new models / edited by
    Jason L. Porter and Mary Kay Cunningham.
Description: Lanham : Rowman & Littlefield, [2021] | Includes bibliographical references and index.
Identifiers: LCCN 2021038252 (print) | LCCN 2021038253 (ebook) | ISBN 9781538148594 (cloth) |
    ISBN 9781538148600 (paperback) | ISBN 9781538148617 (ebook)
Subjects: LCSH: Museums—Educational aspects. | Museums and community—United States. |
    Museums—Social aspects—United States. | Multicultural education.
Classification: LCC AM7 .M863 2021 (print) | LCC AM7 (ebook) | DDC 069.071—dc23
LC record available at https://lccn.loc.gov/2021038252
LC ebook record available at https://lccn.loc.gov/2021038253

∞™ The paper used in this publication meets the minimum requirements of American National Standard for Information Sciences—Permanence of Paper for Printed Library Materials, ANSI/NISO Z39.48-1992.

To my colleagues and former colleagues. I'm certain I would never have gotten here without you.

To my partner in this endeavor, Mary Kay. It is so rare that a great idea you have with a friend actually comes to pass. I attribute this project's existence largely to your dedication, wisdom, and passion.

And to Mark, who always reminds me to lift up my sails.

Jason L. Porter

To Jason:

When I chose this profession I had no idea that I'd meet colleagues that would become dear friends and mentors (or, as you call them, "frien-tors"). I never imagined I would share professional interests so deeply with a colleague that I'd embark on a several year journey to create a book that elevates voices about important issues in our field.

Unfortunately, I also could not have foreseen that several members of my family would become ill and caring for them while desperately trying to sustain my own mental health during a global pandemic would profoundly impact my capacity to equitably share the work of shepherding this book across the finish line.

Luckily, there is one thing I do know: Having a friend and colleague like you is a gift beyond measure. This book may have been inspired by our shared passion and vision, but it was your determination and extraordinary commitment that has made it a reality. It is hard to know if a book can change the field, but people like you most certainly do.

Mary Kay Cunningham

Contents

Preface

This book is not exactly the book we set out to write. When we pitched this project in the fall of 2019—a book for practitioners that would provide practical tools and strategies for meeting the needs of twenty-first-century visitors—we didn't know anything about social distancing. We had yet to don our first N95 masks and we had yet to attend a museum program populated not by eager crowds but by faces in Zoom boxes. During the early part of 2020, we assembled a cadre of writers whose work we admired, and who were thinking in innovative and creative ways about museum education in the twenty-first century. Some were people we had worked with previously, some were people we'd seen only from afar at conferences, others were people we admired for their writing (or their Twitter posts), but whom we didn't know. Their work for which we knew them was based in museum education practice during times when groups gathered in the galleries, when students attended courses in school buildings, and when most of us commuted to offices, cubicles, and museum classrooms to do our work. Then everything changed.

CONTEXT FOR THE BOOK

In early March of 2020, museums (and most other businesses and organizations) shut their doors, travel slowed to a standstill, and our usual interactions with visitors and with each other migrated online because of the COVID-19 pandemic. The anxiety about the moment, for reasons that included physical, financial, emotional, and other worries, rose to a collective hum that drowned out any sense of normalcy. The question of whether museums would be able to do much of the work that the authors were discussing in their proposed chapters seemed anything but certain, and we considered whether it made sense to engage in the process of writing and publishing at all.

Then in May, police officers in Minneapolis killed George Floyd, which ignited protests and amplified calls for action across the world for dismantling institutionalized racism in law enforcement, government, and other community organizations. As trusted civic institutions, many museums were called on to respond to racial injustice (by their audiences and by members of their staff). How to address equity and inclusion in the field (and contribute in meaningful ways to activism and civic engagement in their regions) became an urgent topic for institutions in the field at large—for institutions from science centers to historic homes to art museums. And for many of these organizations, being closed to visitors further challenged how and in what formats they could communicate with their communities in authentic ways (and take actual steps to address systemic racism). This confluence of events in and out of the field caused us and our authors to question whether what they were originally planning to write had relevance in light of a moment that appeared as an upheaval and recalibrating of the field.

As the summer of 2020 wore on, and it became clear that the conversations about the need for change within museums would not be resolved by statements of solidarity or actions that fell well short of a true dismantling of existing power structures, the campaign for the U.S. president ramped up and brought an added level of rancor to our national discourse. Issues of importance to cultural institutions such as immigration, civil rights, and education were topics of political conversations that didn't reflect effort toward honest dialogue and solutions but instead divisive political sloganeering. This heightened environment of partisanship and uncertainty impacted many authors who, in discussion of topics like critical race theory, civic engagement, and informed facilitation of dialogue with visitors, felt like they needed to frame their chapters in somewhat different terms than they'd initially planned.

At its core, this book asserts a central tenet about the importance of museum educators, who, the authors argue throughout, are best poised to meet the needs of visitors in the twenty-first century. The role of the educator (or interpreter) continues to evolve as audiences diversify, as technology becomes more central to the gallery experience and to alternative modes of content, as knowledge about how people learn—individually and in groups—shifts, and as museums embrace the role of facilitating dialogue about contemporary issues that matter to our communities. We hope that this perspective about educators doesn't come off as devaluing other aspects of museum work or as elevating educators to some vaunted place that presumes they alone can ensure that museums will thrive in the future. But as we have seen during the pandemic, museum educators are essential to maintaining connections with visitors through the programs, content development, and conversations that they uniquely have expertise in executing. We believe this connection to the public represents a core function of the museum and thus is an important area to focus on with respect to preparing museums to meet the challenges of the future. This book argues that educators, using a multiplicity of methods and approaches, will lead museums into the future.

Museum education can often be a challenging and isolating experience, and it is not uncommon for interpreters at one institution to feel disconnected from the field at large and limited in their abilities to explore new ways of approaching their work, to keep up-to-date on issues and practices across the field, and to follow the latest research and academic study. Our hope is that museum educators, managers, academics, museum studies and informal education students, and those interested in strategies for working with visitors at diverse institutional types will find this collection of ideas and strategies useful to their work.

Although there have been other books that discuss the methods and the philosophical underpinnings of museum education, none of those have been written to specifically address the changing nature of audiences in the twenty-first century and the ways in which museum interpretation can further the issues the field is grappling with: access, equity, adaptive technology, decolonization, diversified visitorship, and civic participation. This book will dive deeply into many of the most urgent issues facing twenty-first-century educators and provide ideas, strategies, and models to transform practice.

HOW THE BOOK IS ORGANIZED

When we thought about the most useful way to structure this book, given that we wanted it to be as useful as possible to practitioners, we thought in terms of storytelling, something familiar to us as educators and museum interpreters. In the first part of this book's story, we invited authors to discuss who museum visitors are in the twenty-first century, what they expect from museum experiences, and how interactions with educators are evolving based on their needs and curiosities. This section, titled "Changing Expectations of Visitors: Inclusion, Participation, Technology," serves as the first act of the story, a setting of the scene and establishing of characters. This section opens with a case study, written by Enrico G. Castillo, Hallie Scott, and Theresa Sotto, about a partnership between an art museum and a medical school training for psychiatric students that uses museum education techniques to discuss bias and cultural competency in the medical field. The next chapter, written by Veronica Alvarez, Elizabeth Gerber, Sarah Jencks, and Catherine Awsumb Nelson, shares two ambitious case studies that respond to changing needs of the student and teacher audience. They discuss a gallery space operated and utilized by a museum and its staff of educators in conjunction with a local public school and an in-depth program for teachers focused on oratory at a historic theater. These chapters provide ideas for embedding museum practice in work with audiences and argue for a shift in thinking from the perspective that museum experiences are enrichment to encouraging a long-term investment in transformation and deep learning with audiences.

This section continues with Beth Redmond-Jones discussing an innovative partnership between a group of young adults on the ASD spectrum who worked with museums in Balboa Park, San Diego, to create "social stories" that were used by other visitors with sensory needs to help support their visits. This type of innovative "shared authority" provides a model for working collaboratively with audiences that have typically been left out of partnerships that specifically address the needs of visitors with sensory disabilities. The final chapter in this section of the book, written by Mark Osterman, provides a rationale and lays out a step-by-step approach to creating dynamic and effective digital learning plans for museums, something that has become essential during the pandemic.

The second section of the book, titled "Training and Educator Preparation," addresses the middle of the story, where a lot of the action of readying educators to work with audiences takes place. In this section, written by Mac Buff, we begin with a discussion of the needs of LGBTIA+ visitors (and staff and volunteers) and how museums can best prepare their education teams to work inclusively with members of a community that have often felt erased or ignored by museums. The second chapter, by Anna Schwarz and Rachel Stark, is a case study of one museum's approach to adapt one of its core in-person school programs to virtual during the pandemic and the ways in which their educators took advantage of the otherwise challenging circumstances to expand and broaden civic engagement. The next chapter addresses the particular needs of family audiences. Scott Pattison and Smirla Ramos-Montanez use the research they conducted at a science center to discuss the unique approaches to facilitation that museum educators can take to effectively work with groups of diverse learners. To address educator preparation, the next chapter looks at the current state of academic preparation through conversations with active faculty and administrators of museum studies graduate and certificate programs. The fifth chapter in this section, by Lorie Millward, presents an innovative approach to the structure of education and interpretive departments, arguing that through new structures, we can provide educators with the pedagogy, training, and autonomy that are key to effective visitor learning. And in the final chapter in this section, Beth Maloney breaks the notion of professional development for museum educators wide open with a new model for thinking about skill building, networking, and mentorship, and expanding the perspectives of education staff.

For the third section of the book, the part of the story in which we look to the future, we wanted to present a number of ideas that would push conversations about museum education into new and unexpected places. These chapters, in a section titled "New Models, Anticipating the Future," suggest new ways to think about the practice of museum education, suggesting how museums can shift structurally and philosophically to new expectations of visitors, new challenges to the old ways museums do things, and to our latest understanding of how people learn. The first in this section, by Teresa Valencia, argues that museum educators need to have fluency with cultural competency to undo decades of structural racism in museums. She provides foundational research on culturally competent practice as well as suggestions for creating training programs and resources for museum educators. The next chapter looks at children's learning in museums with a particular focus on play-based, self-directed learning. This case study by Tomoko Kuta, explores how a children's museum collaborates with artists on installations that position educators as facilitators of the self-directed learning experiences of young visitors and their families. The third chapter by Julie Smith applies a systems thinking approach to educational design and suggests ways to improve the way educators solve structural problems as a pathway to improving visitor learning.

One often overlooked aspect of museum education is brain science. When was the last time you considered what happens in the brain as you planned an educational museum experience? Jayatri Das and Mickey Maley explain the way learning happens in the brain, dispel myths and misconceptions about cognitive science, and suggest ways in which museum experiences can be crafted to get synapses firing, engage memory-making centers, and balance sensory stimulation for visitors. The next chapter, by Melanie Adams and Kayleigh Bryant-Greenwell, presents ideas for transformative museum work by applying the practice of Critical Race Theory. It provides a case study of one museum that has transformed its approach to exhibits, programs, and education by utilizing CRT as an underpinning methodology. This shift has led to a whole new level of community involvement and collaboration, a core value at one particular museum. The sixth chapter in this section looks back at the impact of the pandemic on museum education. Based on a study undertaken in the first six months after lockdown, Juline Chevalier analyzes the impact of the closures, of social distancing and mask wearing, and the pivot to digital programming and considers how these changes will impact the field long-term. Finally, Lauren Zalut and Sean Kelley of Eastern State Penitentiary share their journey transforming their interpretive strategy, incorporating formerly incarcerated people into their education team and moving away from prison history interpretation to a focus on the inequities and racism of our prison system.

USING THIS BOOK IN YOUR PRACTICE

While the chapters in this book are informed by theory and research, we asked the authors to think of practitioners as its main audience. We wanted this book to be full of practical tools that could be adapted to a variety of museum settings and contexts, so the authors have taken the elements of their case studies or their programs and extrapolated their takeaways to other settings so they could be applied in a variety of settings. Chapters were written to provide deep dives into each topic and to spur thinking about practice rather than to depend upon one another as part of one linear narrative, so feel free to read the book cover-to-cover, select just the chapters that interest or apply to you, or source them when you need them to share with colleagues in other departments. Our intention was to create a collection of chapters that would provide inspiration for thinking about how to apply these ideas directly to practice. In that interest, the authors have included tables, photographs, diagrams, and plans that we encourage readers to examine and adapt for their own purposes. Look for these and other resources on the website that accompanies this book (www.evolvemuseumed.com) as well as discussion questions at the end of each chapter to probe your thinking about the topics. These questions can be used to frame discussions you have as you read specific chapters with your colleagues or classmates or book club or as part of your own self-examination related to the topics covered in each chapter.

Editing and writing this book during the pandemic posed a number of challenges. In her chapter about how she transformed the structure of her education team, Lorie Millward states a maxim that "change is constant," and this phrase sums up the process of putting this book together during an especially tumultuous time. A number of the authors that we approached early on were laid off during the pandemic (or saw their responsibilities increase as other museum workers around them were let go). Many struggled to balance life, work, and writing while their entire families were stuck at home. Still others felt compelled to prioritize their activism and organizing over writing a chapter during a particularly politically charged year.

This is all to say that there are topics that are essential to the discussion of the future of museum education that are absent from this book. There is no chapter on docent teaching or on working with virtual reality or engaging teens. There is no chapter specific to decolonizing education and programs or one on innovative forms of evaluation. And there are voices missing as well—frontline educators, museum workers living with disabilities, classroom teachers, zoo and aquarium educators—which would have furthered the reach and representation of topics in this book. What is certain is that given the complexity of museum education and the people who work within the discipline, the number of chapter topics and voices we could have included far outweighs what we have. This, perhaps, is in part, a testament to the fact that museum education is neither static nor uniform; it is responsive to sociocultural factors, to current events and trends, and to the ongoing churn of new research and new theories. There is much to learn from what is here, and as educators are so adept at doing, we invite you to take inspiration and tools and structures you read about here and find ways to use them in your own work.

Our goal is that this convening of authors, however incomplete, will serve as the beginning of an ongoing project, started decades ago by our museum elders and educational practitioners, of creating a community of learners who will remain engaged in conversation and reflection about practice well into the future. This book scratches the surface, but it is up to all of us who are invested in the field of museum education and its people to continue to dive deeper.

Acknowledgments

This book represents the work of a group of accomplished and brilliant museum and arts educators, researchers, and administrators. We owe a debt of gratitude to each of them for writing about their work during a time of anxiousness and uncertainty. All of them experienced challenges during the writing period for this book, and the fact that each of them managed to articulate a future-looking vision of museum education at a time when things often seemed so bleak, is a testament to their passion for their work and their resilience. Writing a chapter of a book like this does not have many tangible rewards, so their belief in this project, their fortitude to persist with the work they write about, and their desire to share their insights as a part of this book are qualities we'll always be grateful for.

We never would have taken on a project like this if we had not participated in extracurricular activities across the field for a long time. Both of us have had the good fortune to be exposed to a number of professional networks that provided us with opportunities to meet incredible people. These relationships, built over time at conferences, on panels, via special projects, and through connections made through our friends and colleagues, have inspired us to think about our own work and dig deeper into practice. This inspiration led directly to the two of us meeting in Los Angeles, working on a project in San Diego, then having regular phone calls about staff training and educational pedagogy, and later to a few glasses of Prosecco in Portland and a couple of bowls of spaghetti and meatballs in Las Vegas, and finally, to conceiving of and pitching this book. Without members of the American Alliance of Museums and EdCom (AAM's education professional network), the Western Museum Association, Museum Next, the Association of Science and Technology Centers, and the Journal of Museum Education, we would never have had the audacity to think we could assemble such a supergroup of authors to write this book. For us, these professional development opportunities have provided entry into a community of practitioners that has proved valuable both personally and professionally, and this project would never have come about without the support of that community.

Professional friendships, especially among museum educators, have always been special to both of us; our colleagues get us, they speak our language, they feel our feels. They always show a willingness to share resources, to process frustrations and problem-solve challenges, to celebrate accomplishments, and to help us stay motivated to do this work, day after day. We are indebted to these colleagues for their years of support and encouragement. At the risk of inadvertently leaving someone out, we wanted to specifically recognize a few colleagues who—knowingly or unknowingly—shaped, challenged, and/or supported this specific endeavor, including (but not limited to): Cynthia Robinson, Gretchen Sorin, Jessica Luke, Brian Hogarth, Susan Spero, Gregory Stevens, Lotte Lent, Carol Stapp, Dina Bailey, Tony Pennay, Gail Andersen, Mike Murawski, Robert Rutherford, Regan Pro, Cynthia Taylor, Ben Garcia, Sondra Snyder, Kelly McKinley, Wendy Ng, Brandie Macdonald, Abigail Diaz, Sheri Bernstein, and Wendy Abelmann.

Thanks also go to the team at Rowman & Littlefield whose guidance and support was both hands-off and extremely hands-on (appropriately so and at the right moments) and helped us to shape this project and not just edit it. We still marvel that our proposal was accepted, so we deeply appreciate the leap of faith to trust us in bringing this book to fruition. Charles Harmon and Erinn Slanina were a pleasure to work with on this project. Apologies for all the thousands of questions.

We also owe tremendous thanks to our families and friends. Editing a book during a pandemic meant the dogs, kids, and parents were always with us in our offices, workout rooms, kitchens, living rooms, and so forth, seemingly at all times. Our spouses and families were extremely supportive, despite these conditions, sometimes by going to the store themselves, sometimes by just clearing out of the house, other times by forcing us to close our laptops (or on occasion forcing us to open them), and frequently by inviting us to go outside for walks. All of these small acts of kindness allowed us to come back to this book and keep going. Mark, Dan, Wyatt, and Karen—this project could not have been completed without your support and love.

Finally, as two educators, we are naturally collaborative people; we like to take on group projects, we get jazzed by brainstorming on a whiteboard with a whole team, we light up when we co-teach a gallery experience, and we love to talk shop. As a result, we often call on the educators we've worked alongside for ideas, for support, for validation and inspiration, for truth-telling, and when things get rough, for compassion. There are too many of you to name here, but both of our careers have been shaped by the amazing colleagues with whom we have worked.

This book came about because of a conversation we had as we were both immersed in working directly with museum educators on training, skill-building, and program development. These educators led history tours, facilitated activities at science carts, sang and danced at a children's museum, worked alongside docents to teach school children, and zoomed into classrooms to teach about architecture. Their desire for new ideas, for opportunities to experiment, for deep dives into content, for trust in being creative and passionate and political, spurred our thinking about what museum educators in the twenty-first century need and want to make their work in this field have impact. They serve the public, educate children, teach the history, science, and culture so many people take for granted, tell the truth (even when people don't want to listen), and they create experiences that make people want to visit museums. It is our fellow educators that have furthered our thinking about practice and challenged us to reconsider the needs of the audience. They have encouraged us to experiment with new technologies and to establish much bolder visions of inclusion. It is educators who have remained connected with our audiences through the pandemic when many of us were shut out of our beloved museum spaces. We owe educators as much knowledge and vision as we can muster, because if there continue to be visitors in the twenty-first century (and we sincerely hope there will), it will be educators who will be there to make the experience worthwhile. This book is for them.

Introduction

PRACTICING RESILIENCE IN MOMENTS OF CHANGE

Dina A. Bailey, CEO, Mountain Top Vision

Change is a constant. Everything changes all the time. Some seasons of change cause barely notice-able twinges, and others are so seismic that we may never regain our footing. These moments of flux might bring joy, belonging, love, creativity, sorrow, anger, frustration, and/or fear. Change might be experienced individually and/or collectively; it might even be experienced globally. This book is being published as we live through one such season of change, a moment where the rippling effects are being felt in every part of the world—and within every part of ourselves. Regardless of the pandemics' shifting epicenters, as those also seem to have changed multiple times, human beings across the world have found themselves participants in multiple interrelated, interdependent, and indivisible pandemics that will forever change how people live and work. In the United States, these dual pan-demics—namely COVID-19 and racism—have changed how we understand what we find relevant; what we find valuable; what we want to hold tightly to; and, ultimately, what we are willing to sacrifice not just for ourselves, but for others.

There is a broad spectrum when it comes to how the pandemics have impacted the museum field within the United States. Individual communities have unique relationships with their local in-stitutions when it comes to the intersectional impacts of health, race, class, economics, education, and politics—to name a few. From a thirty thousand-foot view, there are certainly aspects that cross all of our communities and have caused both alarming trends as well as optimistic ones; at the same time, the historical and contemporary complexities of each museum's space within the context of the communities it participates in must be taken into consideration. How museums were showing up in the "before times" has certainly affected the resiliency they have shown in the present season.

When did this season begin? Museums have become increasingly more vulnerable as the twen-ty-first century has progressed. As the world has become more accessible because of technology, transportation, media, and so forth, museum visitors have brought a diversity of lived experiences, backgrounds, knowledge, insights, and biases with them. Expectations have shifted as inequities are laid bare. And, museums—and their staff—have been under increasing scrutiny to be more representative, more equitable, and more transparent in their truth-telling. Neutrality is impossible and bias is inescapable.

Some museums have just now begun to see more clearly their vulnerabilities (and responsibili-ties) within various systems of power. Other museums have sensed their vulnerabilities but haven't strongly grasped onto opportunities to build a practice of resilience. Yet others have been intentionally acting in resilient ways for decades. In reality, resilience isn't a linear process for museums; it is not an identity marker that a museum can proudly display like a certification. In this way, I am considering resilience as a verb (though it is also a noun); it is something that we must continue to practice and consciously nurture. That practice and nurturing is often heavily influenced by external pressures (like the bubbles and busts of the economy) and internal pressures (like the mindsets of executive teams and board members). We are continuously moving back and forth along a spectrum.

As museum finances and funding have been affected by various social, political, and economic ripples, museum boards and executive staff have made decisions about what to stop, start, and continue. Sometimes decisions have been made in *response* to pressure; many more times, those decisions have been made in *reaction* to pressure. A reaction is almost instantaneous; it is driven by beliefs, biases, and prejudices of the unconscious mind.[1]

Reactions are based in the moment and don't leave space to consider the long-term effects of a decision; they are essentially defense mechanisms focused on immediate survival. Responses may also be quickly made but are generally a bit slower and take into account information from both one's conscious and unconscious mind; they take into account you, those around you, and the long-term effects of the decision you are making. Responses more often stay in line with your core values while reactions may be more centered in fear, bypassing your values in a need to fight for survival—whether that fight is perception- or reality-based.[2] Practicing resilience shows up in being responsive; it is hampered every time we react.

Museum educators have always been at the forefront of moments of change. That doesn't mean that we, as a whole, have always been the change-makers. We are human; we, too, have been known to swing between reaction and response, between gate-keeping and bridge-building, between implicit bias and radical empathy. That said, as the director of museum experiences at the National Underground Railroad Freedom Center; as the inaugural director of educational strategies at the National Center for Civil and Human Rights; as the director of methodology and practice at the International Coalition of Sites of Conscience, as the current chair of the American Alliance of Museums' Education Committee (AAM EdCom); and, as a consultant who has worked with over seventy-five museums and cultural organizations domestically and internationally, I can tell you emphatically that it is a *deep honor* to identify as a museum educator. Identifying in this way does not necessarily mean that you have a title that incorporates "education" specifically. I, personally, welcome into the fold all who authentically and deeply embrace the work of education within the depth, breadth, and complexity of our museum spaces.

Museum educators are often the first to embrace challenges as opportunities, to take conflict and transition it into a teachable moment, to figure out ways to experiment and innovate regardless of how few or how many resources we have at the time. We can scaffold complex concepts for multiple ages and abilities because we recognize that certain ages or abilities don't directly connect to making an experience "better" or "worse." We truly believe that curiosity can lead to knowledge, knowledge can lead to empathy, and empathy can lead to positive actions that will change the world. We work in a diversity of institutional types and spaces and we, by-and-large, inspire cross-pollination through communities of practice. We often start organizational ripples by grappling with what it means to be diverse, equitable, accessible, inclusive, decolonized, and antiracist—not just as individuals, but as individuals who comprise institutions. And, as institutions that uphold the nation's public trust.

As the world continues to shift, technology and cognitive science are providing new insights for museum education staff in terms of how to effectively engage at the intersection of learning and audience(s). We must consider the current expectations that our visitors are bringing with them; these expectations will affect our own professional development and the co-creation of successful models for future learning. As we consider both our audiences and their expectations, cultural competency, relevancy, reciprocal practice, partnership, and universal design all come to mind as necessary to successfully laying the foundation for the new educational models we are co-creating. As we move from the foundation to the framing, our models will be more resilient (in weathering change) if we incorporate intergenerational learning, civic engagement, and lived experiences into the ways that

Dina A. Bailey

we empower educators—ourselves and teachers more broadly—to practice growth mindsets, encourage flexibility and nimbleness, and support continuous learning across the professional life cycle of a museum educator—from wherever they may enter. From grad students to emerging museum professionals, from seasoned staff members to those on the verge of retiring, we must become even more adept at anticipating the future and "filling in" our frameworks in ways that complement both the present and the future of museum education. These new models depend on building bridges, leveraging human-centered design, and improving practices for equitable engagement and inclusion.

You will read more about laying the foundation, building the framework, and filling in the details of educational models throughout the rest of this exceptional book. The contributors have melded theory and practical application in ways that will support both how you think and the actions you take moving forward. I appreciate being able to directly name some of the challenges of our present *and* point toward multiple opportunity pathways for our collective future. As we progress through the twenty-first century, I must say that I never thought that I would see so much engagement in virtual museum spaces, so many successful online professional development opportunities, such a massive shake up of museum executives (and museums more broadly), and such generosity through mutual aid networks. That said, I also didn't expect to see such tightening of control, such reactive decisions, or so many people leaving the field (or considering leaving the field) due to untenable staff experiences. We have much work to do.

I wish you the best on this particular educational journey and feel confident in the future knowing that there are museum educators like you out there in the present! May we each find ways to embrace seasons of change, practice resilience, support moments and movements, and honor the endearing (and enduring!) complexities of the positions that we hold as museum educators.

NOTES

1. James, Matt. "React vs. Respond: What's the Difference?" *Psychology Today* (blog), September 1, 2016, https://www.psychologytoday.com/us/blog/focus-forgiveness/201609/react-vs-respond.
2. James, Matt. "React vs. Respond: What's the Difference?" *Psychology Today* (blog), September 1, 2016, https://www.psychologytoday.com/us/blog/focus-forgiveness/201609/react-vs-respond.

Part I

Changing Expectations of Visitors: Inclusion, Participation, Technology

1

Building Community and Structural Competency through Art

AN ART MUSEUM AND PSYCHIATRY PARTNERSHIP

Enrico G. Castillo, Hallie Scott, and Theresa Sotto

ABSTRACT

Several museums across the country have long-running partnerships with medical schools that are aimed at enhancing medical skills through the observation of art. In recent years, however, pioneering medical education programs have foregrounded the need for medical professionals to develop expertise in the structural determinants of health—legislation, institutional policies, neighborhood characteristics, distribution of social resources—so as to better comprehend and address the root causes of inequities in health and health care experienced by diverse and vulnerable patients. How can museum educators respond to this shift by using works of art as tools to unpack bias and racial and socioeconomic injustices with participants? Hammer Museum educators Theresa Sotto and Hallie Scott, and psychiatrist Enrico Castillo, will describe how they have collaborated to build community and cultural awareness among current and prospective UCLA psychiatry residents and then modified their program in form and content in response to two deadly pandemics: COVID-19 and systemic racism. This chapter will also suggest ways that the strategies used in this program can be applied to other partnership programs, internal museum initiatives, and to gallery education more broadly.

INTRODUCTION

A group of psychiatry residents look closely at a painting featuring four figures who are gazing at a mysterious sculptural object that towers above them (see figure 1.1). All of the figures are depicted with their backs to the viewer: two faces are partially visible and the other two figures are rendered with few details other than their hooded sweatshirts. Prompted by an educator, the residents begin to share observations about the work and questions about its subject matter and meaning. They note the moody colors, the distancing effect of encountering the figure's backs, and they pose possible interpretations of the large sculptural form. After everyone has had a chance to respond to the work and to each others' observations, the educator shares the artist, title, and date of this work—Noah

3

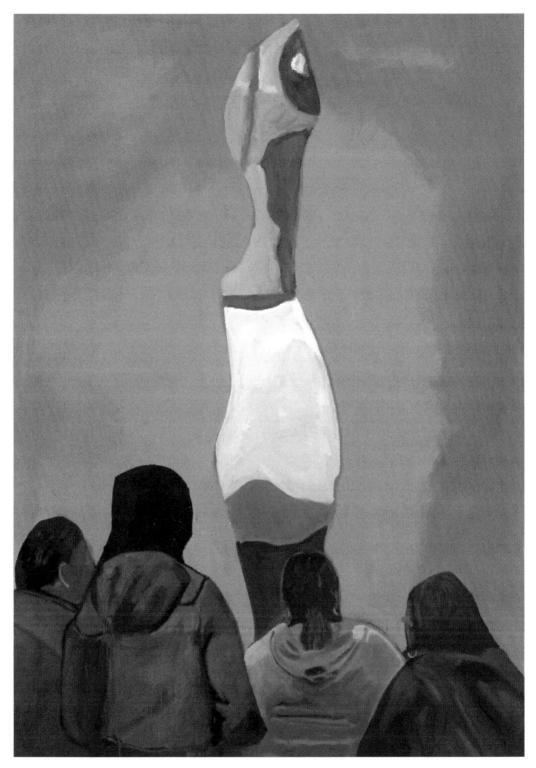

Figure 1.1 Noah Davis, Pueblo del Rio: Public Art Sculpture, 2014. Oil on canvas, 72 x 48 in. (182.9 x 121.9 cm), Hammer Museum, Los Angeles. Purchase. © Noah Davis. *Photo by Joshua White.*

Davis, *Pueblo del Rio: Public Art Sculpture,* 2014—and explains that Pueblo del Rio is a housing project in South Los Angeles that was initially celebrated as a modernist triumph, but is now overcrowded and underfunded. This information shifts the conversation; residents begin to discuss the ways in which this painting raises questions about segregation, urban planning, housing inequities, cultural access, and injustices in the healthcare system.

Facilitated by Hammer Museum educators, this conversation occurred on Zoom in June 2020 as part of an orientation for new psychiatry residents (postdoctoral trainees), organized in partnership with the UCLA Community and Global Psychiatry (CGP) resident-faculty group. Titled "Building Cultural Awareness of Los Angeles and Community through Art," the orientation gathered seventeen residents and faculty for dialogues about works of art and activities geared toward building camaraderie among residents and facilitating an understanding of diverse Los Angeles communities and the ways in which those communities are impacted by structural inequities.

Several museums have long established partnerships that translate museum education techniques to training in other fields such as K-12 formal education, medicine, and law enforcement. These partnerships traditionally focus on building observation and analysis skills through discussions of works of art. We posit that museum educators are also particularly poised to facilitate another competency that partners and collaborators are now beginning to look for: awareness of systemic and structural inequities. This chapter analyzes the UCLA CGP orientation session for new psychiatry residents as a case study of a program focused on building this "structural competency." In writing about the orientation, we hope to offer museum educators and potential partners tangible teaching strategies for facilitating this awareness.

In the first section of this chapter, we contextualize the emerging emphasis on structural competency within both the museum and medical fields. In the second section, we share and offer commentary on the strategies used during the orientation to build understanding of bias and inequity. We end the chapter by suggesting ways to apply these strategies to other potential partnerships and to gallery education more broadly.

We approach this collaboration from a range of backgrounds. Enrico writes from the perspective of a cisgender, second-generation, Filipino American man. Born and raised in rural southwestern Virginia, Enrico experienced racism from peers and educational systems, which has informed his work to be a strong ally for diverse populations with mental illness, to improve the public systems that serve them, and to train physicians in public service and health equity. A white, cisgender, able-bodied woman, Hallie strives to use her privileged positionality to facilitate programs that center the goals and ideas of diverse young people in art spaces. She is committed to working against the deprioritization of teaching within museums and academia. Theresa, a cisgender and able-bodied woman, approaches this work through the lens of a Filipinx American woman and daughter of immigrants who came of age in predominantly white neighborhoods and schools. Passionate about the arts but frustrated by the cultural sector's lack of diversity, she has devoted her career to making museums and other arts organizations more diverse, accessible, and inclusive.

SHIFTING THE CONVERSATION IN MUSEUM EDUCATION: EMPHASIZING INEQUITY

Museum educators intentionally, proactively, and thoughtfully make space for diverse voices. This is the heart of our work. When we teach, we draw out observations and insights about museum objects from multiple perspectives. Those of us who facilitate conversations about art can skillfully draw visitors' attention to facial expressions or the quality of a line and know when to zoom out to remark on representational portrayals, disorienting perspectives, or the relationship of figures to the space around them. We pose questions that encourage people to observe more than they did at first glance and make connections to historical or cultural contexts that are referenced in the work.[1] In doing so, we guide a process of collective meaning-making, leading participants to weave visual evidence, contextual information, and inferences into an informed interpretation.

Put another way, we actively collect details from multiple sources, aggregate context and evidence, and leverage collective wisdom to arrive at a knowledge-based opinion. The process has parallels in many other professions, including law, history, and medicine. However, what makes gallery teaching unique among the aforementioned fields is the emphasis on subjectivity. We find deep satisfaction in hearing multiple interpretations and are quick to point out that there cannot be just one correct answer when it comes to analyzing art. This emphasis on subjectivity enables museum educators to use art to foster understanding of others' perspectives and empathize with their experiences. Taken further, discussions about art have the potential for raising awareness about the systems and structures that impact individual perspectives.

In the past half decade, educators have increasingly focused on the power of objects as tools to discuss structural inequities. Writing in 2016, educators Marit Dewhurst and Keonna Hendrick posited that we must view objects as "opportunities to talk about power and privilege in our society." Educators can do this by using "contextual information about each artwork or artifact to access conversations about racism and oppression" (Dewhurst and Hendrick, "Dismantling Racism"). This reframing of objects as sites for critical analysis of oppression and inequality represents a powerful shift from the dominant paradigm in museum education, which has tended to view objects as neutral vessels for observation and inquiry.[2] Educators can expand their teaching practice by broadening the context provided to visitors in order to draw attention to systems of oppression, whether referenced in selected objects, located within the museum walls, or reflected in individuals' lived experiences. Although it may seem like a tall order, museum educators already do this work—albeit not usually in explicit ways. We have honed the skills necessary to navigate difficult conversations through countless conversations with visitors, who may share responses that are grounded more in bias than in visual evidence. During these moments, we might draw attention back to an object to ground comments in visual evidence, refer to another perspective to draw out different understandings, or bring in additional context that will nudge a conversation into more productive terrain, to name a few techniques.

While many museum educators have become better versed in understanding the connections between collections and systems of oppression, they have been slow to implement gallery-based programs and educational partnerships specifically geared toward building understanding of inequity. Some notable exceptions can be found in the programmatic offerings of historic and cultural institutions. In 1999, for example, the United States Holocaust Memorial Museum in Washington, D.C. established Law Enforcement and Society: Lessons of the Holocaust (LEAS), a program presented in partnership with the Anti-Defamation League and the DC Metropolitan Police Department. LEAS engages law enforcement professionals in dialogue about the role of police in Nazi Germany and reflection about their role in society.[3] Similarly, the Museum of Tolerance in Los Angeles offers Tools for Tolerance*, a professional development program for law enforcement and criminal justice communities with courses such as cultural diversity, racial profiling, and hate crimes.[4] Additionally, the National Museum of African American History and Culture, in partnership with the Metropolitan Police Department and the University of the District of Columbia, launched a training course in 2018 aimed at informing police officers of African American history and culture, including histories of injustices in policing.[5] Finally, the Science Museum of Minnesota stands out among science learning institutions in its range of equity goals across programming, including a professional development initiative called the IDEAL Center, which helps professionals across a range of fields gain strategies for disrupting inequities and fostering transformative change.[6] In the past couple of years, a small handful of art museums have begun to offer tours and one-off programs that specifically use artworks to discuss structural inequities.[7]

At the Hammer Museum at UCLA, museum educators are more explicit and intentional about raising awareness about inequities through discussions about art. The Hammer Museum's mission

Enrico G. Castillo, Hallie Scott, and Theresa Sotto

is: "We believe in the promise of art and ideas to illuminate our lives and build a more just world." Stemming from its mission, the museum exhibits works that address pressing social, cultural, and political issues. Social and systemic inequities frequently recur as thematic concerns in the museum's collections and exhibitions, which allow educators the opportunity to discuss potentially controversial topics rooted in an artist's perspective. Although the museum is most known for its provocative contemporary exhibitions, including its *Made in L.A.* biennial highlighting artists based in Southern California, its founding Armand Hammer Collection comprises European and American paintings from the sixteenth to twentieth centuries. Whether examining an Old Master painting or a work by a contemporary Los Angeles artist, museum educators at the Hammer find ways to further our mission by bringing awareness to inequities—whether they are explicitly addressed in an artwork, revealed through context, or made apparent through thematic connections to present-day issues.[8]

EVOLVING MEDICAL EDUCATION: STRUCTURAL COMPETENCY AND HEALTH EQUITY

Museum-based medical education is part of a larger tradition of medical humanities and arts education programs in undergraduate (medical schools) and graduate (residencies and fellowships) medical education. These programs span medical disciplines—psychiatry, ophthalmology, family medicine, nursing, and palliative care as examples—and draw on art to teach medical competencies. Using Kolb's framework of experiential learning, museum-based education excels at creating knowledge through the transformation of experience, guiding the trainee through cycles of *concrete experience* (encounters with art), *reflective observation* (discussions of art), *concept formation* (reflections on new skills and problem-solving strategies), and *active experimentation* (application of new skills and strategies with the next work of art or patient encounter) (Armstrong and Parsa-Parsi 680–84).

This experiential learning in museum-based education has traditionally focused on developing skills in observation, where the trainee draws lessons from the processes of observing and analyzing works of art that can be generalized to the detail-oriented activities of medical history-taking and physical examination. Other museum-based and arts education programs have focused on critical thinking, empathy, teamwork, and most recently as a wellness intervention to address physician burnout.[9] Broadly speaking, these programs have sought to help medical trainees better serve their individual patients or medical teams, while doing little to challenge trainees' understanding of their place in society or their roles in addressing injustices in health care.

In contemporary American health care, the doors to health and healthcare services remain closed for many due to factors like health insurance status, zip code, language, citizenship, education level, and race. U.S. inequities in COVID-19 cases, hospitalizations, and deaths experienced by Black and Brown communities in every major city reflect long standing systemic problems in American laws, healthcare systems, and social safety nets that have disproportionately, and in many cases intentionally, affected minority communities.

Structural competency, coined in 2014 by Hansen and Metzl, views these systemic problems as essential to medical expertise and practice: "Structural competency seeks to expand medical educational approaches to social realms by infusing into medical canon scholarship on the hierarchies, economies, and networks through which health and illness are produced and maintained" (129). Structural competency urges physicians to comprehend illness not just biologically but sociostructurally, as arising out of unequal laws, social forces, and institutions. Health equity is a parallel public health and medical movement focused on the "commitment to reducing disparities in health and its determinants; health equity is social justice in health" (Braverman et al. S150).

Health equity and structural competency critically examine physicians' roles in their local communities and demand that physicians learn new skills to heal laws and institutions, the root causes of health inequities. These new skills include understanding implicit and explicit bias by race and gender; structural awareness of political and socioeconomic forces that drive illness; knowledge of local public health challenges and social movements; community partnerships; and physician advocacy (Castillo et al. 1817–22). These new physician competencies have taken on greater urgency in light of recent uprisings for racial and social justice and calls for antiracism transformations of American institutions, including academic medicine and museum interpretation (Trouillot). More undergraduate and graduate medical education programs are adopting antiracism, structural competency, and health equity into their curricula.[10] As medical education continues to evolve toward collectivism, antiracism, health equity, and structural competency, this creates new opportunities for museum-based education.

In 2016, Yale University's psychiatry residency training program developed a three-day structural competency initiative as part of their social justice and health equity curriculum (Bromage et al. 244–47). The initiative paired psychiatry residents with community members and included an art museum-based education component with the Yale University Art Gallery. The gallery component of the initiative centered on works of art that reference racial and economic inequities, for example, works of art depicting or created by enslaved people on the Yale campus. This exercise helped to build relationships between the residents and community members and introduced the topic of structural competency in a way that was rooted in their immediate institutional context. The exercise also helped residents confront personal implicit biases and formulate ways that they, as physicians, would work to address systemic inequities.

Around the same time, residents in the UCLA psychiatry program founded resident-faculty collaboratives focused on "Community and Global Psychiatry" and "Justice, Equity, Diversity, and Inclusion."[11] Our UCLA residency program has developed leading educational and recruitment initiatives focused on health equity, structural competency, social responsibility, physician advocacy, and antiracism. Inspired by Yale's structural competency partnership with the Yale University Art Gallery, UCLA's Community and Global Psychiatry (CGP) group partnered with the Hammer Museum in 2019, in large part due to the museum's reputation of exploring social justice and civic engagement in the arts.

AN ART MUSEUM-BASED MEDICAL EDUCATION PARTNERSHIP EMPHASIZING STRUCTURAL COMPETENCY: A CASE STUDY

Background on Hammer Collaborations with Medical Faculty

The Hammer Museum's partnership with the UCLA CGP group drew on gallery teaching activities that we had been implementing with various groups. We first collaborated with faculty in the David Geffen School of Medicine at UCLA in 2018, when we partnered with professors who teach a Diagnostic Skills course to third and fourth year medical students. In two sessions of a ten-week course focused on essential skills in the medical field—observation and empathy—we engaged approximately thirty medical students with a combination of discussion-based and drawing activities that were designed to strengthen attention to visual details, supported deductive reasoning based on visual evidence, and encouraged empathy, perspective-taking, and reflections on how personal associations bias the way we interpret what we see.

In designing the activity that explores personal associations and bias, we drew from a focused training on bias and privilege, which Theresa had been leading for internal staff and museum colleagues since 2017. In this training, participants engage in interactive activities with works of art in order to unpack how aspects of our identity and lived experiences give rise to biases that may impact our work. Although the training was designed originally for museum professionals, our medical school partners thought one of the training activities would be valuable to incorporate into the Advanced Diagnostics course. After all, research has uncovered racial bias in the treatment of patients, such as a disturbing study published in the *Journal of General Internal Medicine* in 2007, which revealed that white doctors with increased implicit bias were less likely to treat a Black patient experiencing chest pain

Enrico G. Castillo, Hallie Scott, and Theresa Sotto

with a drug that reduces blood clots, and thus less likely to prescribe a potentially effective treatment (Green et al. 1231–38).

The Hammer's first foray into helping raise awareness of future doctors' biases through art received positive anecdotal feedback; however, it wasn't until the Hammer's partnership with the Community and Global Psychiatry group that a session on bias could be more seamlessly integrated into larger pedagogical and programmatic goals of health equity and structural competency.

Our partnership began informally. In January 2019, Enrico reached out to the Hammer Museum to request a tour of a current exhibition for a group of psychiatry faculty and medical students who were taking part in a special equity, diversity, and inclusion residency recruitment day hosted by the UCLA David Geffen School of Medicine. The day aimed to encourage candid dialogue with residency applicants on topics related to structural competency and health equity.

The exhibition, an installation by New York–based artist Shadi Habib Allah, used objects and sound to investigate government welfare policies and their impact on disenfranchised populations. Enrico's interest in this exhibition points to the strong thematic connection between the Hammer's mission and the CGP group's emphasis on structural competency. In response to Enrico's request, museum staff arranged for a curatorial walkthrough followed by a discussion about the exhibition. The generative conversation, in which the participants discussed the ways in which the work explored racial and economic disparity, pointed to the potential for an educator-facilitated dialogue in the galleries in a future collaboration.

After meeting to discuss these potential future connections, we arranged a more formal partnership program, facilitated by Theresa and Hallie. This program took the form of two sessions in November and December 2019 as part of a second student recruitment day. This training had three parts: (a) a discussion of the role of medical professionals within society through an analysis of John Singer Sargent's *Dr. Pozzi at Home* (1881); (b) a discussion of trauma through an analysis of two works in the Fall 2019 exhibition *Lari Pittman: Declaration of Independence;* and (c) a debrief about ways that the conversations in the galleries resonate with their psychiatry practice. Each time we debriefed with the students, they shared a range of insightful reflections, describing perceptive parallels between psychiatric care and the process of discussing art together. They highlighted the importance of taking time to uncover more details, the process of developing an interpretation from different observations, and the ways in which group dialogue in the galleries is akin to the process of determining patient care in collaboration with other doctors. Following the experience, one participant shared, "it made me reflect on the human body as a work of art, scars telling a story, and all the layers."

RESIDENT ORIENTATION: BUILDING CULTURAL AWARENESS OF LOS ANGELES AND COMMUNITY THROUGH ART

Planning a Program during Two Pandemics

Building off of the success of our initial collaborations, we decided to expand beyond recruitment to incorporate a museum-based session into the annual Summer orientation week for new residents in June 2020. We planned a two-hour session in the Hammer Museum's galleries as part of the multi-day orientation. We aimed to help establish the tone and agenda for residents' four years in the UCLA residency program through this event, which focused on building community, cultural awareness, and structural competency and to encourage the types of thoughtful insights and critical reflections that were shared during recruitment days. However, like most museums across the country, the Hammer closed in March 2020 as a result of the COVID-19 pandemic and remained closed for over one year. All parts of the new resident orientation that could take place digitally were reimagined, including the Hammer's session. Meanwhile, the murders of George Floyd, Breonna Taylor, Ahmaud Arbery, and countless others fueled social uprisings throughout Los Angeles and across the country, and calls for racial justice spread across all sectors of society. The orientation event was scheduled to take place just twenty-eight days after the murder of George Floyd.

In the weeks leading up to the orientation, the museum and medical fields were being called to task in more public ways than ever before to confront the systemic racism that plagues all of our institutions, and we were each having daily conversations, respectively, about how our fields and our employers in particular could further equity and antiracism efforts internally and externally. Knowing that the two pandemics of COVID-19 and systemic racism loomed large in everyone's minds, we knew that our two-hour orientation session had to explicitly address anti-Black racism in addition to our initial goals. Our challenge: How do we strike a balance between addressing the current moment while being sensitive to those who might be triggered by the discussion—all while helping to build community over Zoom for individuals who are just starting to get to know one another during a fraught time?

To overcome this challenge, we carefully selected which works of art to feature in our discussions. For our discussions with psychiatry residents who are embarking on a program that foregrounds structural competency, we selected works from our collections, recent exhibitions, and the 2020 rendition of *Made in L.A.* (originally scheduled to open in Summer 2020) that would provide context about histories of racism and uprisings in Los Angeles, particularly in Black communities. By focusing on works by artists who examine these subjects in nuanced ways, we felt confident that the process of sharing our perspectives of art together, freed from expectations of discipline-specific knowledge, would broaden the residents' understanding of Los Angeles histories and thus build structural competency while fostering community-building rooted in our shared experience of the year's global challenges.

ACTIVITY 1, PART A: DRAWING GAME TO BUILD OBSERVATION AND LISTENING SKILLS, FACILITATED BY HALLIE

We began the orientation with a drawing game that we often employ during sessions with medical student groups as a means to practice observation, verbal description, active listening, and collaboration. We used Noah Davis's *Pueblo del Rio: Public Art Sculpture* (2014) (see figure 1.1) as the focus for this game. After debriefing the game, we transitioned into the discussion that we described at the beginning of the chapter. Table 1.1 includes directions for facilitating this activity online and in the galleries, followed by questions for reflection.

Commentary

This serves as a generative warm-up activity because it functions on multiple levels. Drawings typically differ significantly from the original work, which often results in amusement and helps to break the ice. The activity also encourages close looking and meta-cognition about the ways that we look and talk about what we see. The process of practicing putting visual information into words and conveying it clearly to others helps to build collaboration and sets the group up to continue to bring awareness to their observational processes throughout the orientation. During the group discussion, residents reflected on the challenge of determining the right details to prioritize and choosing accurate descriptive language. In connecting this activity to psychiatric care, they discussed the need to communicate detailed descriptions, perspective-taking, and the importance of posing clarifying questions to further understanding.

ACTIVITY 1, PART B: MOVING BEYOND DESCRIPTION, TOWARD ANALYSIS AND CULTURAL AWARENESS, FACILITATED BY HALLIE

We followed the drawing exercise with a guided conversation about Noah Davis's painting, as described at the beginning of this chapter. The conversation is designed to build on the looking and

Enrico G. Castillo, Hallie Scott, and Theresa Sotto

Table 1.1. Drawing Game to Build Observation and Listening Skills

Directions on Zoom	*Directions in Galleries*
Preparation • Prepare a slide or document featuring the object that you want to focus on. We have found that this activity is best suited to representational works. The slide or document should be shareable by hyperlink. Have a link to the slide ready to share with the breakout rooms. Implementation • Host forms breakout rooms and instructs participants to gather a piece of paper and a writing utensil before entering the rooms. • Each room should select one participant to be a "describer." • The facilitator shares a link to the image with the describer. • The describer has 3–4 minutes to describe the artwork while the others in the breakout session try to draw it based on the description. • Share drawings. • Leave breakout rooms and come back together as a full group to discuss.	Preparation • Choose a gallery or set of adjoining galleries for this activity. We have found that this activity is best suited to representational works. • Gather pencils, clipboards with paper, and gallery stools for participants. Implementation • Form pairs. Each pair should determine a "describer" and a "draftsperson." • The describer chooses a work to focus on and leads the draftsperson to it. (Or the educators preselect works.) The draftsperson should avoid looking at the work. (This works best if both pairs set up gallery stools, the describer facing the work, the draftsperson facing away from the work.) • The describer describes the work while the draftsperson draws a copy based on the description (without looking). This should take 3–5 minutes. • Look together at drawing and artwork, reflect on the process. • Pairs switch roles with new work.
Discussion Questions • Look together at the work and compare the drawings. What worked and what felt challenging in this process? • How does this type of process translate to working collaboratively in psychiatric care?	

describing skills required in the drawing game, encouraging participants to make observations and inferences that move beyond description and into analysis as well as to learn about an aspect of Los Angeles history that is referenced in the title of the work. In facilitating this conversation, I used the inquiry-based gallery teaching pedagogy that we typically adhere to at the Hammer, supplementing the residents' observations with context about the work and artist as a means to raise cultural awareness about Los Angeles. Table 1.2 lists the questions that we used to facilitate the conversation about Davis's work.

Commentary

This discussion built on the drawing exercise, encouraging the residents to continue to make observations and inferences that move beyond description and into analysis. They eagerly responded to my open-ended questions. Psychiatry residents have previously shared that it feels refreshing to be in a dialogue where there are no right or wrong answers to questions, in contrast to medical school

Table 1.2. Moving Beyond Description, Toward Analysis and Cultural Awareness

Instructions on Zoom	*Instructions in Galleries*
Preparation • Create a slideshow with images of the object and images that illustrate any context you wish to share. Think about including details of the object, photographs of the artist at work, and objects that show comparison. If you choose to make a comparison, put both objects next to each other on one slide to easily facilitate comparative looking.	Preparation • Research the contextual history of the object. If you have supplemental images that you would like to bring in to illustrate this context, print them or save them on an iPad so that you can share them in the gallery.
Questions for Group Discussion and Reflection	
• Take a minute to look again at this work. What are you noticing now as you look for a second time? • What questions do you have? • [Share the title of the work and provide context for the title, share photos of the project if on Zoom] Knowing that context, what other inferences can you make? • [Share information about the artist's interests and share a photo of the artist if on Zoom.] Does the information change or add to your understanding of the work?	

classes. It seemed that this same reaction was at play during the orientation—the residents were excited to hear their peers' insights and contribute their own. The ambiguous subject and setting of Davis's painting also seemed to encourage the open-ended nature of their contributions. I found that asking them to share their questions ("What questions do you have?") was a helpful way to segue into sharing some contextual information about the work. A benefit of facilitating this type of conversation on Zoom is that I was able to include photographs of the Pueblo del Rio housing projects and other images that help to contextualize the works. I shared the shifting history of this local housing project—from its initial vision as a garden city built by notable architects, to the closure of nearby factories and decades of systematic under-resourcing by the local government. This led the residents to make thoughtful inferences about the ways in which the painting elicited questions of housing, cultural access, and other social inequities in Los Angeles. They connected it to Los Angeles' present-day affordable housing crisis and social movements to address these racial and social inequities. The residents' reflections mirrored those of participants in similar sessions we have facilitated. In another program with medical students, one participant shared that she interpreted the painting as invoking the history of anti-Black racism in American medicine and the parallel developments of alternative care networks within Black communities.

Notes about Object Selection

The drawing activity (part A) works well with objects with representational subject matter, rather than abstraction, which can be frustrating to describe. However, I recommend choosing a representational subject with some level of ambiguity in terms of interpretation. This will engender an evolving and nuanced process of collective observation and meaning making during the guided conversation (part B). To fit with the theme of our orientation, the work I chose also had to address a history and legacy of racial inequity in Los Angeles. Noah Davis's *Pueblo del Rio: Public Art Sculpture* poses questions about access to culture and addresses housing inequities in Los Angeles. The work's title locates it at a 1940s modernist public housing project designed by a team of architects including one of the few

Enrico G. Castillo, Hallie Scott, and Theresa Sotto

Black modernist architects working in Los Angeles, Paul R. Williams. Pueblo del Rio was built in Central-Alameda as low-income housing primarily for Black families who worked in defense industries. The project fell into decline in the 1960s and 1970s due to expansion and overcrowding coupled with a lack of governmental funding for upkeep, as well as job losses for residents as factories closed. Davis was drawn to this project as a subject through which he could explore the intersections between modernist painting, architecture, and Black culture.[12]

Noah Davis's *Pueblo del Rio: Public Art Sculpture* was especially productive for this conversation because it not only fits the orientation theme, but it also portrays a process of looking, and therefore invites meta-reflection on that process for viewers. In addition, it contains a charged racial symbol that might provoke bias—people wearing hoodies. Educators working in museums with historic European collections might try using an Impressionist painting for this activity—Impressionists often focused on acts of looking and class signification in response to the rapid restructuring of both the built environment and the social stratifications of the late nineteenth century. For more advice on selecting objects that address current issues from collections that don't prioritize contemporary art, see textbox 1.1.

ACTIVITY 2: EXAMINING IMPLICIT BIASES WITH IMAGES, FACILITATED BY THERESA

The second activity is designed to draw awareness to residents' implicit biases through word association exercises. We believed that including an activity about bias in the orientation session would help set the stage for the importance of critical reflection in patient care, and ultimately, encourage residents to be more aware of any biases that might impact their diagnoses. For this session, we implemented two-word association exercises with two different groups of artworks. The first group included sculptures, photographs, and mixed media works that utilized or represented everyday objects or comprised geometric forms. Participants were asked to select works that they felt matched the words *valuable, comforting, poor,* and *powerful.* The second group included paintings, photographs and prints depicting people, which participants were asked to match with the words *beautiful, strong, safe,* and *successful.* The resulting matches revealed an individual's subjective associations between words and images. More detailed instructions for implementing this exercise over Zoom or in the galleries are listed in tables 1.3 and 1.4.

Commentary

Every time I facilitate this activity, at least two people will select two different images for the same word and will share completely different reasons for their selections. Or they may select the same image for two opposing words. Participants speculate as to why they associated the image with the word, and without fail, a fascinating discussion ensues about what characteristics we associate with certain descriptive words and whether those associations are grounded in stereotypes or an individual's lived experience. Individuals may share, for example, that they associated a tall, cylindrical form with the word "powerful" or that their socioeconomic privileges shaped their connotations of the word "valuable." After I completed this activity with the psychiatry residents, we discussed how implicit biases might affect patient care in Los Angeles communities. Following the program, several residents shared that exploring bias was one of the most valuable aspects of the orientation. One resident stated in the follow-up survey: "I felt it was a great way to reflect on our roles as psychiatrists and how our biases can affect us, while connecting to art." Another wrote: "I appreciated the opportunity to link our discussion about implicit bias to our work with members of the LA community."

For psychiatry residents, especially those embarking on a new program, sharing moments of vulnerability is not commonplace. As professor and author Brené Brown stated in her book *Dare to Lead*, "We need to trust to be vulnerable, and we need to be vulnerable in order to build trust" (35). By modeling a genuine interest in learning other perspectives from the beginning of the session (see

Table 1.3. Examining Implicit Biases with Images

Instructions on Zoom	Instructions in Galleries
Preparation • Prepare a slide of 7–8 images of a range of works of art or other collection objects that you think people will associate with a variety of loaded descriptive words (e.g., valuable, poor, beautiful). • Number the images. • Determine 4–5 descriptive words that you think participants would match with the selected images in different ways depending on their lived experiences and aspects of their identity. Implementation • Present the slide of 7–8 images. • Give participants approximately one minute to familiarize themselves with the images. • Provide the following instructions: *I will state a few words. For each word, select an image that you feel is the best match for the word. Write down the word and the number of your selected work on a piece of paper.* • Encourage them to select the first image that comes to mind when they hear each word rather than spending time thinking about the selection. • State the predetermined words, pausing briefly between each word for just enough time for participants to make a quick selection. • Compare and contrast choices.	Preparation • Select 1–3 galleries that contain works of art or other objects that you think people will associate with a variety of loaded descriptive words (e.g., valuable, poor, beautiful). • Determine the descriptive words that you think participants would match with the images in different ways, depending on their lived experiences and aspects of their identity. • Write each word on a slip of paper. Duplicate each word 2–3 times to ensure that more than one person will receive the same word. Implementation • Invite participants to take 5 minutes to walk around the preselected galleries to familiarize themselves with the works in the space. • Distribute two different words to each participant. • Ask them to select a work that they feel best matches the word. • Encourage them to make quick decisions to select their matches rather than spending time thinking about the selection. • Once selections are made, regroup and compare and contrast choices.
Discussion Questions • Which aspects of your lived experience or identity may have influenced your decision? (See table 1.4.) • What experiences, knowledge, or background led you to associate the word and the object? • How do our personal associations bias the way we interpret what we see?	

above activities), we begin to build trust among the group, which is further enhanced by facilitators also sharing personal stories about their identities and how they shape associations. Setting the stage for trust and vulnerability through our orientation session helped to build community among the new cohort of residents. In fact, 90.9 percent of participants who completed a follow-up survey (10 out of 11) agreed or strongly agreed that the session helped them to build community with co-residents. One resident stated in the survey: "It was wonderful to be with my co-residents and hear their thoughts

Enrico G. Castillo, Hallie Scott, and Theresa Sotto

Table 1.4. Aspects of Lived Experience or Identity

Which aspects of your lived experience or identity may have influenced your decision?		
Values	Politics	Sexuality
Upbringing	Race	Socioeconomic status
Lived experience	Ethnicity	Religion/faith
Education	Age	Ability
Profession	Gender	Culture
Media	Urban/suburban residence	Weight/height

about a particular piece and how it relates to their own life experiences." Moreover, because the activity was implemented over Zoom, participants were able to comment swiftly and contemporaneously through the chat function, which allowed for more residents to share and hear a range of perspectives in a brief amount of time.

Although this activity was successful in building community and reflecting on biases, there are certainly limitations to facilitating an activity designed to increase awareness of bias in just thirty minutes. During the second exercise, almost all individuals selected a painting of a white woman petting a dog for the word "safe." This image was one of two images that portrayed a white woman, out of eight total images depicting figures. During the discussion, I shared that previous facilitations of this exercise resulted in similar findings—that individuals of diverse races selected the painting of the white woman for the word "safe." However, I did not have the time to unpack the reasons why. Following the orientation session, faculty and museum staff discussed whether it would've been useful to take the time to discuss why participants associate whiteness with safety, but ultimately felt that such a discussion would be more productive in a longer, focused session on bias as opposed to one thirty-minute activity within a two-hour orientation session that had multiple goals.

Notes about Object Selection

The effectiveness of this activity is contingent on the selections of works and words. If implementing the activity in the galleries, select galleries that contain a variety of works, ideally created by different artists. After trying a variety of types of works with different groups over time, I've found that the most productive discussions occur when the word associations are made with works that incorporate everyday objects, depictions of objects, or abstract forms (as opposed to portraits or landscapes). Historical artifacts, architecture, furniture, tools, clothing, assemblage, and minimalist sculpture would all work well, especially if their appearance might elicit associations with gender, race, or class norms. When the works depict people, participants tend to be more reticent to share not only the associations they made but also why they made them. Indeed, no one wants to be perceived as biased against certain groups of people. Focusing on everyday objects or abstract forms lessens the fear of judgment, and yet results in nuanced self-reflections nonetheless. Since this activity was implemented over Zoom, I was able to select objects that I felt were most conducive to discussions of biases; however, I needed to bear in mind additional considerations: objects and forms should be clearly recognizable when reproduced digitally and sized small enough so that eight can fit on a computer screen.

One work that has been effective in both the galleries and in Zoom is Michael Queenland's *Untitled* (2017), a seemingly quotidian straw broom with a wooden handle, which is the centerpiece of a work of conceptual art. If I were to share background information about the work, residents would learn that the broom is purposely placed in an upright position, precariously balanced on the tips of the straw and likely to fall down and surprise visitors in the galleries. However, because the purpose of the activity is to raise awareness of bias as opposed to learning about the artworks, I do not share background information with the residents. Participants will need to make associations purely from visual cues. Depending on their lived experiences, they may associate a broom with the word "powerful" or "poor." For example, they may have a close relationship with someone they respect who cleans houses for a living, or they may have grown up in a wealthy household where someone was hired for cleaning services.

A final word of advice: It's helpful to test your selected words and images with a few people before implementing the activity. If everyone selects the same work to match a word, select a different work. The differences in selections result in the most productive conversations.

ACTIVITY 3: CLOSE LOOKING, ANALYSIS, AND BUILDING UNDERSTANDING OF HISTORIES OF RACIAL INEQUITIES IN LOS ANGELES, FACILITATED BY HALLIE

The final activity of the orientation returns to the mode of facilitated, inquiry-based conversation used in activity 1, part B. We discussed two works of art that address histories of racial inequity in Los Angeles, and then planned to culminate with a reflection on the thematic connections between these two works and the Noah Davis painting from the first activity.

The first, Mark Bradford's *Rebuild South Central* (2015), addresses the cycles of police brutality, social and cultural trauma, and uprising in the city.[13] To make the large, mixed media on canvas work, Bradford layered text and materials that he scavenged and preserved from the streets of the South Central neighborhood of Los Angeles in the aftermath of the Rodney King uprisings in the early 1990s. The resulting artwork is a visual palimpsest of the urban environment in that moment, preserving records of both mundane daily experiences and violent struggles. Centered in the 43 x 96 inch canvas are brightly colored letters that read "REBUILD SOUTH CENTRAL WITHOUT LIQUOR STORES!! RECONSTRUIRAL SUR CENTRAL SIN NEGOCIOS DE BEBIDAS ALCHOHOLICAS!!"

The second, *Mr. Rene # MAN POWER* (2011) by Fulton Leroy Washington (aka MR. WASH), is a portrait of a bearded Black man with large tears running down his face, rendered in a photorealistic style in oil paint on a 24 x 20 inch canvas. Two miniature portraits are contained within his tears.[14] The painting is one of a series of portraits of fellow prisoners that the artist painted while incarcerated. The series offers a counternarrative to the dehumanization perpetrated by the carceral system. MR. WASH sought to honor the lives of his inmates by depicting their emotions, families, triumphs, and sufferings. The artist's own experience also reflects racial inequity within the carceral system—in the late 1990s, he was sentenced to life imprisonment after being convicted of a nonviolent drug offense, the mandatory minimum that had been set during the era of the "War on Drugs." Table 1.5 includes questions used to facilitate the conversation about the two works.

Commentary

These works provide a strong framework for practicing close-looking, sharing observations, and collectively making meaning around works of art. As in the first activity, the residents were eager to share observations and build off of each other's comments. Again, I included contextual images, such as photographs of South Central during the aftermath of the Rodney King uprisings, to help to illustrate the historic context. Similarly, I was also able to include images of details in the works, allowing for closer analysis than is possible in the galleries. A pivotal moment happened during the close observation of Mark Bradford's *Rebuild South Central* (2015). One resident bravely raised their virtual hand to ask, "What is South Central?" The resident demonstrated an essential curiosity about context, both in art and in health care. That question led to an informative dialogue about histories of

Enrico G. Castillo, Hallie Scott, and Theresa Sotto

Table 1.5. Close Looking, Analysis, and Building Understanding of Histories of Racial Inequities in Los Angeles

Instructions on Zoom	Instructions in Galleries
Preparation • Create a slideshow with images of the objects and images that illustrate any context that you wish to share. Think about including details of the object, photographs of the artist at work, and objects that you want to bring in as comparisons. If you choose to make a comparison, put both objects next to each other on one slide to easily facilitate comparative looking.	Preparation • Research the contextual history of the objects. If you have supplemental images that you would like to bring in to illustrate this context, print them or save them on an iPad so that you can share them in the gallery.

Questions for Group Discussion and Reflection:

Work A:
• Take a minute to look at this work. What stands out to you?
• [Context for text] What does knowing that context do for your understanding of the work?
• What else do you notice?
• What can you observe about the materials used in the work?
• [Context for materials] Why do you think the artist chose these materials? What effect do they have?
• [Background on the artist] Does this information bring up any new insights or questions for you?

Work B:
• Again, let's look at the work for a minute before we talk about it. What do you see?
• What do you notice about the way it is painted?
• What are your questions about this work?
• [Provide context about the work and artist] Knowing that context, are there any other inferences that you can make?

Comparison works A, B, and the work from Activity 1:
• Looking at these three works together, do you have any additional reflections about connections between them?

systematic exclusion and under-resourcing of South and Central portions of Los Angeles, fueled by racism and unfair systems, alongside histories of strength and resiliency in predominantly Black and Brown communities, fueled by innovation, community organizing, entrepreneurship, and art. Exploring art that was made in Los Angeles by Black artists about local social movements to address systemic injustices taught psychiatry residents about the communities they are joining and serving and their social responsibility as physicians.

It seems important to note here that spending just a couple of minutes providing context on each work felt very cursory. The works address complex histories of both racial inequity and community uplift that require more research and nuance than I was able to provide in the format of a gallery conversation. This orientation was designed with the knowledge that the group of participants will continue to build on the insights that they gained from our conversation throughout their residency. However, this also points to the potential for a longer and more focused partnership program that could encompass other artworks and readings to build a broader understanding of this history.

Unfortunately, we ran out of time for a culminating discussion of the comparison between the three works. We have found that ending online tours and programs with a slide of all of the works discussed is a generative way to invite final reflections that draw connections between the works.

Notes about Object Selection

This activity works well with objects that explore different facets of the topic at hand through divergent perspectives. In this case, I selected artworks with two different artistic approaches and subjects, but both contributed to a larger understanding of systemic inequities that impact Black people living in Los Angeles. The contrasting artistic approaches allowed participants to process and interpret two different visual and material languages. We also wanted to include a work from activity 2, so that participants could reflect further on a work that they were initially asked to respond to just through association. An educator might also choose to facilitate the activity with two objects that illuminate structural inequity through a more direct contrast. A pair of objects that serve or represent two different audiences in the same time period—a scientific tool that represents an important technological advancement and a photograph of a community harmed in the development of the technology, for example—can be very effective in illuminating inequities in terms of class, race, and gender. Objects that reveal change over time can function in similar ways. For example, a pair of maps could demonstrate how a city has changed over the course of a century to favor businesses and wealthy residents. See textbox 1.1 for more ideas about selecting objects for these activities.

Final Debrief

We had planned a fifteen-minute closing discussion to foster participants' reflections on how the topics explored throughout the session connect to their profession. We were prepared to pose the following questions:

- In what ways do the conversations that we had about these objects connect to your work as psychiatrists?
- Did our conversations and activities make you think differently about the communities that you might work with in Los Angeles?

Unfortunately, each of the planned activities, which we had facilitated for the first time over Zoom, needed more time than anticipated, and we only had five minutes left for a wrap-up. Such concluding discussions are incredibly important not just for participants to make further connections to what they experienced (see "Background on Hammer Collaborations with Medical Faculty" section), but also so that facilitators have an immediate sense of participants' takeaways. In future sessions, we will be sure to allow enough time for this important moment of sharing and introspection.

ASSESSMENT AND REFLECTIONS

Survey Findings

Following the orientation session, we emailed an online survey to the residents to determine the effectiveness of each activity in reaching our goals. Eleven out of fifteen residents who attended the orientation session completed the survey, and the findings were overwhelmingly positive. Ten out of eleven (90.9 percent) survey respondents selected "yes" in answer to the question, "Do you feel the Hammer Museum session during your orientation was valuable to you?" Additionally, almost all respondents agreed or strongly agreed with the following statements:

Tips for Selecting Objects to Address Current Times

There are a range of ways to connect museum objects of all kinds to current public discourse about systemic racism and societal inequities more broadly.

- Find a transhistorical theme that is reflected across your collection and has contemporary resonance, such as discrimination, power and privilege, class and labor, or revolution, and discuss the ways the theme has evolved or stayed stagnant over time.
- Choose a work that depicts a historic rebellion or uprising. Ask visitors how the image compares to media images of civil unrest today.
- Pair an object with a problematic history with a contemporary perspective on that history, such as a quote from a local artist, scientist, or scholar or a video produced by activists.
- Select an object that represents privilege (e.g. wealth, patriarchy, white privilege, heteronormativity). Discuss whether the person or people who created the object share the privilege and how contemporary audiences may react to the object in different ways, depending on whether they share similar privileges.
- Contextualize objects related to the accomplishments of key figures in history and science with information about diversity and inclusion, or lack thereof, in their respective fields.
- Choose a work by a white maker and analyze in terms of codes of whiteness. Educators tend to share and discuss racial identity only when the maker is BIPOC (Black, Indigenous, and People of Color), but, in reality, every object can be analyzed in terms of its racial context.[1]
- Select a work or exhibit that could reveal inequities in labor and compensation or in recognition of labor. Discuss who is credited in didactics and who else may have contributed to the work or exhibit but is not credited, which may include collaborators who are unnamed, fabricators of a plinth or frame, or factory or studio workers who made all or part of the object.
- Discuss whose voices are missing in your collection and why that might be the case (e.g., colonialist history of the museum, biases of museum founders, the continuing emphasis on eurocentric canons, and white supremacy limiting access to opportunities in your field).

NOTE

1. This strategy is adapted from Marit Dewhurst and Keonna Hendrick. See "Decentering Whiteness," 459.

- I learned about an aspect of Los Angeles history and/or culture that I didn't know before. (*7 strongly agree, 3 agree, 1 neutral*)
- The activities helped me to build community with my co-residents. (*4 strongly agree, 6 agree, 1 neutral*)
- Closely analyzing works of art as a group helped me reflect on processes of observation in psychiatry. (*4 strongly agree, 6 agree, 1 disagrees*)
- I increased my awareness of my implicit biases. (*4 strongly agree, 5 agree, 2 neutral*)

Comparisons of the above findings reveal that we were most effective in our goal to increase understanding about histories of diverse LA communities through art. In fact, one survey respondent wrote in an open field in the survey that, "[I] learned about LA racial history that I was completely ignorant of." However, most statements in response to the question "What was the single most valuable aspect of the session?" related to either building community with peers (several wrote that they enjoyed time with co-residents) or sharing and learning different perspectives (i.e., from one another, from artists). Even the person who felt that the session was not valuable overall wrote that "spending time with classmates" was the single most valuable aspect of the session.

The survey also indicated one area of the session that needs improvement. In response to the statement, "I felt I could speak up and actively participate," responses were the most mixed relative to the other survey questions: 4 respondents strongly agreed, 2 agreed, 3 were neutral, 1 disagreed, and 1 strongly disagreed. Notably the individual who did not find the overall session valuable selected "strongly disagree" in response to this statement. Unfortunately, it is not clear why several respondents were either neutral or did not agree with this statement since no specific reasons were provided.

Lessons Learned

Based on survey findings and reflections from UCLA faculty and Hammer staff during a post-session debrief, we concluded that the orientation session was effective in achieving all goals: to build community among a new group of residents, discuss and reflect on individual biases, and build structural competency by learning about inequities impacting Los Angeles communities. Our collective planning discussions leading up to this orientation event and the adaptations that we made in light of the pandemic, the murder of George Floyd, and the uprisings for racial and social justice in Los Angeles made this event successful by bringing our institutions (academic medicine and museums) into dialogue with contemporary sociopolitical movements. Furthermore, the calls for racial justice that became more vociferous and widespread in May 2020 encouraged us to more directly discuss systemic racism, which is essential to comprehending structural inequities in health care.

All parties agreed that we should continue to incorporate a similar session in the next resident orientation—whether online or in person. Although talking about digital images of art online is not the same as discussing original works of art together in the space of the museum, the Zoom platform afforded us the opportunity to select works that we felt would best address our goals rather than being limited to the works on view in the galleries and also bring in contextual images that would reinforce background information about topics explored in the artworks. Future in-person programs could include the best of both worlds: a combination of in-gallery experiences with supplemental images shared via iPad and discussions in a classroom with slides projected to reinforce points as necessary.

One aspect of our session that we will continue to examine and strengthen relates to the survey finding that several participants did not agree or were neutral about feeling that they could speak up and fully participate in the program. Although it was unclear from the survey why participants felt this way, anecdotal information suggests that participants may have felt uncomfortable discussing art in general due to a lack of prior experience in museums or that their predisposition toward science may have limited their comfort level with the subjectivity of art. Other reasons could be that the residents were just starting to get to know one another and that community-building over Zoom has its own limitations. One component that we would like to incorporate in future sessions, whether online or on site, is taking the time in the beginning of the session to share community guidelines, such as Glenn E. Singleton and Curtis Linton's Four Agreements of Courageous Conversations (Gonzalez). We would also like to include more ways to share responses anonymously, such as incorporating a poll or sharing a whiteboard that participants could annotate. If the session takes place in person, we could ask participants to write responses on individual slips of paper, collect them, and then share them without identifying who wrote them. Indeed, any facilitated discussion that engages with personal reflections on bias, privilege, and inequities would benefit from a balance of group discussions and opportunities to respond anonymously.

CONCLUSION

Medicine is often incorrectly understood as occurring within a vacuum, that physicians administer pharmaceuticals or other therapeutics to organ systems or intracellular targets in ways that are blind to elements outside of the body (Greene and Loscalzo 2493). This view of medicine understands illness biomedically but fails to comprehend how much of illness arises from sociostructural and historical contexts. But medicine, like art, does not occur within a vacuum. To vigorously combat reductionism in medical education and foster structural competency and health equity, transformative educational experiences are needed, and art museum-based education is one arena in which these types of experiences are available. Art museum-based programs have traditionally focused on observation, using tools like close reading to powerfully teach new ways of looking that can be generalized to patient care. These same tools, redirected to focus on social movements, local histories, and systemic injustices have the potential to engage trainees in the work of partnering with communities to address the root causes of health injustices.

Our partnership between UCLA Community and Global Psychiatry and the Hammer Museum was in and of itself a critical ingredient to the success of this educational program during this challenging time. On the topic of partnerships in medical education, Hansen and Metzl write, "Ultimately, it is only by preparing clinical trainees to partner with entities outside the clinic that we can empower them to influence the social determinants of their patients' health and reduce health inequalities" (281). Partnerships bring medical trainees into dialogue with expertise and perspectives outside of health care. When a community leader teaches a class to residents, we model the importance of humility and multidisciplinary expertise to solve the most complex challenges facing patients. The mutual respect held between the museum and UCLA CGP made this event successful and demonstrated to residents the value that the residency program places on humility—that the role of structurally competent physicians is not to medicalize structural problems, but to learn from and support community-based organizations and efforts.

Although not an initial goal for the program, we came to realize that our work together also addresses physician burnout, albeit through a different route than the aforementioned movement to use art to address physical burnout in medical education (see "Evolving Medical Education: Structural Competency and Health Equity" section). Recent wellness literature formulates burnout as arising not only from overwork, but from instances of moral injury, when one's actions run counter to one's values or beliefs, especially in the absence of organizational support or due to unjust institutional arrangements (Kopacz et al. e28). Our program addresses this type of burnout by inspiring physician advocacy in our residents through art that was created in reaction to racial and social injustices. Art helped the residents know that they were not alone in witnessing injustices, that they could be allies to larger, local social movements.

We believe that this transformative process can be extended beyond collaborations between medical schools and art museums. We write this chapter at a time when institutions are being called upon to understand and acknowledge the ways in which they operate within and replicate systems of oppression. Cultural institutions are clear culprits within this discourse. The civil unrest of 2020 and ensuing calls for dismantling systemic racism at every level have exacerbated pressure on museums to claim solidarity in the movement for Black lives and racial justice.[15] But museums must also move beyond making performative statements. As Yesomi Umolu and others have pointed out, they must reimagine their role in society as spaces that center and care for communities, rather than objects (Umolu). They must find ways to equitably support, partner with, and program for neighbors, young people, families, teachers, organizers, and other community members that are often overlooked in institutional decision making.

We hope that the focus on structural competency within our collaboration can serve as a model for other educators striving to do this work. Regardless of what type of objects or collections you work with at your museum, we hope that you can apply the strategies that we shared to other programs and partnerships such as those with K–12 school systems, higher education groups, local organizations, and other groups who are also looking to build structural competency during this political and social moment. Educators at a children's museum might, for example, use these strategies with a set of objects that highlight disparities in educational access to facilitate a conversation with a group of school administrators about inequities impacting K–12 education. A history museum might lead a dialogue about access to urban spaces for a group of developers by applying the close looking and analysis strategies to historic records of their city. High school students might tour a natural history museum with an educator who shares not only collection highlights, but also discusses the colonial power dynamics that brought the collection into being. The Examining Implicit Biases with Images activity, in particular, might be helpful for educators leading an executive training focused on understanding hiring biases.

However, we also acknowledge that this work cannot just be external—internally, museums must dismantle staffing hierarchies, funding inequities that prioritize collections and high level donors over education and community engagement, white supremacist leadership and communication structures, and other systemic inequities that are pervasive within our cultural institutions. We believe that our strategies can be readily adapted to the internal trainings focused on antiracism, inclusive leadership, and implicit bias that are in such high demand in this political moment. Although our institutions frequently look to outside consultants to lead these trainings, we advocate that they should better value, utilize, and remunerate museum educators' skills in this area.

Finally, in demonstrating educators' ability to facilitate structural competency, we hope that we have made an argument for the critical need for educators' skills in today's museums. The COVID-19 pandemic has resulted in devastating furloughs and layoffs within education departments, signaling a deprioritization of our skills within our institutions. If museums truly want to address both internal and external inequities, they can begin by learning from their education staff.

DISCUSSION QUESTIONS

1. How might you apply the strategies outlined in this article to your programs?
2. What works in your collection might work well for facilitating conversations about structural inequities?
3. Which museum educators' skills and competencies are transferable to other disciplines and how can these cross-disciplinary connections help to build community partnerships?
4. How can museums best utilize the skills and competencies of their staff and work together to raise awareness of societal inequities inside and outside of museum walls?
5. What other strategies might you develop in order to build structural competency with partners and audiences?
6. As community partners shift in pedagogical focus and programmatic goals into the twenty-first century, how can museum educators stay abreast of these changes so that museums can be more effective partners?

NOTES

1. This inquiry-based, dialogic practice is informed by constructivism, referring to learners constructing their own meaning based on experience; it offers an alternative to the oppressive "banking" concept of education articulated by Paolo Freire in *Pedagogy of the Oppressed* (1970). Rika Burnham and Elliott Kai-Kee elaborate on gallery teaching pedagogy in *Teaching in the Art Museum* (2011): asking open-ended questions, paraphrasing responses, inviting participants to share inferences and the visual evidence they drew upon, and layering in information when it is necessary to move the conversation forward.

Enrico G. Castillo, Hallie Scott, and Theresa Sotto

2. La Tanya S. Autry and Mike Murawski led the field in challenging this paradigm beginning in 2017 through their #museumsarenotneutral initiative, a call to museums to counteract the self-perpetuated myth that they are "neutral" institutions that exist outside of political, social, and economic systems.

3. See "Law Enforcement," United States Holocaust Memorial Museum, last accessed November 30, 2020, https://www.ushmm.org/outreach-programs/law-enforcement.

4. See "Tools for Tolerance® for Law Enforcement and Criminal Justice," Museum of Tolerance, last accessed November 30, 2020, https://www.museumoftolerance.com/for-professionals/programs-work shops/tools-for-tolerance-for-law-enforcement-and-criminal-justice/.

5. See "National Museum of African American History and Culture Hosts Metropolitan Police Department in New Training Program," National Museum of African American History and Culture, last accessed November 30, 2020, https://www.si.edu/newsdesk/releases/national-museum-african-american-his tory-and-culture-hosts-metropolitan-police-department-0.

6. See "IDEAL Center," Science Museum of Minnesota, last accessed March 13, 2021, https://www.smm.org/ideal-center.

7. Some examples of tours include the Blanton Museum of Art's "Doing Social Justice" tours and *Race and Social Justice in Art* primer; the Institute of Contemporary Art Boston's "Power and Representation" virtual visits; and the "Race and Gender in American Art" tours at the Whitney Museum. It is difficult to find instances of longer-term programs or partnerships focused on these topics. One exception is the Empowered Educator program that the Carnegie Museum of Art has been hosting since 2017 in partnership with the Center for Urban Education, the Western Pennsylvania Writing Project, the Learning Instigator, and Remake Learning. Empowered Educators is a forum for teachers, administrators, counselors, and others to discuss topics like race, equity, and bias and explore how they relate to teaching. Many museum educators leading teen programs also incorporate discussions of inequity and cultural access into their work with this age group. For example, educators at the National Portrait Gallery discuss issues of representation in their collection with teen program participants and the teens curate an alternative exhibit of portraiture in response. For more on the latter, see Blake and Coren.

8. Examples of our programming include Art without Walls, a partnership with the Los Angeles Public Library that connects exhibitions, social justice themes, and children's literature; and "Exploring Social Constructs" K–12 tours, which center on issues of difference, inequality, race, gender, class, social justice, and activism. See "Black Voices, Black Joy: A Reading Series with the Los Angeles Public Library," Hammer Museum, last accessed December 1, 2020, https://hammer.ucla.edu/programs-events/2020/black-voices-black-joy-reading-series-los-angeles-public-library; "Tour Options," Hammer Museum, last accessed December 1, 2020, https://hammer.ucla.edu/edu/k-12-tours. In addition to our exhibition-based programs, the Hammer has long offered public programs that examine social inequity, including Hammer Forum, a series of events that have explored timely social and political issues since 2007. See "Programs & Events," Hammer Museum, last accessed March 13, 2021.

9. For more on these programs, see Katz and Khoshbin 331, Orr et al. 361.

10. See Gabrielle Redford, "AAMC Releases Framework to Address and Eliminate Racism," AAMC, October 6, 2020, https://www.aamc.org/news-insights/aamc-releases-framework-address-and-eliminate-rac ism; "Structural Competency: New Medicine for Inequalities That Are Making Us Sick," last accessed November 30, 2020, https://structuralcompetency.org/.

11. See "UCLA Community and Global Psychiatry," last accessed November 30, 2020, https://www.uclacgp.com/; "UCLA Psychiatry Office of Justice, Equity, Diversity and Inclusion," last accessed November 30, 2020, https://diversity.semel.ucla.edu/.

12. *Public Art Sculpture* is one of a series of works by Davis that focus on Pueblo del Rio. These thematic interests in the work, which recur throughout his oeuvre, also led Davis to start his own cultural institution. In 2012, he founded the Underground Museum in the predominantly Black and Latinx neighborhood of Arlington Heights, Los Angeles, as a space for the community to have free, walkable access to museum-quality art. Davis died of cancer at the age of thirty-two in 2015; the Underground Museum continues to thrive.

13. See "Mark Bradford, *Rebuild South Central*, 2015," Hammer Museum, accessed April 27, 2021, https://hammer.ucla.edu/sites/default/files/styles/large/public/migrated-assets/media/exhibitions/2015/Mark_Bradford/MB.13.jpg.jpeg?itok=wyOGU0tl. The Hammer exhibited this work as part of *Mark Bradford: Scorched Earth* in 2015.

14. See "Fulton Leroy Washington (aka 'MR. WASH'), *Mr. Rene # MAN POWER*, 2011," Hammer Museum, accessed April 27, 2021, https://hammer.ucla.edu/sites/default/files/styles/large/public/2020-12/MRWASH_mila_5817.jpg.jpeg?itok=QIZeQ2U_.
15. The @changethemuseum Instagram account, for example, provides a platform for museum workers to confront the effects of white supremacy on our cultural institutions, and ultimately on the public we aim to serve.

BIBLIOGRAPHY

Armstrong, Elizabeth, and Ramin Parsa-Parsi. "How Can Physicians' Learning Styles Drive Educational Planning?" *Academic Medicine*, vol. 80, no. 7, 2005, pp. 680–84.

Autry, La Tanya S., and Mike Murawski. "Museums are Not Neutral." *Art Museum Teaching,* August 31, 2017, updated July 2020, https://artmuseumteaching.com/2017/08/31/museums-are-not-neutral/. Accessed 1 April 2021.

"Black Voices, Black Joy: A Reading Series with the Los Angeles Public Library." *Hammer Museum*, https://hammer.ucla.edu/programs-events/2020/black-voices-black-joy-reading-series-los-angeles-public-library. Accessed 1 December 2020.

Blake, Caitlin, and Ashleigh D. Coren. "We Love Our Work, Therefore It's Our Responsibility to Critique It." *Viewfinder: Reflecting on Museum Education E-Journal*, no. 13, March 2021, https://medium.com/viewfinder-reflecting-on-museum-education/we-love-our-work-therefore-we-have-a-responsibility-to-critique-it-fcb421e8c8d5. Accessed 1 April 2021.

Braveman, Paula A. et al. "Health Disparities and Health Equity: The Issue Is Justice." *American Journal of Public Health*, vol. 101, no. S1, 2011, pp. S149–55.

Bromage, B. et al. "Understanding Health Disparities Through the Eyes of Community Members: A Structural Competency Education Intervention." *Academic Psychiatry,* vol. 43, no. 2, 2019, pp. 244–47.

Brown, Brené. *Dare to Lead: Brave Work, Tough Conversations, Whole Hearts.* New York, Random House, 2018.

Burnham, Rika, and Elliott Kai-Kee. *Teaching in the Art Museum: Interpretation as Experience.* Los Angeles, J. Paul Getty Museum, 2011.

Castillo, Enrico G. et al. "Reconsidering Systems-Based Practice: Advancing Structural Competency, Health Equity, and Social Responsibility in Graduate Medical Education." *Academic Medicine: Journal of the Association of American Medical Colleges*, vol. 95, no. 12, 2020, pp. 1817–22.

Dewhurst, Marit, and Keonna Hendrick. "Decentering Whiteness and Undoing Racism in Art Museum Education." *The Palgrave Handbook of Race and the Arts in Education,* edited by Amelia M. Kraehe, Rubén Gaztambide-Fernández, and B. Stephen Carpenter II. Cham, Switzerland, Palgrave Macmillan, 2018, pp. 451–67.

Dewhurst, Marit, and Keonna Hendrick. "Dismantling Racism in Museum Education." *Journal of Folklore and Education*, vol. 3, 2016, https://www.locallearningnetwork.org/journal-of-folklore-and-education/current-and-past-issues/journal-of-folklore-and-education-volume-3-2016/dismantling-racism-in-museum-education/. Accessed 1 April 2021.

Freire, Paolo. *Pedagogy of the Oppressed.* Translated by Myra Bergman Ramos. New York, Continuum, 2006.

"Fulton Leroy Washington (aka 'MR. WASH'), *Mr. Rene # MAN POWER*, 2011." Hammer Museum. Accessed April 27, 2021, https://hammer.ucla.edu/sites/default/files/styles/large/public/2020-12/MRWASH_mila_5817.jpg.jpeg?itok=QIZeQ2U_.

Gonzalez, Jennifer. "How One District Learned to Talk about Race." *Cult of Pedagogy,* 28 April 2019, https://www.cultofpedagogy.com/courageous-conversations-about-race/. Accessed April 1, 2021.

Green, Alexander R. et al. "Implicit Bias among Physicians and Its Prediction of Thrombolysis Decisions for Black and White Patients." *Journal of General Internal Medicine*, vol. 22, no. 9, September 2007, pp. 1231–38, https://www.ncbi.nlm.nih.gov/pmc/articles/PMC2219763/. Accessed 1 April 2021.

Greene, Jeremy A., and Joseph Loscalzo. "Putting the Patient Back Together—Social Medicine, Network Medicine, and the Limits of Reductionism." *The New England Journal of Medicine*, vol. 377, no. 25, 2017, pp. 2493–99.

Hansen, Helena, and Jonathan M. Metzl. "New Medicine for the US Health Care System: Training Physicians for Structural Interventions." *Academic Medicine: Journal of the Association of American Medical Colleges*, vol. 92, no. 3, 2017, pp. 279–81.

"IDEAL Center." *Science Museum of Minnesota*, https://www.smm.org/ideal-center. Accessed 13 March 2021.

Katz, Joel T., and Shahram Khoshbin. "Can Visual Arts Training Improve Physician Performance?" *Transactions of the American Clinical and Climatological Association,* vol. 125, 2014, pp. 331–42.

Kopacz, Marek S., Donna Ames, and Harold G. Koenig. "It's Time to Talk about Physician Burnout and Moral Injury." *The Lancet Psychiatry*, vol. 6, no. 11, 2019, pp. e28.

"Law Enforcement," United States Holocaust Memorial Museum, https://www.ushmm.org/outreach-programs/law-enforcement. Accessed 30 November 2020.

"Mark Bradford, *Rebuild South Central*, 2015." Hammer Museum. Accessed April 27, 2021, https://hammer.ucla.edu/sites/default/files/styles/large/public/migrated-assets/media/exhibitions/2015/Mark_Bradford/MB.13.jpg.jpeg?itok=wyOGU0tl.

Metzl, Jonathan M., and Helena Hansen. "Structural Competency: Theorizing a New Medical Engagement with Stigma and Inequality." *Social Science and Medicine,* no. 103, 2014, pp. 126–33.

"National Museum of African American History and Culture Hosts Metropolitan Police Department in New Training Program." National Museum of African American History and Culture, https://www.si.edu/newsdesk/releases/national-museum-african-american-history-and-culture-hosts-metropolitan-police-department-0. Accessed 30 November 2020.

Orr, Andrew R. et al. "The Fostering Resilience through Art in Medical Education (FRAME) Workshop: A Partnership with the Philadelphia Museum of Art." *Advances in Medical Education and Practice*, vol. 10, 2019, pp. 361–69.

"Programs and Events." *Hammer Museum,* https://hammer.ucla.edu/programs-events?start_date=04%2F01%2F2021. Accessed 13 March 2021.

Redford, Gabrielle. "AAMC Releases Framework to Address and Eliminate Racism." *AAMC*, 6 October 2020, https://www.aamc.org/news-insights/aamc-releases-framework-address-and-eliminate-racism. Accessed 1 April 2021.

"Structural Competency: New Medicine for Inequalities that Are Making Us Sick." *Structural Competency,* https://structuralcompetency.org/. Accessed 30 November 2020.

"Tools for Tolerance® for Law Enforcement and Criminal Justice." *Museum of Tolerance*, https://www.museumoftolerance.com/for-professionals/programs-workshops/tools-for-tolerance-for-law-enforcement-and-criminal-justice/. Accessed 30 November 2020.

"Tour Options." *Hammer Museum*, https://hammer.ucla.edu/edu/k-12-tours. Accessed 1 December 2020.

Trouillot, Terence. "Pushed to Address Systemic Racism, Museums Face a Reckoning." *Artsy*, 16 July 16 2020, https://www.artsy.net/article/artsy-editorial-pushed-address-systemic-racism-museums-face-reckoning. Accessed 1 April 2021.

UCLA Community and Global Psychiatry, https://www.uclacgp.com/. Accessed 30 November 2020.

UCLA Psychiatry Office of Justice, Equity, Diversity and Inclusion, https://diversity.semel.ucla.edu/. Accessed 30 November 2020.

Umolu, Yesomi. "On the Limits of Care and Knowledge: 15 Points Museums Must Understand to Dismantle Structural Injustice." *artnet news,* 25 June 2020, https://news.artnet.com/opinion/limits-of-care-and-knowledge-yesomi-umolu-op-ed-1889739. Accessed 1 April 2021.

2

Shared Authority

SCHOOL AND MUSEUM PARTNERSHIPS FOR THE TWENTY-FIRST CENTURY

Veronica Alvarez, Elizabeth Gerber, Sarah Jencks, and Catherine Awsumb Nelson

ABSTRACT

Museum and school partnerships have taken on many different forms, although the majority of museums engage their school communities through field trips. This chapter will describe two innovative, multi-year, partnerships between cultural institutions and their school and teacher communities. In the first case study, the education team at Los Angeles County Museum of Art partnered with an elementary school to create a museum-quality gallery at their school site. Through shared authority and collaboration, exhibitions at the site are inclusive of the interests of the local community. In the second case study, Ford's Theatre's education department created the National Oratory Fellows program (NOF), an intensive professional development program for educators from across the country. Teachers collaborate with Ford's teaching artists to develop and implement a range of oratory content and techniques as part of their existing classroom practice. Through these long-established relationships, Ford's has created a national learning community of education professionals that are both ambassadors for Ford's as well as professional leaders within their own communities. Both of these examples illustrate the benefits of shared authority between cultural institutions and the communities they serve.

INTRODUCTION

This chapter will grapple with some of the most urgent issues facing twenty-first-century museum educators. Through reflective analysis of two case studies, it will provide ideas, strategies, and models that address the changing educational challenges facing both museum and school communities.

In 1980, the American Association of Museums (AAM) appointed a commission tasked with ensuring the relevance of museums and their responsiveness to changing conditions in society. The commission noted that to maintain their germaneness, "it is essential that museum professionals understand that the educational role of museums is as important as the museum's collecting responsibilities"[1] and stated that "museums have an opportunity to contribute to the national agenda for education" and should be included in national efforts to reform education for they would "contribute greatly to excellence in the educational system."[2] Although AAM has since changed its name to the American Alliance of Museums, their mandate still resonates today, forty years later—perhaps even more so, as America's demographics, the educational landscape, and a global pandemic have all contributed to deep introspection within museums about their roles as facilitators of dialogue about contemporary issues that matter to our communities.

Almost from their inception, art museums were seen as educational institutions[3] and thus often served as partners to school communities.[4] Coupled with recent research that has shown that the arts increase student performance in other subject areas, improve the health and mental well-being of students, and lead to an increase in student empathy,[5] principals and teachers have sought innovative ways to include the arts in the curriculum.[6] However, as state, district, and federal budgets drastically cut funding to arts education, classroom educators have had to rely on philanthropies, arts organizations, and other nonprofits—including museums—to fund and facilitate arts education in schools.[7]

However, museums and schools are natural partners, and there are numerous instances of meaningful collaborations across the country. When museums and schools partner, students learn through multiple formats—"reading" (works of art) and writing, looking and questioning, analyzing, and thinking critically. Museums can provide the transformative power of encounters with works of art, historic artifacts, scientific specimens, and hands-on interactives, all of which have the potential to complement ideas discussed in the classroom. Museum educators also provide professional development opportunities for teachers that create supportive networking communities that extend beyond the museum walls. Museums can also enhance the subject areas not addressed within a school setting and build students' skills and provide them with unique opportunities that are not available within the formal, school environment.

This chapter will present two case studies of long-term museum partnerships, one from an art museum and another from a historic site. One case study, from the Los Angeles County Museum of Art, will discuss a unique museum/school partnership in which the museum invested in a museum-quality gallery on the school site, the evolution of the partnership, the benefits and challenges for each, and concludes with a discussion of lessons learned and possible implications for the broader educational system. The other case study, from Ford's Theatre, will discuss how the education department responded to the COVID-19 pandemic by enhancing their online learning, reengaged with their constituents to build an accessible online community, and address their goals of civic engagement.

We end with some concluding remarks about what we learned through these partnerships and how these case studies have the potential to impact museums as they seek to collaborate with their school communities; ones that reflect best practices in teaching, accessibility, and community building. Both of these case studies propose that as a field we broaden the ways that museums engage with audiences beyond their physical spaces by sharing authority and engaging communities through dialogue on contemporary issues.

BEYOND THE MUSEUM'S WALL: A UNIQUE SCHOOL ANDS MUSEUM PARTNERSHIP

Veronica Alvarez and Elizabeth Gerber

Setting the Context

Almost all, or 96 percent of art museums offer single-visit school field trips, and those trips make up a significant number of their audience attendance.[8] Of the museums that offer such trips, the majority, 45 percent serve an urban audience (followed by suburban at 30 percent), and 57 percent of art museums reach out specifically to Title 1 schools[9] (Title 1 provides federal funds to schools with high percentages of low-income students). But what are the possibilities when museum education departments go beyond the single-visit field trip? What is necessary to make off-site museum experiences successful? How can lasting partnerships change and influence the museum, and in turn, impact the K–12 educational landscape?

Early in my museum career, I (Veronica) was in a big conference room in a session on community engagement, listening to a panel of prominent speakers, one of whom was Lisa Sasaki, the current director of the Smithsonian Asian Pacific American Center. Much of the discussion centered on defining "community" and what that meant and implied for museums. At one point, Lisa said, "sometimes, you just have to put a ring on it." After laughing at the reference to the famous Beyoncé song, I was deeply impacted by that statement. Up to that point, I had mostly only experienced single-visit school field trips or what I called the "parachute in" strategy to outreach. The museum would parachute into a community who we thought would benefit from our presence with art instruction or workshops, and then quickly we would parachute out, never making the long-term, deep commitment that could make the most impact. It was only much later in my career that I got an opportunity "to put a ring on it"—as illustrated by the following case study.

A Nascent Partnership

Charles White Elementary School is located less than five miles from the largest art museum in the western United States, the Los Angeles County Museum of Art (LACMA). The school resides across the street from MacArthur Park, in the Westlake district, a densely populated area just east of Koreatown.[10] The elementary school is located in the buildings of Otis Art Institute, which vacated the location in 1997 in favor of a campus on the west side of the city. (Otis Art Institute later became Otis College of Art and Design.) The college's departure from the neighborhood was part of a broader exodus that included other businesses and organizations. In 2004, Charles White Elementary School opened its doors on the former Otis campus, named for the American artist and educator Charles White (1918–1979), who taught at Otis Art Institute from 1965 until his death. The art school's large professional gallery—previously used to display student and alumni artwork—was left intact.

Inspired by the Mexican Muralists and deeply affected by the Civil Rights Movement, artist Charles White portrayed the universality of human experiences through his portraits of African-Americans. In the spirit of White's commitment to social change and civic engagement, LACMA staff was excited by the possibility of collaborating and partnering with Charles White Elementary (named in honor of the artist) around those shared goals, especially through exhibitions in the school's gallery.[11] At the time we initiated the partnership, our goals, typical of other school and museum collaborations of the time, included, "sharing works from the museum's permanent collection with the community in the school's gallery, while simultaneously providing educational programming, offer(ing) LACMA the chance to build an audience, grow ties with the MacArthur Park neighborhood, and perhaps help strengthen this community." When we embarked on the partnership, we did not foresee how it would evolve, the commitment it would entail, and most importantly, that we wouldn't strengthen the community, but rather, that the community would strengthen us.

The collaboration initially sought to create an exhibition at the school featuring objects from LACMA's encyclopedic collection alongside newly commissioned work. Los Angeles artists Mark Bradford and Ruben Ochoa developed the first exhibition, SWAP (2007), based on themes and physical references from the surrounding neighborhood. Reflecting on their collaboration, Ochoa said, "We looked at the area around MacArthur Park, near the school. The principal let us know how a lot of the students came from the area and how their parents shopped at the swap meets and stores around the park. I was drawn to the merchants there, and so was Mark. We found a common denominator with our merchant-class backgrounds." Concurring, Bradford added, "We use materials that have a commonality, that have memory of place, community, accessibility. And both of us embed our work with class issues." Because the neighborhood consisted of novice museum-goers, Bradford and Ochoa approached the project with the hope that the installation would help demystify art—both contemporary art as well as historical examples from LACMA's collection. Displaying works reflecting themes centered within the school community inspired them and provided the groundwork for future exhibitions; and shifted an understanding of art and artists away from finished, concrete objects toward art-making as a process, reflecting issues such as community and identity.

As the partnership developed, LACMA's work at the Charles White Elementary School[12] gallery sought to address some of the key concerns facing museums in the twenty-first century. Best practices in museum education such as object-based, student-centered, and experiential learning, along with exhibitions and workshops that connect directly with curriculum, or reflect pedagogical approaches more broadly, anchor much of this work. But by including the community from the outset in its programming at this specific location, inviting artists to be part of creating exhibitions and programs, and structuring tours and workshops as integral parts of an active gallery experience, LACMA seeks to develop and implement innovative ways to display the museum's collection by sharing authority to engage with the community.

Key Program Characteristics

While this partnership has evolved considerably over nearly fifteen years, five core characteristics have remained at its heart. Exhibiting LACMA's collection at the school, using the expertise of museum educators to guide the exhibition process, working with contemporary artists, incorporating a dedicated art workshop space, and aligning each exhibition with curricular goals have always been fundamental aspects of the partnership. High-quality exhibition and educational programming, coupled with LACMA's deep experience working with artists, schools, and communities, has ensured relevant and sustained engagement over the years while providing opportunities for the museum to refine the partnership based on the needs and desires of the school community.

Exhibitions of LACMA's Collection

Exhibiting works from LACMA's permanent collection has allowed unprecedented deep engagement with original works of art, both for students and their teachers. The capacity for careful looking, learning to think and talk about observations and interpretations, and creating meaning from objects all take time to develop. Students and teachers discover the details, nuances, and complexities through dedicated and prolonged encounters with works of art because the exhibits of the work are located directly on the school site; therefore, their museum experience extends far beyond the museum's walls.

One major lesson for the museum from these exhibitions, however, was scheduling. Initially, the schedule for the Charles White gallery was incorporated into the museum's exhibition schedule. However, LACMA's calendar, which was more seasonal than responsive to the school calendar, did not allow for teachers and students to engage with the art objects as much as we, and they, would have liked. For example, for one show, the gallery installation took place during the fall with a February opening date, which meant that students only had the months of February through early June to engage with the show. Given state-mandated testing and spring break, the exhibition overlapped with only about ten to twelve weeks of instructional time. These kinds of logistics and considerations were something the museum did not initially plan for and had to adjust to meet the needs of the school community.

The Role of Museum Educators

Another unique and important aspect of the Charles White exhibitions throughout the program's history is that educators lead the exhibition and program planning process. The expertise of the museum's conservation, curatorial, design, and marketing departments, among others, are essential to creating shows, but it is the museum educators that initiate the planning process, starting with considering strategies for achieving student learning goals and increasing community accessibility. Museum educators bring their expertise in child development and teaching strategies, knowledge of curriculum standards, and understanding of the school's culture to the development and implementation of each exhibition. In addition, the process involves sustained collaborative work with the school and community; educators often work with school administrators, leaders at partner organizations, and community stakeholders to discuss new initiatives and share knowledge and expertise. For example, museum educators made it a priority to hire gallery guides from the local community and train them in object-focused, conversation-based tours. In this way, community engagement becomes an essential and integral part of each exhibition from its initial conception. Throughout this partnership, LACMA educators have gleaned a strong understanding of the necessary components and strategies required to achieve the desired goals and outcomes for these exhibitions.

The Role of Contemporary Artists

A particular feature of the exhibition program is the partnership with contemporary artists for each exhibition's development and display. During fifteen years of exhibitions, this has taken several different forms, but it has always included a dialogue with the artists. Some artists are commissioned to create new work to be displayed alongside objects from the museum's collection, while others embrace an approach of co-creating work together with the school's students. Exhibitions have also displayed student work in response to a particular theme from the exhibition. Respective exhibitions have involved local, national, and international artists.

The commissioning of work by contemporary artists has at times provided students with the opportunity to not only meet and develop relationships with acclaimed artists but also to gain an up-close view of the artistic process. The planning schedule is developed intentionally to allow time for the artists to research, brainstorm, and receive feedback; ideas percolate as the artists engage in conversations with community members, school administrators, students, and teachers. These innovative collaborations have thus encouraged LACMA to be more responsive to its audiences, while also providing more meaningful access to the creative process. (See table 2.1.)

A Dedicated Space for Creating Art

As exhibitions have evolved, LACMA has adapted the space to include an art-making area for students, their families, and the broader public. Beginning with the gallery's second exhibition (*Journeys|Recorridos*, 2008), tables and benches for art-making were incorporated into the exhibition design, and a part-time teaching artist was hired to develop and lead art workshops. Originally a component of the school's after-school program, workshops are now a dedicated classroom-time experience for all Charles White students during the school day. Art workshops can extend the experience of looking at art in multiple ways. Specifically, they broaden the ideas and concepts discussed while viewing artworks in the exhibition, and they allow them to be explored in hands-on ways by the students. Paired with gallery discussions, the workshops' hands-on activities also engage multiple learning styles. For a school comprising a significant number of English Language Learners, the workshops provide opportunities to develop critical-thinking skills and a means for students to express themselves creatively while demonstrating their understanding beyond the written word.

Alignment with Curricular Goals

Similar to the rest of the country, arts education in Los Angeles had been adversely affected by California's economic and budgetary constraints, along with shifting priorities, which has resulted in an

Table 2.1. History of Exhibitions at Charles White Elementary School

Title of Exhibition	Description	Dates
SWAP: Mark Bradford and Ruben Ochoa	The installation was inspired by the neighborhood that frames MacArthur Park, where the school is located and included art from LACMA's collection as well as installation pieces created by Ochoa and Bradford.	November 7, 2007–June 8, 2008
Journeys | Recorridos	LACMA commissioned Marysa Dowling to work with students to explore their local areas, the journeys they make, the people they meet, and how they choose to express themselves through photography.	December 12, 2008–February 26, 2010
L.A. Icons: Urban Light and Watts Towers	The exhibition featured historic photographs of Watts Towers and a selection of photographs, drawings, and collective poems from 3rd, 4th, and 5th grade students.	October 15, 2010–March 31, 2011
A Is for Zebra	An exhibition about alphabets that make sense and non-sense, which included a variety of art from artists such as John Baldessari, Francisco de Goya, to commissioned works from Michele Dizon, Camilo Ontiveros, and Stephanie Taylor.	December 2, 2011–March 29, 2012
Shinique Smith: Firsthand	The exhibition juxtaposed objects Smith selected from LACMA's Costume and Textiles collection, new work based on her experience within the school and community, and student art.	February 9–July 19, 2013
Kaz Oshiro: Chasing Ghosts	For this exhibition, Oshiro selected artworks from the museum's collection, created new work based on his interactions at the school, and student art.	January 24–June 7, 2014
Bari Kumar: Remembering the Future	The exhibition included ten original works by the artist, including oil paintings and cloth constructions as well as ancient South and Southeast Asian artworks.	January 30–June 13, 2015
A Universal History of Infamy: Those of This America	Featured sixteen U.S. Latino and Latin American artists across a range of media—from installation and performance to drawing and video.	January 27–October 6, 2018
Life Model: Charles White and His Students	Featured artwork in diverse media such as sketchbooks, photographs, and archival footage that illuminate Charles White as an art educator.	February 16–September 14, 2019
Rufino Tamayo: Innovation and Experimentation	The exhibition included prints by Tamayo and a selection of Mesoamerican sculpture from LACMA's collection.	December 21, 2019–July 11, 2020

emphasis on teaching strategies to increase reading and math test scores and a de-emphasis on art instruction. Despite partnership efforts between regional school districts and local arts organizations, a majority of students throughout the Los Angeles area still do not receive a robust arts education program.

The Charles White program seeks to address the lack of access to arts education as its exhibitions are designed to connect to the school's educational goals and curriculum standards. By aligning with California's Common Core and arts standards, teachers can more easily incorporate the arts into their classroom teaching. And by providing high-quality and consistent arts education through gallery discussions and art-making workshops, the LACMA/Charles White collaboration cultivates creative and critical thinking, fosters personal relationships among students, their families, the school, the community, and the museum, and reinforces the idea of the museum as an accessible resource—all while filling a critical need in the school's curriculum.

Recent Changes: A Committed Partnership

In 2015, the museum received a significant grant from the county earmarked for making upgrades to the gallery at Charles White Elementary. LACMA's Education Department saw this as an opportunity to strengthen and refine its ongoing partnership with the school district, nearby neighborhood organizations, and community members. To "put a ring on it," the museum and LAUSD also signed a new ten-year memorandum of understanding, formalizing this relationship for another decade. Thus, through *physical improvements* and the creation of the Visual Arts Magnet Center, LACMA expanded and deepened its services in a meaningful way to a significantly broader audience.

Physical Improvements to the Gallery

One of the primary areas that received physical improvements with the 2015 grant was the entrance area, which allowed increased access to the gallery for the general public, both physically and conceptually. Specifically, the entrance gate was relocated so that the gallery could be open to the public during non-school hours. While the safety of the students and the artwork was the main priority, the gallery's appearance from the street was made more welcoming. Access on evenings and weekends allows for greater participation and a branded entrance publicly announces the partnership between the school and the museum.

Charles White Visual Arts Magnet Center

In tandem with the physical enhancements, there was also an opportunity to focus on an area that thus far had not been adequately addressed—teacher professional development. To this end, LACMA staff was an integral partner in the application process for Charles White to become an LAUSD Visual Arts Magnet. The process was long, intense, but deeply collaborative. In the beginning, no one foresaw magnet status as a stated goal. However, as the partnership deepened and financial and personnel investment in the project continued, it seemed like a natural evolution of the partnership to become an arts magnet that would be mutually beneficial.

Once the magnet application was approved, LACMA staff worked with the new principal (the principal that started the application process was transferred to another school in the middle of this process) and other team members to interview, observe, and hire new magnet teachers. Once this core group was in place, we developed an intensive teacher professional development program for the entire school site. We created two distinct strands: art as a content area and arts integration. Guided mostly by the Kennedy Center's definition[13] of arts integration, we modeled ways in which teachers can integrate the arts in other subject areas. Obviously, LACMA educators capitalized on the fact that students had access to actual objects on-site, so the approach to learning and teaching centered on object-based, student-driven questioning, interpretation, and experiential learning within their immediate school setting. With the museum's deep involvement in the school becoming a visual arts magnet center, LACMA educators were now even more aware of, and sensitive to, the various needs and goals of the school and community.

Due to the COVID pandemic, the professional needs of the teachers shifted, naturally, and LACMA educators shifted in response. Currently, a LACMA educator is working closely with the teachers to focus on literacy and the arts to support students during virtual learning. Working one-on-one with teachers to plan their lessons, a LACMA teaching artist works with students to build their drawing and illustrating skills to support literacy and writing skills across different subject areas. For example, students created a graphic novel of Los Angeles when the Tongva (the indigenous peoples that originally lived at the site of the school) inhabited the region as part of their social studies lesson. To cite another example, with the guidance of the teaching artist, teachers are exploring the relationship between the arts and different types of writing such as informative, narrative, and opinion writing. Thus, students are using the arts to support learning in social studies and language arts to demonstrate their learning at a time when engagement and maintaining their literacy skills is an enormous challenge.

What We've Learned

We reflected on the fact that the application for magnet status was successful due to factors that had been cultivated over a long period of time—a long-standing commitment between the school and the museum; mutually respectful relationships established between the stakeholders; and the unique opportunity of having a museum gallery directly on the school site. This last part became even more important for the museum as this satellite campus provided LACMA the opportunity for additional gallery space when portions of the main museum were demolished to make way for a renovated building,[14] and even more importantly, situating a physical art space within the community.

With the myriad of recent changes, including the remodeled site and the school's magnet status, LACMA educators continue to envision ways to improve aspects of the program and respond to lessons learned. Recent changes include an advisory group composed of school and community leaders to guide the development of the main themes and goals of future exhibitions—an example of the museum letting go of its traditional role as the sole arbiter of curatorial authority. Responding to the needs of teachers and the learning styles of students at Charles White Elementary School and other neighborhood schools, LACMA continues to design programming that aligns with arts education and broader curriculum goals. Skills vital for success in the twenty-first century, such as creativity, critical thinking, collaboration, communication, and innovation, with a special emphasis on literacy, remain at the core of this programming.

As the LACMA and Charles White Elementary School partnership continues to expand and strengthen, all involved are working together to foster the skills and knowledge to prepare students to be successful and become participants in civic life. Providing students and community members with ongoing access to original works of art, a role in the development of exhibitions, and a wide array of related programming outside the traditional museum's walls is unprecedented. Establishing mutually respectful relationships, learning together by seceding control and sharing authority—this is what is possible when you put a "ring on it."

THE NATIONAL ORATORY FELLOWS PROGRAM AT FORD'S THEATRE

Sarah Jencks, Director of Education and Interpretation, Ford's Theatre Society and Catherine Awsumb Nelson, Independent Researcher

Setting the Context

When thinking about ways for cultural institutions to engage the K–12 education system, there are opportunities for intervention at the student, teacher, school, and district level, or through resources—like partnering with a vendor like a media or curriculum company. Depending upon goals and capacities, each institution makes decisions about how it can best effect changes aligned with its mission and vision. Ford's Theatre Society decided to intervene primarily at the teacher level for many reasons, some of which were strategic and others determined by circumstance, all of which led to a long-standing and successful educational program.

The mission of Ford's Theatre Society, the independent nonprofit partner of Ford's Theatre National Historic Site, is to celebrate Abraham Lincoln's legacy and explore the American experience through theater and education. As both the National Park Service–owned site of Abraham Lincoln's 1865 assassination and an operating, producing theater, Ford's has found its programming sweet spot at the intersection of history and theater. One important manifestation of this sweet spot is its oratory programs, the most intensive of which is the National Oratory Fellows (NOF) program. In 2010, teachers who had participated in Ford's Theatre summer institutes expressed a desire to remain connected with one another and to continue learning together. In response, the Ford's education team created the National Oratory Fellows (NOF) program. NOF is a multi-year, intensive professional development initiative through which primarily upper elementary and middle school teachers collaborate with Ford's teaching artists and one another to develop and implement a range of oratory content and techniques as part of their existing classroom practice, usually in a history or contained classroom. NOF offered dedicated teachers the opportunity to partner with Ford's teaching artists via videoconference to build a primarily virtual professional learning community focused on integrating public speaking, the study of historical speeches, and writing of original ones into their core classroom practice. Almost ten years later, this professional learning community is still flourishing.

A word of explanation: While this program is both expansive and extensive, it was executed by a staff of 2.5 FTE with significant additional responsibilities, working with five to seven part-time teaching artists hired on a contract basis. The vast majority of costs associated with this program went to pay for hotel and travel expenses, which allowed this program to be national in scale. However, it could be executed locally or regionally for a fraction of what we were able to spend. The most important "expense" was not dollars at all but the ten years of iterative programming as the teachers and teaching artists learned, built, and revised the program.

PROGRAM JOURNEY

The National Oratory Fellows program was created in 2011 when teachers who had participated in week-long summer institutes at Ford's contacted us, asked how they could remain connected with the professional learning community they had forged at the institute. It started as a six-month pilot with four history teachers—from Maryland, Nebraska, Idaho, and Missouri—who had remained in regular touch with the Ford's staff and had expressed a particular interest in extending one aspect of the summer institute curriculum, doing close readings of historical speeches with students and using a simple performance rubric to get the students up on their feet performing these speeches. They partnered with theater and writing teaching artists (TAs), using video-conference technology, to bring the TAs into their classrooms over ten visits to model and co-teach the historical speeches—implementing a model of engagement that extends beyond the physical space of the Ford's Theatre campus.

In the nine years since then, the program has grown to support more than fifty teachers in fifteen states across the country, who have created a professional learning community that, as they report, provides them with support and opportunities to stretch their teaching outside of school politics. As the Fellows progress, many become instructors and ambassadors for the work and are paid to offer workshops and lead model classes to hundreds of teachers in their regions each year. The Oratory Fellows are now differentiated into four areas of expertise (Novice, Emerging, Veteran, and Master), depending on both their number of years in the program and their confidence and acumen with teaching oratory. Because Ford's Theatre staff sought to share authority, over the years, Fellows have shaped the program through the articulation of their own needs and ideas for improvement, so that they feel a great deal of ownership over it. Master Oratory Fellows have worked with staff and teaching artists to co-create model lessons and resource materials that are spotlighted on the Ford's website.

Beginning in 2017, an IMLS Museums for America grant allowed Ford's Theatre to contract with researcher and independent evaluator Catherine Awsumb Nelson, in order to collect and analyze data on teacher and student change as a result of the program. Additionally, and perhaps more importantly, Nelson did ethnographic interviews with teachers, students, and school administrators and supported the Fellows and staff in articulating which program elements were most crucial to program success. From this data, and through working sessions, staff and Master Fellows clarified the Ford's Theatre Approach to Oratory Instruction, which is a comprehensive framework that incorporates close reading, performance, research, original writing, and collegial feedback. The framework fills a long-standing gap in teacher preparation and classroom instruction in literacy that precedes but was highlighted by the Common Core State Standards (CCSS).[15] The CCSS set explicit student goals not only for reading and writing but also for speaking and listening, recognizing all four as crucial forms of literacy needed across subject areas and for college and career readiness. However, current curriculum and instructional frameworks focus much more on reading and writing, at least in part because speaking and listening are not typical sections on standardized tests. The Ford's Theatre Approach to Teaching Oratory gives teachers tools to address that gap, providing a high-engagement way for students to interact with texts while building skills in all four domains of the standards.

FORD'S THEATRE APPROACH TO TEACHING ORATORY

Oratory integration is an approach to teaching and learning that focuses on the power of the spoken word, throughout history and in our present time. Students

- learn to analyze written texts and primary source documents;
- learn to perform historic and original speeches;
- develop the skills to speak and write in a clear, civil, and concise manner;
- cultivate their voices as writers and speakers;
- gain knowledge and language to critique other speakers for content and presentation; and
- hone their literacy skills as they dig into complex text.

These tools accomplish multiple curricular goals, from analyzing historical speeches to writing persuasive speeches, to speaking more effectively, to listening and critiquing constructively. Oratory integration empowers students to be thoughtful, responsible citizens in a global community.

Many teachers and students assume public speaking is an innate talent. Ford's Oratory tools provide a structure for all students to learn and cultivate speaking skills. A multi-year evaluation shows that this approach builds student skills and confidence in speaking and deepens their understanding of effective persuasion. Teachers also report that the Ford's Approach helps build a classroom culture of civil discourse and constructive feedback, supporting students in becoming active participants in our democratic society.

Working together, Nelson and the Master Fellows determined that the following four elements are essential to the effective implementation of the Ford's Approach:

1. Speaking using the Podium Points: A framework for coaching students in nine specific oral and physical elements of effective speaking.
2. Responding with Warm and Cool Feedback: A technique for building a classroom culture of constructive feedback in which students support each other's development as effective speakers.
3. Arguing and Analyzing with the Rhetorical Triangle: A model, dating back to Aristotle, for recognizing and deploying three key elements of persuasion, whether students are analyzing historical speeches or writing and performing their own.
4. Connecting to Texts with an Actor's Approach: A theater-based technique for close reading (adapted from the work of Uta Hagen) which helps students understand the historical context and motivation behind speeches.

NATIONAL ORATORY FELLOWS PROGRAM STRUCTURE

National Oratory Fellows are selected through a competitive admissions process. They work together as a professional learning community over multiple years to learn and practice the Oratory Approach. All of the Fellows find out about the program either by participating in a summer institute or through a colleague. Each annual program cycle consists of four major elements, two of which take place throughout the school year, and two of which bracket it.

1. **Summer "Pretreat."** Before schools begin in August, Fellows attend a two-day orientation and planning retreat at Ford's Center for Education and Leadership. Fellows develop their skills with oratory/performance integration and work with Ford's staff and their teaching artist to plan their unit for the school year. Some points for the Fellow to consider before meeting with the teaching artist include:
   - Which areas of my curriculum provide an organic integration of written and spoken text?
   - Are there any literacy skills that warrant focus throughout the school year? How might a teaching artist help me to focus on these skills?
   - What does my teaching artist need to know about the logistics of my school-day schedule in order to make our time together run smoothly?
   - What are the best means of communication between me and my teaching artist?
2. **Teaching Artist/Teacher Collaboration.** National Oratory Fellows are partnered with a Ford's Theatre teaching artist. This teaching artist, an expert in the performing arts, will collaborate regularly with the teacher, conduct virtual lessons within the Fellows' classroom, and will provide coaching and feedback to the Fellow in regard to their oratory-integrated lessons.
   Modeled on the Gradual Release of Responsibility framework (Pearson & Gallagher 1983), which was originally intended to support literacy teaching, over a period of years the teaching artist leads model lessons observed by the teacher; then co-teaches with the teacher; then observes the teacher teaching oratory lessons; and finally, the teacher teaches both content and strategies independently, and in some cases begins teaching others.
   The Oratory Fellow and teaching artist will have:
   - Monthly planning sessions in which they discuss focus skills, lesson objectives, and implementation.
   - Virtual classroom visits (up to 960 minutes per year for Novice Fellows). Visits are at first student-centered and later observations of the Fellow teaching, followed by reflection and coaching. The number of student-centered teaching artist minutes decreases each year, in

consultation with Ford's staff, while the number of minutes dedicated to planning and coaching increases year over year.

- The length of planning sessions and classroom visits is at the discretion of the Fellow and teaching artist, based on the most effective use of each to achieve desired student learning outcomes.

3. **Monthly Group Sessions.** From September to April, Fellows participate in scheduled monthly discussions via video conference. Staff and Master Fellows colead, sessions for newer Fellows. Master Fellows hold a separate monthly session to discuss their practice, which staff may attend. Between the sessions, Fellows contribute to ongoing discussions and sharing resources on the project management platform Basecamp.

4. **Culminating Retreat.** In early May, Ford's Theatre hosts the Fellows for a weekend retreat. Emerging and Veteran Fellows may bring two student delegates to the retreat. Fellows must be available to attend the May Retreat to be eligible for the program. The retreat is both a celebration and an intensive learning experience, including master classes with teaching artists for the student delegates and the Fellows, working sessions for the Fellows, speech performances at both the Lincoln Memorial and the stage of Ford's Theatre, and chances to visit a few sites on the Mall and see a musical at the theatre.

A MULTI-YEAR LEARNING TRAJECTORY

Almost all Fellows choose to remain with the program for multiple years, recognizing that integrating the Oratory Approach into their teaching takes time and practice. As the program developed, Ford's education staff scaffolded the content to introduce teachers to increasingly advanced oratory approaches, while gradually reducing the amount of teaching artist support they receive. By the time teachers become Master Fellows, they are not only implementing all of the techniques independently in their classrooms, but they are also taking on increasing leadership, teaching, and mentoring roles with more junior Fellows. As the cadre of Master Fellows has grown, they have taken on the bulk of professional development leadership, both at the in-person retreats and in monthly online sessions. Working with FTS staff to develop and implement these professional development sessions for other Fellows, as well as for colleagues in their schools and regions, helps to develop them as teacher leaders, an increasingly important, albeit originally unintended outcome of the program.

PROGRAM OUTCOMES

The external evaluation found that 89 percent of Fellows reported that the professional development they received as an Oratory Fellow had a "Major" or even "Transformative" impact on their practice.[16] Specifically, as seen in table 2.2, the evaluation identified the outcomes for teachers, students, and schools.

WHAT WE'VE LEARNED

One might wonder what would compel a teacher to dedicate so much unpaid time to an organization, while holding down an already demanding full-time job. The teachers that choose to become National Oratory Fellows (NOF) are ambitious and searching. They are all dedicated to their practice and their students, but they are also looking for something beyond their classrooms and their schools in which to ground their work. Observationally, this is generally true of teachers that choose to participate in summer institutes run by cultural institutions, and even more so for those that take on the project of joining the NOF professional learning community. The external evaluation of the program confirms that being part of a national professional learning community of like-minded teachers is greatly valued

Table 2.2. The National Oratory Fellows Program Outcomes

Teachers	Students	Schools
• Expanded toolkit for addressing speaking and listening standards • Integration of oratory throughout the curriculum (as opposed to a standalone unit on "public speaking") • Language, structure, and tools for improving student speaking skills • Teacher leadership opportunities • Supportive professional learning community	• Confidence in speaking (in formal and informal settings) • Ability to give and receive feedback • Increased civility and peer support in classroom culture • Students finding their voice to speak about the issues that matter most to them.	• Dissemination of oratory strategies beyond Fellow classrooms • Creation of school-wide or community-level oratory events

by participants.[17] In addition to this important but abstract return on investment, the Fellows are (except for the pandemic year) flown to Washington, D.C., twice a year for programming retreats for at least four years, if they stick with the program. During the May retreat, Emerging and Veteran Fellows bring two student delegates who serve as work samples, in addition to participating in an exciting long weekend of master classes and meeting and exploring D.C. with a small cadre of dedicated young orators from around the country.

It has at times been hard to convince the Fellows' school administrators that this program is not meant to be a speaking contest that culminates in sending two students to Washington, especially when "their" Fellow moves to Master status and is no longer eligible to bring students. The reasoning behind this decision is in part philosophical but is also driven by logistics: Ford's has limited classroom space, and listening to more than thirty middle schoolers deliver even short, two-minute speeches on the Ford's Theatre stage can feel like too long. Aside from the logistics, by limiting the number of years any Fellow can bring students, Ford's sends the message that this program is really about teacher growth and not an opportunity for schools to offer a free trip to the nation's capital.

Beyond bringing students to Washington to speak on the stage, each year the staff asks the Fellows to write a speech in response to a prompt—usually, something that connects to current events, self-expression, and their growth and work over the course of the year. The Fellows deliver their speeches to one another during the May retreat and offer one another warm and cool feedback. They then vote on two Fellows to speak as part of the student performance on the last day of the retreat. Asking the Fellows to take the risks that their students are taking, both by writing in their own voices and speaking in front of a crowd, has become an important part of the Fellows' journeys.

Meeting together each month via Zoom started as a requirement; not all the participants fully understood or embraced it. It was an opportunity to check-in, and we talked about what they were trying in their classrooms and what was and wasn't working. As the Fellows became more comfortable with one another and built both skill and trust, they have come to find the evening gatherings to be deeply supportive and meaningful. They now lead exercises and try out new ideas for one another, and the Master Fellows provide on-boarding and support for the newer Fellows. Additionally, by beginning video-conference teaching artist residencies in 2011 and meeting by Zoom starting in 2013, the Fellows developed capacity and creativity with distance learning, which became valuable resources in their schools during the pandemic.

By creating a long-standing community of practice that teachers can opt into and build skills over a period of years, Ford's Theatre has developed a cadre of education professionals across the country that are both ambassadors for our work and professional developers based in communities of all kinds. From upstate New York to Toledo to Kansas City, Sacramento to rural Nebraska to small-town Kentucky, National Oratory Fellows are finding commonalities and building networks that strengthen the union Abraham Lincoln worked so hard to save; they are extending the mission of Ford's Theatre beyond our site's physical space. When their students meet each spring in Washington, they break down stereotypes about people from different parts of the country and form lasting networks.

A project like the National Oratory Fellows requires a clear vision, but it began with a nugget of an idea, nurtured by feedback from end-users—that is, teachers. While Ford's is a small- to medium-sized institution (a pre-pandemic staff of around fifty), the director has given the education team the freedom to seek funding opportunities to pilot new programs, and it took a few years of pitching to get the money for the pilot. The scope and range of the program allowed Ford's to cultivate relationships with teachers across the breadth of the country. These long-term partnerships are a win-win for the teachers and for Ford's Theatre. (See figure 2.1.)

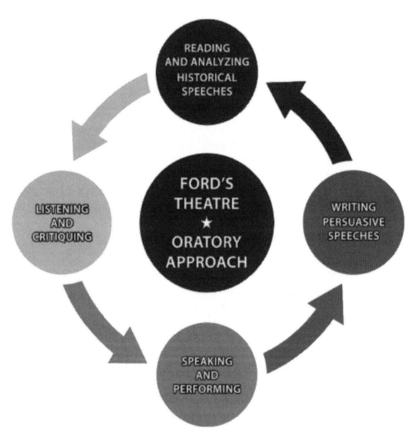

Figure 2.1 The Ford's Theatre Approach to Oratory Instruction framework, a comprehensive approach that incorporates close reading, performance, research, original writing, and collegial feedback. *Catherine Awsumb Nelson*

SHARED AUTHORITY: TOWARD A MORE INCLUSIVE AND ACCESSIBLE MUSEUM

Museums are tasked with being more accessible, inclusive, diverse, relevant, transparent, and welcoming.[18] The intricate work of public engagement is a critical component of a museum's overall programming, especially if it is to remain vital to its audiences and communities. As these two case studies demonstrate, for both institutions it has meant sharing authority with our constituents and creating programs that extend beyond our walls.

For LACMA, the partnership with Charles White Elementary School has allowed it to deepen relationships with multiple communities. Additionally, the collection has been presented in new and dynamic ways, the creative process has been supported and fostered, and the project educates, in the broadest possible sense. All programs are presented free of charge in this location, eliminating barriers for participation—both real and perceived. As students, teachers, and administrators are part of the planning process, the work of the museum becomes more collaborative and transparent. The range of possible ways to engage with works on view at the Charles White gallery allows for opportunities to engage deeply with culture—both our own and others—in efforts to strengthen the museum's capacity to be created by the communities in which it is situated and for its diverse, local constituents.

For Ford's Theatre, an intentional and deliberate engagement with teachers across the country allowed it to build a community of practitioners that has strengthened its capacity to achieve its mission. Through the use of technology and capitalizing on the investment it made in building relationships with teacher communities, Ford's Theatre was well prepared to deal with the transition to an online format that a global pandemic forced on so many other institutions to also adapt to. And through a continued commitment to reflective assessment, Ford's Theatre could change and iterate aspects of the program in response to their constituents by implementing a model of shared authority.

While it is true that these initiatives take money, time, and human resources—resources that some museums may not have—more importantly, they take a vision for, and commitment to, a process of continual refinement, reevaluating, and adapting. This includes prioritizing the voices and perspectives of multiple stakeholders, adapting program components, and a willingness to allow the project to evolve in unexpected directions. Both of these case studies demonstrate museum educators' willingness to respond to their communities' needs and a willingness to evolve in response to lessons learned or unanticipated challenges.

Museums are seen as trusted institutions,[19] viewed as both reliable sources of information and as community resources for lifelong learning. Many continue the work of presenting and interpreting topics of cultural, civic, and social significance and develop programming designed to encourage thoughtful consideration of multiple and diverse experiences and perspectives. By actively engaging with and building trust with communities through collaborative educational programming, museums can be spaces for dialogue and shared authority with the communities they serve.

DISCUSSION QUESTIONS

1. When thinking about your museum, can you think of a time or program when your museum seceded authority? How was that manifested? What were the outcomes?
2. This chapter highlights some benefits when museums secede authority—better partnerships, increased learning opportunities, and stronger programs. What other benefits arise when museums give up some of their authority?
3. Due to the COVID-19 pandemic, education departments have faced challenges in programs (as described in the LACMA case study where teacher professional development had to shift entirely online), staffing (such as furloughs and layoffs), or some opportunities, such as the Ford's ability to capitalize on bringing teachers together virtually from across the country. Did your museum support the education department during the pandemic? If so, how?

NOTES

1. Mary Ellen Munley, "Museums as Learning Environments: A Prospectus for a New Century," 1984: 29.
2. Munley, "Museums as Learning Environments," 1984: 30.
3. Rika Burnham and Elliott Kai-Kee, *Teaching in the Art Museum,* 2011; Tracie E. Costantino, "Training Aesthetic Perception," 2004; George H. Hein, *Learning in the Museum,* 1998; Anna M. Kindler, "Aesthetic Development and Learning in Art Museums," 1997.
4. Costantino, "Training Aesthetic Perception," 2004; David Ebitz, "Qualifications and the Professional Preparation and Development of Art Museum Educators," 2005; Nick Rabkin, Michael Reynolds, Eric Hedberg, and Justin Shelby, *A Report on the Teaching Artist Research Project,* 2011.
5. Susanne Garvis and Christopher Klopper, "Something Old, Something New, Something Borrowed but not Blue," 2014; Mary Ann Reilly, "Finding the Right Words," 2008.
6. Liane Brouillette, Karen Childress-Evans, Briana Hinga, and George Farkas, "Increasing Engagement and Oral Language Skills of ELLs through the Arts in the Primary Grades," 2014; Rabkin, Reynolds, Hedberg, and Shelby, *A Report on the Teaching Artist Research Project,* 2011.
7. Rabkin, Reynolds, Hedberg, and Shelby, *A Report on the Teaching Artist Research Project,* 2011; Randi Korn & Associates, *Summary of Results Survey of Single-Visit K–12 Art Museum Programs,* 2015.
8. Randi Korn & Associates, *Summary of Results Survey of Single-Visit K–12 Art Museum Programs,* 2015.
9. Ibid.
10. MacArthur Park is comprised of mostly Latinos (69.2 percent), followed by 20 percent Asian, 5 percent white and 4.5 percent Black. The median annual household income is $29,300, less than half the $62,474 average median income in Los Angeles, https://statisticalatlas.com/zip/90057/Race-and-Ethnicity.
11. Beyond the scope of this chapter, the invitation to install an exhibition in the school's gallery coincided with the launch of a new initiative at LACMA to provide art classes at many schools and libraries in this region of the city.
12. Student body of Charles White: Latino students (94 percent); White and Black students make up less than 3 percent (2.1 percent and 2.7 percent respectively). Eighty-eight percent of students are English Learners (ELs) as compared to 55 percent of students in the Los Angeles Unified District, https://explorelausd.schoolmint.net/school-finder/schools/1219/charles-white-elementary-school.
13. S. Layne and L. Silverstein, *What is Arts Integration?*, Kennedy Center, 2021, https://www.kennedy-center.org/education/resources-for-educators/classroom-resources/articles-and-how-tos/articles/collections/arts-integration-resources/what-is-arts-integration/.
14. Deborah Vankin, "LACMA Demolition: Three Buildings Down, One More Begins Tear-Down," *Los Angeles Times,* August 19, 2020, https://www.latimes.com/entertainment-arts/story/2020-08-19/lacma-demolition-update-summer-2020.
15. CCSS, National Governors' Association Center for Best Practices, 2010.
16. Catherine Nelson, *Evaluation of Ford's Theatre Oratory Fellows Program, Year One Summary of Findings,* 2018.
17. Catherine Nelson, *Ford's Theatre Oratory Fellows Case Study Addressing Common Core State Standards,* 2019.
18. Munley, "Museums as Learning Environments: A Prospectus for a New Century," 1984.
19. Wilkening Consulting, April 9, 2018, http://www.wilkeningconsulting.com/datamuseum/trust-and-museums. (Survey conducted March 2018 on behalf of American Association for State and Local History from a sample of Americans across the country.)

BIBLIOGRAPHY

Brouillette, Liane, Karen Childress-Evans, Briana Hinga, and George Farkas. "Increasing Engagement and Oral Language Skills of ELLs through the Arts in the Primary Grades." *Journal for Learning through the Arts,* 10, no.1 (2014): 1–25. Retrieved from https://escholarship.org/uc/item/8573z1fm.

Burnham, Rika, and Elliott Kai-Kee. *Teaching in the Art Museum: Interpretation as Experience*. Los Angeles: Getty, 2011.

Costantino, Tracie. E. "Training Aesthetic Perception: John Dewey on the Educational Role of Art Museums." *Educational Theory* 54 (2004): 399–417. https://doi:10.1111/j.0013-2004.2004.00027.x.

Ebitz, David. "Qualifications and the Professional Preparation and Development of Art Museum Educators." *Studies in Art Education,* 46 (2005): 150–69. *JSTOR.*

Garvis, Susanne, and Christopher Klopper. "Something Old, Something New, Something Borrowed but not Blue: The Educational Impact of the Arts." In *Representations of Working in Arts Education: Stories of Learning and Teaching,* edited by Narelle Lemon, Susanne Garvis, and Christopher Klopper, 71–90. Chicago: Intellect, University of Chicago Press, 2014.

Hein, George H. *Learning in the Museum.* London: Routledge, 1998.

Kindler, Anna M. "Aesthetic Development and Learning in Art Museums: A Challenge to Enjoy." *Journal of Museum Education* 22, no. 2/3 (1997): 12–16. https://doi:10.1080/10598650.1997.11510353.

Layne, S. and L. Silverstein. *What is Arts Integration?* Kennedy Center, 2021. Accessed February 26, 2021, https://www.kennedy-center.org/education/resources-for-educators/classroom-resources/articles-and-how-tos/articles/collections/arts-integration-resources/what-is-arts-integration/.

Munley, Mary Ellen. "Museums as Learning Environments: A Prospectus for a New Century." *Museum Education: Past, Present, and Future* 9, no. 2/3 (1984): 29–32. *JSTOR.*

National Governors Association Center for Best Practices, Council of Chief State School Officers. (2010). Common core state standards, English language arts. National Governors Association Center for Best Practices, Council of Chief State School Officers, Washington, D.C., http://www.corestandards.org/ELA-Literacy/introduction/key-design-consideration/.

Nelson, Catherine. *Evaluation of Ford's Theatre Oratory Fellows Program, Year One Summary of Findings,* 2018.

Nelson, Catherine. *Ford's Theatre Oratory Fellows Case Study Addressing Common Core State Standards,* 2019.

Pearson, P. David, and Margaret Gallagher. "The Gradual Release of Responsibility Model of Instruction." *Contemporary Educational Psychology* 8 (1983): 112–23.

Rabkin, Nick, Michael Reynolds, Eric Hedberg, and Justin Shelby. *A Report on the Teaching Artist Research Project: Teaching Artists and the Future of Education.* Chicago: University of Chicago Press, 2011.

Randi Korn & Associates. "Summary of Results Survey of Single-Visit K-12 Art Museum Programs" (Unpublished manuscript). Reston: National Art Education Association, 2015.

Reilly, Mary Ann. "Finding the Right Words: Art Conversations and Poetry." *Language Arts,* 86 (2008): 99–107. Retrieved from http://www2.ncte.org/resources/journals/languagearts/.

3

The Spectrum Project

SOCIAL STORIES, MUSEUM EDUCATORS, AND YOUNG ADULTS WITH AUTISM

Beth Redmond-Jones

ABSTRACT

Museums provide opportunities for individuals, families, and groups to spend quality time together in an interactive environment that aims to foster a sense of community and enjoyment. However, many museums are loud, crowded public spaces that can be difficult to navigate and over-stimulating for individuals with an autism spectrum disorder (ASD). Though policies on inclusive practices for individuals with autism have resulted in the development of successful practices and advances in formal education and early childhood settings, museums have been slow to provide approaches for supporting those with autism, especially adults. This chapter will provide museum educators with some valuable tools for engaging young adults with autism at their museum, based on the Social Stories Sectrum Project at the San Diego Natural History Museum (The Nat), which provided a structured opportunity for high-functioning verbal young adults (ages 18–25) with ASD to meet up with their peers and practice social skills, participate in organized trips to seven museums in Balboa Park in San Diego, and work together to create "social stories" for the museums visited.

THE SPECTRUM PROJECT

There is a saying in the autism community, "if you've met one person with autism, you've met one person with autism." Being part of the autism community (my oldest daughter is on the spectrum), I knew this quote, but hadn't really grasped the entire meaning of it until 2017 when the Social Stories Spectrum Project was implemented at the San Diego Natural History Museum (The Nat). This project brought museum education staff and a group of young adults on the Autism spectrum together to create descriptive visitor engagement tools that could be used by other visitors on the spectrum and their families. The project was designed to be a social experience for the youth as well as a valuable effort by the museum to learn more about engaging with visitors on the Autism spectrum.[1]

WHAT IS AN AUTISM SPECTRUM DISORDER?

Autism spectrum disorder and autism are both general terms for a group of complex disorders of brain development. People with ASD may communicate, interact, behave, and learn in ways that are different from most other people. These symptoms fall on a continuum, with some individuals showing mild symptoms and others having much more severe symptoms, including the inability to communicate verbally at all.

MUSEUMS' VISITORS WITH AUTISM

Museums provide opportunities for individuals, families, and groups to spend quality time together, experience and learn something new, and provide a community of like-minded individuals. But many museums are loud, crowded public spaces that are over-stimulating for individuals with autism. Though museums have stepped up their engagement for kids under the age of ten with autism,[2] they have been slow to provide approaches for supporting adults with autism.

Though museums work to design inclusive environments that reflect universal design parameters, the field is unprepared to accommodate the growing number of adults with ASD. A study from the Centers for Disease Control and Prevention (CDC) estimated the prevalence of ASD among adults aged eighteen years and older in the United States in 2017 at 5,437,988 (2.21 percent) of adults in the United States.[3]

Given that the Social Stories Spectrum Project did not exist elsewhere, we built it from the ground up. The Nat's intention was to invite the beneficiaries of the project—young adults with ASD—to serve as partners and co-creators in the development of the social stories for seven different museums. Our hope was that this project would:

- exemplify the museum field's effort to share authority with a special segment of the public that historically had been overlooked,
- identify whether creating social stories for different types of museums required different strategies or methodologies,
- encourage the partner organizations to better serve individuals with ASD, and
- provide needed scaffolding for those with ASD to visit museums they may never have visited before.

This chapter describes this project in detail. At the end it also provides a number of lessons learned for museum educators in a variety of settings and museum disciplines that can be utilized in similar types of programs for people living with ASD or other neurological conditions.

RUNNING THE PROJECT

When we learned that the Social Stories Spectum Project was funded by the Institute for Museum and Library Services (IMLS), The Nat team was excited about the work ahead of us, but we were also hesitant. None of us had ever run this type of program before and we did not have a model to emulate. We acknowledged that we would make mistakes along the way and recognized that we would need to be nimble to make this project successful for the young adults, the San Diego autism community, the museum community, and ourselves.

APPLICATION AND INTERVIEW PROCESS

We first implemented an application and interview process for the participants of the project. The application gave us insights to their level of education completed, their writing ability (phrases vs.

complete sentences), as well as conversation starters like their special interests. We wanted to be sure that the young adults were verbal and high functioning enough to engage with the group independently, without an aid or a parent's support, for two reasons. First, The Nat facilitators were not trained in working with lower functioning individuals with ASD. It would not have been fair to the facilitators nor the participants to create a situation where both parties could not be successful. Second, most services and activities for those with autism expire at age eighteen or upon graduation from high school. This project allowed individuals older than that to contribute to society and a need within the San Diego museum community.

The interview process, which was conducted by phone, was critical, though we realized later that all of the conversations with the young adults should have been facilitated either face-to-face or via video chat. The interviews did give The Nat facilitators an understanding of the young adults' verbal capabilities and focus, but we were not prepared for parent prompting of the young adult during the interviews. In hindsight, those that required parent prompting also ended up requiring prompting from the facilitators as well as the occupational therapist (OT) for basic communication and interaction during the meetings that took place later.

However, each of the young adults was motivated, passionate, and looking forward to exploring museums, working on their social skills, making friends, and creating social stories for their community. They came from a variety of backgrounds. They were musicians, artists, collectors, gamers, volunteers, animal lovers, college students, world travelers, and historians. Each participant had a wide range of special interests, which they were excited to share with us and with their peers (see figure 3.1).

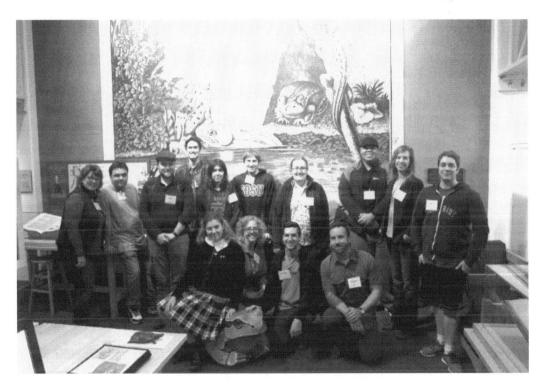

Figure 3.1 Group expectations were reviewed at the beginning of each meetup to reinforce the skills the young adults were to work on. *Photo courtesy of the San Diego Natural History Museum (The Nat).*

ADVISORY GROUP

Our advisors for the Social Stories Spectrum Project included an accessibility advocate from Museum of Science, Boston, the director of the accessibility program at the Smithsonian Institution, a local researcher and professor at San Diego State University in the field of severe intellectual disabilities, an autism advocate that worked for a local nonprofit that provided services that instill community-wide autism inclusion, and a local occupational therapist (OT) who specialized in working with individuals with autism on life skills in the "real world." We also included our Balboa Park partners, who were comprised of designated staff members from the Fleet Science Center, Museum of Photographic Arts, San Diego History Center, San Diego Museum of Art, Museum of Us (formerly known as the San Diego Museum of Man), and Japanese Friendship Garden so they could take advantage of the expertise being brought together for this project.

During the two-day kick off meeting, The Nat team, the OT and the advisors spent time getting to know each other better, getting everyone on the same page with regard to the scope of the project, exploring three of the museums (The Nat, Museum of Photographic Arts, and Museum of Us), and learning about autism. Through presentations and dialogue, the group began to come to a basic understanding of the unique characteristics and needs of individuals with autism including support with sensory processing challenges, life skills, and social interactions. We discussed how we, as The Nat facilitators and the occupational therapist, could best support the participants through structured meetups, facilitated experiences, and opportunities to work on social skills, so we could all be successful in visiting the museums and supporting the creation of the social stories.

We also discussed our hopes and fears. We hoped that the young adults would feel empowered and amplified by the project; that The Nat facilitators and project partners would gain a broader understanding of visitors with ASD; that this project would have long-term positive effects in regard to inclusive practices within the San Diego ASD community; and that the project would become a model for other museums who want to co-create a project with members of the autism community. We also had fears about the project which we needed to reframe as "challenges"—these could be mitigated by educating ourselves, being nimble and ready to change course as needed, and accepting that we would learn a lot from this project, which would then inform our respective future practices and hopefully that of the museum community.

PROVIDING STRUCTURE FOR EACH MEETUP

As we prepared for our first meeting with the young adults, The Nat team worked to answer the following question: How do you structure a meetup for young adults with autism whom you have never met, who do not know each other, and who are probably as nervous as we are? Our answer: break it down to basics.

We always had an agenda at each meeting. It outlined the time of the meetup and broke down the activities, including restroom breaks and snack time, into time frames. This structure was very beneficial to the young adults as they knew exactly what would be happening and when. It gave them a routine.

During our first meetup, we co-created a list of "Group Expectations" (see textbox 3.1). Since communication and understanding social cues can be challenging for individuals with autism, we felt it was critical to define Group Expectations for collaborating. It was so rewarding to see how the group began to work together to define these expectations and to agree upon them. At the end of the exercise, one of The Nat team members stated "these are the same expectations that we, as museum professionals, try to abide by when working with our colleagues." It was a wonderful moment of reflection, but also a realization by the young adults that the skills they were going to work on were also those that neurotypical individuals also work on. These expectations were reviewed at the beginning of each meetup to reinforce these concepts for everyone.

Beth Redmond-Jones

Group Expectations
- *Respect each other's differences.*
- *Everyone's voice should be heard.*
- *Respect someone else's perspective.*
- *Be honest and polite.*
- *Take a break when you need it.*
- *Let The Nat staff know if you are leaving the room.*
- *Be a good listener—practice active listening (eye contact, turn body toward the person who is talking).*
- *Feel free to ask a question, repeat something, or say it in a different way.*
- *Phone OK for project work or for coping.*
- *Advocate for yourself!*
- *Contact The Nat staff if you can't come to a meetup.*
- *Be kind and forgiving to yourself and others.*
- *Use of stress relievers (fidgets, engine changers) are encouraged.*
- *Have fun!*

At that first meetup, we also co-created the 5-point Feelings Check-In (see table 3.1), a tool the OT brought to the project (modified here to be in table format). She uses this scale to help individuals with autism self-manage behavior and emotional regulation. It's a way to make abstract concepts and feelings visual, concrete, and personal. Since we had several young adults with sensory processing

Table 3.1.

	5 Point Check-In	*Strategies to help mitigate feelings*
5	• *Overwhelmed* • *Panic attack* • *Confusion* • *Loss of verbal abilities* • *Can't process thoughts* • *"Shut Down"* • *Meltdown*	• *Deep breathing* • *Deep pressure* • *Think of things that make you feel better* • *Remove myself from situation with a NAT team member or OT*
4		
3	• *Frustrated* • *Irritated* • *Nervous* • *Anxious*	• *Music* • *Mantras* • *Positive Statements* • *Counting*
2		
1	• *Happy* • *Calm* • *Excited* • *Relaxes* • *Content*	

challenges, we felt it was critical to develop a common language and scale so we could all "check in" with one another and provide support as needed. So as a group, the young adults defined what each point represented and different ways someone could mitigate those feelings.

So, at the beginning of each meetup, each person checked in with the group to say how their day had been going and how they were currently feeling (tired from an exam, hot and tired from walking in the heat, hungry, happy, feeling great, etc.). Most days, everyone was in the 1-2 point range, but there were a few occasions when someone would be a 3 or 4. On those days, we saw the young adults trying to "check in" with that person to see if they could get them a snack, carry something for them, or ask them something about a special interest. For us facilitators, these were magical moments as the young adults demonstrated empathy, not a usual trait seen or expressed by those with autism.

Icebreakers were also a regular part of our meetup agenda as they connected us to each other before we started on that day's activity and provided a great way for us to explore our commonalities and differences. It was a big hit with the participants as they learned about the things they shared in common, especially music and movies. For one of the icebreakers, we invited everyone to share what their favorite food was. This allowed everyone to see commonalities as there were some enthusiastic "me too's" from the participants followed by smiles.

ADDRESSING SENSORY DIFFERENCES

Some individuals with autism have sensory processing disorder, a condition in which the brain has trouble receiving and responding to information that comes in through the senses. This may include being oversensitive to things in their environment such as bright lights, common or loud sounds, or even the touch of a specific type of clothing material such as polyester or wool.

We found that some of the young adults had diverse sensory needs which required our own nimble mindset to adapt and change to meet their challenges. The participants arrived by train, bus, cars, and Uber/Lyft drivers from various parts of the city and county. They gathered together for four hours, explored museums, and co-created social stories together. All of this activity was very challenging, especially for those young adults in our group that had sensory processing challenges. Within a few meetups, it became apparent that we needed to make adjustments to our environment to help the participants feel more centered, focused, and regulated emotionally and behaviorally for increased learning opportunities and social interactions.

We adjusted our meeting room design, from the overhead lights that were harsh and had a tendency to flicker to standing lamps with softer light that could be adjusted up or down depending upon the needs of the group. We also reconfigured the seating arrangements. Those that needed movement input could choose office chairs that spinned and rocked, or therapy balls to sit and gently bounce on. This variety of physical movement was alerting to the nervous system and helped participants engage more in the learning process. Participants also learned to advocate where they would like to sit in the group to be most comfortable. We supplied engine changers (see figure 3.2) and fidgets (see figure 3.3) baskets to further support individual sensory needs. The baskets typically contained gum; hard candy for sucking; sour candy to increase alertness; chewy candy to work the jaw; and fidgets in different shapes and sizes, and with a variety of textures, like sculpting wax and spinners, to keep fingers busy. The use of engine changers and fidgets helped participants sustain their attention to the tasks at hand.

ENGAGING AN OCCUPATIONAL THERAPIST WITH A SPECIALIZATION IN AUTISM

As we developed the project, we knew that having an occupational therapist (OT) who was experienced working with young adults with autism would enhance the effectiveness and success of the project. But what we didn't realize was the critical role the OT would play. Besides addressing any

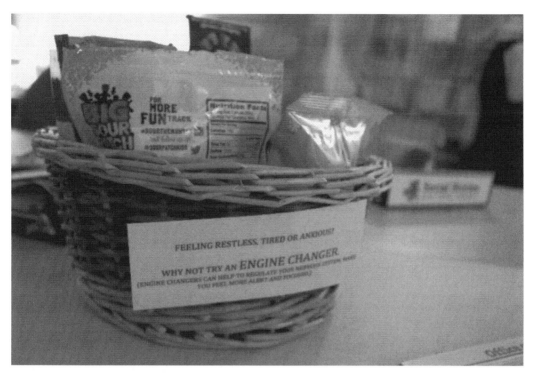

Figure 3.2 Engine Changers. *Photo courtesy of the San Diego Natural History Museum (The Nat).*

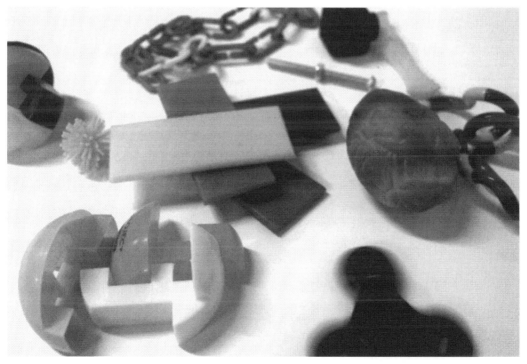

Figure 3.3 Fidgets. *Photo courtesy of the San Diego Natural History Museum (The Nat).*

The Spectrum Project

challenges the participants had, she modeled behavior, techniques, language and methodology for The Nat facilitators so we could provide better support for the young adults throughout the project. Here are two examples of tools our OT brought to the project that proved invaluable.

- Teaching Social Skills—Social skills (looking someone in the eye when speaking to them, shaking hands, saying hello and goodbye, not interrupting) are something we, in the United States, learn about and then practice intuitively throughout our lives. But these are not intuitive skills for those with autism. Through role play, conversation, and situational awareness, the OT was able to effectively teach the young adults social skills and provide The Nat team with the tools to help support and facilitate these teaching moments.
- Managing Autism Meltdowns (a 5 on our "5 Point Check-In" chart)—Our OT came with the experience and skills to identify the signs early and to navigate meltdowns, which became invaluable to the whole group. An autism "meltdown" is a powerful experience for everyone. These meltdowns are characterized by an intense response to an overwhelming or stressful situation in which an individual is unable to maintain control. An autistic meltdown is more emotional and prolonged, and with no underlying intention to gain anything from a situation. They are often preceded by indicators of distress—an individual becomes less responsive, visibly uncomfortable and requests to be left alone.[4] Alternatively, there could be less discrete physical signs such as placing their hands over their ears, particularly in an overwhelming sensory environment. By having the OT teach The Nat team the signs of potential meltdowns and provide us with tools to help in these situations, we were able to mitigate and supersede any emotional events. We utilized a quiet room, alone time, and fidgets to support the young adults. One of our participants, however, needed a different type of intervention which required her autism service dog to lie on her lap to apply deep pressure. This lowered her sensory system and allowed her body to relax so she could return to a balanced and functional state.

SCAFFOLDING: BUILDING A FRAMEWORK FOR MUSEUM VISITS

So, how did we go about getting ten young adults with autism, who had never worked together, to co-create a social story for a museum? "Much of contemporary learning theory rests on the idea of 'instructional scaffolding,' by which educators or educational material provides supportive resources, tasks, and guidance upon which learners can build their confidence and abilities," writes Nina Simon in *The Participatory Museum*.[5] For The Nat team, this was a critical point. It was important that each young adult have a framework or tool to document both the easy and challenging aspects of the visit for them (bright lights, loud sounds, couldn't find the bathroom, didn't like talking with floor staff, loved the squishy couch, etc.). We also felt it was critical that each individual have a voice, as each of them is unique and their autism manifests in individual ways. The aforementioned phrase "if you've met one person with autism, you've met one person with autism," was becoming readily apparent in our group.

The framework we developed—knowing very well we might need to refine it as we went along—was based on four phases of a museum visit. As we introduced this framework, or scaffolding, to the young adults, we asked them to help us brainstorm things to think about, or activities they may do during each of these four phases.

Phase 1: Before the Visit

- Look at the museum's website: exhibitions, rules to follow
- Get your money or museum pass ready
- Make sure you have your phone and wallet
- Route or map to the museum

- Open hours
- Cafe hours

Phase 2: Arriving at the Museum

- Buy a ticket
- Show your ID/Museum pass
- Interact with person at desk
- Wait in line
- Possibly see security
- Explain about your service dog if asked
- Get a map
- Where are restrooms?
- Check your bag
- Ask about rules about photography

Phase 3: Moving Around the Museum

- Crowds—school groups!
- Noises
- Lights
- Docents
- Volunteers
- Big things
- Moving things
- Not moving—Art
- Gift shop
- Restrooms
- Classes/programs
- Movies
- Places to sit
- Food and water
- Loud spaces
- Quiet spaces!!

Phase 4: Leaving the Museum

- Gift shop
- Restrooms
- Find exits
- Get your backpack
- Make sure you have all your stuff
- Find your car/bus

With this framework fresh in everyone's mind, the group headed to a museum to give the framework a try. We met up with our museum project partner, who welcomed the group and invited them all in. We asked the young adults to lead the way, then go their separate ways to explore the museum and fill out their framework worksheets. We let them know that The Nat team and museum project partner would be available for questions as needed. Each museum visit provided unique insights, including where to stand in line to get your museum ticket ("Why did the admission's person just give me a sticker?"), discoveries about light levels being too high or too low, the locations of the quiet and loud areas, places to sit, where the gift shop was located, how to leave, and/or where to stand in line to play with an interactive.

After completing the museum visit, the museum project partner returned with the group back to our meeting room to debrief about the time spent in their space. This proved interesting for all involved, as some things that were challenging for some of the young adults were not for others, and vice versa. The museum project partner answered questions and provided clarifications which were helpful for many of the young adults. The Nat staff provided probing questions here and there to be sure that all aspects of the visit were covered.

For the subsequent museum visits, the young adults started asking the museum project partner questions when they first met, such as "Are cell phones allowed?" and "Are we wearing appropriate clothing to go into your museum?" (This question still makes me smile; the young adult showed up looking ready for an interview but wanted to be sure he conformed to the dress code.) As the young adults entered the second museum, we realized that entry and going through admissions was very different than the first museum visited and required some coaching on our staff's part. At the second debrief, it was interesting to see some of the young adults move out of their own experience at the museum and think about the experience of other visitors who may have autism. This demonstration of their ability to empathize was another great sight to behold.

After working through the framework, the young adults sorted through the information, determining what was critical for physical movement through the particular museum that would be important for future visitors on the ASD spectrum (for instance, interactions with staff or volunteers when entering the museum, the location of elevators or restrooms) versus what were sensory challenges (loud entryways and atria, narrow and potentially crowded museum entrances) versus "good to know" items (no flash photography, cannot touch anything, no food allowed). We also discussed the language and tone that would be used in writing their social story. We called the resulting document our "shot list."

On a subsequent visit, we took our "shot list" and visited the museum again to photograph elements of the social story that we could tell pictorially, which would provide visual cues for users. When we started the photographic process, we asked questions of the group: "Who would like to take the photo," "Who would like to be an actor," "What is the photo we need to take," and "Is this the right angle." After photos were taken, we asked the young adults to crowd around the iPad and make a decision about which photos to keep so we could edit on the spot. But we found this process disjointed and confusing for the young adults. It was too unstructured and didn't keep everyone focused on the task at hand. It was also difficult to get ten or more people around an ipad, which led to some wandering off, others saying they were bored, and others requiring encouragement to participate.

So, once again, we embraced being nimble and changed our photography review strategy. For each photography day, we identified:

1. A project manager, who managed the "shot list" and led the group in pursuit of our various photograph needs;
2. A scout, who identified potential locations for the photographs;
3. The photographer, who took multiple photographs from different vantage points; and
4. "Actors," to help show the different procedures for moving through the museum (e.g., buying tickets at an admission desk, locating an elevator, etc.).

After all the photos were taken, we returned to our meeting room, but did not look at the photos until the next meetup when we could display the "shot list" and project the photos onto the wall. This enabled the group to look at the photos together and discuss which image fit what we were trying to show the best. This change in strategy proved to be important and helpful as it provided everyone with a "role" in the process. It also required the participants to collaborate and cooperate with their peers, gave them a purpose for the day, and required discussion and consensus. As a result, we saw a dramatic increase in the young adults' self-esteem and ability to work as a group and care for and communicate with one another.

In the end, the group visited all seven museums twice to work through the framework and take photographs. We visited a couple of the museums a third time to shoot a photograph we missed or to improve on the original photograph. Each of the seven social stories contained between twenty-two and thirty-one photographs and each social story was translated into Spanish. The design layout and translation of the social stories was completed by The Nat team, but the young adults reviewed each finished product prior to publication. All of the social stories can be found under The Nat's accessibility web page (www.sdnhm.org).

WHAT WE LEARNED

When recruiting museums to participate in this project, we were surprised to hear that most of the museums in Balboa Park were not addressing the needs of visitors with autism. Some stated that they had had groups come in from local autism organizations and others had children with autism in their summer camp programs, but that was the extent of the involvement and investment. Those museums that did join the project were eager and open to learning from the young adults. They wanted to learn how their institutions could become more welcoming, inclusive, and accessible.

After their multiple visits to the museums, the young adults identified several challenges common at the institutions that exacerbated feelings of a lack of welcoming, inclusion, and accessibility.

- Some of the museum's accessibility web pages were difficult to find and none of them had social stories.
- The entrance to the museum was often difficult to find.
- Paying for admission was confusing and there was often a lack of directional signage that explained where to go.
- Most admission staff were not trained to accommodate service animals and those individuals with autism that visited with them.
- There was not enough seating and/or quiet areas for down time.
- For those with sensory issues, the museums with loud, flashy exhibits and/or open architectural spaces with hard surfaces where sound could bounce were particularly difficult to navigate for an extended amount of time.

The Nat contracted with Randi Korn & Associates (RKA) to conduct the evaluation of this program. The evaluation explored outcomes for young adult participants, museum staff, and project partners from other Balboa Park museums. RKA conducted in-depth, naturalistic observations of three meetups; individual interviews with a few participants; and interviews with museum staff and partners. They also developed feedback worksheets, both to share interim findings and to collect a second round of participant feedback before the program finished.

Our goals for the young adults were for them to feel that their perspective was valued, they were contributing to society, to build social and communication skills, with an end result of building confidence and self-esteem. Overall, the evaluation showed that the project was successful in supporting participants in two of the three goals, most noticeably in building social and communication skills as well as confidence and self-esteem.

But young adults feeling and knowing they were contributing to society and their perspective was valued, was not as effectively achieved. We emphasized "co-creation of social stories" but that became our challenge. The evaluation found that:

> Several participants suggested providing participants greater license to control the program's structure, such as simply giving them the authority to suggest activities to break up the day. Perhaps allowing participants to have greater input on the day's agenda, goals, and the process of achieving these goals would have promoted greater feelings of value in participants' perspectives.[6]

But as the facilitators, we felt it was necessary to create the meetup structure to give the young adults a "routine" for our time together so we could achieve our end goal of producing social stories for seven museums. To have the agenda created at the meeting, or by selected young adults, would have caused challenges for other young adults who needed consistency, and change to the routine would have provoked anxiety and distress. After reflecting on this, though, maybe we were too hung up on the end goal of producing social stories, rather than really looking at effective ways to work with young adults with autism and, specifically, how to support those who were rigid in their thought process to manage that change in routine.

> Another barrier to participants feeling and knowing they are contributing to society relates to what "co-creation" looks like for this program. For instance, in the beginning of the program, staff provided a great amount of scaffolding for project work and social communication; but over time, staff provided less, which seemed successful given the group dynamics evident at the end of the program. Program staff regularly reflected on this approach to "co-creating" project work. Yet, staff expressed concerns about if/how to encourage agency for participants to structure the program design (e.g., agenda, activities).[7]

In our desire to truly engage these young adults with autism, we may have done them, and ourselves, a disservice by emphasizing "co-creation." We envisioned this project with good intentions but with a neurotypical perspective and strategy, not with a neurodiverse lens. Basically, we created a "co-creation" expectation that we had already envisioned that would work by our standards, not allowing for the input by the young adults who thought differently from us. We were trying to facilitate a project for a group of individuals that typically needed structure but, not all of them needed that structure. Yet, due to our inexperience working with young adults with autism, we were not knowledgeable nor nimble enough to change course.

As I reflect on this project, I think the young adults may have been better served if the project had been facilitated by educators who facilitate classroom programs and tours versus a combination of exhibits staff and educators. Educators have an advantage of being more connected to the community in addition to having the tools for facilitating programs with individuals who have a diverse set of learning styles and abilities. Did the Spectrum Project fail with our staffing structure? No, not at all. But educators would have an advantage—they are connected to local organizations and can create partnerships that are not a one-time offering, like this project, but something that can grow and be sustained over time.

With educators having those critical connections to the community, they can open doors to creating a similar project to this without the need for a large grant. The framework for the social stories has been developed and tested, and additional tools for collaborating with young adults with autism have been described. Now what is needed are individuals with ASD to help define the experience of visiting your organization, whether it is a museum, zoo, aquarium, historic site, or botanical garden. This framework works for all disciplines of informal learning institutions, it just needs to have individuals with the right needs to represent their community and help you create your social story.

Beth Redmond-Jones

TAKEAWAYS FOR EDUCATORS

Although it might be challenging to replicate this project, there are several takeaways that educators can utilize in their practice when working with young adults with autism.

1. Your museum, zoo, or aquarium can create a social story by utilizing the four-phase framework developed during this project.
   a. This could be accomplished by staff, but by engaging individuals in the autism community to assist you, they will identify challenging elements of your institution that you may not notice.
   b. The final social story can be simply designed in a word processing program with text and photographs and saved as a PDF; it does not have to be a highly designed product. Remember to keep the text short and to the point, and have the image reflect what is being stated in the text.
   c. Post your social story on your website, share it with programming materials for summer camp, share it with local autism organizations and community partners and post on your social media channels with hashtags for the ASD community (#ASD, #autism, #autismspectrum-disorder #aspergers #inclusion, #socialstory).
2. When running tours, public programs, and group visits for young adults with autism, provide scaffolding to ensure their success.
   a. Providing an agenda or schedule will give structure to their visit and during their program.
   b. Developing expectations as a group can be beneficial and defines behavior parameters. It defines what is expected of them and where the boundaries lie.
   c. The 5-point Feelings Check-In list is invaluable. As educators, you have no idea what each young adult has faced that day, and this is a good way for participants and educators to have a baseline for mood and capacities on a given day.
   d. Providing a fidget basket or bag is an easy tool to have available. It allows hands to stay busy so minds can focus.
   e. Assess the room and ancillary spaces where the program is taking place. Can lighting be adjusted up or down? Are their different types of seating? Is there a way to make the room more welcoming to the senses?
   f. Provide a quiet space for those who need to "take a break" as needed. It might be a nook in the corner of the room, a small table next to a window, or an empty office. Giving that space will allow the young adult to regroup, then rejoin the program when ready.
   g. Staff your programs appropriately. One of The Nat facilitators, Erica Kelly, reflected that "we learned that someone always needed to be 'on duty' on any specific day. . . . It might be [for] one of the young adults who would wander off, or another who needed focused attention when she/he got overwhelmed at a museum, or another who needed 'alone time' to regroup."[8] An extra staff member can assist any stressed individual without disruption to the others while the program continues.
3. Not everyone has access to an occupational therapist to provide insight to working with those on the spectrum, so seek out ways to train staff. Reach out to local autism organizations and ask them if they would be willing to come in and share their knowledge of working with individuals with autism and how your organization can better serve them. But don't only train education staff, be sure to include floor, security, frontline, cafe, and store staff so your organization will be working together with a unified knowledge and language.
4. It is important to understand that many individuals with autism also have comorbid conditions that they struggle with including ADHD, gastrointestinal disorders, bipolar, depression, seizures, schizophrenia, obesity, and/or anxiety.[9] Several of the young adults that we worked with strug-

gled with an additional physical or mental health condition which at times were their dominant challenge, more so than their autism.

CLOSING THOUGHTS

As facilitators of the Social Stories Spectrum Project, we encouraged the young adults to express their own needs as well as recognize and support the needs of other individuals and the group as a whole. It was a joy to observe them progress individually, and to, over time, see themselves as part of a larger group. They learned how to be leaders, how to express their opinions, how to accept feedback, how to manage their time, and how to show respect toward others. They created social stories for their community, the autism community, by providing written and photographic information about what might happen at a particular museum and some guidelines for behavior. This critical information increases structure for a person with autism, and thereby reduces anxiety.

Incorporating the community which a museum is trying to serve is a critical step in being more inclusive. By creating these social stories, the young adults facilitated an important outcome—they helped each museum take the next step in becoming more inclusive, accessible, and welcoming.

This project reaffirmed that the museum community needs to engage the audiences they are trying to serve, and to not have the mentality of "build it and they will come."[10] Implementing inclusion practices is more than engaging in formative evaluation and focus groups—it's giving a specific audience a defined and active role in the process and giving them a voice which we listen to, then adjust accordingly. As one of the young adults said to me, "I live with autism, you don't. But thanks for asking me to give my opinion to help create these social stories. I hope you learned something too."[11]

DISCUSSION QUESTIONS

1. What are steps that you would need to take to engage young adults with autism and create a social story for your museum?
2. What steps would you need to take to work with colleagues to audit your existing community partnerships and then brainstorm projects that would allow for shared authority (and result in making those communities feel more welcomed at your museum)?
3. Which of the Takeaways for Educators are ones that you could easily implement? Which would take a little more effort?
4. What are ways that you can use some of the tools outlined in this chapter to make your programs more accessible and welcoming for individuals with autism?
5. What ways do you and your colleagues imagine engaging the autism community at your museum?

NOTES

1. The Social Stories Spectrum Project was funded by the Institute of Museum and Library Services, Museums for America Grant #MA-20-16-0257-16-0, in addition to the National Foundation for Autism Research and the Balboa Park Cultural Partnership.
2. Wyld, Nancy. "San Diego Natural History Museum Autism Research Report." October 2014 (unpublished).
3. CDC. "CDC Releases First Estimates of the Number of Adults Living with ASD." Centers for Disease Control and Prevention, April 27, 2020, https://www.cdc.gov/ncbddd/autism/features/adults-living-with-autism-spectrum-disorder.html.
4. National Autistic Society. "Meltdowns: A Guide for all Audiences," https://www.autism.org.uk/advice-and-guidance/topics/behaviour/meltdowns/all-audiences.
5. Simon, Nina. *The Participatory Museum*. Museum 2.0, 2010.

6. Randi Korn & Associates. "Program Evaluation Social Stories SPECTRUM Project," February 1, 2018, https://www.informalscience.org/program-evaluation-spectrum-social-stories-project-san-diego-natural-history-museum-2016-17.
7. Randi Korn & Associates. "Program Evaluation Social Stories SPECTRUM Project," February 1, 2018, https://www.informalscience.org/program-evaluation-spectrum-social-stories-project-san-diego-natural-history-museum-2016-17.
8. Kelly, Erica. Email to author, December 5, 2020.
9. Children's Hospital of Philadelphia, "Autism's Clinical Companions: Frequent Comorbidities with ASD," July 1, 2013, https://www.chop.edu/news/autism-s-clinical-companions-frequent-comorbidities-asd.
10. *Field of Dreams*. Universal Pictures, 1984.
11. Young Adult Participant. Conversation with author, January 12, 2018.

BIBLIOGRAPHY

CDC. "CDC Releases First Estimates of the Number of Adults Living with ASD." Centers for Disease Control and Prevention, April 27, 2020. https://www.cdc.gov/ncbddd/autism/features/adults-living-with-autism-spectrum-disorder.html.

Children's Hospital of Philadelphia. "Autism's Clinical Companions: Frequent Comorbidities with ASD," July 1, 2013. https://www.chop.edu/news/autism-s-clinical-companions-frequent-comorbidities-asd.

Field of Dreams. Universal Pictures, 1984.

Kelly, Erica. Email to author, December 5, 2020.

National Autistic Society. "Meltdowns: A Guide for all Audiences." https://www.autism.org.uk/advice-and-guidance/topics/behaviour/meltdowns/all-audiences.

Randi Korn & Associates. "Program Evaluation Social Stories SPECTRUM Project," February 1, 2018. https://www.informalscience.org/program-evaluation-spectrum-social-stories-project-san-diego-natural-history-museum-2016-17.

Simon, Nina. *The Participatory Museum*. Museum 2.0, 2010.

Wyld, Nancy. "San Diego Natural History Museum Autism Research Report." October 2014 (unpublished).

Young Adult Participant. Conversation with author, January 12, 2018.

4

Digital Decisions to Evolve, Change, and Adapt

Mark D. Osterman

ABSTRACT

The COVID-19 pandemic and recent nationwide protests against police violence have exacerbated what were already important issues of diversity, equity, inclusion, and accessibility (DEIA) facing our communities. This has resulted in a demand for the cultural sector and its leaders to act with greater urgency than they have to date to address these matters directly. In addition, the field has experienced enormous disruption from the pandemic including layoffs, furloughs, financial distress, and public closures. As a result, people's relationship with technology has deepened as we rely more on digital connections for work, cultural experiences, education, health care, and social interactions. To handle this disruption, many museums are attempting to increase their capacity for digital experiences. An investment in digital capacity can help with the challenges organizations face to reach new and expanded audiences while addressing relevancy, social impact, and DEIA. This chapter explores how arts institutions can use technology to evolve, change, and adapt to proactively address these challenges.

INTRODUCTION

As museums continue to focus more on visitors, community, and co-participation, their education departments have a lead role to play. Museum educators have training, knowledge, experience, and networks that can help build relevant and impactful experiences. As stated in AAM's *Excellence in Practice: Museum Education Principles and Standards,*[1] "Museum educators are specialists who help museums fulfill their educational mission. They recognize that many factors affect the learning that occurs in museums. Educators seek to promote the process of individual and group discovery and to document its effect. On museum teams, museum educators serve as audience advocates and work to provide meaningful and lasting learning experiences for a diverse public." With a focus on accessibility, accountability, and advocacy, the role of museum educators in holistic digital transformation within museums should be central.

Some of the challenges for museums in developing digital transformation, identified in the Knight Foundation's 2020 report *Digital Readiness and Innovation in Museums: A Baseline National Survey*[2] include limited dedicated digital staffing, siloed digital projects, outcomes that are poorly tracked,

Challenges

audience insights that are not robust and/or poorly integrated, and emergent or undefined digital strategies. Museums are also challenged by a large digital divide in our local communities and around the world. Three and a half billion people (almost half the world's population) remain unable to access the Internet.[3] Many lower socioeconomic neighborhoods in the United States have limited access to technology exasperating a digital divide as communities are now challenged to live and work online. Digital technologies have also created new challenges for museums, developing viable business models that can be monetized.[4]

CREATING A DIGITAL STRATEGY

A first step to address these challenges is developing a digital strategy. A digital strategy can help create digital transformation by building literacy and raising awareness of how digital approaches might contribute to the advancement of a museum's mission.[5] When choosing to develop such a strategic document, staff must decide whether an institution will benefit most from a digital strategy that is integrated into other strategic documents or one that is separate. Coerver, in his 2017 publication, *On Digital Content Strategy*,[6] posits that a digital strategy should not be distinct from an analog or a human-to-human strategy but rather should be fully integrated into a museum's practice and viewed as an extension of a visitor's natural experience. The decision of whether a digital strategy is separate or integrated into other strategic documents is typically dependent upon an organization's digital maturity.[7] When beginning to develop a digital strategy an organization needs to assess their own level of digital maturity. This begins by looking at how a museum manages, creates, and understands its application of digital across the institution. This reflection process includes an internal assessment of your organization's digital literacy and work culture, how digital is applied to mission and strategy across all departments, and a careful assessment of the current use of technologies for exhibitions, collections, communications, advancement, education, interpretation, and operations. To do this type of assessment, it is recommended that museum staff collaborate with a technologist from within and outside the field who can aid an institution in understanding their level of digital maturity and identify what steps are necessary for future growth. Some examples of existing digital strategies that can serve as models include the Smithsonian Institution's *Web and New Media Strategy*,[8] John Stack's *Tate Digital Strategy 2013–15: Digital as a Dimension of Everything*,[9] Rippleffect's *Derby Museums Digital Engagement Strategy*,[10] the National Portrait Gallery's *Digital Strategy*,[11] and the UK National Archives' *Digital Strategy*.[12]

An interdepartmental working group should lead the development of a digital strategy, ensuring an integrated plan that involves all museum departments.[13] In addition to working across departments, museums should reach out to technology innovators and community leaders to explore, discuss, and recommend how technology can best advance a museum's mission. This group can eventually serve as members of an advisory committee.

At a minimum, a digital strategy should:

- Outline how technology can create moments of discovery that adds relevancy to museum visitors and the institution;
- Build staff digital literacy and maturity;
- Build staff awareness about DEIA and the role technology can play in enhancing DEIA initiatives;
- Enhance audience research practice;
- Enhance audience outreach and participation;
- Outline project management practices such as co-creation, prototyping, and iteration;
- Build awareness of the digital divide and the challenges related to digital literacy and digital access internally and across the community;
- Increase and enhance access to collections and improve ongoing management of object collections and digital assets:

Mark D. Osterman

- Outline how technology can be used to ensure and enhance ongoing preservation and conservation efforts; and
- Outline how technology can be used to enhance communication internally and with the community.

DEFINING DIGITAL TERMINOLOGY

It is important to have standardized and shared definitions of terms such as "digital transformation," "digital maturity," and "digital literacy." The One-by-One project has worked to develop its own shared understanding of these terms in their Culture 24 report *The Digital Transformation Agenda and GLAMs: A Quick Scan Report for Europeana*.[14] They are:

- **Digital transformation** is the act of adopting digital technology or digital thinking to significantly transform an organization's operation and/or the reframing of the organization to be inherently digital in its purpose.
- **Digital maturity** is an individual's or an organization's ability to use, manage, create, and understand digital, in a way that is contextual (fit for their unique setting and needs), holistic (involving vision, leadership, process, culture, and people), and purposeful (always aligned to the institution's social mission).
- **Digital literacy** is the ability to reflect upon an individual's or organization's competency with digital (using digital tools) and their capability with digital (achieving tasks with digital), and also how they understand and review this digital practice in an informed way within the wider contexts of their institution, professional networks, sector, and society.

A shared understanding of these terms among staff helps to create a foundation upon which an institution and its community can build digital capacity and maturity. In sum, the development of digital strategies should build organizational competencies in staff, strategic integration, digital literacy and advocacy, adoption of new practices and processes, and the ability to utilize audience insights.[15]

KEY CONSIDERATIONS

Social Impact and Change

Digital culture is now a leading factor in shaping social change as technology platforms have become centers for the debate of societal issues. As museums embrace the use of technologies, they can no longer avoid being part of challenging conversations and must choose their role and define their social impact. Thus far, many museums have chosen to remain impartial, a stance that is now often viewed as representing a status quo that is not equitable and representative of systemic bias that alienates many community members. La Tanya S. Autry and Mike Murawski have co-produced a global advocacy initiative called *Museums Are Not Neutral* that demands transformation across institutions and pushes museums to acknowledge that not only must they cultivate new points of view but that historically, they have always had a point of view that affected public perception and reception.[16] The public is demanding change through more social engagement, and they are questioning the relevance of museums and cultural institutions that attempt to remain neutral and do not engage and accept responsibility for past and current practices. As stated by Finnis and Kennedy in the *Digital Transformation Agenda and GLAMs: A Quick Scan Report for Europeana* these changes raise a lot of important questions for galleries, libraries, archives, and museums (GLAMs)[17]:

- "How do GLAMs behave in the digital social space—what is their voice and purpose?"
- "What are the ethics and politics of the digital space—do GLAMs understand these?"

- "How do GLAMs equip their workforce and their communities to operate in these spaces?"
- "What is the role of contemporary collecting in this environment?"
- "How can GLAMs document societal change?"

While exploring social change through digital can offer new ways of connecting and collaborating with more diverse communities, outreach is not simple, and the cultural sector faces numerous challenges ahead. For example, people of color are 82 percent more likely than non-Hispanic Caucasians to state they would not participate in cultural activities because those activities do not reflect people of diverse backgrounds.[18] Museums have a history of exclusivity along with institutional practices that have not engaged people of color and indigenous populations.[19] Those practices must be reassessed to open more opportunities for engagement and relevance for formerly excluded communities. This includes the digital divide as well as exhibition content, interpretation and education, collection management practices, public programs, online resources, social media practices, and community outreach must all be reevaluated to meet the new demands of public discourse and change happening all around us. One recommended resource the field can look to for enhancing inclusive practice and social impact is the MASS Action Toolkit. Mass Action is a "collaborative project that seeks to align museums with more equitable and inclusive practices."[20] The toolkit asks practitioners to consider[21]:

- "What is the role and responsibility of the museum in responding to issues affecting our communities locally and globally?"
- "How do the museum's internal practices need to change in order to align with, and better inform, their public practice?"
- "How can the museum be used as a site for social action?"

The MASS Action Toolkit helps to promote DEIA practices that can reflect a cultural institution's values to a community. It is more important than ever that communities understand and can relate to a museum's values, mission and vision. By taking real action steps as outlined in resources such as the MASS Action Toolkit, organizations can make clear how their efforts—and thereby the institution itself—is interested in social impact, engagement, and relevancy.

Audience Insight

Audience insight gained from assessment and evaluation should be a consideration from the outset of any project. Today there are a multitude of digital tools to help with audience research; museum practitioners should leverage these tools to enhance program development, audience engagement, and reflection. Almost every major social media and website platform has an analytics program such as Facebook Audience Insights, Instagram Insights, Twitter Analytics, and Google Analytics. These tools should be coupled with staff-managed formative and summative onsite, online, and programmatic impact evaluation so that organizations can gain robust audience insights from their digital outputs. The Knight Foundation recently found that "lack of audience research was endemic across museum types. Less than 25 percent of museums reported having audience research processes in place like community feedback, co-creation and impact evaluation. Similarly, 78 percent of institutions do not set goals and outcomes at the beginning of a project or systematically examine the impact of their work, which undermines the ability to design for audience needs or evaluate success of digital projects."[22] The lack of audience research and co-creation practices indicates that museums are still not engaging and adequately representing their communities.

While technology can facilitate enhanced and expanded audience insights, museums need to find, understand, and value their digital audience. It is likely your digital audience will be different from your physical one. Audiences may exist in different locations, have different motivations and needs, and respond differently to your collection and educational offerings based on their personal backgrounds and experiences. Museums need to be aware of these nuances and other motivations when designing digital engagement. In addition to audience insights, museums need to consider larger investments in research and development for the creative use of new technologies. Museums need to cater to a combination of physical and digital production and presentation moving forward.[23]

Museum educators should play a lead role strategizing how audience insight can help the institutions they serve achieve more diverse participation and broader access. Educators' experience working directly with audiences, designing and conducting assessment and evaluation, and analyzing data can help mentor peers and expand institutional capacity for audience research. Building audiences should include using technology to conduct analysis of participation patterns that highlight existing mechanisms of success while also revealing factors that may inadvertently promote social exclusion and economic marginalization. Educators, along with all other museum departments, need to take advantage of improved and continuous data collection. Museums should seek the use of Customer Relation Management (CRM) and Point of Sale (POS) systems, in addition to the previously mentioned analytic tools, to help collect and analyze visitor, donor, and engagement data that is accessible across departments and teams. This software can also help with the implementation of public health and safety measures onsite, including visitor flow monitoring and management due to post-pandemic concerns.[24]

Co-creation

Co-creation is the practice of involving the community in the development of what museums do. This includes, but is not limited to interpretation, the curating of artworks and artifacts, the development of exhibitions, exhibition design, social media engagement, the crafting of educational resources, and the origination and implementation of guided experiences.[25] Those involved in co-creation include a mix of museum staff and individuals or groups that belong to the community. Co-creation is challenging and requires staff resources and funding equivalent to standard museum practices to be successful, but it usually results in outcomes of high quality.[26] Co-creation is a model best practice related to building community relevancy and having community impact. By involving community members in program planning, exhibition planning, and digital initiatives, the community is gaining a sense of co-ownership of the museum space, therefore they have more invested and will want to participate.

The growth of social networking platforms and Internet access has enhanced the possibilities for transparency, a shifting of authority, and the development of co-creation practices. While a digital divide exists and offers challenges, using technology can make it easier for museums to invite participation and contributions to a museum's programmatic and educational efforts.[27] However, implementing these participatory projects can be challenging due to limited staff, community resources, budgets, technologies, and a lack of motivation from community members to participate. To develop and implement co-creation projects, museums must reassess their own digital practices and be willing to share authority. Some useful ideas identified by Medhavi Ghandi[28] to keep in mind when developing co-creation projects include:

- "Identifying what interests audiences or what are areas of curiosity."
- "Identifying what are areas of relevancy for audiences."
- "Understanding the audience's motivations to participate or contribute to co-creation projects."
- "Identifying who your audience should be for each co-creation project and why."
- "Identifying the level of digital literacy of your co-creators and eventual audience."

An example of a successful co-creation project is the Brooklyn Museum's *Click!*.[29] As outlined on the museum's website, *Click!* is a photography exhibition that invited the online community and the general public to participate in the exhibition process. The project started with an open call. An online forum was then opened for audiences to evaluate anonymous submissions. *Click!* culminated in an exhibition where the artworks were installed according to how the artworks were ranked by the public. More about this project can be found at https://www.brooklynmuseum.org/exhibitions/click/.

Another cogent example of a co-creation approach is represented by the Derby Museum Trust. The Derby Museum adopted a human-centered design methodology into its *Re: Make*[30] project as they encouraged visitors and volunteers to become citizen curators, designers, and makers; applying skills to support the redevelopment of Derby's Silk Mill. More about this project can be found at https://remakemuseum.tumblr.com/.

The Montreal Museum of Fine Arts offers the opportunity for the public to propose projects for co-creation with the museum on their website. Focus areas for co-creation include health and art therapy, schools and universities, wellness, and accessibility and inclusion. The museum's website, https://www.mbam.qc.ca/en/education-wellness/propose-a-project-for-co-creation-with-the-museum/, offers a form that can be filled out and submitted by the public for proposed projects that can use the museum's collection to enhance a project and enrich participants' engagement.

Museums that invest in co-creation are effectively extending their roles from that of expert to that of host. Museum educators can take the lead in this process by advancing opportunities to engage communities where they are and in many different areas of interest. In the examples provided, institutions are involving their audiences in storytelling. It is through this direct interaction between the museum and the public that learning can be amplified by museum educators and made more personal and relevant. When advocating for co-creation, especially in digital formats, educators also need to fight against the fear that by being inclusive and/or responsive to the audience that they are denigrating the museum's expert authority.[31] Educators must work closely with other staff and make them understand how both can coexist and be beneficial to expanding engagement and opportunities for learning.

For real change, museums will need to conduct community outreach to those they are not reaching and have real conversations with community members to understand how best to serve new audiences. Again, museum educators have the experience and understanding more than other positions within an institution to frame how this outreach is done. Nina Simon's *The Art of Relevancy*[32] offers great insights in how to build relevancy with audiences through community engagement and outreach. Another resource to look to for co-creation practices is The OF/BY/FOR ALL Change Network. This is an online program that provides a framework designed to make civic and cultural organizations more inclusive, equitable, and relevant. The construct of the program is that OF is board, staff, partners, and content are representative of the community; BY is programs, events, projects, and strategies are co-created by the community; ALL programs, projects, events, and spaces are welcoming for the community (OF/BY/FOR/ALL).[33]

Iteration

A challenge that often exists in museums related to digital initiatives is that significant attention is mostly paid to highly visible and large-scale projects. This can set unrealistic benchmarks for budgeting, staffing, and resources, and can work against smaller institutions' ability to grow digital capacity.[34] To be agile and better serve the community, projects should be local in context, iterative, and modest in scale. At the same time, they should be focused on impact and replicability. To achieve these ends an iterative approach to project development makes sense.

Iteration is the process of making continuous improvements and is primarily done through observation, evaluation, and responding to trends in data. Iterative design is a way of finding out unknown user needs and behaviors and is intended to improve overall quality and functionality while making the museum more agile and responsive to the needs of constituents. To achieve an iterative methodology, a museum must cultivate an environment of continuous enhancement through learning and experimentation.

A good example of an iterative project is London's Victoria & Albert (V&A's) *Explore the Collections* tool. The online collections database brings together data, stories, images, and content. The platform is much more than a digital catalog with detailed information on objects. Users are now encouraged to see connections between related objects deepening the possibilities for learning across collections. New features offer suggestions for related search keywords, the ability to filter and map objects on display, and offers a digital visualization of related objects for each search. This all encourages a more intuitive and organic experience when looking through the collection.

The project launched in February 2021 in beta form and is using an iterative approach as the V&A continually develops and updates the platform. The V&A is also approaching this project from a co-creation perspective by encouraging the public to provide feedback on their experiences, which can be incorporated into future iterations of the project.

Advanced Discovery

After decades of digitization, museums and other cultural institutions have emerged with very large digital archives of multimedia content. This increase in digital assets offers the opportunity for museums to develop new modes of analysis and increased levels of access and engagement. Museums should treat the production and refinement of collection data as an ongoing creative practice that is inclusive and representative of many perspectives.

For advanced discovery, museums should develop a unique set of search filters that not only includes the typical search fields but also appeals to a variety of users with diverse backgrounds and experiences. How museums have developed data description determines what information, perceptions, and histories people take away. In many museums, implicit and systemic bias related to data input has excluded a variety of perspectives that are germane to collection content. Careful review and reflection of this data can improve how diversity is surfaced in collections and improve overall discovery by making collections more inclusive.[35] The development of new discovery tools and the incorporation of inclusive editing practices requires the need to conduct community outreach to identify perspectives, vocabulary, and search criteria based on the interests, needs, and personal experiences of community members.[36] This involvement of the public enhances transparency and leans toward co-creation practices. Description that includes the terms community members are familiar with (vs. curatorial or academic language) leads to more relevant search results. To make changes in how data is input, and better document diversity, museums must be thoughtful in their practice and make this part of a larger process of collections management and access.[37]

A number of institutions that have explored areas of advanced discovery include:

- The Barnes Collection created an innovative search experience which allows audiences to search the collection by visual characteristics to cluster and filter images in unique ways rather than using names of artists or art historical movements (https://collection.barnesfoundation.org/).
- SMK Open, in Solvgade, Copenhagen offers every artwork its own digital page with multimedia content such as videos, articles, audio, and information on related events and exhibitions. Additionally, SMK is making all digital material available through an API allowing others to include the data directly in their own websites, apps, and so forth (https://www.smk.dk/en/article/smk-open/).
- London's Victoria & Albert Museum *Explore the Collections* tool brings together data, stories, images, and content, providing a narrative-led approach in which users can search for specific objects or allow the site to recommend content based on the user's interests (https://www.vam.ac.uk/collections?type=featured).

- The Cleveland Museum of Art created ArtLens. This experiential platform encourages engagement on a personal and emotional level. ArtLens Gallery uses gesture-sensing projections that respond to bodily movements and facial recognition to create an immersive experience (https://www.clevelandart.org/artlens-gallery/artlens-exhibition).
- The Tate museum allows users to browse the collections and then collate their discoveries into albums that can be published to the Tate's website. Uploaded albums can be annotated with notes and also embedded with images, video, and audio from other sites. Once published to the Tate's website, users can share with other website visitors and allow visitor-curated perspectives to be seen. Furthermore, users can allow comments to public albums in order to further idea generation and discourse (https://www.tate.org.uk/art/albums/how-use-albums).
- The Metropolitan Museum of Art's Ceramics Lookbook uses an API to compare the textures of ceramic objects in the museum's collection. The museum collaborated with graduate students in a Master of Science in Data Visualization program at Parsons' School of Art, Media, and Technology (https://azuic.github.io/the-met-ceramics-lookbook/).
- William College Museum of Art's (WCMA) Mellon Digital Project promotes WCMA's collection as an open resource for teaching, learning, and creative expression. The digital platform shows the ways the collections are used by faculty, students, and community (https://artmuseum.williams.edu/wcma-digital-project/).
- The Smithsonian Institution's Open Access allows users to download, share, and reuse (2.8 million at February 2020 launch) 2D and 3D objects from their collections (https://www.si.edu/openaccess).

These examples show organizations experimenting with traditional modes of search and interactivity making attempts to increase relevance to the user through interfaces that go beyond traditional search filters such as artist's name, date, medium, and year. Museums are attempting to make searching a more intuitive experience that employs multiple ways of exploring a collection that can connect and relate with a wide spectrum of audiences. This is the direction all museums need to move in relation to digital collections management and access.

Revenue Generation

Museums are searching for ways to monetize digital experiences. In the early months of the COVID-19 pandemic, organizations began by offering most, if not all, digital content for free. Many struggled to find ways to generate revenue with museum closures and with the shut down in-person education and programming offerings. This has created user expectations that digital content should/could always be free. However, museums will likely need to recalibrate this perception and gain deeper insights into their audiences to be able to drive revenue from their digital engagements. Museums must also create content that is differentiated and unique, does not have an already established market and is of a quality level for which people are willing to pay. Due to the relatively low price point of many streaming services, people are conditioned to not pay a lot for engaging digital content. Unfortunately, there is no quick answer to this challenge and there are also no one-size-fits-all solution to relying on digital programming for income with a public accustomed to getting it for free or at low-cost. Some general considerations include:

- Embracing entrepreneurship, innovation, and partnerships;
- Embracing a broader interpretation of mission and content;
- Embracing online ticketing for user-friendly, friction-limited transactions;
- Creating innovative membership models;

Mark D. Osterman

- Developing fee-based special access to new content;
- Offering early access to high-value digital content;
- Providing online courses/certifications;
- Adapting professional development content for corporate clients; and
- Using social media to build an engaged community and transition an audience into a source of revenue.

In AAM's *Trends Watch 2021: Navigating a Disruptive Future,* Elizabeth Merritt discusses how museums are starved for income yet have few examples of how digital engagement can be used to replace or supplement traditional revenue streams tied to physically interacting with the museum.[38] Merritt asks us to consider, "how, in the short term, digital solutions can help the museum survive and, in the long term, which digital solutions can offer lasting improvements in the museum's mission delivery and financial success."[39] The challenges that museums face in a revenue-driven marketplace that looks for relevancy and social impact will only increase. In response, museums must create educational offerings, public programs, exhibitions, and other experiences that are impactful, representative, and inclusive. Culture Track 17 points out generational and cultural challenges that compound the economic ones. "Millennials are uniquely interested in human rights and equality, where their giving doubles that of Gen X, Baby Boomers, and Pre-Wars. People of color are similarly committed to these issues, being 44 percent more likely to donate to human rights causes and 71 percent more likely to donate to equality organizations than non-Hispanic Caucasians. It is therefore increasingly important to focus on culture's role in sparking social change and engaging in civil and human rights."[40] Museums that invest in removing barriers and expanding programs and missions can potentially increase avenues of revenue streams from digital programs. Redefining how museums serve their communities will help them continue to attract the necessary revenue, support, and funding needed to stay operational.

CONCLUSION

As the cultural sector continues to contend with a crippling global pandemic, extreme financial exigencies, and systemic racism, museums increasingly will need digitally literate leadership who embrace DEIA practices. Institutions must consider technology investment alongside other critical priorities and can no longer be funded as an afterthought.[41] To be successful, museums will need to restructure and train their staff to address the needs of not just digital literacy and digital maturity, but digital content production and distribution and the development of new channels for income generation.[42] These new structures and formats will almost certainly impact the work of museum educators in ways that museums are only now beginning to explore.

In this process, museum educators must help museums move beyond traditional methods as they embrace existing and emergent technologies to stay relevant and maintain sustainability. Educators are uniquely qualified to help their institutions and colleagues explore partnerships and collaborative opportunities that better serve their communities. Educators' experience with pedagogy and andragogy along with their historic roles as audience researchers and advocates for museum visitors can help institutions use technology to build a digital practice that better understands who their communities are and how they can be served. Using audience insight, community feedback, and co-creation with community members, museum educators along with their colleagues can help ensure that technology investments are impactful and meaningful to those communities. As people grapple with multiple societal and global crises, shifting habits will demand change. Technology can assist museums during this time and help institutions build new audiences of the future. We must remember that digital can be part of the solution, but it should not be assumed to be the solution. Technology can act as a support for museums while helping to build better relationships with audiences. As a field and at our individual organizations, we have an opportunity before us to leverage this moment to build a better and different future. Let us take advantage of this moment.

DISCUSSION QUESTIONS

1. In what ways can you cultivate a workplace culture of innovation and experimentation, especially around digital tools?
2. How are you currently working with your communities? What opportunities exist for more co-creation practices? Among your existing digital content, how could you include community voices and perspectives?
3. How do you make digital experience and content unique and differentiated from onsite content and experiences?
4. What do you know about your audiences for digital content? What do they want? What do they value? What tools could you use to learn about your audience's appetites for digital content?
5. How do you make collections data and access represent complex, multilayered narratives? Audit your own online collection and resources for language, representation, and bias. Where are the blind spots or opportunities for a more inclusionary approach to your digital collecting practices?
6. How can your museum use digital technology to elevate voices that have been historically marginalized and begin to share authority?

NOTES

1. AAM's *Excellence in Practice: Museum Education Principles and Standards,* p. 6.
2. Knight Foundation's 2020 report *Digital Readiness and Innovation in Museums: A Baseline National Survey,* p. 2.
3. Finnis, Jane; Kennedy, Anra. *The Digital Transformation Agenda and GLAMs: A Quick Scan Report for Europeana,* Culture24. 2020, pp. 7–9.
4. Wallace Foundation. *Arts Organizations' Early Response to COVID-19 Uncertainty: Insights from the Field,* 2020, p. 7.
5. Stein, Rob. *Museums and Digital Strategy Today,* Alliance Labs, American Alliance of Museums, 2017.
6. Coerver, Chad. *On Digital Content Strategy.* 2017.
7. Stein, Rob. *Museums and Digital Strategy Today,* Alliance Labs, American Alliance of Museums, 2017.
8. Smithsonian Institution's *Web and New Media Strategy,* 2009.
9. Stack, John. *Tate Digital Strategy 2013–2015: Digital as a Dimension of Everything,* Tate Papers, no.19, Spring 2013.
10. Rippleffect. *Derby Museums Digital Engagement Strategy,* 2013.
11. National Portrait Gallery. *Digital Strategy,* 2016.
12. UK National Archives. *Digital Strategy,* 2017–2019.
13. Merritt, Elizabeth. *Trends Watch: Navigating a Disruptive Future.* American Alliance of Museums, 2021 p. 20.
14. Finnis, Jane; Kennedy, Anra. *The Digital Transformation Agenda and GLAMs: A Quick Scan Report for Europeana,* Culture24. 2020, pp. 7–9.
15. Knight Foundation. *Digital Readiness and Innovation in Museums: A Baseline National Survey.* 2020, p. 3.
16. Autry, La Tanya S. and Murawski, Mike. *Museums Are Not Neutral.* 2021.
17. Finnis, Jane; Kennedy, Anra. *The Digital Transformation Agenda and GLAMs: A Quick Scan Report for Europeana,* Culture24. 2020, p. 29.
18. Culture Track '17. *Culture + Community in a Time of Crisis: A Special Edition of Culture Track.* 2017, Online. 13 March 2021, p. 15.
19. Bunch, Lonnie G. *Flies in the Buttermilk: Museums, Diversity, and the Will to Change.* 2000.

20. MASS Action Project. 2016.
21. MASS Action. *Mass Action Toolkit.* 2017.
22. Knight Foundation. *Digital Readiness and Innovation in Museums: A Baseline National Survey.* 2020, p. 9.
23. Wallace Foundation. *Arts Organizations' Early Response to COVID-19 Uncertainty: Insights from the Field,* 2020, p. 33.
24. Wallace Foundation. *Arts Organizations' Early Response to COVID-19 Uncertainty: Insights from the Field,* 2020, p. 33.
25. Share Museums East. *Co-creating Community Projects: An Introductory Guide.* 2018, p. 4.
26. Share Museums East. *Co-creating Community Projects: An Introductory Guide.* 2018, p. 9.
27. Gandhi, Medhavi. *Museums and the Practice of Digital Co-creation.* 2020.
28. Gandhi, Medhavi. *Museums and the Practice of Digital Co-creation.* 2020.
29. Brooklyn Museum, *Click!.* 2008.
30. Derby Museums. *Derby Museums Digital Engagement.* 2016.
31. Nelson, Tonya. *The Digital Future of Museums: Conversations and Provocations.* By Keir Winesmith, Suse Anderson. Routledge, 2019, p. 175.
32. Simon, Nina. "The Art of Relevance." *Museum 2.0*, 2016.
33. OF/BY/FOR/ALL Change Network. 2021.
34. Knight Foundation. *Digital Readiness and Innovation in Museums: A Baseline National Survey.* 2020, p. 10.
35. Berry, Dorothy. Introduction to Conscious Editing. 2020, Online. 13 March 2021, p. 8.
36. Berry, Dorothy. Introduction to Conscious Editing. 2020, Online. 13 March 2021, p. 9.
37. Lloyd-Banes, Frances. *Documenting Diversity: How Should Museums Identify Art and Artists?* 2019.
38. Merritt, Elizabeth. *Trends Watch: Navigating a Disruptive Future.* American Alliance of Museums, 2021, p. 14.
39. Merritt, Elizabeth. *Trends Watch: Navigating a Disruptive Future.* American Alliance of Museums, 2021, p. 14.
40. Culture Track '17. *Culture + Community in a Time of Crisis: A Special Edition of Culture Track.* 2017, Online. 13 March 2021, p. 38.
41. Knight Foundation. *Digital Readiness and Innovation in Museums: A Baseline National Survey.* 2020, p. 3.
42. Wallace Foundation. *Arts Organizations' Early Response to COVID-19 Uncertainty: Insights from the Field,* 2020, p. 4.

BIBLIOGRAPHY

American Alliance of Museums. *Excellence in Practice: Museum Education Principles and Standards.* AAM, 2005, Online. 13 March 2021, p. 6. Available at https://www.aam-us.org/professional-net works/education-committee/edcom-resources/.

Autry, La Tanya S., and Murawski, Mike. *Museums Are Not Neutral.* 2021, Online. 13 March 2021. Available at https://www.museumsarenotneutral.com/.

Berry, Dorothy. Introduction to Conscious Editing. 2020, Online. 13 March 2021, pp. 8–9. Available at https://sunshinestatedigitalnetwork.wordpress.com/2020/09/16/introduction-to-conscious-ed iting-series/. Retrieved recording: https://youtu.be/XGCTtDgNty4 and slides: https://drive.google .com/file/d/1nOKbyU3K-nn2Y4GNh0OI96KD8d-ZOAtN/view?usp=sharing.

Brooklyn Museum, *Click!.* 2008, Online. 13 March 2021. Available at https://www.brooklynmuseum .org/exhibitions/click/.

Bunch, Lonnie G. *Flies in the Buttermilk: Museums, Diversity, and the Will to Change.* 2000 (originally appeared in the July/August 2000 issue of Museum News, a publication of the American Alliance of Museums). Online. 19 April 2021. Available at https://www.aam-us.org/2019/05/29/flies-in -the-buttermilk-museums-diversity-and-the-will-to-change/.

Coerver, Chad. *On Digital Content Strategy.* 2017, Online. 13 March 2021. Available at https://www .sfmoma.org/read/on-digital-content-strategy/.

Culture Track '17. *Culture + Community in a Time of Crisis: A Special Edition of Culture Track*. 2017, Online. 13 March 2021, pp. 15, 38. Available at https://2017study.culturetrack.com/home.

Derby Museums. *Derby Museums Digital Engagement*. 2016, Online. 13 March 2021. Available at http://collectionstrust.org.uk/wp-content/uploads/2016/11/Derby-Museums-Digital-Engage ment-Strategy1.pdf.

Finnis, Jane; Kennedy, Anra. *The Digital Transformation Agenda and GLAMs: A Quick Scan Report for Europeana*. Culture 24. 2020, pp. 7–9, 23, 29. Online. 13 March 2021. Available at https://pro.eu ropeana.eu/files/Europeana_Professional/Publications/Digital%20transformation%20reports /The%20digital%20transformation%20agenda%20and%20GLAMs%20-%20Culture24%20 findings%20and%20outcomes.pdf.

Gandhi, Medhavi. *Museums and the Practice of Digital Co-creation*. 2020, Online. 13 March 2021. Available at https://www.theheritagelab.in/podcast-museums-digital-cocreation/.

Knight Foundation. *Digital Readiness and Innovation in Museums: A Baseline National Survey*. 2020, pp. 3, 9-10. Online. 13 March 2021. Available at https://knightfoundation.org/wp-content/up loads/2020/10/Digital-Readiness-and-Innovation-in-Museums-Report.pdf.

Lloyd-Banes, Frances. *Documenting Diversity: How Should Museums Identify Art and Artists?* 2019, Online. 13 March 2021. Available at https://medium.com/minneapolis-institute-of-art/documen ting-diversity-17f55a4118da.

MASS Action. *Mass Action Toolkit*. 2017, Online. 13 March 2021. Available at https://www.museum action.org/resources.

MASS Action Project. 2016, Online. 13 March 2021. Available at https://www.museumaction.org/.

Merritt, Elizabeth. *Trends Watch: Navigating a Disruptive Future.* American Alliance of Museums, 2021, pp. 14, 20. Online. 13 March 2021. Available at https://www.aam-us.org/programs/center-for-the -future-of-museums/trendswatch/.

Montreal Museum of Art. 2021. Online. 19 April 2021. Available at https://www.mbam.qc.ca/en/edu cation-wellness/propose-a-project-for-co-creation-with-the-museum/.

National Portrait Gallery. *Digital Strategy*. 2016, Online. 13 March 2021. Available at https://www.npg .org.uk/assets/files/pdf/strategic-plan/NPG_Digital_Strategy_Digest_v4_1.pdf.

Nelson, Tonya. *The Digital Future of Museums: Conversations and Provocations.* By Keir Winesmith, Suse Anderson. Routledge, 2019, p. 175.

OF/BY/FOR/ALL Change Network. 2021, Online. 19 April 2021. Available at https://www.ofbyforall .org/change-network-overview.

Rippleffect. *Derby Museums Digital Engagement Strategy*. 2013. Online. 13 March 2021. Available at http://collectionstrust.org.uk/wp-content/uploads/2016/11/Derby-Museums-Digital-Engage ment-Strategy1.pdf.

Share Museums East. *Co-creating Community Projects: An Introductory Guide.* 2018, pp. 4, 9. Online. 13 March 2021. Available at http://sharemuseumseast.org.uk/wp-content/uploads/2018/07/Co -creating-Community-Projects.pdf.

Simon, Nina. "The Art of Relevance." *Museum 2.0*, 2016.

Smithsonian Institution's *Web and New Media Strategy*, 2009. Online. 13 March 2021. Available at https://www.si.edu/content/pdf/about/web-new-media-strategy_v1.0.pdf.

Stack, John. *Tate Digital Strategy 2013–15: Digital as a Dimension of Everything*. Tate Papers, no. 19, Spring 2013, Online. 13 March 2021. Available at http://www.tate.org.uk/research/publications/tate-pa pers/19/tate-digital-strategy-2013-15-digital-as-a-dimension-of-everything.

Stein, Rob. *Museums and Digital Strategy Today*. Alliance Labs, American Alliance of Museums, 2017. Online. 13 March 2021. Available at https://www.aam-us.org/2017/07/10/museums-and-digital -strategy-today/.

UK National Archives. *Digital Strategy*, 2017–2019. Online. 13 March 2021. Available at https://www
.nationalarchives.gov.uk/documents/the-national-archives-digital-strategy-2017-19.pdf.

Wallace Foundation. *Arts Organizations' Early Response to COVID-19 Uncertainty: Insights from the Field.*
2020, pp. 4, 7, 21, 33. Online. 13 March 2021. Available at https://www.wallacefoundation.org
/knowledge-center/pages/arts-organizations-early-response-to-covid-19-uncertainty-insights
-from-the-field.aspx.

Part II

Training and Educator Preparation

5

Training for the Rainbow

PREPARING EDUCATORS TO BE LGBTQ-INCLUSIVE

Mac Buff

ABSTRACT

Lesbian, gay, bisexual, transgender, and queer (LGBTQ+) people make up approximately 5 percent of the U.S. population, with numbers growing significantly among youth and young adults. LGBTQ+ issues have become more visible in the first two decades of the twenty-first century due to political fights about marriage equality, military service, and transgender rights. With this increased visibility, more LGBTQ+ folks live openly and expect to see their sexuality and/or gender identity included in the public sphere. As these demographics of our visitors, participants, and staff change, museum educators must change their ways of interacting. How can we effectively prepare staff and volunteers to engage in a safe, inclusive manner with colleagues, visitors, and program participants?

This chapter will draw on the author's personal experience as an openly transgender and queer person in the museum field, as well as a variety of training models the author has experienced and/or implemented. After an overview of LGBTQ+ identity and issues, the chapter examines three elements of an effective training method: personal reflection on identity, an understanding of broader systems of hetero- and cis-normativity, and an introductory "inclusion script" for person-to-person interactions. While this model was initially developed to foster LGBTQ+ inclusion, its principles are generally transferable to other topics such as racial justice. As a baseline for training, it has proven effective at a variety of institution types and is scalable to different institution sizes. Though inclusion training must always be an ongoing process, this three-pronged model provides a broad platform from which to begin.

INTRODUCTION

Fifty-one years ago from the time of this writing, transgender women of color, gay men, and butch lesbians fought back against a police raid on the Stonewall Inn, a popular New York City gay bar. Though this 1969 event was not the first such response in the United States, it was the spark which ignited the gay rights movement. Remembrances of the Stonewall uprising morphed into Pride parades, eventually giving rise to LGBTQ Pride celebrations in cities and towns around the world.

The ongoing struggle for LGBTQ rights over the past fifty-plus years has often brought this community into national awareness here in the United States. More and more lesbian, gay, bisexual, transgender, queer, and other non-heterosexual/non-cisgender people—otherwise known as LGBTQ+ people—now live openly. Social acceptance for LGBTQ+ people has generally increased. In a 2013 Pew research study, 92 percent of LGBT adults felt that society was more accepting of them since the turn of the millennium.[1] Since 2000, LGBTQ+ legal issues have frequently dominated news wavelengths. Individual states voted on marriage equality for same-sex couples before a national Supreme Court ruling established it as the law of the land.[2] The discriminatory military policy of Don't Ask, Don't Tell was challenged and repealed.[3] The state of California mandated LGBTQ+-inclusive school health curriculum, amid a flurry of controversy.[4] The Supreme Court ruled that discrimination on the basis of sexuality or gender identity is covered under Title VII's "sex discrimination" for the purposes of employment, allowing legal recourse for those who believe they have been fired for being LGBTQ+.[5]

Of course, this progress did not come without obstacles and setbacks. In 2016, forty-nine people were killed in a homophobic mass shooting at the Pulse gay nightclub in Orlando, Florida.[6] Beginning that same year, the Trump administration consistently undermined or rolled back legal protections for LGBTQ+ people.[7] The number of transgender people killed, especially murdered transgender women of color, increases every year.[8]

Museums do not sit apart from the sea changes of society. As LGBTQ+ people enjoy more visibility and more acceptance, we expect the same from the cultural institutions we love and patronize. As LGBTQ+ people have seen the backlash which comes with social progress, we have also learned to watch our surroundings for signs of acceptance and safety or discrimination and danger. LGBTQ+ people are involved in every facet of museums: as staff, volunteers, visitors, donors and supporters, and program participants. Museum education programs must effectively prepare staff and volunteers to engage in an inclusive manner with all whom they work alongside and come into contact with.

As museum educators, we want to create connections between our visitors and our content. LGBTQ+ inclusion is key to this endeavor. Non-inclusive practices create barriers, often making LGBTQ+ people feel unsafe or unwelcome in the space, and therefore unable to learn. This can be as simple as using binary language like "ladies and gentlemen" when greeting visitors, as far-reaching as unintentional omission (or intentional erasure) of LGBTQ+ identities in exhibit interpretation, or as overt as anti-gay statements from a tour guide. Connections are also hampered when educators themselves feel unsafe at work; if LGBTQ+ staff or docents are not welcomed by an institution, they may well tip-toe around and conceal parts of their identity which, if openly expressed, could aid in connecting with visitors.

This chapter will address specific considerations for the LGBTQ+ community and share a training model to prepare educators to welcome this community. As the author, I approach this topic from several angles. I am myself a member of the LGBTQ+ community, as a queer, non-binary transgender person in a "same-sex" marriage. Many of the political battles of the past twenty years have directly impacted my life. I have spent much of my professional career in museum education and have seen many aspects of the field, from part-time educator positions to middle management. In nearly every role, I have spoken out as an advocate for myself and others, working to make each museum more inclusive. I believe this is necessary work for each of us, regardless of identity, as we move forward into the twenty-first century.

LGBTQ+ 101: SOME CONTEXT

Language and Terminology

To outsiders, the LGBTQ+ community seems to have a lexicon all its own. Words used to describe identity and presentation are constantly changing, as new words are added and old ones develop—or shed—negative connotations. It may seem like new identities are being invented, but in reality, each of these identities has existed for generations: we just now have more precise language to describe our experience.

For a number of years, LGBT (lesbian, gay, bisexual, and transgender) was the accepted umbrella term to refer to the community. "Queer" has been a part of the LGBT movement since the beginning but was popularized in the 1990s. By the beginning of the twenty-first century, the umbrella acronym had expanded to LGBTQ, with the "Q" variously (and sometimes simultaneously) representing Queer or Questioning. Since that time, a whole host of other labels have emerged for non-heterosexual and non-cisgender identities. ("Cisgender" describes someone whose gender identity aligns with the gender they were assigned at birth, or someone who is not transgender—more on this in a moment, when we discuss gender in more detail.) Asexual, aromantic, pansexual, non-binary, genderqueer, genderfluid, Two-Spirit, and many more people are now accepted as part of the LGBTQ+ community. Sometimes the "+" sign represents these identities in the acronym, and sometimes the acronym is expanded, as in LGBTQIA2. For many years, "queer" was a derogatory term; more recently it has been reclaimed by many, especially younger generations who have come of age since the inception of the activist group Queer Nation in the early 1990s.[9] It is occasionally used within the community as an umbrella term for those who identify as LGBTQ+, as well as an individual identity.

For many LGBTQ+ folks, their sexuality or gender identity is an important part of how they understand themselves. Many choose to be "out," living openly and not concealing their identity. Others choose to be "in the closet" in some or all of their life, hiding their sexuality/gender or opting not to discuss it openly. This may be a decision based on physical, emotional, or financial safety, fear of discrimination, a desire to maintain the status quo, or simply because they consider their sexuality or gender to be a private part of their lives. Because being "out" can result in repercussions, the choice whether to come out or remain in the closet is a highly personal one, may change based on situations, and must be respected.

While many aspects of the LGBTQ+ experience are similar no matter one's queer identity, transgender people face an additional set of challenges. A transgender person is someone whose internal felt sense of gender does not align with the gender they were assigned at birth. Typically, when a baby is born, the doctor determines whether the child is male or female based on external genitalia: this is someone's assigned gender. For many people, as they grow up, their internal felt sense of gender matches up with their assigned gender—for example, a child assigned male at birth who continues to understand himself as a boy/man throughout his life. Such people are cisgender. However, for some people, their internal felt sense of gender is different than their assigned gender. Such people are transgender. Some transgender people identify with the binary gender "opposite" the one they were assigned at birth—for example, someone who was assigned male at birth but understands herself to be a woman. Some transgender people identify with both genders to some degree, or neither gender, or feel themselves to be entirely without gender. These people generally fall under the category of "non-binary," and may use additional words to describe their identity such as genderqueer, genderfluid, bigender, or agender. Many, but not all, transgender people undergo social, legal, and/or medical transition to align their life more closely with their internal sense of gender. Like other LGBQ+ people, transgender folks may be out in some parts of their lives and not in others. (See figure 5.1.)

Central Issues of the Early Twenty-First Century

The first two decades of the twenty-first century have seen many advances for LGBTQ+ rights and equality. All of these advances were hard-won, revealed systemic inequities, and were incomplete enough that many LGBTQ+ folks do not enjoy their full benefits. At the time of this writing, too, most advances are recent enough that even LGBTQ+ people who have gained additional rights still worry that these rights could be taken away again. Changes in the Supreme Court in late 2020 motivated

The Transgender Umbrella

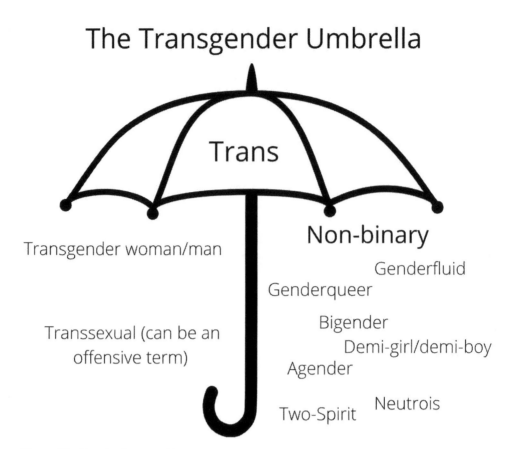

Figure 5.1. *Creative Commons License*

many U.S. residents in same-sex marriages to legally protect their partnerships by drawing up wills and powers of attorney, fearing that marriage equality may be overturned. Though this section focuses on political, legal, and social issues in the United States, similar struggles have played out around the world.

Perhaps the most sweeping and well-known reform was the movement for marriage equality. The prohibition of same-sex marriages was first legally challenged in the 1970s, but came into the spotlight for the LGBTQ+ community during the AIDS crisis of the 1980s. When hospitals restricted the visitors of dying AIDS patients to family only—including legal spouses but not including committed non-legal partners—many gay men died alone, without the companionship of their beloved. This began to galvanize what would become the movement for marriage equality.[10] As the United States entered the twenty-first century, the Defense of Marriage Act prohibited federal recognition of same-sex marriages. (In fact, at the turn of the millennium, same-sex activity between consenting adults was still illegal in some states.) Individual states legalized same-sex marriage beginning with Massachusetts in 2004, and the Defense of Marriage Act itself was struck down in 2013.[11] Two years later, the Supreme Court again ruled in favor of same-sex couples, declaring all state bans on same-sex marriage unconstitutional.[12] On a practical level, not only did this signal growing acceptance for lesbians and gay men, it also allowed same-sex couples to enjoy the financial security of spousal benefits and marriage tax credits.

Predictably, marriage equality was not the end of the road. Though a lesbian could now list her wife as her spouse on employment benefits, she could still be fired for being lesbian. The same year as the Defense of Marriage Act was struck down, a national employment nondiscrimination act covering LGBTQ+ people failed in Congress. The Supreme Court stepped in again in 2020, ruling that employers cannot discriminate based on sexuality or gender identity.[13] Of course, discrimination can be hard to prove, so many LGBTQ+ people fear they could still be unfairly fired and their employer hide the discrimination under frivolous excuses.

For transgender people, the stakes are often even higher. In 2018, the Human Rights Campaign called anti-transgender violence "a national epidemic."[14] Increasing numbers of transgender people were reported murdered each year from 2013–2020. Most of these were Black transgender women, whose social position put them at the intersection of violence from anti-Black racism, misogyny, and transphobia. (In fact, this is such a concern that there is now a word for the specific oppression focused at this intersection: transmisogynoir, from the word "misogynoir" coined by Moya Bailey.) Nearly half of transgender people surveyed in 2015 by the National Center for Transgender Equality reported experiencing verbal harassment for their gender identity in the previous year, and almost 10 percent had been physically attacked.[15]

In the same way that the legal battle for marriage equality brought gay, lesbian, and bisexual issues onto the national stage, the second decade of the twenty-first century directed a spotlight on transgender issues. Transgender celebrities like Laverne Cox, Janet Mock, and Caitlyn Jenner brought their identities into the public eye. *Time* magazine proclaimed the "transgender tipping point" in 2014, indicating that public opinion was shifting in favor of trans folks.[16] Very shortly thereafter, a wave of legislation known as "bathroom bills" swept the country. These state bills and initiatives sought to restrict trans folks' access to public bathrooms and changing rooms, requiring people to use the facilities corresponding with their assigned gender at birth. In most areas, the bills were rejected by voters or legislature. However, conflicting guidance from the Department of Education during the late 2010s resulted in some transgender students being barred from using the school bathroom aligning with their gender identity.[17]

Bathroom debates are, fundamentally, not about gendered restrooms. They are about the legitimacy of transgender identity: if I am not allowed to pee in public restrooms, I am not allowed to exist in public life. Bathroom bills are about policing "proper" expressions of gender: my wife, a handsome woman who dresses androgynously, received visual scrutiny in women's restrooms when a bathroom bill was on the ballot in our home state. Bathroom bills are about perpetuating the myth that paints transgender women as dangerous, deceitful men cross-dressing to gain access to women's safe or sacred spaces. And while public policy like bathroom bills may seem far removed from museums, truthfully, it is not. Museums usually have public restrooms, which can be a site of safety or danger for transgender folks regardless of legal restrictions on restroom usage. Inclusive restrooms should not be the only step museums take to welcome LGBTQ+ folks, and they need not be the first; but inaccessible restrooms create a significant barrier to access for any population, including transgender and gender-nonconforming people.

Another prevalent issue for transgender folks is gender transition. As mentioned earlier, many (but not all) transgender people undergo some form of social, legal, and/or medical transition. This may include such things as: asking people to use a different name or pronouns to refer to them, changing their legal name or gender marker, taking hormones, or getting gender-affirming surgery. No two transitions look alike. Each person makes decisions about which transition steps to take based on practicality, cost, personal preference or comfort level, and a host of other considerations. Some people take most of their visible transition steps within a couple of years; others spread their transition out across decades. Regardless, the active transition process is often a vulnerable one for transgender people. There may be legal or logistical barriers to transition, especially regarding medical treatment. The people around them, such as coworkers and friends, are learning new ways of relating to the person; this often brings feelings of uncertainty, fear, or anger for everyone involved. At certain points in their transition, the person may be more readily seen as transgender by strangers, which often puts them at higher risk for gender-based violence. For more information on how to support transgender people undergoing transition at your institution, check out the American Alliance for Museums' *Toolkit for Gender Transition*.[18]

Intersection of Identity

Of course, LGBTQ+ people are not *just* LGBTQ+. There are Black transgender men, white lesbian women, Latinx intersex folks, and so on. So, while an issue may impact all members of the LGBTQ+ community, it will likely not impact all equally. Marriage equality was a giant leap forward for gay and lesbian people but did little or nothing to help transgender people. And, in the United States, disability laws mean that many disabled people (queer or not) cannot marry their partner without losing their disability benefits.[19] Marriage equality still has not arrived for disabled queer folks.

Museums are often perceived as a "liberal" field, one open to gay and lesbian workers. Many gay men have made their careers in the art world. Yet, our field as a whole remains white-dominated, and disproportionately male in positions of leadership. A focus on increased LGBTQ+ inclusion must take into consideration the myriad of identities queer folks bring with them and welcome the whole person.

WHY SHOULD MUSEUMS CARE?

At least 4.5 percent of the population identifies as LGBTQ+.[20] This number is growing, especially among youth, and it does not reflect people who may internally identify as LGBTQ+ but would not respond in that way on a survey. LGBTQ+ people are already part of our institutions, whether we know it or not. They visit our museums, attend our programs, serve on our boards, volunteer, and work alongside us. Even the smallest museums in the most conservative of areas will encounter an LGBTQ+ person at least occasionally. Because the percentage of LGBTQ+ identity is higher among youth, educators are even more likely to work with students who identify as queer. LGBTQ+ inclusion is not only about inviting new visitors or workers in, but creating a safer space for those who are already here.

LGBTQ+ visitors expect a certain level of inclusion and seek out institutions which welcome them. I will use an example from my own life outside of museums. My relationship to restaurants is similar to many visitors' relationship to museums: I go to a restaurant for entertainment, for socialization, or to experience something new. When I go out to eat, I prioritize restaurants that have gender-inclusive bathrooms (such as a single-stall gender-neutral restroom). If a server repeatedly makes assumptions about my gender, I am less likely to patronize that establishment again. If, in attempting small talk, the server makes jokes that strike me as homophobic or transphobic, I will avoid the restaurant.

The same is true of museums. We know that people must have their needs met in order to learn. If physical safety is in question (for example, if a trans visitor is worrying about whether they can safely use the restroom), people will not be able to focus on new information. If they feel excluded, they cannot form the emotional connection required for following their curiosity or assimilating new ideas. When visitors feel anxious about their physical safety, or even ostracized for their identity, they will not likely return to the museum nor recommend that others visit.

Representation is also important for effective interpretation and learning. As a visitor, I must be able to connect the content with my lived experience. If an artist's gay identity is key to his work, then it should be mentioned when discussing that artist. If two apparently single Victorian women shared a household, it does both them and visitors a disservice to assume heterosexuality and speak of them only as "close friends" without including any nuance about their relationship or identities. There will be LGBTQ+ visitors who can relate more closely to content when queer identity is openly discussed; similarly, all visitors, regardless of identity, lose out when we conceal a piece of the story.

Staff and volunteers have the same needs as visitors. Just as we cannot effectively learn if our needs are not met, we are more effective teachers when we can show up with our whole selves. My most awkward moments as an educator have been when a student asks me a question such as "Do you have a husband?" or "Are you a boy or a girl?" when I am unsure of my institution's stance on queer identity. I spend a moment wondering whether I should lie to the student, violating the trust they have in me as a teacher, or whether I should answer honestly and risk discipline, perhaps even the loss of my job. On the other hand, when I know that I have my institution's support and can speak the truth, such moments create an opportunity for deeper connection with students.

The American Alliance for Museum's *LGBTQ Welcoming Guidelines* implores member organizations:

> Museums are community anchors, trusted places to safely encounter and find meaning in cultures, art, people and ideas different from our own. The significance we experience at museums comes from our innate ability to forge connections deeper than taste, opinion or belief. Sexual orientation and gender identity are threads in the vibrant, variegated tapestry of any community. Museums benefit from interweaving or even highlighting those threads, among many others, in our work. Let's continue to make museums welcoming for everyone.[21]

Beyond ethical or philosophical reasoning, non-inclusive policies or practices can create real harm. For staff or volunteers, it takes an emotional toll to remain closeted day after day. The stress of hiding one's private life often creates barriers between coworkers if, for example, gay staff cannot talk openly about their partner in the break room while people are sharing what they did over the weekend. Particularly for transgender people, even the ability to be "out" at work does not necessarily indicate an inclusive working environment. When staff repeatedly use the wrong pronouns to refer to a transgender person, that can create an environment of emotional harm where the person feels unseen or disrespected. This may lead a transgender staff person or volunteer to leave the organization for a more inclusive one or may result in a transgender visitor deciding not to visit again. There are real financial, as well as relational, consequences to a lack of inclusion.

TRAINING STAFF AND VOLUNTEERS

While facilities such as bathrooms can be important for welcoming LGBTQ+ people, they are not enough on their own. A museum with gender-neutral restrooms can still alienate LGBTQ+ visitors through exhibit signage or staff/volunteer behavior; a museum which cannot adapt its restrooms to be gender-neutral (for example, in historic buildings with renovation restrictions) can still create a culture of inclusion. Plus, big facility changes require buy-in from many different stakeholders across the institution; yet training can start small, in your own department.

An inclusive mindset is essential, no matter what other steps toward inclusion the museum may take. Without a baseline understanding provided by training, other changes will appear surface-level and be vulnerable to the whims of institutional and leadership shifts. If one educator is dedicated to creating a welcoming environment, and then that educator leaves, programming can easily revert to exclusionary practices. On the other hand, if the whole team is committed to inclusive processes and is well-trained in its methodology, that imbues the overall effort with resilience.

The following training model is one I have used many times, with a variety of sizes and types of institutions. The model works with museum educators, classroom teachers, and youth workers; with folks from small organizations and big ones. The end of this section will include some notes on scaling this model for a variety of contexts and expanding it to talk about other historically minoritized identities such as race or disability.

This training model relies on three parts: personal reflection on identity, a broader understanding of systems of cis-normativity and heteronormativity, and practical steps for application. There is plenty to dig into with these topics, and if you have time, each could be its own day-long training session. But overall, the most common delivery for the training described here is a single two-hour workshop, either virtual or in-person.

THE MODEL

Trainers

This workshop can be facilitated by staff from within the institution, by an outside consultant, or by some combination thereof. I have found it helpful to have two facilitators for any workshop on identity and inclusion: one who can speak from the societally targeted position, and one from the societally advantaged position. For example, I am a white, queer, transgender person. When I facilitate workshops on LGBTQ+ identity, I prefer to have a straight, cisgender co-facilitator. This co-facilitator can give some additional context to straight cisgender participants if needed and can step in to answer some basic questions if they get too invasive for me to comfortably respond to. My role in that workshop is to provide a personal perspective of the queer experience, and to speak from a knowledge that is deeper than my co-facilitator can have. On the other hand, I will not facilitate workshops on racial equity by myself; I always work with a co-facilitator who is a person of color. In that case, my role is reversed. If at all possible, workshops about marginalized identities should *not* be taught only by facilitators who have no personal experience with that identity. This may require looking outside your institution, to consultants or organizations in your area. When partnering with an outside consultant, it is often helpful to have them co-facilitate with a staff member, who can provide the particular context for your institution. Regardless of who is facilitating, be sure they are appropriately compensated for their time and energy.

Prelude: Setting the Scene

As with any conversation about difficult, personal, or political topics, begin with guidelines for conversation. The training should be a space where people can engage at whatever level they are currently at, where they can ask awkward questions, and where they can take risks. At the same time, it should be a space where offensive language is not tolerated, and where LGBTQ+ participants feel supported. (For more on supporting LGBTQ+ participants, see later in this section.)

I. Personal identity reflection

Sexual orientation and gender identity are at once deeply personal and socially experienced. Both are socially constructed identities, influencing how one moves through and interacts with the world. As with any identity category, there are "marked" and "unmarked" sexual and gender identities. This concept of markedness comes from linguistics, where a "marked" word needs additional modification to clarify meaning while an "unmarked" word needs no description. As Deborah Tannen put it in her 1993 essay "Marked Women, Unmarked Men," the unmarked meaning is "what you think of when you're not thinking anything special."[22] (See table 5.1.)

Table 5.1.

Unmarked	*Marked*
Lion	Lioness
Nurse	Male nurse
Man	Gay man
Woman	Transgender woman

Some social identities are the "unmarked" default. People are presumed to be heterosexual and cisgender (i.e., not transgender) until proven otherwise. This is perhaps most obvious with babies and young children. Gender reveal parties assume that the unborn child will continue to identify with the revealed gender throughout their life. Baby boys are dressed in onesies that say "Chick Magnet" and baby girls in onesies that read, "Sorry boys, Daddy says I can't date until I'm married." Those with unmarked identities often do not realize how identity is constructed or the deep impact these early presumptions can have on their lives.

I have found it useful to begin trainings with an opportunity for all participants to investigate their own identities. In order to preserve a sense of safety and create an environment where people can do some deep reflection, this is a largely individual process. Partner and large-group sharing, useful for some to process their thinking, emphasizes that people should only share what they are comfortable with.

There are many tools available for this purpose, but my personal favorite is the Gender Unicorn.[23] Developed by Trans Student Educational Resources, the Gender Unicorn investigates gender identity (in the categories of identity, expression, and sex assigned at birth) as well as sexual orientation (in the categories of who one is physically and emotionally attracted to). Unlike some other resources available, the Gender Unicorn breaks out of the popular binary-spectrum visualization of identity. Rather than having the participant place their identity at a singular point along a spectrum with "male" at one end and "female" at the other, the Gender Unicorn allows the participants to mark how strongly they identify with each category: male, female, and other. (See figures 5.2 and 5.3.)

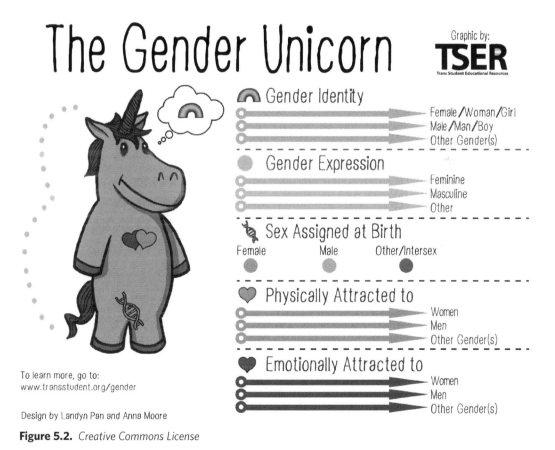

To learn more, go to:
www.transstudent.org/gender

Design by Landyn Pan and Anna Moore

Figure 5.2. *Creative Commons License*

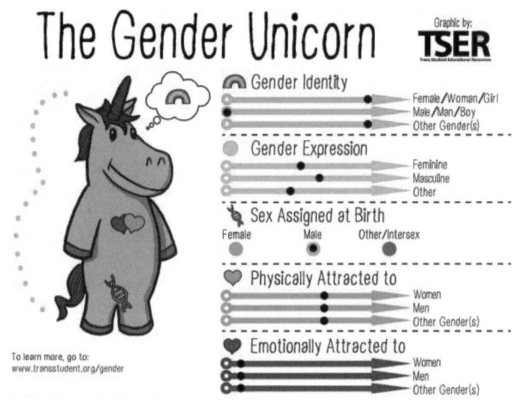

Figure 5.3 *Creative Commons License*

Once participants have had the opportunity to identify their own identities, a set of questions guide personal reflection, partner conversation, and/or whole-group discussion. These questions should provide opportunities for participants to interrogate how their identities affect how they show up in the world, as well as any "ah-ha!" moments. I often use questions such as:

- What was this exercise like for you?
- What did you notice about yourself?
- What did you notice about social gender roles/norms?
- How have your sexual or gender identities impacted your experience of education?

Some straight cisgender participants may find the last question especially challenging. Unmarked identities are often experienced without noticing them. So, a straight, cisgender person from a family with straight parents likely went through school learning about families that looked more or less like theirs, hearing stories about characters (both historical and fictional) whose identity aligned with theirs, easily figuring out which bathroom to use during the school day, and so forth. They may not have even noticed the ways in which these experiences affirmed their sexual and gender identity. A discussion about these impacts can help to reveal the ways unmarked identities continually reconstruct the dominant narrative.

Grounding the training in personal work helps participants connect to the content, relating it to their own lives. As Freeman Tilden says in the classic *Interpreting Our Heritage*, "the visitor's chief interest is whatever touches [their] personality, [their] experiences, and [their] ideals."[24] The same can be said of educators, volunteers, staff, and so forth. However, it is important to connect this personal work to larger social norms/expectations, as a segue to the following section.

II. Understanding the systems of cis-hetero-normativity

"Heteronormativity" is another word for the unmarkedness described above. The heterosexual is "normal." People must "come out" as gay, as different from the norm. An unmarried woman gets asked if she has a boyfriend, and an unmarried man about his girlfriend. Families are assumed to have a father and a mother, rather than two fathers or two mothers. Similarly, "cisnormativity" describes the unmarkedness of cisgender identity. One's gender is assumed to align with that typically associated with one's genitals and other sex characteristics. People are expected to be either male or female, and further, to conform with general expectations about how men and women should behave.

Heteronormativity and cisnormativity are distinct from homophobia and transphobia, but they often create oppressive environments for LGBTQ+ people. Take, for example, a lesbian couple having a child. In some states, the non-gestational mother cannot be listed on the birth certificate since she is not technically the father, and the birth certificate only allows one place for "Mother" and one for "Father." If, later, the gestational mother dies or the couple divorces, the non-gestational mother may face legal difficulties in maintaining custody of her child.

Museums, like all other institutions, are not immune from cis-hetero-normativity. We see it when an educator greets a class field trip with, "Good morning, boys and girls!" We see it when early childhood programs are labeled "Mommy and Me." We see it when a discussion about artwork assumes that two male figures in a painting are friends, but a male and a female figure in another painting are dating or married. This section of the training, depending on institutional context, may focus on systems of cis-hetero-normativity at the organization, local/state level, national level, or some combination thereof. Some possible discussion questions to consider:

- Where in our museum/programming do we make assumptions about people's partners, family structures, or gender?
- Where in our museum/programming do we require someone to identify their gender with only binary options?
- For parts of our museum/programming where people are required to identify their gender, do we know how we will respond if someone identifies with a gender different from how they appear or different from that assigned to them at birth (for example, if a child assigned male at birth wants to join the girls' science program)?
- How do we talk about ambiguous figures in our content? What assumptions do we make about them? For example:
  ○ Figures of indeterminate gender in an artwork
  ○ Two unrelated people of the same sex making close physical contact in a historic photograph
  ○ Animals whose biological sex and/or sexual practices do not align with human ideas of gender binary or heterosexuality
- In each of these cases, how could we shift our language, assumptions, or practices in order to reduce cis-hetero-normativity?

While breaking down societal systems of cis-hetero-normativity is unfortunately beyond the scope of one-off educator trainings, language use can help to disrupt some of these norms. A language shift, while not easy, is possible to implement at any institution if all involved are committed to it. For examples of inclusive language guides, see Margaret Middleton's Family Inclusive Language Guide[25] or the Gender Inclusive Language Guide provided in the online resources associated with this book.[26] Some possible discussion questions around an inclusive language guide:

- Read through the guide. What stands out to you?
- What do you have questions about?
- What language shifts might be easy for you to implement? What shifts might be harder?

III. Practical application

Every training needs a practical application that participants can put to use in their work. For some programmatic contexts, such as for educators whose role primarily involves direct facilitation, the introduction of inclusive language models may fit this bill. For others, participants may want further applications.

If participants come from a variety of different settings or roles, I have found it useful to have a general discussion with a question such as, "how might you apply this to your work?" This allows each participant the flexibility to engage at whatever level they feel comfortable and adapt to their particular needs. Deepening questions such as "what supports would you need to feel successful (and how can you call in those supports now)?" or "what are you excited and anxious about?" may be helpful as well.

Another method of creating practical application is with role-play or scenario discussion. The trainer generates scenarios (real or hypothetical) which may arise in context, allowing participants to discuss or role-play how they might respond. This method is particularly beneficial if a few specific instances occur with some frequency (for example, educators discussing the scenario of talking about students' families, and how they could avoid making heteronormative assumptions in that conversation).

LGBTQ+ inclusion starts from within the institution, so participants should also be equipped to address non-inclusive behavior coming from fellow staff and/or volunteers. Practice how to respond when a colleague says "good morning, boys and girls!," for example, or when you hear someone use the wrong pronouns for a transgender colleague. (In the case of advocating for a specific other person, it's often best to check in with that person to see how they would like you to support them first. If a recurring issue at your institution involves a staff member or volunteer, see the next section for more information on how to support them.)

Supporting LGBTQ+ Participants

For many straight cisgender participants, a lot of the concepts and language in this training will be new. They may be used to outdated terminology that is now considered offensive (such as "transsexual" or "transgendered"), or not have the words to describe what they are trying to say. They may have real, genuine questions about biology or identity which they feel are necessary to know the answers to before moving forward. This is all part of the learning process, but it can be exhausting or even triggering for LGBTQ+ people in the room. (I use the word "triggering" intentionally, as in, it can trigger a trauma response in people who have experienced trauma related to their identity in the past. If someone has experienced a particular line of questioning leading to a yelling match or even a physical assault, their body may react to that line of questioning as if it were the assault, going into fight, flight, or freeze mode.) The facilitator must balance the learning needs of those who are new to this topic with the emotional safety of those most affected.

Setting agreements for dialogue at the beginning is key. The facilitator must also be prepared to step in and correct someone's terminology (for example, saying "Some years ago, 'transsexual' was an accepted term, but now most people prefer 'transgender'") or stop a line of questioning altogether (for example, "it's really not important to know whether a gay person is sexually active with their partner. The point is that we shouldn't assume someone is straight until proven otherwise").

Sometimes the practice of caucusing or affinity groups may be helpful. LGBTQ+ participants can be grouped separately from straight cisgender participants, or there can be a time for LGBTQ+ participants to break away from the main group to have their own discussion. Depending on your group, you may even caucus further, putting (for example) cisgender LGB participants in a different group from transgender participants, or LGBTQ+ participants who are people of color in a different group from white LGBTQ+ participants. This caucusing often happens naturally when meeting in person—you may notice that the queer folks often sit at the same table, so a "table talk" discussion as part of the training can allow them to have time and space to connect with like-peers. However, to preserve the emotional safety of the space, do not require participants with marginalized identities to sit apart from each other except for very good reason. Allow natural caucusing to happen.

LGBTQ+ folks are often put in the position of being the "queer hotline" for colleagues, friends, and family. They are approached with sometimes invasive or offensive questions about their identities, their communities, and their bodies. People assume that just because I am queer, I know everything about sexual and gender identity. But the fact of the matter is, there is no test to become LGBTQ+. Identifying with that community does not magically give one knowledge about every aspect of even one's own identity, never mind others within the community. And it can be tiring to have to answer the same questions over and over again. So, while queer folks should have the opportunity to share their experiences if they wish, do not rely on them to answer questions that may arise. And, similarly, LGBTQ+ folks themselves can learn from a training like this. Even though I have facilitated these trainings, I find value in participating in them as well. If nothing else, I can learn from how others present the material, and practice advocating for queer folks in new ways.

If there is a particular recurring issue related to one or more staff/volunteers, talk with those affected before the training. Take their lead on how to address the issue. For example, imagine that one of the volunteers at your organization is a transgender man (someone who was assigned female at birth and identifies as male) who is starting his transition. Other volunteers and staff frequently refer to this person using "she" pronouns and his old name. You likely want to address this in the training, and even if you don't, it will probably come up. The volunteer in question may not want to attend the training—or he might want to attend, and possibly even talk about his own experience with the group. He may want people not to correct others in front of him, leaving it up to him whether he will say anything. Or he may want people to correct others for him, so that he doesn't have to take on that emotional labor. All of these should be his decision, and you should make sure that they align with him prior to the start of the training.

And finally, do not assume that no one in your group is LGBTQ+ just because you are not aware of anyone. Such an assumption is cis-hetero-normative. Some people may choose not to be out in their work lives, be in the process of coming out, or be in the closet entirely. In fact, assume that you have several LGBTQ+ people involved with your organization; statistically, that is fairly likely.

Scaling the Training Model

Each institution has its own set of concerns, based on staffing models, location, size, and so forth. A museum with two paid staff and a corps of occasional volunteers has very different training needs than a large museum with a multi-million-dollar budget and many departments. Fortunately, this training structure can be scaled in a variety of ways. It can be done with small or large groups, over a single workshop or multiple sessions, as a collaborative study group or a facilitated training. The key part is the structure: first, self-reflection on one's own identity and how that impacts one's interaction with the world; second, learning about societal systems of cis- and heteronormativity; third, application to daily work and/or life. If you choose to have a collaborative study group, take care to choose predominantly (if not exclusively) study material produced by LGBTQ+ people. Some suggested resources are included in the online supports associated with this book.

Further, LGBTQ+ identity is just one of many historically marginalized identities. The basic structure of this training model can be applied to learning and thinking about inclusion for other identity groups as well. For example, a similar workshop on racial equity might ask participants to think about their own racial identity and how that has impacted their life experiences, then moving into learning about structural racism (such as red-lining), and finally examining ways to disrupt white supremacy in one's everyday work.

MAKING THE CASE

What if you are not a decision maker at your organization? It can sometimes feel daunting or even impossible to make the case for inclusivity training to your supervisor, director, or board. Hopefully, the opening sections of this chapter will aid you in finding the language to advocate for LGBTQ+ inclusion.

But most importantly, begin where you are. Engage in your own personal study, following the training model outlined here. Begin to change your own behavior. Encourage your colleagues to do the same—you might even bring together a workgroup to share your learning, or an article or book club to guide discussion. At one institution I worked for, museum-wide change started when a few passionate educators began meeting up once a month after work to discuss an equity-themed book we had all read. If you are a supervisor of a team, or even a person with informal authority on the team, try implementing a small change like an inclusive language guide. Embedding LGBTQ+ inclusion in small ways can have ripple effects.

In many institutions I am familiar with, inclusion efforts started with the education department. We are often the ones who have the closest contact with visitors and can see the effects of non-inclusive practices firsthand. We are attuned to educational research that emphasizes the need for safe and welcoming spaces for learning. Educators impact many aspects of the museum, so when the education department makes changes, others pay attention. Because we are skilled at facilitation, educators are often recruited to assist with museum-wide training efforts and may have a hand in determining the organization's training needs. No matter how large or small your sphere of influence, start there; but don't stop making the case to others as well.

MOVING FORWARD

LGBTQ+ inclusion training is not the end-all solution; it is a piece of the equity puzzle. One workshop will not solve all of your problems. But knowledge is power, and frequently a lack of knowledge is what (consciously) holds people back from implementing equity and inclusion.

For this reason, it is crucial to end trainings with a robust section on practical applications. New learning must effect a change in behavior. As Maya Angelou reportedly said, "You did [then] what you knew how to do. And when you knew better, you did better."[27] Training should help museum professionals not only *know* better, but *do* better—and continue doing better, well beyond the initial scope of the training.

I end this chapter as I do my training sessions. What is one thing you are committed to doing in order to further LGBTQ+ inclusion in your context? This could be as simple as learning more about something, a small change you could make in your language, a person you could talk with about this. Or it could be as large as rewriting official policy, committing to an institution-wide training workshop, developing a partnership with an LGBTQ+ organization. Write down the thing you are committed to doing on a notecard or piece of paper, as well as a quick note about why you think this is important to do. Leave this somewhere you will see it regularly, as a reminder to continue taking action and remaining accountable to your own commitment.

No matter how small your first step, you can begin the journey toward LGBTQ+ inclusion. Under this rainbow is a world where all people are welcomed and included in museums, no matter who they are or how they love.

DISCUSSION QUESTIONS

1. Complete the Personal Identity Reflection activity using the Gender Unicorn. What was this exercise like for you? What did you notice about yourself and/or about social norms?
2. Based on what you read in this chapter, why is it important to be intentionally LGBTQ-inclusive? What are some potential consequences of being non-inclusive? What are some potential benefits of being inclusive?
3. What other examples of cis-hetero-normativity can you think of in your daily life? In museums you've visited or worked in?
4. What is your current sphere of influence? What one or two things could you do to increase LGBTQ inclusion in your sphere of influence?

When you envision using this training model, what questions or concerns do you still have?

NOTES

1. Pew Research Center, "Social Acceptance," *A Survey of LGBT Americans,* June 13, 2013, https://www.pewsocialtrends.org/2013/06/13/chapter-2-social-acceptance/.
2. See, for example: Massachusetts, Goodridge v. Department of Public Health (2004); Washington state Referendum 74 (2012); Confederated Tribes of Coos, Lower Umpqua, and Siuslaw Indians repeal of Tribal Code Section 4-7-6 (c) (2014); U.S. Supreme Court, Obergefell v. Hodges (2015).
3. U.S. Department of Defense, "Repeal of 'Don't Ask, Don't Tell' Quick Reference Guide," October 28, 2011, https://archive.defense.gov/home/features/2010/0610_dadt/Quick_Reference_Guide_Repeal_of_DADT_APPROVED.pdf.
4. California Senate Bill 48 (Chapter 81 of the Statutes of 2011).
5. U.S. Supreme Court, Bostock v. Clayton County (2020).
6. Lucas Grindley, "What the Media Gets Wrong about Pulse," *Advocate,* June 12, 2018, https://www.advocate.com/commentary/2018/6/12/what-media-gets-wrong-about-pulse.
7. National Center for Transgender Equality, "The Discrimination Administration: Trump's Record of Action Against Transgender People," https://transequality.org/the-discrimination-administration.
8. Elinor Aspegren, "An 'Epidemic of Violence': HRC Counts Record Number of Violent Transgender Deaths in 2020," *USA Today,* October 15, 2020, https://www.usatoday.com/story/news/nation/2020/10/14/transgender-murders-reach-least-32-year-surpassing-record/3639313001/.
9. Merrill Perlman, "How the Word 'Queer' Was Adopted by the LGBTQ Community," *Columbia Journalism Review,* January 22, 2019, https://www.cjr.org/language_corner/queer.php.
10. Kelsey Louie and Jordan Sang, "Marriage Equality and HIV: What's Love Got to Do With It?," *POZ,* September 29, 2015, https://www.poz.com/article/marriage-equality-HIV-27852-9116.
11. U.S. Supreme Court, Windsor v. United States, 570 U.S. 744 (2013).
12. Obergefell v. Hodges, 576 U.S. 644 (2015).
13. Bostock v. Clayton County.
14. Human Rights Campaign, "A National Epidemic: Fatal Anti-transgender Violence in America in 2018," https://www.hrc.org/resources/a-national-epidemic-fatal-anti-transgender-violence-in-america-in-2018.
15. Sandy E. James, Jody L. Herman, Susan Rankin, Mara Keisling, Lisa Mottet, and Ma'ayan Anafi, *The Report of the 2015 U.S. Transgender Survey,* National Center for Transgender Equality (Washington, D.C.: National Center for Transgender Equality, 2016).
16. Katy Steinmetz, "The Transgender Tipping Point," *Time* (May 29, 2014), https://time.com/135480/transgender-tipping-point/.

17. See, for example, G.G. v. Gloucester County School Board (2015).
18. American Alliance of Museums, *Gender Transition and Transgender Inclusion in the Museum Workplace: A Toolkit for Trans Individuals, Insitutions, and Coworkers* (2019), https://www.aam-us.org/professional-net works/lgbtq-alliance/resources/.
19. Eryn Star, "Marriage Equality is Still Not a Reality: Disabled People and the Right to Marry," *The Advocacy Monitor,* November 14, 2019, https://advocacymonitor.com/marriage-equality-is-still-not-a-reality-dis abled-people-and-the-right-to-marry/.
20. Frank Newport, "In U.S., Estimate of LGBT Population Rises to 4.5%," *Gallup,* May 22, 2018, https://news.gallup.com/poll/234863/estimate-lgbt-population-rises.aspx.
21. American Alliance of Museums, *Welcoming Guidelines for Museums* (Washington, D.C.: American Alliance of Museums, 2016), 1.
22. Deborah Tannen, "Marked Women, Unmarked Men," *New York Times Magazine* (June 20, 1993), https://static1.squarespace.com/static/5523ffe4e4b012b2c4ebd8fc/t/5617e224e4b0ae0940 4129f4/1444405796395/marked+woman.pdf.
23. Trans Student Educational Resources, "The Gender Unicorn," 2015, http://transstudent.org/gender.
24. Freeman Tilden, *Interpreting Our Heritage,* 4th ed. (Chapel Hill: University of North Carolina Press, 2007), 36.
25. Margaret Middleton, "Family Inclusive Language Chart," https://www.margaretmiddleton.com/family -inclusion.
26. Also available here: Mac Buff, "Beyond Bathrooms: Including All Genders through Language," *View- finder,* March 6, 2019, https://medium.com/viewfinder-reflecting-on-museum-education/beyond -bathrooms-including-all-genders-through-language-300580834384.
27. Quoted in Oprah Winfrey, "The Powerful Lesson Maya Angelou Taught Oprah," October 19, 2011, https://www.oprah.com/oprahs-lifeclass/the-powerful-lesson-maya-angelou-taught-oprah-video.

BIBLIOGRAPHY

American Alliance of Museums. *Gender Transition and Transgender Inclusion in the Museum Workplace: A Toolkit for Trans Individuals, Insitutions, and Coworkers.* Washington, D.C.: American Alliance of Museums, 2019, https://www.aam-us.org/professional-networks/lgbtq-alliance/resources/.

American Alliance of Museums. *Welcoming Guidelines for Museums.* Washington, D.C.: American Alliance of Museums, 2016.

Aspegren, Elinor. "An 'Epidemic of Violence': HRC Counts Record Number of Violent Transgender Deaths in 2020." *USA Today.* October 15, 2020, https://www.usatoday.com/story/news/nation /2020/10/14/transgender-murders-reach-least-32-year-surpassing-record/3639313001/.

Buff, Mac. "Beyond Bathrooms: Including All Genders through Language." *Viewfinder.* March 6, 2019, https://medium.com/viewfinder-reflecting-on-museum-education/beyond-bathrooms-including -all-genders-through-language-300580834384.

Grindley, Lucas. "What the Media Gets Wrong about Pulse." *Advocate.* June 12, 2018, https://www .advocate.com/commentary/2018/6/12/what-media-gets-wrong-about-pulse.

Human Rights Campaign. "A National Epidemic: Fatal Anti-transgender Violence in America in 2018," https://www.hrc.org/resources/a-national-epidemic-fatal-anti-transgender-violence-in-america -in-2018.

James, Sandy E., Jody L. Herman, Susan Rankin, Mara Keisling, Lisa Mottet, and Ma'ayan Anafi. *The Report of the 2015 U.S. Transgender Survey.* National Center for Transgender Equality. Washington, D.C.: National Center for Transgender Equality, 2016.

Louie, Kelsey, and Jordan Sang. "Marriage Equality and HIV: What's Love Got to Do With It?" *POZ.* September 29, 2015, https://www.poz.com/article/marriage-equality-HIV-27852-9116.

Middleton, Margaret. "Family Inclusive Language Chart," https://www.margaretmiddleton.com/family -inclusion.

National Center for Transgender Equality. "The Discrimination Administration: Trump's Record of Action Against Transgender People," https://transequality.org/the-discrimination-administration.

Newport, Frank. "In U.S., Estimate of LGBT Population Rises to 4.5%." *Gallup.* May 22, 2018, https://news.gallup.com/poll/234863/estimate-lgbt-population-rises.aspx.

Perlman, Merrill. "How the Word 'Queer' Was Adopted by the LGBTQ Community." *Columbia Journalism Review.* January 22, 2019, https://www.cjr.org/language_corner/queer.php.

Pew Research Center. "Social Acceptance." *A Survey of LGBT Americans.* June 13, 2013, https://www.pewsocialtrends.org/2013/06/13/chapter-2-social-acceptance/.

Star, Eryn. "Marriage Equality Is Still Not a Reality: Disabled People and the Right to Marry." *The Advocacy Monitor.* November 14, 2019, https://advocacymonitor.com/marriage-equality-is-still-not-a-reality-disabled-people-and-the-right-to-marry/.

Steinmetz, Katy. "The Transgender Tipping Point." *Time.* May 29, 2014, https://time.com/135480/transgender-tipping-point/.

Tannen, Deborah. "Marked Women, Unmarked Men." *New York Times Magazine.* June 20, 1993, https://static1.squarespace.com/static/5523ffe4e4b012b2c4ebd8fc/t/5617e224e4b0ae09404129f4/1444405796395/marked+woman.pdf.

Tilden, Freeman. *Interpreting Our Heritage.* 4th ed. Chapel Hill: University of North Carolina Press, 2007.

Trans Student Educational Resources. "The Gender Unicorn." 2015. http://transstudent.org/gender.

U.S. Department of Defense. "Repeal of 'Don't Ask, Don't Tell' Quick Reference Guide." October 28, 2011, https://archive.defense.gov/home/features/2010/0610_dadt/Quick_Reference_Guide_Repeal_of_DADT_APPROVED.pdf.

Winfrey, Oprah. "The Powerful Lesson Maya Angelou Taught Oprah." October 19, 2011, https://www.oprah.com/oprahs-lifeclass/the-powerful-lesson-maya-angelou-taught-oprah-video.

6

Building a Better World

RETHINKING A MUSEUM'S CIVIC ENGAGEMENT MODEL

Anna Schwarz and Rachel Stark

ABSTRACT

Civic engagement, meaning values-based programs that encourage all visitors, even the youngest among us, to take small, consistent actions for the good and well-being of our community, is central to the identity of the Skirball Cultural Center. In the Build a Better World school programs, developed in conjunction with the award-winning exhibition Noah's Ark at the Skirball, educators lead activities that foster human connections, inspire hope, and invite people to take action in some way, be it responding with kindness, encouraging people to see themselves in others, or starting community campaigns to support people struggling with homelessness. These passionate educators often partner with like-minded classroom teachers and community organizations to be of direct service. However, given the heightened vulnerabilities of our students during the pandemic, the challenges of virtual learning, and the questioning of democratic principles in our politics, we paused to look critically at our work. As an arts and culture provider rooted in Jewish tradition and American democratic ideals, what is our role in the community—in this moment and in the long term? How can we respond to the needs of teachers, students, and their families now, and in ways that are sustainable for the future? How can we reimagine and expand the training and support our museum educators need? This chapter will explore the evolution of Build a Better World programming and the evolving roles of our museum education team.

PANDEMIC PANDEMONIUM

It had been a long ten months from March 2020 to January 2021. Zoom fatigue had set in. In a virtual after-school classroom, several young students were rolling around on the floor, others were not on camera. One was playing with his bouncing puppy. Another was looking past the screen and yawning. Then Skirball educators Lori Nierzwick and Mario Ibarra appeared in their Zoom boxes, and in an easy exchange of English and Spanish, brought the online room to life with an activity about storytelling and creative writing. Through a mix of interactive storytelling, visual analysis, and creative expression, these skilled educators waged battle on the fatigued learning environment, bringing joy and compassion to a group of fifty pre-K–grade 2 students (and occasionally their siblings and caregivers who were drawn in to participate).

Similar to institutions around the world, the role of museum educators at the Skirball Cultural Center in Los Angeles is evolving. For the time being (though hopefully only temporarily), gone are the days of blithely greeting busloads of children at our front steps, watching the swirl of little bodies having animal dance parties aboard the permanent exhibition Noah's Ark at the Skirball, or assembling in the hundreds for dynamic music and dance performances. Yet this collective shift to distance learning was the enormous challenge facing America's teachers when stay-at-home orders went into effect in early 2020. At the Skirball, in the wake of more than one hundred field trip cancellations, and with no plans to resume in-person programming anytime soon, museum educators have shifted their practices as well. With technology now the central means of communication, our entire mode of interdisciplinary teaching has been overhauled by necessity.

How did we move forward when the world seemed to be spiraling out of control? We turned to what we know best—the strengths of our educators, our community of teachers, and Noah's Ark at the Skirball's messages of hope and resilience.

A SNAPSHOT OF THE SKIRBALL

The Skirball Cultural Center in Los Angeles is an American Jewish institution rooted in the value of welcome and committed to creating cultural experiences that celebrate discovery and hope, foster human connection, and call upon participants to help build a more just society. Since opening to the public in 1996, the Skirball has established itself as a dynamic Jewish cultural institution and among the leading cultural venues in Los Angeles. It includes a world-class museum that holds a collection of objects representing four thousand years of American Jewish life and regularly presents a range of engaging changing exhibitions and public programs.

Noah's Ark at the Skirball, the permanent children's and family destination that opened in 2007, is the heart of the institution and an embodiment of its mission. The ancient story of Noah's Ark aligns with the Skirball's conviction that by working together and caring for one another, people can weather life's storms or challenging times and help build a better world. The gallery features a floor-to-ceiling ark and three hundred-plus whimsically designed animal puppets and sculptures—all handcrafted from recycled materials and everyday objects, including bottle caps and sofa springs. This emphasis on repurposed materials reminds us of the value of second chances.

Both in the physical design and in the programming, Noah's Ark at the Skirball is filled with open-ended experiences that invite visitors of all ages to bring the messages, meaning, and story to life. Whether working together to "conduct" a storm on a wall of sound effects, caring for the animals on the ark, or learning about ways they can help the environment or participate in community service projects, visitors to Noah's Ark learn by doing and are invited to make the experience their own.

Informed by this values-based foundation, the team of museum educators has developed a distinct approach to teaching and learning, using the arts to foster hope, connection, and action. The Skirball's team of educators is made up of experienced museum facilitators, former classroom teachers, actors, dancers, musicians, and puppeteers! Through a lively mix of oral storytelling (they each research and present age-old flood tales), close looking (a combination of Visual Thinking Strategies and the See-Think-Wonder framework, originated by Harvard's Project Zero), movement, music- and art-making, they delight young audiences and create a joyful, immersive learning experience.[1] At the same time, they focus on the critical work of inspiring students to see themselves as active participants in society.

We call this part of our work civic engagement. It is central to our mission as a cultural center. To us, it means values-based programs that encourage all visitors, even the youngest among us, to take small, consistent actions for the good and well-being of communities. In the Build a Better World program for students and teachers, which is developed to correspond to the Noah's Ark experience, educators lead activities in the galleries that invite participants to take action in some way, be it small

Anna Schwarz and Rachel Stark

acts of kindness, encouraging people to see themselves in others, or starting community campaigns around pressing issues such as homelessness or global warming. But we can't (and don't) do this work alone. Through partnerships with local nonprofits such as LA Family Housing (which assists families struggling with homelessness), The Refugee Children's Center, Children's Hospital Los Angeles, or even the Theodore Payne Foundation for Wildflowers and Native Plants, we bring real needs and challenges in communities in Los Angeles to first and second graders in age-appropriate and direct ways.[2] On field trips to Noah's Ark, students begin service-learning programs and then return to school to continue the projects. These programs have resulted in school-wide community campaigns and donation drives. But in the world of COVID-19, we quickly found ourselves reimagining what it means to "build a better world" and how we could engage students and teachers strictly via a digital platform.

QUESTIONS WE ASKED OURSELVES

As we collectively reeled from the pandemic in Spring 2020, Skirball educators joined colleagues around the world in rethinking our models of student and teacher engagement. We began by asking questions, a practice central to Jewish teaching and tradition.

- How could we translate our strengths—including our educators' unique skill sets, values-driven content, and the participatory nature of our programs—to build community in the digital realm?
- How could we be responsive to students' and teachers' needs when school closures and the very real economic and emotional stresses of the pandemic were in effect?[3]
- How could we help the museum education team do their work digitally, and do it well? What additional training or support would they need?
- With community partners tied up with the very real need of feeding and housing people, and trying to keep their doors open in a major recession, how could we reimagine the Build a Better World model and fulfill the social justice aspect of the Skirball's work?
- Was it possible that we would be able to do certain things even better or achieve things we couldn't achieve with analog programs?

Embracing a spirit of adaptability—and inspired by the Jewish story of survival over four millennia—we asked ourselves how could we adapt our educational programs to meet the challenges of this time while retaining the essence of the Skirball's values and approach?

OUR JOURNEY FORWARD (SO FAR)

As we write this article in March 2021 after a full year of school closure in Los Angeles, more than six hundred thousand students in LA County are experiencing some form of distance learning. Despite this catastrophic shift in educational experience, what remains the same for Skirball museum educators is a commitment to values-based teaching and learning, celebrating creativity, and empowering students as storytellers and change-makers.

Go to the source, our community of classroom teachers—You can't teach about building a better world if you can't get the kids in the room, even a virtual room. Removed from the day-to-day reality of distance learning, we wanted to hear directly from teachers about how they were doing and where we might offer support.

In Spring 2020, we surveyed over 3,500 educators on our mailing list. While the responses were useful, we knew we had to go deeper and issued an open call for advisors. Our goal was not only to gather input on resources appropriate for distance learning in a pandemic, but also to give educators a virtual space to come together as a community of learners. Of our large network of teachers, seven pre-K to fifth grade teachers, who were similarly committed to teaching through storytelling, became the inaugural members of the Skirball's Teacher Advisory Council (STAC). While we've long been committed to teachers as experts and co-creators of museum education experiences, the pandemic afforded us the opportunity to formalize that commitment.[4] The council is a collaborative, resource-sharing group of local teachers and leaders who champion LA County's diverse student populations and share in the Skirball's mission to foster empathy, collaboration, and community. (See figure 6.1.)

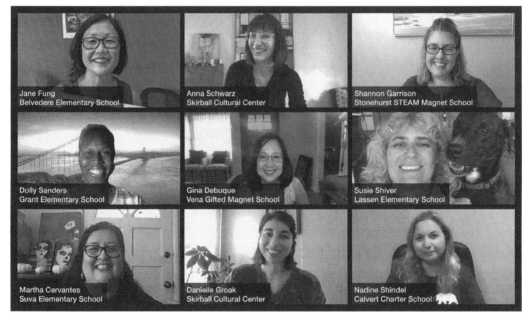

Figure 6.1 Skirball Teacher Advisory Council, 2020–2021. *Courtesy of Skirball Cultural Center.*

Over regularly scheduled Zoom meetings, we covered a wide range of questions: How are teachers doing with distance learning? Is Google Classroom more user-friendly than Schoology? Are pre-recorded videos preferred over live educator-led activities? How many students lack and/or have access to tools needed for distance learning? How can we help bridge the digital divide?

What we learned was that while the school districts were working to provide laptops and Wi-Fi hotspots to students, teachers looked to us to provide content and engagement to students in front of their screens. What they requested were short videos to help with vocabulary building and lessons to support critical thinking and connect abstract themes to students' daily experiences. They emphasized that video content could not just be livestreamed; it would have to be posted online for students to view if and when they could. The opportunity to show a clip repeatedly held another advantage: children in lower elementary grades would have multiple chances to deepen their understanding of the material, boosting their confidence along the way. Other practical insights emerged: visual aids would enhance storytelling sessions, especially for emerging bilinguals; worksheets should be fillable PDFs, not require printing or scanning; videos should be short-format; and the chat function was a must for reengaging students who seemed less likely to speak up if they felt disconnected from their peers.

The teacher advisors allowed us to see where our strengths would be most useful and effective. Most significantly, they regularly invite Skirball educators into their virtual classrooms, co-teach and test lesson plans, and offer insightful feedback on an ongoing basis. Their help could not be more foundational.

Adapt instruction to the platform and audience needs—Our educators participated in regular virtual meetings with the teacher advisors. They then developed a series of digital training sessions where we learned how to best use the tech to prioritize student learning while maintaining a safe online learning environment (hello Zoom waiting rooms and chat!), how to activate oral stories on a small screen, and how to capture the immersive experience in video clips and PowerPoint slides.

We've always used a co-teaching approach at the Skirball, which allows educators to naturally bounce off of each other, and supports collaborative teaching and learning.[5] We had hoped to continue with this model, but what we didn't know was that Zoom would practically require it! We found it was essential to have one lead educator/storyteller and one host/co-teacher to oversee the chat and slides. So, we began by practicing virtual co-teaching and working to align the content of our virtual field trips to each museum educator's own skills and abilities.

This was a challenging time exacerbated by the steep learning curve for digital programming. All of the educators were isolated at home and had to do this work remotely with whatever tools they had for work. Some were more tech-savvy than others. Some had ongoing WiFi and connection issues. Some needed light (ring lights for everyone!). But ultimately, out of necessity, our team of educators became video producers, writing scripts, contracting production companies, working through the intricacies of filming in the galleries while abiding by COVID-19 safety protocols.

Create new content suited for this moment and digital learning—Building on invaluable input from STAC teachers, who piloted the lesson plans, and our museum educators' expertise, we developed *Noah's Ark at the Skirball: The Art of Imagination* in 2020 for pre-K through grade 5 with an emphasis on storytelling and social and emotional learning.[6] This set of resources includes six streaming videos (including one in Spanish), seven downloadable lesson plans, virtual teacher PD programs, and live virtual field trips. (See figure 6.2.)

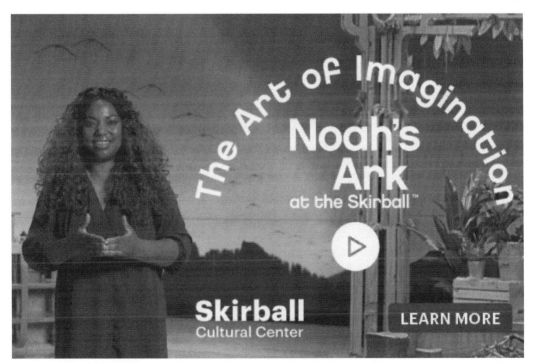

Figure 6.2 Noah's Ark at the Skirball: The Art of Imagination. Photo by WolfDog Creative. *Courtesy of Skirball Cultural Center.*

In developing this set of resources, and piloting it with STAC teachers, we learned that our approach to the civic engagement component of our programs had to change. Students' attention spans are limited. To keep them engaged on big ideas around the importance of empathy, collaboration, community service, and action, we needed to provide content that sparked joy through imaginative play, art-making, and creative writing and not just talking or presenting. To even get to empathy, we needed to provide tools that increased focus and allowed students to cope with stress; thus we emphasized mindfulness activities. And finally, with our community partners tied up with direct service, we no longer had access to their time in support of our programs. Instead, we pivoted to other resources such as *Taking Action Together* that gives students tools to make their own service-learning action plan.

Although the modality changed, the Build a Better World messages of hope and resourcefulness have not. In the live virtual field trips in particular, educators like Lori and Mario are still able to bring moments of joy, capturing those impactful lessons by telling timeless flood stories from around the world. On tiny screens, students travel through huge storms by embodying rain and wind—swaying side to side or rolling energetically on the floor (yes, it's okay to go off screen and move around in your physical space!)—they create safe shelters through community council style share-outs and celebrate new beginnings with an animal dance party (have you ever danced like a baby duckling?). In some tales we are on a large boat with many creatures, in others, on a little walnut shell or inside a hollowed-out pumpkin. Students are encouraged to let their imaginations run wild and become part of the story! These stories result in giggles and cheers, but also serve as a reminder that throughout history, people have experienced hard times and overcame challenges by working together.

In another live virtual field trip, educators lead students in an exploration of the whimsical hand-crafted animals aboard Noah's Ark, made from repurposed materials and everyday items. In lessons about caring for the earth, students analyze what the animal sculptures are made of, have deep conversations about second chances, and create artwork out of found objects. The lessons inspire conversations about global warming and have led to community campaigns about recycling, for example.

As we began the virtual field trips, we were mindful (and curious) about how best to retain students' attention for forty-five to sixty minutes. What we found was that students were so engaged, they wanted to continue the conversation beyond the allotted time! Teachers reported back that the stories told by the educators were so rich, full of hopeful messages, and centered on student participation, that class participation in their regular Zoom classes increased after the field trip. Many students return to their regular virtual class eager to share their own stories with their peers. For some students, like a child named Lorenzo, participation in the virtual field trip led him to turn on his camera for the very first time in the school year. Other students are eager to participate in the chat. And still others, like a group of nonverbal kindergartners, are thrilled to be featured in a spotlight dance party. This type of active participation, even from afar, validates the team's hard work and reminds us that building a better, more just society starts with a classroom community that values kindness, compassion, and offers safe spaces for creative expression.

All in all, programs are designed to center the voices of students and foster a sense of agency. The youngest members of our community are learning that they are not alone, and that they can take small, but substantive actions to make a difference in their own lives and in their communities. Students can select a cause *they* care about and determine what actions to take as a class, be it postcard writing campaigns or interviewing family members and highlighting the heroes in their own homes. This is student activism in this moment. It may be smaller in scale and less visible than the hundreds of care packages assembled in our gallery-based programs for nonprofits that provide services to our unhoused neighbors, but it is as effective a tool in demonstrating to students that they have a voice and that their actions matter.

Build Reflection into the Process—For the museum education team, reflection has always been central to the way we create and sustain programs. So, during our shift to virtual programs, we made sure to build collaborative reflection into our ongoing programming process. We held ongoing meetings with the teacher advisors that helped shape the daily virtual field trips. Through these meetings we were continually learning about what was landing and what needed to be adjusted, especially as we entered a perhaps extended period of hybrid instruction. But what remained clear from student and teacher feedback was that the civic engagement aspects of our programming were resonating with students.

On visiting Noah's Ark on a virtual field trip, fifth-grade students said:

- "[The Noah's Ark animals showed me that] every single thing can have value no matter what it is."
- "[The Skirball educators] appreciate what we say. They want us to participate and to feel welcome. . . . They really got us to use our voice, to speak up."

On what the fifth-graders reported that they took away from the flood stories:

- "That you're going to face challenges in life . . . and with perseverance and strength you can always get through them, no matter what challenge it is. And if you never give up, you'll always be able to persevere and get through it."
- "I think it's teaching us not only to reuse and recycle but to love what we have and to appreciate what we have . . . our planet, our animals, our family."

Fifth-grade teacher and Skirball teacher advisor Shannon Garrison noted that the flood tale's storyline—of weathering storms, fostering community, and building a better world—is an effective way to guide her students through these hard times. For Skirball educators, it was humbling and heartening to learn that the virtual experience could be as rich from the perspective of teaching these values as the on-site experience.

Digital learning is challenging, and we are all learning how to be better Zoom hosts, how to keep learning interactive and engaging (Zoom fatigue is real), and how digital tools have their own standards of effective use and practice. We've kept the pre-COVID tradition of meeting before and after tours to prepare for and then reflect on the co-teaching experiences. In this way, our commitment to being a community of learners as a staff has remained. Don't get us wrong, the creation of this set of resources, and the process of reframing museum educators' roles and shifting to a digital platform has been extremely challenging. Many tears have been shed in the process, many hours wasted on lessons that didn't see the light of day, many frustrated Zoom calls where setbacks happened. But with those challenges came the pleasure of knowing that this new set of virtual programming was effective and was having its desired impact. Our reach has the potential to be so much greater than ever before. Without the restrictions of bus funding and limited gallery space, we can access classrooms as far and wide as we want. And the depth of our interactions with students—multiple visits to the same classroom—is increasing. While many museums are closing their doors permanently and furloughing staff out of necessity, we recognize just how lucky we are to be able to do this work in partnership with teachers.[7] We have been fortunate to be able to take this opportunity not only to respond to the challenges of the moment, but to deepen our practice as well.

LESSONS LEARNED ALONG THE WAY (AND STILL LEARNING)

We can all agree—remote learning is stressful. Teachers are dedicated to their students, but they do this work in the face of growing burnout (for themselves and their students), and battle unexpected power outages, Zoom crashing nationwide, lack of access to laptops and reliable Internet.[8] Let's be honest, our educators can't solve these major issues single-handedly nor can they address every challenge remote teaching presents. But the demands of distance learning present opportunities to define our strengths and rethink how to engage with our audiences.

While the pandemic has forced us to reevaluate our priorities, it has also laid bare the necessity of active civic engagement. Although we recognize that not every museum could offer a program like this with the same degree of authenticity (not everyone has a Noah's Ark), some of the larger themes around civic engagement could be applied by a variety of types of museums for virtual programming with young students and via teacher partnerships. Here are some things to consider.

Identify institutional values and amplify them. Take time to reflect on what your institution prioritizes. What are your foundational values that can help build a better world? If you work at a science museum, perhaps your focus is on conservation and the active role young people can play in advancing that cause. If at a historic site, perhaps you are focused on the pressing issues of racial justice and equality. Pick the area you want to focus on, make sure it is aligned with your institutional values, and go! At the Skirball, in refining programs to a digital format (and with a slashed budget), our educators asked themselves: What is quintessentially Skirball about this? Can we focus on "Build a Better" messages with this project?

Teacher well-being and expertise are invaluable. The success of museum education programs lies in deep relationships with teachers that are mutually beneficial and based on shared values and concerns for students. Form a teacher advisory council if you don't already have one. The teachers will tell you what you need to know. And co-teaching between museum educators and classroom teachers allows programs to be even richer. At the Skirball's bimonthly STAC meetings, teachers help us stay on track, brainstorm with us new avenues for online engagement, reinforce the co-teaching model—we regularly visit their virtual classrooms and have the privilege not only to observe these skilled educators in action but also to teach side-by-side with them. And perhaps most important, create space where we can all be human. We can vent about a bad day, laugh, share mindful moments, talk about family stories and traditions, have an occasional stretch/yoga session, and ultimately see that we are all connected by a shared commitment to students and their families.

Students are changemakers. Students are passionate! Create space for the youngest members of our community to express themselves, artistically and intellectually. Give them the tools and the platform to consider ways that they can take action in their families, schools, neighborhoods, and beyond.

Reach out to your neighbors. Find out what the local direct service nonprofits in your area are doing to feed people, support families experiencing homelessness, advocate for refugees, or help the environment, and how you can support their efforts. Since monetary donations aren't usually realistic for a nonprofit museum, consider ways to offer mutually beneficial programming. It could be an effort to get out the word about what that organizaton is doing through a poster-making or postcard-writing campaign. For example, encourage young people to write *Cards of Kindness*, with messages of hope and gratitude for someone they've never met. In doing so, students will foster empathy, broaden their horizons, and strengthen community connections.

Online is here to stay. While we are eager to return to our gallery spaces soon, we know that digital learning will continue in one form or another. In many ways, digital allows us to extend our reach even further and demonstrate our commitment to civic engagement. Skirball educators like Lori and Mario are now on the digital front lines, along with like-minded heroes in online classrooms, eking out substantive and hopeful learning experiences designed to open hearts and minds. We're off the hill, literally (since the Skirball is located atop the Santa Monica Mountains). Beaming in from our homes, we are joining our constituents of students, teachers, and families who share the same values and

Anna Schwarz and Rachel Stark

vision for building a better world together. The work is challenging, iterative, and takes resilience, but we are hopeful that it makes all of us, museums and educators and humans, more actively involved in shaping our future.

DISCUSSION QUESTIONS

1. In developing programs, ask yourself: Does this content feel relevant, appropriate, most needed, authentic? Is it in line with your values? How does it connect to the values of your institution?
2. Education in this country is in crisis. What role are you playing as museum educators to support students and teachers? What are you uniquely positioned to contribute to student learning and teacher sustainability? And how can you utilize your skills to instill joy, hope, and compassion?
3. What does civic engagement mean to you and your institution? Who is the community with whom you are engaged? How can you create and strengthen collaboration with community partners that share similar values and that ultimately bring people together to actively shape a more just, equitable future?
4. Pre-COVID, did your institution offer stipends or fee waivers to schools in need? Knowing that significant financial constraints persist, how can you make digital content available to the widest possible audience?

NOTES

1. Teaching strategies are drawn from Visual Thinking Strategies (VTS): Critical Thinking and Inclusive Discussion, Vtshome.org and Harvard's Project Zero Visible Thinking, pz.harvard.edu/projects/visiblethinking.
2. "Comfort and Hope: A Partnership with LA Family Housing" and "Messages of Welcome and Hope," skirball.org.
3. Esquivel and Blume, "Tens of Thousands of L.A.-Area Students Still Need Computers or Wi-Fi 6 Months into Pandemic," *Los Angeles Times*.
4. Kletchka and Carpenter, *Professional Development in Art Museums*, 167–70.
5. Stark, "Cultivating Shared Leadership with Docents and Staff," 22.
6. *Noah's Ark at the Skirball: The Art of Imagination*, skirball.org.
7. Kenney, "From Bad to Worse," *The Art Newspaper*.
8. Johnson, "Up to 1 Million California Students May Still Lack Connectivity during Distance Learning," EdSource.

BIBLIOGRAPHY

"Cards of Kindness." 2020. Skirball Cultural Center, https://www.skirball.org/sites/default/files/lesson7-noahsark-cardsofkindness.pdf.

"Children Are Citizens." n.d. Harvard's Project Zero Visible Thinking | Project Zero, http://pz.harvard.edu/projects/children-are-citizens.

"Citizen University." n.d., https://citizenuniversity.us.

"Comfort and Hope: A Partnership with LA Family Housing." 2018. Skirball Cultural Center, https://www.skirball.org/comfort-hope.

"Community Council." 2020. Skirball Cultural Center, https://www.skirball.org/sites/default/files/2-lesson-noahsark-communitycouncil.pdf.

"The Definition of Civic Engagement." n.d. *New York Times*, https://archive.nytimes.com/www.nytimes.com/ref/college/collegespecial2/coll_aascu_defi.html.

Esquivel, Paloma, and Howard Blume. 2020. "Tens of Thousands of L.A.-Area Students Still Need Computers or Wi-Fi 6 Months into Pandemic." *Los Angeles Times*, https://www.latimes.com/california

/story/2020-09-15/tens-of-thousands-of-la-county-students-still-need-computers-and-hot -spots-six-months-into-school-closures.

"For Your Students." n.d. Skirball Cultural Center, https://www.skirball.org/education/for-your-stu dents.

Johnson, Sydney. 2020. "Up to 1 Million California Students May Still Lack Connectivity during Distance Learning." EdSource, Highlighting Strategies for Student Success, https://edsource .org/2020/california-still-lacks-connectivity-for-more-than-300000-students-during-distance -learning/641537.

Kenney, Nancy. 2020. "'From Bad to Worse': Over Half of US Museums Have Laid Off or Furloughed Staff, Survey Shows." *The Art Newspaper*, November 17, 2020, https://www.theartnewspaper.com/news /from-bad-to-worse-over-half-of-us-museums-have-laid-off-or-furloughed-staff-survey-shows.

Kletchka, Dana Carlisle, and B. Stephen Carpenter II. 2018. *Professional Development in Art Museums: Strategies of Engagement through Contemporary Art*. N.p.: National Art Education Association.

The Learning Accelerator. 2020. "Driving Quality in Remote Learning: A Framework for Research-Informed Remote Experiences for K–12 Learners." 20-09-TLA: Quality Drivers for Remote Learning, https://docs.google.com/document/d/1f7VErrahG_wDm5O2rgZFc1MANB6r6779eSiHGwJEqJ8 /edit#.

Lewis, Barbara. 1998. *The Kid's Guide to Social Action: How to Solve the Social Problems You Choose—And Turn Creative Thinking into Positive Action*. N.p.: Free Spirit Publishing.

"Messages of Welcome and Hope." 2018. Skirball Cultural Center, skirball.org/education/build ing-better-world/messages-welcome-hope.

Murawski, Mike. 2021. *Museums as Agents of Change: A Guide to Becoming a Changemaker*. N.p.: Amer-ican Alliance of Museums.

Murawski, Wendy W. n.d. "Five Keys to Co-teaching in Inclusive Classrooms." AASA, The School Superintendents Association, https://www.aasa.org/SchoolAdministratorArticle.aspx?id=4906.

Pennay, Anthony. 2021. *The Civic Mission of Museums*. N.p.: American Alliance of Museums (AAM).

Stark, Rachel. 2016. "Cultivating Shared Leadership with Docents and Staff." *Journal of Museum Educa-tion* 41, no. 1 (February), https://www.tandfonline.com/doi/abs/10.1080/10598650.2015.1134396.

"Taking Action Together." 2020. Skirball Cultural Center, https://www.skirball.org/sites/default/files/ lesson6-noahsark-takingactiontogether.pdf.

"Visual Thinking Strategies." n.d. Visual Thinking Strategies (VTS): Critical Thinking and Inclusive Discussion. vtshome.org.

7

Facilitating Family Learning in Museums

RETHINKING OUR ASSUMPTIONS AND APPROACHES

Scott Pattison and Smirla Ramos Montañez

ABSTRACT

Although museums have long valued and catered to families as an audience, museum educators have not always had the tools or training to support the unique nature of family learning or to develop family-specific approaches that are distinct from classroom teaching. In this chapter, we outline a series of research-based principles for understanding family learning and provide examples to illustrate how these principles play out in museums. Specifically, we highlight the importance of (a) recognizing that families have multiple goals, (b) appreciating the central role of parents and other adult family members, and (c) understanding how a museum visit is a brief moment in a family's long-term learning trajectory. We then explore how these principles might be used to inform new approaches to the facilitation of family learning in museums and provide an example of a professional development resource intended to help educators incorporate these principles into their practice.

INTRODUCTION

Museum educators have often struggled with a simple paradox. On the one hand, as learning institutions, museums are rooted in the educational system of our society, which is dominated by formal schooling. This has made it difficult for museums to define their approaches and measures of success independent of the school system. At the same time, the audience and learning context of museums is fundamentally different from school. Rather than teaching classrooms of children of similar age in a relatively structured learning environment with often narrowly constrained learning goals and content, museums offer open, free-choice spaces for intergenerational groups to learn and explore when they want, the way they want, for as long as they want.[1] In short, museum educators often face the challenge of applying formal schooling models to support learning in an environment that could not be more different.

One critical difference that distinguishes museum learning from school is the opportunity for families to learn together. Families—which we define broadly to encompass any intergenerational group of adults and children visiting together, regardless of their biological relationship—are one of the most fundamental social structures in our society. And they have long served as a primary audience for museums. Although most museums offer classes or field trip opportunities, families and other informal visitor groups remain a central part of how museums define and support themselves.[2] The study of families has also been a central focus of museum scholarship and research. Investigators have explored why families come to museums, what family learning looks like in these settings, ways that museum exhibits can be designed to support family conversations and learning, and, in some cases, how museum educators can facilitate family learning.[3]

This focus on families is well justified—not only from a financial perspective but also based on the mission of most museums to support learning, advance knowledge, and help children and adults become engaged and informed citizens.[4] Families are central contexts for human learning in our society—across cultures and throughout the world. When children are young, adult family members are the primary drivers of learning and development, providing safety and security, supporting children's natural curiosity and exploration, and modeling and scaffolding during learning experiences.[5] Even after children enter the formal school system, the home and family context continue to be central determinants of children's long-term learning and well-being.[6] As these children become adults, they in turn form their own families and pass along their knowledge, values, and cultural practices to their children, shaping how our society re-creates itself and evolves over time.[7] In the current context of the global pandemic, the critical importance of family has been starkly highlighted as communities have seen the cascading effects of disrupting family support systems and routines.

Although museums have long valued and catered to families as an audience,[8] museum educators have not always had the tools or training to support the unique nature of family learning. As with school, education and learning are central to the family experience. However, the two learning contexts are fundamentally different. Formal schooling, especially as it has traditionally been structured in the United States, focuses on creating educational learning experiences for large groups of children of similar age. The focus and structure of these learning experiences are controlled by a central adult figure (the teacher), whose choices are also informed by curriculum and policy at the local, state, and federal level. Children's progress and outcomes are assessed through standardized tests, and educational content and tasks are organized in ways that may only vaguely resemble learning situations that individuals encounter outside of school.

In contrast, family learning, even though it varies greatly across communities, is by definition intergenerational and social and often arises spontaneously through everyday conversations and interactions. There is rarely any formal assessment, and the goals of these experiences, whether implicit or explicit, are often multiple and complex—including not only learning new knowledge and skills, but also building individual and group interests and identities, creating positive memories and social bonds, reinforcing family values, and having fun together.[9] As part of the broader phenomenon of "informal" or "free-choice" learning, families have control over what, how, when, and with whom they learn.[10] Unfortunately, much of the approaches and research that has informed museum education comes from schools, despite the many differences between these two learning institutions.

In this chapter, we hope to help resolve this paradox by providing more background about family learning to inform the work of museum educators. Based on existing research and our experience studying and working with families over the last several decades, we outline a series of research-based principles for rethinking family learning in museums. For each principle, we describe the research that has informed our understanding of families and provide examples to illustrate how these principles play out in museums. We then explore how these principles might be used to inform new approaches to the facilitation of family learning at museum exhibits, drawing from research funded by the National Science Foundation.[11] Although our own perspectives are informed primarily by our work in science centers and our research in the field of informal STEM education, we believe these principles are relevant across museum types and learning settings. (See the end of the chapter for examples of family-centered facilitation approaches developed in other types of museums.)

Scott Pattison and Smirla Ramos Montañez

PRINCIPLES OF FAMILY LEARNING FOR MUSEUM EDUCATION

The study of families and family learning is broad and extends well beyond the world of museums or even education. In this section, we highlight just a few principles of family learning that we believe are particularly relevant to the work of museum educators.

The examples provided for each principle come from the National Science Foundation–funded Researching the Value of Educator Actions for Learning (REVEAL) project (www.terc.edu/reveal). The three-year research study was conducted at the Oregon Museum of Science and Industry (OMSI) and was designed to develop and test effective staff facilitation strategies for supporting family learning at interactive math exhibits. In particular, we draw from video recordings captured as part of the project of staff-family interactions at one of the exhibits included in the study: *Balancing Art* (see figure 7.1). The *Balancing Art* exhibit challenges visitors to create balanced sculptures by hanging weights on each side of a rod suspended on a central fulcrum. Distances from the center of the rod and the weight of each sculpture piece are quantified so that visitors can explore, discover, and use both qualitative and quantitative understandings of the mathematical relationship between distance, weight, and balance. In the REVEAL project, museum educators were also provided specific tools and materials to help them support family learning—what we called "facilitation affordances." For example, at *Balancing Art*, educators had a series of "mystery weights" that they could share with visitors and challenge them to either create balanced configurations with the new pieces or use the exhibit to determine the value of the mystery weights.

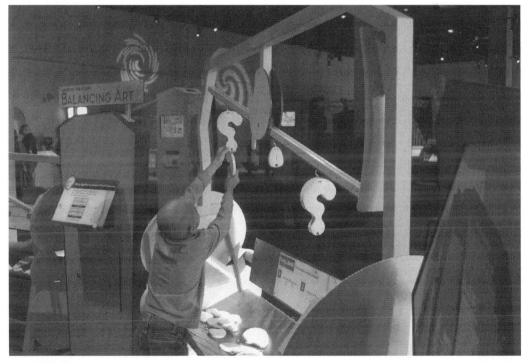

Figure 7.1 *Balancing Art* exhibit used as part of the REVEAL project. *Image © Oregon Museum of Science and Industry 2013.*

(1) Families Have Multiple Goals

A critical piece to understanding and supporting family learning is to appreciate that families have multiple goals in any educational or learning context—and that those goals may or may not align with the objectives of the educators in that setting. Research has long demonstrated that individuals have multiple reasons for visiting a museum.[12] In their influential work on identity and museums, Falk and colleagues described five "identities" that may motivate individuals to visit museums: explorers, facilitators, experience seekers, professionals/hobbyists, and rechargers.[13] For example, a parent might be primarily motivated to visit a science center with their family in order to facilitate enjoyable learning experiences for their children. Or a couple might frequent their local art museum in order to recharge and refresh after a busy work week. Subsequent research has highlighted how these "identity-related motivations" influence the ways that visitors explore a museum and the outcomes of that experience.[14]

The same dynamics and diversity of goals and motivations can be seen within families. As noted above, families visit museums to learn, have novel and enjoyable experiences, spend time together, reinforce family traditions and cultural values, take a break and get out of the house, and more. In fact, families often balance various goals simultaneously in any given interaction or experience. A good example of this comes from research on how families engage in mathematics outside of school, such as shopping at a grocery store, talking about budget at the dinner table, or reinforcing a math concept for their children at a math-related museum exhibit.[15] In these situations, research shows that families actively balance multiple goals beyond the sole focus on completing the mathematical task, including building social relationships or efficiently managing time and effort.[16] In some cases, the teaching and learning of the mathematical concept might be a primary focus. But in most cases, this may be an important but secondary goal, such as when family members prioritize the efficiency of a mathematical strategy (e.g., estimation) in order to complete an everyday task quickly or when an adult family member decides to move on to another museum exhibit when they see their children becoming distracted—in other words, prioritizing the goal of overall visit enjoyment over specific content or learning goals at each exhibit.

One misconception about families is that they either come to a museum to learn or they come to a museum to have fun. In fact, research shows that these two goals are not at odds with each other or mutually exclusive.[17] Nor would we expect them to be—especially in an informal learning environment like a museum where learning is driven by our own motivations, interests, identities, and enjoyment.[18] As Falk and Dierking noted long ago, there is a reason that many families choose to visit museums as opposed to the other entertainment opportunities available to them.[19] Museums are spaces that simultaneously offer the chance for family bonding, fun shared experiences, and learning driven by curiosity and interests. What we and others have observed in our research is that families are often quite adept at balancing these different goals, tailoring and selecting their experiences throughout a museum visit to both create learning opportunities and help ensure a fun, enjoyable experience for the whole group.[20] On the other hand, family goals can also be in conflict with each other in the same experience. For example, Rowe analyzed an example of a family at an interactive science exhibit in which visitors were encouraged to explore the idea of angular momentum as they tested different wheels on several inclined ramps.[21] Rowe documented how the adults and children continuously negotiated between the goals of understanding the scientific principles at the exhibit, exploring these principles using a more open-ended approach, and turning the activity into a racing competition.

The following example provides another illustration of this complex dynamic of multiple family goals and how these relate to the goals of a museum educator. In the interaction, the family begins to engage with the *Balancing Art* exhibit as a museum educator watches nearby:

> A family with two adults and one boy (about 10 years old) approaches the exhibit. The child immediately starts hanging weights from the balance bar. The man starts to intervene ("So Landen,

look at the numbers on them") but the woman stops him ("He's gonna do what he wants, let him think"). The boy continues to hang weights on both sides of the rod, naming the weights as he hangs them and talking quietly to himself (e.g., "See if I can match them"). The two adults and a museum educator watch closely nearby. After a few minutes, the woman steps up to the exhibit and tries to guide the activity ("Can I show you something? Look at the numbers."). She helps the boy add up the weights on each side of the rod, seeming to focus on a deeper understanding of the mathematical relationship in the exhibit ("So, you have twelve over here and sixteen over here and it's still not heavier. Why is that?"). The boy continues to explore on his own, trading out different weights and checking the balance of the rod. The educator and adults watch closely, chatting about the temperature of the room. The whole group exclaims when the boy gets the rod to balance, and the educator confirms ("I would say that's balanced. As long as it's touching any of that blue there"). At this point, the educator tries to engage the boy in a more direct exploration of the mathematical relationship, starting with a question ("Do you think how far out it goes matters?"). He then facilitates an "experiment" to highlight this relationship with a simplified configuration of weights. However, the boy seems more focused on balancing the rod with all the available weights ("We have an extra one!"). The group continues to explore the activity for several minutes. After the boy and woman leave, the man stays for another minute to talk to the educator and briefly try out the activity on his own. (Watch the full interaction here: https://tinyurl.com/BalancingArt1)

In this example, we see multiple goals at play, both within the family and between the family and the museum educator. At the outset, the boy jumps right into the exhibit, appearing to engage in an open-ended, perhaps tactile or aesthetically driven exploration of the weights and balancing rod. The man begins to intervene, starting to guide the boy to focus more on the underlying mathematical principle of the exhibit. But the woman stops him, perhaps recognizing the boy's more exploratory goal. Later, the woman seems to align herself with the man's focus and begins explaining the math relationship to the boy. At this point, the museum educator joins the interaction and proposes an experiment to test the relationship between weight and distance. The boy initially resists, insisting on his personal goal of finding a way to hang all the weights. The group continues exploring, with the boy sometimes focusing on the goal proposed by the educator and sometimes returning to his own exploration. When the woman and boy leave, another overlapping goal is revealed—the man's own interest in the mathematical relationship. He stays a few minutes to confirm his own thinking and chat with the museum educator before following the rest of his group.

As shown in this example, appreciating that families have multiple goals has important implications for the work of educators. Museum professionals are often taught to focus on the pedagogical goals of the experience, perhaps in pursuit of a series of learning or content objectives that we have mapped out in advance.[22] And, as in the example above, families may very well share these goals and be eager to work with the educator to create learning opportunities for the group. However, families are often balancing these types of goals with other priorities, such as ensuring that everyone has an enjoyable experience. Individual family members may also be pursuing their own goals, as appeared to be the case in the interaction above. In order to successfully facilitate family learning, museum educators must remain aware of and help families balance these multiple goals. We have seen in our own research that adult family members can be quite skillful in shifting, redirecting, or even ending an interaction when they feel that it is not achieving this balance for the whole group.[23] In the interaction above, the educator perhaps had this in mind as he gave the family space initially to negotiate their own goals and provided the boy time to explore the activity in his own way. Later, he seemed to try to follow the adult's attempt to focus more on the mathematical relationships in the exhibit—although we might debate on how well this was received by the boy. He reserved his most detailed explanation of the mathematics for the end of the exhibit, when the man remained behind and clearly communicated his desire to learn more about the math underlying the activity.

(2) Parents Play Unique Roles

Another critical consideration when supporting families in museums is recognizing the unique role of parents and other adult caregivers in family learning. Unlike a typical school classroom, families are not made up of individuals of similar age and experience. Instead, families are complex groups in which parents (defined broadly to include any primary adult caregiver in a child's life) play a central role as teachers, learning facilitators, resource brokers, and more.[24] Parents are their children's first teachers, and they remain one of the most powerful influences on their children's educational trajectories throughout the school years.[25] At home, in museums, and across other learning contexts, parents support their children's learning and development by modeling skills and practices, providing explanations, guiding and scaffolding children's exploration, and providing new learning resources and experiences based on their children's evolving interests and abilities.[26]

Although many of us would acknowledge the important role of parents, it is also common to hear educators and researchers alike disparage adult family members, highlight their weaknesses, and repeat stereotypes about what "parent engagement" should look like. In fact, research in museums and other settings has repeatedly shown that parents are quite effective at facilitating their children's learning.[27] Of course, the way parents interact with children may not always match our own expectations or approaches as educators. However, this may be just as much about our own culturally-based understanding of what parenting and family learning "should" look like, rather than any research evidence of more or less "effective" parenting approaches. In a classic example, Gaskins studied families in children's museums and described how families from different cultural backgrounds engaged with their children in different ways depending on their cultural beliefs about play and parenting.[28] For example, some families were much more likely to support child-directed play while in other families the parents and adults were more likely to lead the interaction or collaboratively participate with their children. In another revealing study, researchers showed that even parents that appear to be standing back "disengaged" from their children are likely connecting with the experience and supporting children in ways that may be invisible to us as educators.[29]

One of the reasons that parents are often successful at supporting children's learning is because of their unique and intimate knowledge of their children's abilities, prior experiences, and interests.[30] As educators, we know that connecting with prior experiences and knowledge and creating personally relevant experiences is critical for successful learning.[31] However, this is exactly the type of information that museum educators often lack when facilitating experiences for visitor groups. Parents, on the other hand, are well acquainted with their children and are usually highly sensitive to the ways an experience is relevant—especially, as discussed above, as they think about how the experience is fun and enjoyable for the whole family. Prior research has shown the ways that parents in museums frequently help their children connect with prior experiences and build on prior knowledge.[32] Similarly, in our own work with families, we frequently have seen the skillful ways that parents redirect or tailor experiences to be appropriate or engaging for their children, including modifying the suggestions or ideas presented by museum educators to support their children's learning.[33]

The example below at the *Balancing Art* exhibit highlights the powerful role that parents play in family learning in museums, even when a museum educator is present:

> A family with one adult and two girls (approximately 11 and 6 years old) approaches the balancing exhibit. The family is speaking Spanish, and the man immediately begins to facilitate the exhibit for the group, explaining the mathematics to the girls as they explore the activity. He seems to have a clear understanding of the goal and underlying mathematical relationship in the exhibit. Both children appear interested, but his focus is particularly on the older girl and helping her work on the mathematics. The educator stays back and observes. At one point, she prevents another group from interfering with the family's work. After the family has balanced one configuration, she approaches and offers the family a "mystery weight"—a new piece of unknown weight that

the family must add to the rod and try to create a balanced configuration. She acknowledges and supports the man's facilitation role by handing the mystery weight to him and allowing him to continue to lead the group ("Okay, I'm going to give this to your grown-up. You want to put it on over there and she'll put it on over here"). After the family solves this challenge, with the older girl taking the lead and the man providing guidance, the educator offers another. With the third challenge, the educator mixes up the process by offering the new mystery weight to the older girl so that she can place it on the rod and let the adult solve the challenge ("This time, you get to put it on, and your grown-up gets to do the solving"). He seems engaged but somewhat self-conscious about this change. The older girl watches and seems to enjoy the shift in roles. The man successfully solves the challenge, and the group celebrates before saying goodbye to the educator. (Watch the full interaction here: https://tinyurl.com/BalancingArt2)

Like the idea of multiple goals, the unique role of parents in family learning has implications for the work of museum educators. Research suggests that in order to successfully support family learning, museum educators must acknowledge and support, rather than undermine, the multiple roles of parents and engage with them as co-facilitators of the group experience.[34] For educators, as in the example above, this may mean taking a supporting role and providing tools and strategies that adult family members can use to extend their roles as teachers and facilitators—including offering novel learning tools, sharing additional knowledge and insights about the exhibit content, or suggesting different engagement strategies.[35] In the example above, the educator offered support, including "mystery weights" and associated challenges, provided space for the family to engage in the manner and language they were most comfortable with, and engaged directly with the adult without making assumptions about his language abilities or without interfering with his role as group facilitator.

This process can also require reflection and self-awareness for us as educators in order to look beyond our own models of learning and realize that parenting may look very different for families and visitors from different cultural backgrounds.[36] Again, the educator in the example above supported the role of the adult in the family, even if she might have had different ideas about the goals of the exhibit or the ways that the child should be supported (e.g., a more exploratory or child-directed approach). Ignoring the role of parents, on the other hand, can make it difficult for educators to connect with families. In our early research on family learning in museums, we documented a variety of ways that parents can serve as gatekeepers to museum educator involvement, potentially blocking or avoiding the educator's involvement when they feel that their role as parent is being undermined or that the family's goals are not being supported.[37] Similarly, other studies have shown how facilitation by museum educators can shift how parents and other adult family members engage with their children at the exhibits.[38] More broadly, by failing to connect with and support the unique ways that families learn together from different cultures and backgrounds, museums risk exacerbating the barriers to visiting museums that we know already exist for many families.[39]

(3) A Museum Visit Is a Brief Moment in a Family's Learning Trajectory

The last principle that has been highlighted for us working with families over the years is the reality that an interaction with a museum educator, and even the overall museum visit, is just one brief moment in a family's long-term learning trajectory. As educators, this is a sobering reminder that although we spend a great deal of time thinking about and planning for the ways we support families during their visit, our time with families is but a tiny fraction of their cumulative learning experience over time. We know from research that museum visits and other informal learning experiences, even if they are brief, can have a powerful and lasting impact, including the interests and identities of children and adults. And we know that cumulatively museums and other informal learning contexts play a critical role in children's and adult's education, even compared to school.[40] However, for a given family, we know very little about what has happened before their visit, what will happen afterward, and how this unique combination of events will shape the family's experience.

One implication of this principle is that as museum educators we cannot make assumptions about how a family's behavior in a particular moment represents their approach to learning in other contexts. For example, what can we infer if we see a family at a museum exhibit and the adult is standing back watching or even checking their phone? Do we assume the adult is a disengaged parent that doesn't care about their children's education? Do we consider that they perhaps have been working tirelessly to engage their children all day and now need a brief break? Perhaps an emergency has come up that they need to attend to? A variety of studies have actually highlighted how families from different cultural backgrounds may behave one way in a museum but take a very different approach to learning in their own homes.[41] One long-standing misconception in formal education has been the labeling of parents, especially those from traditionally under-represented groups, as not engaged in their children's education if they don't show up to school events or behave in the ways that teachers expect "engaged" families to behave.[42] In fact, it is likely the educational institution itself is creating barriers to family involvement (e.g., lack of transportation or linguistically accessible resources) or making assumptions about what engagement should look like (e.g., parents who can't make it to a school event but are deeply involved in their children's learning at home). Similarly, instead of focusing on "disengaged" parents or "problems" with the ways families use exhibits, museums need to reflect on the ways that they create barriers for families or stereotype the ways that learning "should" look in their institutions.

The example below provides an interesting case of how an educator must navigate these complexities and assumptions as he tries to support family learning at the *Balancing Art* exhibit:

An adult man and two young kids (a boy and girl approximately 5 and 2 years old, respectively) approach the *Balancing Art* exhibit. The man guides the group ("Alright, let's balance this stuff") and helps manage the two kids as the older boy places weights back and forth on each side to try to balance it, with little discussion of the underlying mathematical relationship. At the outset, the man provides tips about balancing ("You need to put some on this side, okay") and suggests the boy should think about addition ("Remember, do addition, okay? See if you can do it"). Throughout, the young girl tries to stay involved, holding on to the weights, watching the older boy, and trying to hang weights on each side. The man occasionally helps manage between the two kids when there is conflict (e.g., "That's a good idea, Deli. Let Deli put them on, too"). The man seems particularly focused on helping the older boy understand the goal of balancing the rod (e.g., "We have to see what we can do to make it go flat. Right now, it is on this side. Let's see if we can get more over on that side"). The three continue to work together for several minutes, with the man switching back and forth between helping balance the rod and managing the two children. At first, the educator primarily stays back and observes. At one point, the educator steps in to help steady the rod to test if it's balanced. After about three minutes, the educator steps up to the activity and provides more specific suggestions about moving the weights, with the man watching a few steps away. At about three and a half minutes, the educator focuses more on the younger girl, asking her to compare the different weights in her hands, while the older boy continues to place weights on either side of the rod to try to get it to balance. Both the educator and the man then help the boy with his "guess-and-check" strategy, suggesting ways to shift the weights slightly on each side (without calculating the overall weight on each side or looking at the relationship between weight and distance). At last, the group is able to find a balanced configuration. The educator high fives with the kids ("I'd say that's balanced there!") and the family moves on. (Watch the full interaction here: https://tinyurl.com/BalancingArt3)

From an educator perspective, this interaction feels very different from the previous two examples. There is little talk about the mathematical relationship between distance and weight at the exhibit, and perhaps we might assume that the educator missed an opportunity by not pursuing his

Scott Pattison and Smirla Ramos Montañez

learning goals, especially with the older boy. But there are also a variety of clues throughout the interaction that highlight how the family's history might have influenced this interaction and the educator's decisions. The man has two younger children, and he is clearly balancing the need to engage both in a way that is appropriate to their ages and interests. At the outset, he brings up addition—perhaps acknowledging that adding the weights on each side might be a more appropriate focus for the age of the boy than multiplication (a judgment that is difficult for a museum educator to make in a brief interaction without more insights about a child's age and prior knowledge). The younger girl also reacts strongly to the older boy several times, which may suggest sibling rivalry or perhaps ongoing conflict between the kids that the adult is trying to manage as they complete their visit. The adult is highly involved from the start, but also takes several breaks as the educator facilitates for the children. It may be that it has been a long day, and this experience is a welcome change of pace for the family. Regardless of the reality of the family's background and experience, the educator uses a light touch, seeming to follow the man's lead and supporting the goals that the family has decided to focus on, regardless of his own educational priorities.

Thinking about a family's long-term learning trajectory, this example also highlights how little control museums and museum educators have over the ultimate outcomes of an individual experience. Partly this is because the nature and outcomes of a museum visit are determined, to a great extent, by what visitors bring with them to the experience, including their values, identities, interests, and prior knowledge.[43] The long-term outcomes of the experience also depend on what happens after the visit, which is well beyond the control of the educator or museum. In our own research, we have seen how a broad range of outcomes can emerge from even a relatively intensive family program with multiple family touch points, based on families' values, interests, and subsequent experiences.[44] In the example above, the educator only engages with the family for a few minutes—likely a small fraction of the family's overall museum visit, let alone their cumulative learning experience over time. Although the museum educator followed the adults lead and did not try to go deeper into the mathematical content of the exhibit, it is impossible to know how these decisions impacted the outcomes of the experience for the family. Perhaps supporting an overall positive experience is just what this family needed—a memory that plants the seed for future visits and ongoing interests.

DEVELOPING FAMILY-CENTERED APPROACHES TO MUSEUM EDUCATION

Developing approaches to supporting family learning in museums that incorporate these principles requires going beyond the models of education and learning that we have been accustomed to in schools. It also requires museum educators to be highly flexible, adaptable, and responsive to the complexities of family learning.

One example of this type of approach was developed in collaboration with museum educators through the Researching the Value of Educator Actions for Learning (REVEAL) project. REVEAL was a three-year research study carried out by the Oregon Museum of Science and Industry (OMSI) between 2013 and 2017. In collaboration with TERC and Oregon State University, the team explored the role of museum educators in deepening and extending family engagement and learning at interactive math exhibits.[45] The primary goals of the project were to (a) iteratively develop and refine a model of how staff facilitation can deepen and extend family engagement and learning at interactive math exhibits; (b) test key components of this model, including the relationship between staff facilitation and the nature of family engagement and learning; and (c) develop and share evidence and research-based tools to support professional development efforts for museum educators.

Through the study, the team developed a model of facilitation within the context of family learning at interactive math exhibits (figure 7.2). The model identifies the three goals that guided the approach, the reflective cycle of facilitation that educators used to pursue those goals and respond to the unique needs and interests of family groups, and the various physical, personal, and social factors

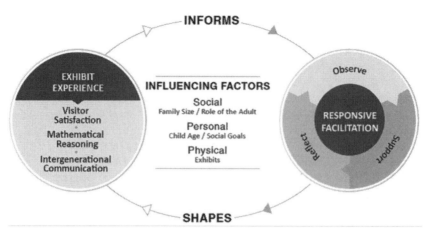

Figure 7.2 REVEAL responsive facilitation model for families in museums. *Image* ©
Oregon Museum of Science and Industry 2014.

that influenced the nature of the interactions. Based on the assumption that museum facilitation is a complex social interaction between educators and visitors that requires acknowledging and building on the interests, knowledge, and experiences of visitor groups, the three learning goals identified in the model guided educators in a continuous process of balancing the more content-focused goal of the interactions (mathematical reasoning) with the more visitor-centered goals (satisfaction and intergenerational communication) that are essential to informal learning in museums.[46] As the model indicates, to achieve this balance the educators followed an ongoing cycle of responsive facilitation, observing visitors and their interactions with the exhibit, making choices about their facilitation strategies, and then reflecting on the impact their facilitation had on the families[47] (see figure 7.2).

The interactions shared in this article are from REVEAL and were documented as part of the video-based professional development guide created through the project.[48] The examples show the complexity of museum educators trying to stay attuned to the unique needs and goals of each family, balance these with their own educational goals, share their role as educator with other family members, and continuously adapt throughout the interaction. As highlighted, this work is never easy or perfect. It is a constant process of reflection, both in the moment and over time, as we learn to better understand and support families. The guide that was developed through the REVEAL project was intended to provide a catalyst for staff facilitators in museums, science centers, and other informal learning environments to discuss, reflect on, and improve their educational practices in order to better support family learning in their settings. The program was particularly designed for staff who engage with families and visitor groups through informal, conversational interactions, such as facilitation at interactive exhibits or activity carts. The guide includes an introduction to the REVEAL project and the video-based professional development program; guidance and facilitation tips for staff members leading the program with their colleagues; five discussion modules, each focused on a different aspect of facilitation and each linked to specific videos of staff-family interactions; handouts for participants, including background readings and video discussion guides; and articles and resources for learning more about each module topic.

The REVEAL project is one example of trying to incorporate the family learning principles outlined in this chapter into approaches to facilitating the unique nature of family learning in museums. The facilitation strategies developed through REVEAL attempt to explicitly recognize the multiple goals that families bring with them to museums and place family-centered goals (e.g., visitor satisfaction and

Scott Pattison and Smirla Ramos Montañez

communication among family members) as equally important to more content-centered goals (e.g., supporting mathematical reasoning). The approach also recognizes the unique role of parents and other adult family members and helps educators explore ways of positioning their role as supporting rather than replacing parents. For example, educators in the project first practiced noticing the facilitation that adults are already doing within the family and making strategic, ongoing decisions about when to step in to provide additional facilitation, offer tools and information to support the adult, or simply step back and observe. Relative to principle three above, the reflection guide provides museum educators with a chance to think about their role in the broader trajectory of a family's learning experiences over time. In our experience, this broader perspective allows educators to better appreciate the importance of what families bring with them to the museum, such as unique interests or routines for learning together, and helps them balance their own educational goals with those of the families. For example, an educator may choose to prioritize satisfaction over content goals during a particular interaction, knowing that a positive memory may encourage a family to continue talking about their experience and return to the museum in the future.

The REVEAL model is designed to be flexibly incorporated into the work of museum educators in many ways. During the REVEAL project, four educators participated in five half-day training sessions over two weeks using the guide and videos. The first session introduced the project and the REVEAL facilitation approach, the next three focused on different exhibits and the mathematics and facilitation strategies specific to those exhibits, and the final session gave the group time to reflect on what they had learned and prepare for data collection. Each session included opportunities for the educators to watch and discuss example videos of expert educators facilitating family learning at the REVEAL exhibits, as well as to practice facilitation with visitors at these exhibits, supported by coaching from the project team. The videos in particular were a critical tool for helping educators step back from an interaction, view it multiple times, and practice noticing family goals, parent roles, and other clues about what the family brought with them to the interaction. The training also provided educators with a broader perspective on family learning, aligned with the three principles discussed in this chapter, and a chance to develop their own toolkit of strategies for supporting families.

CONCLUSION

In this chapter, we argue that museums are critical educational institutions in our society and that museum educators need unique approaches to supporting learning that matches their settings and contexts. In particular, this requires understanding how family learning is different than learning in school and developing educational approaches tailored to families. From our own research, we have suggested three family learning principles that we believe are essential for understanding and supporting families in museums: (1) families have multiple goals, (2) parents play unique roles, and (3) a museum visit is a brief moment in a family's learning trajectory. The REVEAL facilitation approach is one documented method for incorporating these principles into the work of museum education—especially when facilitating family learning at interactive exhibits. However, there are many other approaches appropriate for different museums, audiences, and educational topics. (For example, see strategies developed by the Conner Prairie history museum,[49] and the Boston Children's Museum and Chicago Children's Museum.[50])

The focus of this book is on the central challenges facing museum educators today, and we believe a focus on families provides a powerful lens for thinking about these challenges. As we have described, focusing on the unique aspects of family learning can help museum educators reshape their roles in ways that are complementary to but distinct from schools—especially as the education system tries to redefine itself in the twenty-first century. Similarly, as museums, like all institutions, rethink their practices in response to the changing demographics of our nation and reflect on their own roles in perpetuating social inequity and injustice, a deep appreciation of the different goals, values, and practices of families across communities provides a method for museum educators to increase their cultural competencies to welcome and support a more diverse visiting audience. And finally, adopting new approaches to supporting family learning aligns with the increasing call for museums to explore new approaches to education and replace didactic, one-way models with more open, dialogic, collaborative approaches. By working with families, museum educators must come to recognize the learning and teaching that is already present within these groups and find ways to support, rather than replace, this learning. Through this process, museum educators can develop facilitation approaches that leverage the unique power of informal learning experiences in museums in order to support life-long family learning.

ACKNOWLEDGMENTS

This material is based upon work supported by the National Science Foundation under Grant No. DRL-1321666. Any opinions, findings, and conclusions or recommendations expressed in this material are those of the authors and do not necessarily reflect the views of the National Science Foundation.

DISCUSSION QUESTIONS

1. The principles and facilitation strategies discussed in this chapter are explained in the context of math exhibits at a science center. How might these principles apply to other content areas and other types of museums? How might they be adapted to your own practice and learning context?
2. In this chapter, we discussed the value of reflective practice and the development through the REVEAL project of a guide to help educators engage in this process. What other tools do you think would be useful for educators to better support family learning in museums?
3. Issues of diversity, equity, and inclusion (DEI) are now the foundation of strategic planning across many museums and are influencing approaches to visitor programming and museum education. How do you think the principles in this chapter relate to DEI? How might they need to expand or evolve to better align with DEI efforts?

NOTES

1. John H. Falk and Lynn D. Dierking, *The Museum Experience Revisited* (Walnut Creek, CA: Left Coast Press, 2013).
2. Kirsten Ellenbogen, Jessica J. Luke, and Lynn D. Dierking, "Family Learning in Museums: Perspectives on a Decade of Research.," in *In Principle, in Practice: Museums as Learning Institutions*, ed. John H. Falk, Lynn D. Dierking, and Susan Foutz, Learning Innovations Series (Lanham, MD: AltaMira, 2007), 17–30; Falk and Dierking, *The Museum Experience Revisited*.
3. For example, Louise Archer et al., "Disorientating, Fun or Meaningful? Disadvantaged Families' Experiences of a Science Museum Visit," *Cultural Studies of Science Education* 11, no. 4 (February 15, 2016): 917–39, https://doi.org/10.1007/s11422-015-9667-7; M. Borun et al., "Family Learning in Museums: The PISEC Perspective" (Philadelphia, PA: The Franklin Institute, 1998), https://www.fi.edu/sites/default/files/EvaluationReasearch_4FamilyLearning1998.pdf; Maureen A. Callanan et al., "Family Science Talk in Museums: Predicting Children's Engagement from Variations in Talk and Activity," *Child Development* 88, no. 5 (September 2017): 1492–1504, https://doi.org/10.1111/cdev.12886; Ellenbogen, Luke, and Dierking, "Family Learning in Museums: Perspectives on a Decade of Research"; Joshua P. Gutwill and Sue Allen, "Facilitating Family Group Inquiry at Science Museum Exhibits," *Science Education* 94, no. 4 (2010): 710–42; Catherine A. Haden et al., "Supporting Family Conversations and Children's STEM Learning in a Children's Museum," *Early Childhood Research Quarterly* 29, no. 3 (33 2014): 333–44,

https://doi.org/10.1016/j.ecresq.2014.04.004; Scott A Pattison et al., "The Impact of Facilitation by Museum Educators on Family Learning at Interactive Math Exhibits: A Quasi- Experimental Study," *Visitor Studies* 21, no. 1 (2018): 4–30, https://doi.org/10.1080/10645578.2018.1503879.

4. Institute of Museum and Library Services, "Museums, Libraries, and 21st Century Skills" (Washington, D.C.: Institute of Museum and Library Services, 2009), https://www.imls.gov/assets/1/AssetManager/21stCenturySkills.pdf.

5. National Research Council, *From Neurons to Neighborhoods: The Science of Early Child Development* (Washington, D.C.: National Academy Press, 2000); National Academies of Sciences, Engineering, and Medicine, *Parenting Matters: Supporting Parents of Children Ages 0–8* (Washington, D.C.: National Academies Press, 2016).

6. Remy Dou et al., "Early Informal STEM Experiences and STEM Identity: The Importance of Talking Science," *Science Education* 103, no. 3 (May 2019): 623–37, https://doi.org/10.1002/sce.21499; National Academies of Sciences, Engineering, and Medicine, *Parenting Matters*; National Academies of Sciences, Engineering, and Medicine, *Vibrant and Healthy Kids: Aligning Science, Practice, and Policy to Advance Health Equity* (Washington, D.C.: National Academies Press, 2019), https://doi.org/10.17226/25466.

7. Barbara Rogoff, *The Cultural Nature of Human Development* (Oxford, UK: Oxford University Press, 2003); Carlfred B. Broderick, *Understanding Family Process: Basics of Family Systems Theory* (Newbury Park, CA: Sage Publications, 1993).

8. Robert Brown, Neryl Jeanneret, and Jennifer Andersen, "Are We on the Same Page? Family and Museum Staff Perceptions of Engagement and Learning," *Visitor Studies*, October 4, 2019, 1–20, https://doi.org/10.1080/10645578.2019.1668235.

9. Archer et al., "Disorientating, Fun or Meaningful?"; Brown, Jeanneret, and Andersen, "Are We on the Same Page?"; Ellenbogen, Luke, and Dierking, "Family Learning in Museums: Perspectives on a Decade of Research"; Cecilia Garibay, "Latinos, Leisure Values and Decisions: Implications for Informal Science Learning and Engagement," *The Informal Learning Review* 94 (2009): 10–13.

10. John H. Falk and Lynn D. Dierking, "Reimagining Public Science Education: The Role of Lifelong Free-Choice Learning," *Disciplinary and Interdisciplinary Science Education Research* 1, no. 1 (December 2019): 10, https://doi.org/10.1186/s43031-019-0013-x; National Research Council, *Learning Science in Informal Environments: People, Places, and Pursuits* (Washington, D.C.: National Academies Press, 2009).

11. I. Gontan et al., "REVEALing Findings from the Field: Experiences Developing and Implementing a Staff Facilitation Model at Two Science Centers," *Informal Learning Review* 138, May/June (2016): 15–17; Scott A. Pattison et al., "A Design-Based Research Study of Staff-Facilitated Family Learning at Interactive Math Exhibits," *Visitor Studies* 20, no. 2 (July 3, 2017): 138–64, https://doi.org/10.1080/10645578.2017.1404348; Pattison et al., "The Impact of Facilitation by Museum Educators on Family Learning at Interactive Math Exhibits: A Quasi- Experimental Study."

12. John H. Falk and Lynn D. Dierking, *Learning from Museums: Visitor Experiences and the Making of Meaning*, American Association for State and Local History Book Series (Walnut Creek, CA: AltaMira, 2000); Siëlle Phelan, Inga Specht, and Doris Lewalter, "Visit Motivation as Part of Visitors' Personal Context in a Science Museum," *Visitor Studies* 23, no. 2 (July 2, 2020): 141–61, https://doi.org/10.1080/10645578.2020.1808419.

13. John H. Falk, *Identity and the Museum Visitor Experience* (Walnut Creek, CA: Left Coast Press, 2009).

14. John H. Falk, Joseph Heimlich, and Kerry Bronnenkant, "Using Identity-Related Visit Motivations as a Tool for Understanding Adult Zoo and Aquarium Visitors' Meaning-Making," *Curator: The Museum Journal* 51, no. 1 (January 2008): 55–79, https://doi.org/10.1111/j.2151-6952.2008.tb00294.x; Paichi P. Shein, John H. Falk, and Yuh-Yuh Li, "The Role of Science Identity in Science Center Visits and Effects," *Science Education*, June 27, 2019, https://doi.org/10.1002/sce.21535.

15. Scott A. Pattison, Andee Rubin, and Tracey Wright, "Mathematics in Informal Learning Environments: A Summary of the Literature (Updated)," 2017, http://www.informalscience.org/mathematics-informal-learning-environments-summary-literature.

16. Marta Civil and Emily Bernier, "Exploring Images of Parental Participation in Mathematics Education: Challenges and Possibilities," *Mathematical Thinking and Learning* 8, no. 3 (June 2006): 309–30, https://doi.org/10.1207/s15327833mtl0803_6; Shelley Goldman and Angela Booker, "Making Math a Definition

of the Situation: Families as Sites for Mathematical Practices," *Anthropology & Education Quarterly* 40, no. 4 (December 14, 2009): 369–87, https://doi.org/10.1111/j.1548-1492.2009.01057.x; Roy D. Pea and Lee Martin, "Values That Occasion and Guide Mathematics in the Family," in *Research on Learning as a Human Science*, ed. William R. Penuel and Kevin O'Conner, National Society for the Study of Education Yearbook (New York: Teachers College Press, 2010), 34–52.

17. K. A. Renninger and Suzanne Hidi, *The Power of Interest for Motivation and Engagement* (New York: Routledge, 2016).

18. National Research Council, *Learning Science in Informal Environments*.

19. Falk and Dierking, *Learning from Museums*.

20. Scott A. Pattison and Lynn D. Dierking, "Staff-Mediated Learning in Museums: A Social Interaction Perspective," *Visitor Studies* 16, no. 2 (July 2013): 117–43, https://doi.org/10.1080/10645578.2013.767731; Ellenbogen, Luke, and Dierking, "Family Learning in Museums: Perspectives on a Decade of Research"; Maureen A. Callanan et al., "Exploration, Explanation, and Parent-Child Interaction in Museums," *Monographs of the Society for Research in Child Development* 85, no. 1 (March 2020): 7–137, https://doi.org/10.1111/mono.12412; Smirla Ramos Montañez et al., "Emergent Activity Frames in Facilitated Family Interactions at Math Exhibits" (Portland, OR: Oregon Museum of Science and Industry, 2018), http://REVEAL.TERC.edu.

21. S. Rowe, "Using Multiple Situation Definitions to Create Hybrid Activity Space," in *Discourse in Action: Introducing Mediated Discourse Analysis*, ed. Sigrid Norris and Rodney H. Jones (New York: Routledge, 2005), 123–34.

22. Lynn Uyen Tran, "Teaching Science in Museums: The Pedagogy and Goals of Museum Educators," *Science Education* 91, no. 2 (March 2007): 278–97, https://doi.org/10.1002/sce.20193; Laura W. Martin, Lynn U. Tran, and Doris Ash, eds., *The Reflective Museum Practitioner: Expanding Practice in Science Museums* (Routledge, 2019), https://doi.org/10.4324/9780429025242.

23. Scott A. Pattison and Lynn D. Dierking, "Exploring Staff Facilitation That Supports Family Learning," *Journal of Museum Education* 37, no. 3 (2012): 69–80; Pattison and Dierking, "Staff-Mediated Learning in Museums."

24. National Research Council, *Identifying and Supporting Productive STEM Programs in Out-of-School Settings* (Washington, D.C.: The National Academies Press, 2015); Lori Takeuchi, Sarah Vaala, and June Ahn, "Learning across Boundaries: How Parents and Teachers Are Bridging Children's Interests" (New York: The Joan Ganz Cooney Center at Sesame Workshop, Spring 2019), http://joanganzcooneycenter.org/wp-content/uploads/2019/06/jgcc_learningacrossboundaries.pdf; National Academies of Sciences, Engineering, and Medicine, *Parenting Matters*.

25. Katherine P. Dabney, Devasmita Chakraverty, and Robert H. Tai, "The Association of Family Influence and Initial Interest in Science," *Science Education* 97, no. 3 (May 2013): 395–409, https://doi.org/10.1002/sce.21060; National Academies of Sciences, Engineering, and Medicine, *Parenting Matters*.

26. Callanan et al., "Exploration, Explanation, and Parent-Child Interaction in Museums"; Kevin D. Crowley et al., "Shared Scientific Thinking in Everyday Parent-Child Activity," *Science Education* 85, no. 6 (November 2001): 712–32, https://doi.org/10.1002/sce.1035; Takeuchi, Vaala, and Ahn, "Learning across Boundaries: How Parents and Teachers Are Bridging Children's Interests"; Maureen Vandermaas-Peeler, Melissa Mischka, and Kaitlin Sands, "'What Do You Notice?' Parent Guidance of Preschoolers' Inquiry in Activities at Home," *Early Child Development and Care* 189, no. 2 (January 28, 2019): 220–32, https://doi.org/10.1080/03004430.2017.1310724.

27. Gaea Leinhardt, Kevin Crowley, and Karen Knutson, eds., *Learning Conversations in Museums* (Mahwah, NJ: Erlbaum, 2015); Haden et al., "Supporting Family Conversations and Children's STEM Learning in a Children's Museum"; Scott A. Pattison and Lynn D. Dierking, "Early Childhood Science Interest Development: Variation in Interest Patterns and Parent-Child Interactions among Low-Income Families," *Science Education* 103, no. 2 (2018): 362–88, https://doi.org/10.1002/sce.21486.

28. Suzanne Gaskins, "The Cultural Meaning of Play and Learning in Children's Museums," *Hand to Hand* 22, no. 4 (2008): 1–2, 8–11.

29. Elizabeth Wood and Barbara Wolf, "When Parents Stand Back Is Family Learning Still Possible?," *Museums and Social Issues* 5, no. 1 (April 2010): 35–50, https://doi.org/10.1179/msi.2010.5.1.35.

30. Callanan et al., "Family Science Talk in Museums"; Takeuchi, Vaala, and Ahn, "Learning across Boundaries: How Parents and Teachers Are Bridging Children's Interests."

31. National Research Council, *How People Learn: Brain, Mind, Experience, and School*, ed. John Bransford, Expanded ed. (Washington, D.C.: National Academy Press, 2000).

32. Callanan et al., "Family Science Talk in Museums"; Kevin D. Crowley and M. Jacobs, "Building Islands of Expertise in Everyday Family Activity," in *Learning Conversations in Museums*, ed. Gaea Leinhardt, Kevin D. Crowley, and Karen Knutson (Mahwah, NJ: Erlbaum, 2002), 333–56.

33. Pattison and Dierking, "Exploring Staff Facilitation That Supports Family Learning"; Pattison and Dierking, "Staff-Mediated Learning in Museums"; Scott A. Pattison, "Exploring the Foundations of Science Interest Development in Early Childhood" (Doctoral dissertation, Corvallis, OR, Oregon State University, 2014), http://hdl.handle.net/1957/54783.

34. Susan M. Letourneau, Katherine McMillan Culp, and David Wells, "Engaging Caregivers in Making: The Role of Physical and Social Settings in Museum-Based Making and Tinkering Activities," *Visitor Studies*, January 25, 2021, 1–21, https://doi.org/10.1080/10645578.2020.1863056; Pattison and Dierking, "Staff-Mediated Learning in Museums"; Pattison et al., "A Design-Based Research Study of Staff-Facilitated Family Learning at Interactive Math Exhibits"; Brown, Jeanneret, and Andersen, "Are We on the Same Page?"

35. Ian L. Chandler-Campbell, Kathryn A. Leech, and Kathleen H. Corriveau, "Investigating Science Together: Inquiry-Based Training Promotes Scientific Conversations in Parent-Child Interactions," *Frontiers in Psychology* 11 (August 5, 2020): 1934, https://doi.org/10.3389/fpsyg.2020.01934; Rooske K. Franse, Tessa J. P. Van Schijndel, and Maartje E. J. Raijmakers, "Parental Pre-knowledge Enhances Guidance during Inquiry-Based Family Learning in a Museum Context: An Individual Differences Perspective," *Frontiers in Psychology* 11 (June 10, 2020): 1047, https://doi.org/10.3389/fpsyg.2020.01047; Gutwill and Allen, "Facilitating Family Group Inquiry at Science Museum Exhibits"; Lulu Song et al., "Parents' and Experts' Awareness of Learning Opportunities in Children's Museum Exhibits," *Journal of Applied Developmental Psychology* 49 (March 2017): 39–45, https://doi.org/10.1016/j.appdev.2017.01.006; Aiyana K. Willard et al., "Explain This, Explore That: A Study of Parent-Child Interaction in a Children's Museum," *Child Development* 90, no. 5 (September 2019), https://doi.org/10.1111/cdev.13232.

36. Gaskins, "The Cultural Meaning of Play and Learning in Children's Museums"; Barbara Rogoff et al., "Firsthand Learning through Intent Participation," *Annual Review of Psychology* 54, no. 1 (February 2003): 175–203, https://doi.org/10.1146/annurev.psych.54.101601.145118; Graciela Solis and Maureen A. Callanan, "Evidence against Deficit Accounts: Conversations about Science in Mexican Heritage Families Living in the United States," *Mind, Culture, and Activity* 23, no. 3 (July 2, 2016): 212–24, https://doi.org/10.1080/10749039.2016.1196493.

37. Pattison and Dierking, "Staff-Mediated Learning in Museums"; Pattison and Dierking, "Exploring Staff Facilitation That Supports Family Learning."

38. Susan M. Letourneau, Robin Meisner, and David M. Sobel, "Effects of Facilitation vs. Exhibit Labels on Caregiver-Child Interactions at a Museum Exhibit," *Frontiers in Psychology* 12 (March 12, 2021): 637067, https://doi.org/10.3389/fpsyg.2021.637067.

39. Cecilia Garibay, Steven Yalowitz, and Guest Editors, "Redefining Multilingualism in Museums: A Case for Broadening Our Thinking," *Museums and Social Issues* 10, no. 1 (April 2015): 2–7, https://doi.org/10.1179/1559689314Z.00000000028; Noah Weeth Feinstein and David Meshoulam, "Science for What Public? Addressing Equity in American Science Museums and Science Centers," *Journal of Research in Science Teaching* 51, no. 3 (March 2014): 368–94, https://doi.org/10.1002/tea.21130; Archer et al., "Disorientating, Fun or Meaningful?"

40. National Research Council, *Learning Science in Informal Environments*; John H. Falk and Lynn D. Dierking, "The 95 Percent Solution: School Is Not Where Most Americans Learn Most of Their Science," *American Scientist* 98, no. 6 (2010): 486–93, https://doi.org/10.1511/2010.87.486; John H. Falk et al., "The Contribution of Science-Rich Resources to Public Science Interest," *Journal of Research in Science Teaching* 55, no. 3 (2018): 422–45, https://doi.org/10.1002/tea.21425; Julie Ernst, "Zoos' and Aquariums' Impact and Influence on Connecting Families to Nature: An Evaluation of the Nature Play Begins at Your Zoo and Aquarium Program," *Visitor Studies* 21, no. 2 (July 3, 2018): 232–59, https://doi.org/10.1080/10645

578.2018.1554094; Joshua P. Gutwill, "Science Self-Efficacy and Lifelong Learning: Emerging Adults in Science Museums," *Visitor Studies* 21, no. 1 (January 2, 2018): 31–56, https://doi.org/10.1080/1064557 8.2018.1503875.

41. Gaskins, "The Cultural Meaning of Play and Learning in Children's Museums"; Deborah R. Siegel et al., "Conversations about Science across Activities in Mexican-Descent Families," *International Journal of Science Education* 29, no. 12 (October 8, 2007): 1447–66, https://doi.org/10.1080/09500690701494100; Pattison, "Exploring the Foundations of Science Interest Development in Early Childhood."

42. Christine M. McWayne et al., "Defining Family Engagement among Latino Head Start Parents: A Mixed-Methods Measurement Development Study," *Early Childhood Research Quarterly* 28, no. 3 (July 2013): 593–607, https://doi.org/10.1016/j.ecresq.2013.03.008; Angela Calabrese Barton et al., "Ecologies of Parental Engagement in Urban Education," *Educational Researcher* 33, no. 4 (May 1, 2004): 3–12, https://doi.org/10.3102/0013189X033004003.

43. Falk, Heimlich, and Bronnenkant, "Using Identity-Related Visit Motivations as a Tool for Understanding Adult Zoo and Aquarium Visitors' Meaning-Making"; John H. Falk and Martin Storksdieck, "Using the Contextual Model of Learning to Understand Visitor Learning from a Science Center Exhibition," *Science Education* 89, no. 5 (September 2005): 744–78, https://doi.org/10.1002/sce.20078; John H Falk et al., "Investigating the Cascading, Long Term Effects of Informal Science Education Experiences Report" (Beaverton, OR: Institute for Learning Innovation, 2018).

44. Scott A. Pattison and Smirla Ramos Montañez, "Long-Term Family Interest Development: Retrospective Interviews with Parents One to Two Years after a Family-Based Preschool Engineering Program" (Manuscript in preparation, 2020); Scott A. Pattison and Smirla Ramos Montañez, "Diverse STEM Interest Development Pathways in Early Childhood" (Book chapter in preparation, 2020).

45. M. Benne et al., "REVEAL: Researching the Value of Educator Actions on Learning" (2016 AISL PI Meeting, Bethesda, MD, 2016), http://www.informalscience.org/poster-reveal-researching-value-educator-actions-learning; Gontan et al., "REVEALing Findings from the Field: Experiences Developing and Implementing a Staff Facilitation Model at Two Science Centers"; Pattison et al., "A Design-Based Research Study of Staff-Facilitated Family Learning at Interactive Math Exhibits"; Pattison et al., "The Impact of Facilitation by Museum Educators on Family Learning at Interactive Math Exhibits: A Quasi-Experimental Study."

46. Falk and Dierking, *The Museum Experience Revisited*; National Research Council, *Learning Science in Informal Environments*; National Research Council, *Identifying and Supporting Productive STEM Programs in Out-of-School Settings*.

47. Pattison et al., "A Design-Based Research Study of Staff-Facilitated Family Learning at Interactive Math Exhibits"; Pattison et al., "The Impact of Facilitation by Museum Educators on Family Learning at Interactive Math Exhibits: A Quasi-Experimental Study."

48. E. Andanen et al., *REVEAL Responsive Museum Facilitation: A Video-Based Reflection Guide for Engaging with Families at Interactive Exhibits* (Portland, OR: Oregon Museum of Science and Industry, 2017), https://external-wiki.terc.edu/display/Reveal/Educator+Resources.

49. Lynn Dierking et al., *Opening Doors to Great Guest Experiences: Training DVD for Museum Educators*, 2006, https://www.worldcat.org/title/opening-doors-to-great-guest-experiences/oclc/76801840.

50. T. Porter and T. Cohen, "Learning Together: Families in Museums Staff Training Curriculum" (Boston Children's Museum, 2012), http://www.bostonchildrensmuseum.org/sites/default/files/pdfs/Learning-Together.pdf.

BIBLIOGRAPHY

Andanen, E., Andee Rubin, Scott A. Pattison, Ivel Gontan, and C. Bromley. 2017. *REVEAL Responsive Museum Facilitation: A Video-Based Reflection Guide for Engaging with Families at Interactive Exhibits*. Portland, OR: Oregon Museum of Science and Industry, https://external-wiki.terc.edu/display/Reveal/Educator+Resources.

Archer, Louise, Emily Dawson, Amy Seakins, and Billy Wong. 2016. "Disorientating, Fun or Meaningful? Disadvantaged Families' Experiences of a Science Museum Visit." *Cultural Studies of Science Education* 11 (4): 917–39, https://doi.org/10.1007/s11422-015-9667-7.

Benne, M., Scott A. Pattison, A. Rubin, and Lynn D. Dierking. 2016. "REVEAL: Researching the Value of Educator Actions on Learning." Presented at the 2016 AISL PI Meeting, Bethesda, MD, http://www.informalscience.org/poster-reveal-researching-value-educator-actions-learning.

Borun, M., J. Dritsas, J. Johnson, N. Peter, K. Wagner, K. Fadigan, A. Jangaard, E. Stroup, and A. Wenger. 1998. "Family Learning in Museums: The PISEC Perspective." Philadelphia, PA: The Franklin Institute, https://www.fi.edu/sites/default/files/EvaluationReasearch_4FamilyLearning1998.pdf.

Broderick, Carlfred B. 1993. *Understanding Family Process: Basics of Family Systems Theory*. Newbury Park, CA: Sage Publications.

Brown, Robert, Neryl Jeanneret, and Jennifer Andersen. 2019. "Are We on the Same Page? Family and Museum Staff Perceptions of Engagement and Learning." *Visitor Studies*, October, 1–20, https://doi.org/10.1080/10645578.2019.1668235.

Calabrese Barton, Angela, C. Drake, J. G. Perez, K. St. Louis, and M. George. 2004. "Ecologies of Parental Engagement in Urban Education." *Educational Researcher* 33 (4): 3–12, https://doi.org/10.3102/0013189X033004003.

Callanan, Maureen A., Claudia L. Castañeda, Megan R. Luce, and Jennifer L. Martin. 2017. "Family Science Talk in Museums: Predicting Children's Engagement from Variations in Talk and Activity." *Child Development* 88 (5): 1492–1504, https://doi.org/10.1111/cdev.12886.

Callanan, Maureen A., Cristine H. Legare, David M. Sobel, Garrett J. Jaeger, Susan Letourneau, Sam R. McHugh, Aiyana Willard, et al. 2020. "Exploration, Explanation, and Parent–Child Interaction in Museums." *Monographs of the Society for Research in Child Development* 85 (1): 7–137, https://doi.org/10.1111/mono.12412.

Chandler-Campbell, Ian L., Kathryn A. Leech, and Kathleen H. Corriveau. 2020. "Investigating Science Together: Inquiry-Based Training Promotes Scientific Conversations in Parent-Child Interactions." *Frontiers in Psychology* 11 (August): 1934, https://doi.org/10.3389/fpsyg.2020.01934.

Civil, Marta, and Emily Bernier. 2006. "Exploring Images of Parental Participation in Mathematics Education: Challenges and Possibilities." *Mathematical Thinking and Learning* 8 (3): 309–30, https://doi.org/10.1207/s15327833mtl0803_6.

Crowley, Kevin D., Maureen A. Callanan, Jennifer L. Jipson, Jodi Galco, Karen Topping, and Jeff Shrager. 2001. "Shared Scientific Thinking in Everyday Parent-Child Activity." *Science Education* 85 (6): 712–32, https://doi.org/10.1002/sce.1035.

Crowley, Kevin D., and M. Jacobs. 2002. "Building Islands of Expertise in Everyday Family Activity." In *Learning Conversations in Museums*, edited by Gaea Leinhardt, Kevin D. Crowley, and Karen Knutson, 333–56. Mahwah, NJ: Erlbaum.

Dabney, Katherine P., Devasmita Chakraverty, and Robert H. Tai. 2013. "The Association of Family Influence and Initial Interest in Science." *Science Education* 97 (3): 395–409, https://doi.org/10.1002/sce.21060.

Dierking, Lynn, R. Underhill, Institute of Museum and Library Services, and Conner Prairie. 2006. *Opening Doors to Great Guest Experiences: Training DVD for Museum Educators*, https://www.worldcat.org/title/opening-doors-to-great-guest-experiences/oclc/76801840.

Dou, Remy, Zahra Hazari, Katherine Dabney, Gerhard Sonnert, and Philip Sadler. 2019. "Early Informal STEM Experiences and STEM Identity: The Importance of Talking Science." *Science Education* 103 (3): 623–37, https://doi.org/10.1002/sce.21499.

Ellenbogen, Kirsten, Jessica J. Luke, and Lynn D. Dierking. 2007. "Family Learning in Museums: Perspectives on a Decade of Research." In *In Principle, in Practice: Museums as Learning Institutions*, edited by John H. Falk, Lynn D. Dierking, and Susan Foutz, 17–30. Learning Innovations Series. Lanham, MD: AltaMira.

Ernst, Julie. 2018. "Zoos' and Aquariums' Impact and Influence on Connecting Families to Nature: An Evaluation of the Nature Play Begins at Your Zoo and Aquarium Program." *Visitor Studies* 21 (2): 232–59, https://doi.org/10.1080/10645578.2018.1554094.

Falk, John H. 2009. *Identity and the Museum Visitor Experience*. Walnut Creek, CA: Left Coast Press.

Falk, John H., and Lynn D. Dierking. 2000. *Learning from Museums: Visitor Experiences and the Making of Meaning*. American Association for State and Local History Book Series. Walnut Creek, CA: AltaMira.

——. 2010. "The 95 Percent Solution: School Is Not Where Most Americans Learn Most of Their Science." *American Scientist* 98 (6): 486–93, https://doi.org/10.1511/2010.87.486.

——. 2013. *The Museum Experience Revisited*. Walnut Creek, CA: Left Coast Press.

——. 2019. "Reimagining Public Science Education: The Role of Lifelong Free-Choice Learning." *Disciplinary and Interdisciplinary Science Education Research* 1 (1): 10, https://doi.org/10.1186/s43031-019-0013-x.

Falk, John H., Joseph Heimlich, and Kerry Bronnenkant. 2008. "Using Identity-Related Visit Motivations as a Tool for Understanding Adult Zoo and Aquarium Visitors' Meaning-Making." *Curator: The Museum Journal* 51 (1): 55–79, https://doi.org/10.1111/j.2151-6952.2008.tb00294.x.

Falk, John H, Judith Koke, C Aaron Price, and Scott A. Pattison. 2018. "Investigating the Cascading, Long Term Effects of Informal Science Education Experiences Report." Beaverton, OR: Institute for Learning Innovation.

Falk, John H., Scott A. Pattison, David Meier, David Bibas, and Kathleen Livingston. 2018. "The Contribution of Science-Rich Resources to Public Science Interest." *Journal of Research in Science Teaching* 55 (3): 422–45, https://doi.org/10.1002/tea.21425.

Falk, John H., and Martin Storksdieck. 2005. "Using the Contextual Model of Learning to Understand Visitor Learning from a Science Center Exhibition." *Science Education* 89 (5): 744–78, https://doi.org/10.1002/sce.20078.

Feinstein, Noah Weeth, and David Meshoulam. 2014. "Science for What Public? Addressing Equity in American Science Museums and Science Centers." *Journal of Research in Science Teaching* 51 (3): 368–94, https://doi.org/10.1002/tea.21130.

Franse, Rooske K., Tessa J. P. Van Schijndel, and Maartje E. J. Raijmakers. 2020. "Parental Pre-knowledge Enhances Guidance during Inquiry-Based Family Learning in a Museum Context: An Individual Differences Perspective." *Frontiers in Psychology* 11 (June): 1047, https://doi.org/10.3389/fpsyg.2020.01047.

Garibay, Cecilia. 2009. "Latinos, Leisure Values and Decisions: Implications for Informal Science Learning and Engagement." *The Informal Learning Review* 94: 10–13.

Garibay, Cecilia, Steven Yalowitz, and Guest Editors. 2015. "Redefining Multilingualism in Museums: A Case for Broadening Our Thinking." *Museums and Social Issues* 10 (1): 2–7, https://doi.org/10.1179/1559689314Z.00000000028.

Gaskins, Suzanne. 2008. "The Cultural Meaning of Play and Learning in Children's Museums." *Hand to Hand* 22 (4): 1–2, 8–11.

Goldman, Shelley, and Angela Booker. 2009. "Making Math a Definition of the Situation: Families as Sites for Mathematical Practices." *Anthropology & Education Quarterly* 40 (4): 369–87, https://doi.org/10.1111/j.1548-1492.2009.01057.x.

Gontan, I., Scott A. Pattison, S. Brandon, A. Rubin, E. Andanen, and M. Benne. 2016. "REVEALing Findings from the Field: Experiences Developing and Implementing a Staff Facilitation Model at Two Science Centers." *Informal Learning Review* 138 (May/June): 15–17.

Gutwill, Joshua P. 2018. "Science Self-Efficacy and Lifelong Learning: Emerging Adults in Science Museums." *Visitor Studies* 21 (1): 31–56, https://doi.org/10.1080/10645578.2018.1503875.

Gutwill, Joshua P., and Sue Allen. 2010. "Facilitating Family Group Inquiry at Science Museum Exhibits." *Science Education* 94 (4): 710–42.

Haden, Catherine A., Erin A. Jant, Philip C. Hoffman, Maria Marcus, Jacqueline R. Geddes, and Suzanne Gaskins. 2014. "Supporting Family Conversations and Children's STEM Learning in a Children's Museum." *Early Childhood Research Quarterly* 29 (3): 333–44, https://doi.org/10.1016/j.ecresq.2014.04.004.

Institute of Museum and Library Services. 2009. "Museums, Libraries, and 21st Century Skills." IMLS-2009-NAI-01. Washington, D.C.: Institute of Museum and Library Services, https://www.imls.gov/assets/1/AssetManager/21stCenturySkills.pdf.

Leinhardt, Gaea, Kevin Crowley, and Karen Knutson, eds. 2015. *Learning Conversations in Museums*. Mahwah, NJ: Erlbaum.

Letourneau, Susan M., Katherine McMillan Culp, and David Wells. 2021. "Engaging Caregivers in Making: The Role of Physical and Social Settings in Museum-Based Making and Tinkering Activities." *Visitor Studies*, January, 1–21, https://doi.org/10.1080/10645578.2020.1863056.

Letourneau, Susan M., Robin Meisner, and David M. Sobel. 2021. "Effects of Facilitation vs. Exhibit Labels on Caregiver-Child Interactions at a Museum Exhibit." *Frontiers in Psychology* 12 (March): 637067, https://doi.org/10.3389/fpsyg.2021.637067.

Martin, Laura W., Lynn U. Tran, and Doris Ash, eds. 2019. *The Reflective Museum Practitioner: Expanding Practice in Science Museums*. Routledge, https://doi.org/10.4324/9780429025242.

McWayne, Christine M., Gigliana Melzi, Adina R. Schick, Joy L. Kennedy, and Kevin Mundt. 2013. "Defining Family Engagement among Latino Head Start Parents: A Mixed-Methods Measurement Development Study." *Early Childhood Research Quarterly* 28 (3): 593–607, https://doi.org/10.1016/j.ecresq.2013.03.008.

National Academies of Sciences, Engineering, and Medicine. 2016. *Parenting Matters: Supporting Parents of Children Ages 0–8*. Washington, D.C.: National Academies Press.

———. 2019. *Vibrant and Healthy Kids: Aligning Science, Practice, and Policy to Advance Health Equity*. Washington, D.C.: National Academies Press, https://doi.org/10.17226/25466.

National Research Council. 2000a. *From Neurons to Neighborhoods: The Science of Early Child Development*. Washington, D.C.: National Academy Press.

———. 2000b. *How People Learn: Brain, Mind, Experience, and School*. Edited by John Bransford. Expanded ed. Washington, D.C.: National Academy Press.

———. 2009. *Learning Science in Informal Environments: People, Places, and Pursuits*. Washington, D.C.: National Academies Press.

———. 2015. *Identifying and Supporting Productive STEM Programs in Out-of-School Settings*. Washington, D.C.: The National Academies Press.

Pattison, Scott A. 2014. "Exploring the Foundations of Science Interest Development in Early Childhood." Doctoral dissertation, Corvallis: Oregon State University, http://hdl.handle.net/1957/54783.

Pattison, Scott A., and Lynn D. Dierking. 2012. "Exploring Staff Facilitation That Supports Family Learning." *Journal of Museum Education* 37 (3): 69–80.

———. 2013. "Staff-Mediated Learning in Museums: A Social Interaction Perspective." *Visitor Studies* 16 (2): 117–43, https://doi.org/10.1080/10645578.2013.767731.

———. 2018. "Early Childhood Science Interest Development: Variation in Interest Patterns and Parent-Child Interactions among Low-Income Families." *Science Education* 103 (2): 362–88. https://doi.org/10.1002/sce.21486.

Pattison, Scott A., and Smirla Ramos Montañez. 2020a. "Diverse STEM Interest Development Pathways in Early Childhood." Book chapter in preparation.

———. 2020b. "Long-Term Family Interest Development: Retrospective Interviews with Parents One to Two Years after a Family-Based Preschool Engineering Program." Manuscript in preparation.

Pattison, Scott A., Scott M. Randol, Marcie Benne, Andee Rubin, Ivel Gontan, Elizabeth Andanen, Crosby Bromley, Smirla Ramos Montañez, and Lynn D. Dierking. 2017. "A Design-Based Research Study of Staff-Facilitated Family Learning at Interactive Math Exhibits." *Visitor Studies* 20 (2): 138–64, https://doi.org/10.1080/10645578.2017.1404348.

Pattison, Scott A, Andee Rubin, Marcie Benne, Ivel Gontan, Todd Shagott, Melanie Francisco, Smirla Ramos Montanez, and Lynn D. Dierking. 2018. "The Impact of Facilitation by Museum Educators on Family Learning at Interactive Math Exhibits: A Quasi-Experimental Study." *Visitor Studies* 21 (1): 4–30, https://doi.org/10.1080/10645578.2018.1503879.

Pattison, Scott A., Andee Rubin, and Tracey Wright. 2017. "Mathematics in Informal Learning Environments: A Summary of the Literature (Updated)," http://www.informalscience.org/mathematics -informal-learning-environments-summary-literature.

Pea, Roy D. and Lee Martin. 2010. "Values That Occasion and Guide Mathematics in the Family." In *Research on Learning as a Human Science*, ed. William R. Penuel and Kevin O'Conner, National Society for the Study of Education Yearbook, 34–52. New York: Teachers College Press.

Phelan, Siëlle, Inga Specht, and Doris Lewalter. 2020. "Visit Motivation as Part of Visitors' Personal Context in a Science Museum." *Visitor Studies* 23 (2): 141–61, https://doi.org/10.1080/10645578. 2020.1808419.

Porter, T., and T. Cohen. 2012. "Learning Together: Families in Museums Staff Training Curriculum." Boston Children's Museum, http://www.bostonchildrensmuseum.org/sites/default/files/pdfs /Learning-Together.pdf.

Ramos Montañez, Smirla, Scott Randol, Carla Herran, Scott A. Pattison, Andee Rubin, Todd Shagott, Elizabeth Andanen, and Marcie Benne. 2018. "Emergent Activity Frames in Facilitated Family Interactions at Math Exhibits." Portland: Oregon Museum of Science and Industry, http://REVEAL .TERC.edu.

Renninger, K. A., and Suzanne Hidi. 2016. *The Power of Interest for Motivation and Engagement*. New York: Routledge.

Rogoff, Barbara. 2003. *The Cultural Nature of Human Development*. Oxford, UK: Oxford University Press.

Rogoff, Barbara, Ruth Paradise, Rebeca Mejía Arauz, Maricela Correa-Chávez, and Cathy Angelillo. 2003. "Firsthand Learning through Intent Participation." *Annual Review of Psychology* 54 (1): 175– 203, https://doi.org/10.1146/annurev.psych.54.101601.145118.

Rowe, S. 2005. "Using Multiple Situation Definitions to Create Hybrid Activity Space." In *Discourse in Action: Introducing Mediated Discourse Analysis*, edited by Sigrid Norris and Rodney H. Jones, 123–34. New York: Routledge.

Shein, Paichi P., John H. Falk, and Yuh-Yuh Li. 2019. "The Role of Science Identity in Science Center Visits and Effects." *Science Education*, June, https://doi.org/10.1002/sce.21535.

Siegel, Deborah R., Jennifer Esterly, Maureen A. Callanan, Ramser Wright, and Rocio Navarro. 2007. "Conversations about Science across Activities in Mexican-Descent Families." *International Journal of Science Education* 29 (12): 1447–66, https://doi.org/10.1080/09500690701494100.

Solis, Graciela, and Maureen A. Callanan. 2016. "Evidence against Deficit Accounts: Conversations about Science in Mexican Heritage Families Living in the United States." *Mind, Culture, and Activity* 23 (3): 212–24, https://doi.org/10.1080/10749039.2016.1196493.

Song, Lulu, Roberta Michnick Golinkoff, Amara Stuehling, Ilyse Resnick, Neha Mahajan, Kathy Hirsh-Pasek, and Nora Thompson. 2017. "Parents' and Experts' Awareness of Learning Opportunities in Children's Museum Exhibits." *Journal of Applied Developmental Psychology* 49 (March): 39–45, https://doi.org/10.1016/j.appdev.2017.01.006.

Takeuchi, Lori, Sarah Vaala, and June Ahn. 2019. "Learning across Boundaries: How Parents and Teachers Are Bridging Children's Interests." New York: The Joan Ganz Cooney Center at

Sesame Workshop, http://joanganzcooneycenter.org/wp-content/uploads/2019/06/jgcc_learn
ingacrossboundaries.pdf.

Tran, Lynn Uyen. 2007. "Teaching Science in Museums: The Pedagogy and Goals of Museum Educators." *Science Education* 91 (2): 278–97, https://doi.org/10.1002/sce.20193.

Vandermaas-Peeler, Maureen, Melissa Mischka, and Kaitlin Sands. 2019. "'What Do You Notice?'
Parent Guidance of Preschoolers' Inquiry in Activities at Home." *Early Child Development and Care*
189 (2): 220–32, https://doi.org/10.1080/03004430.2017.1310724.

Willard, Aiyana K., Justin T. A. Busch, Katherine A. Cullum, Susan M. Letourneau, David M. Sobel, Maureen A. Callanan, and Cristine H. Legare. 2019. "Explain This, Explore That: A Study of Parent–Child
Interaction in a Children's Museum." *Child Development* 90 (5), https://doi.org/10.1111/cdev.13232.

Wood, Elizabeth, and Barbara Wolf. 2010. "When Parents Stand Back Is Family Learning Still Possible?"
Museums and Social Issues 5 (1): 35–50, https://doi.org/10.1179/msi.2010.5.1.35.

8

Museum Studies Programs

A CONVERSATION ABOUT THE FUTURE

Jason Porter and Mary Kay Cunningham

In a discussion of the twenty-first-century museum education landscape, one question that comes up repeatedly is that of the contribution and utility of graduate and certificate programs in museum studies or related courses of study. In the last few decades, the number of programs has grown significantly. As of this writing, most major universities offered some program in the discipline—187 currently in the United States alone—according to AAM's searchable directory, including in-person, on-line, and hybridized programs.[1] Now, after the events of 2020, which saw museums around the world shuttered, numerous staff members laid off (especially those in visitor-facing departments), budgets slashed, and programs such as internships, group research projects, and other field experiences typically executed by students discontinued, questions about the role of museum studies programs in the field have become even more timely.

In order to learn more about the state of museum studies, we convened conversations with a number of museum studies faculty and administrators to hear directly from them on the issues facing academic preparation for museum work. It is important to say up front that these conversations were not conclusive and that no crystal balls were consulted in divining what the future will hold for the students, faculty, and for the programs themselves. But the conversations did illuminate important themes as well as nod to some of the key questions everyone in the field of museum education should be concerned with, both in terms of the role of the academy in the pursuit of effective museum practices as well as in providing the field with a skilled and prepared labor force for the future.

A few notes about these conversations and the participants. These groupings of professionals were, in no way, representative of the field of museum studies in its totality, but they do represent a range of academic institutions and a great deal of experience in academia and in museum practice. It is important to acknowledge that the group represented only a limited amount of racial and ethnic diversity; there were no faculty members with disabilities represented, no participants from international schools, and the programs they represent are located mostly in the American northeast. We selected these individuals because we knew them professionally, they were recommended to us by others, or because of the program they work in or their background as educators. We also did not treat the conversations as official focus groups and follow stringent qualitative research protocols, but instead allowed the talk to flow and take whatever turns the participants wanted. We did, however, record the conversations and excerpted quotes from our discussion for this chapter. Because of the fact that we did not treat these conversations as formal research, we have decided not to attribute specific quotes to specific people but to simply list the participant's names at the end of the chapter.

Generally, we can describe the group as composed of program administrators, faculty members, and lecturers at well-established museum studies, museology, informal education programs, and at newer or newly configured degree programs from across the country. One common characteristic we prioritized for all those interviewed was that, prior to working in academia, all of them were practitioners in the field of museum education or in related arts education management. The programs they work in range from small to large, offer coursework across the spectrum of museum disciplines or focus exclusively on education and provide graduates with either certificates or masters degrees or both. Each conversation took up approximately two hours (though they could have gone on for much longer) and mostly followed a protocol of questions we constructed that related to the thesis of this book, though as previously stated, there were issues and questions raised that we didn't plan for or consider in advance.

The hope for this chapter is to contribute to a broader conversation about museum studies in relation to the field of museum education. Between questions about access and equity, to the changing nature of the museum workforce, to the debate as to whether the degree is a professional or academic one, to questions about student debt and the degree's utility in gaining employment in the field, to the preponderance of programs compared to the number of jobs in the sector, this conversation raises many issues that warrant further discussion. What was clear from talking to these museum studies faculty members and administrators was that their aspect of the museum world—namely preparation, training, research, and professional standards—has been impacted by the events of 2020 in many of the same ways that the rest of the field has. The repercussions of the pandemic, the amplified calls for racial justice, and the economic downturn have affected the academic side of museum education in ways comparable to the ways they have impacted museums themselves. Students are all learning at home, their access to in-person experiences—from classes to field experiences—have been severely limited, and the already narrow pathway to employment has contracted even further. The question then is an almost universal one, whether you work in a museum or are studying to do so or teaching those who want to: What will the future hold?

MUSEUM STUDIES PROGRAMS HAVE SHIFTED THEIR FOCUS

The first theme to emerge in these conversations about how museum studies programs have adapted to the needs of the twenty-first century was that today's programs, from both a curriculum and pedagogy perspective, have changed over the course of the last decade or in one program's case, even the last twenty years. All of the panelists agreed—speaking specifically about their own programs—that the focus has shifted from collection stewardship and management to community engagement and education. Most spoke of an emphasis on more visitor-centered aspects of study, including a shift toward social justice, learning, and evaluation. As one faculty member put it, "We teach general museum studies . . . with a focus on learning, community and social justice. We tell students, 'If that's not your focus, then this isn't the program for you.'" Another agreed with this shift in focus. "Some students question why we're talking about engagement and equity and not focusing on objects. But they need to understand the roles of museum curator, registrar, etc. as educators. You can have expertise in these special areas, but you need to understand your role in public engagement first and foremost." There was a lot of agreement that museum studies students are learning more about what it means to be outwardly focused on service to communities rather than inwardly focused on collections.

The panel also spoke about the shift from specialized coursework to more general museum skills-based classes. "We've shifted away," one program director said, "from a focus on collections and registration. Now our goal is to help students build specialist and generalist skills. They need to know how to manage people, programs, and money. And they need experiences in the core competencies such as writing, presenting, and community, using data, and doing research." Another panelist mentioned that "all of the students take education and administration—even human resources—so that if they get into leadership, they have these transferable skills." Another faculty member added, "this (providing instruction in education and other aspects of museum work) allows students to develop a greater sense of the systems that exist across the organization and how independent everything is." This move toward generalization may be the result of the changing landscape of the cultural sector and the reality that certain jobs are in greater supply than others once students finish the program. Preparing students to have skills in multiple areas may make them more marketable once they begin job hunting, as well as providing them with a broader exposure to museum work so that they can later specialize in the area of the field that sparks their interest. But for whatever the reason, the emphasis on centering education and public engagement seems clear as a trend among museum studies programs.

THE JOURNEY TOWARD ANTIRACIST PRACTICES

 In addition to shifting the emphasis toward aspects of museum work that are visitor-centered, the panelists also mentioned that their curriculum has become more responsive to what the panel referred to as the "concerns and interests" of their students. Most of the panelists, especially when asked about how the events of 2020 impacted their programs, discussed an increased focus in classwork, thesis topics, and field experiences, on "social justice and change and how to do it." One faculty member noted, "We are all having to wake up. Now everything (we do) is infused with an activist stance and social values." Although there have been efforts and thinking about how to address inequalities and systemic racism in museums studies programs and the field at large for decades, the public outcry and protests created a spotlight on issues that intensified the commitment of students and faculty (especially non-BIPOC) in demanding change. If the program had not already begun this process before 2020, some more recently adjusted their coursework to respond to their students and to the field's increased emphasis on equity and inclusion so that it was infused in every aspect of the program. "We used to isolate diversity as a course, whereas now we use racial literacy and inclusion as lenses (or frames) that are infused across all the courses." And some significant changes have been made, including creating student-faculty equity teams, reformatting classes to infuse equity into course syllabi, and adding classwork and readings that prepare students to understand antiracist teaching and decolonization practices.

But like most of us in the museum field, grappling to identify and name our roots in white supremacy culture,[2] many of the panelists acknowledged that their work in addressing institutionalized racism and inequities has only begun; the institutional shifts that need to happen have only scratched the surface. "We have changed our recruitment and admissions processes to uplift students of color—at this point 50% identify as BIPOC—but now what? Have we changed our practices to teach to diverse populations? What do we teach and how do we teach it? How do we teach museum studies differently? How do we teach in an anti-racist way? What is enough? Museum studies programs really need to wrestle with variation in experience with racism and whiteness." This self-examination was also present for some of the panelists from a personal perspective. The American Alliance of Museum's publication *Facing Change* was referenced as a tool for starting to do one's own work, especially for the members of the panel who were white-identifying.[3] "As a person, I have become much more aware of my own identity and white privilege and am constantly asking myself what it means to be a white person trying to diversify a program." It's important to reiterate that structural racism is not a new or emergent issue for the museum field on the whole and for museum studies programs. The fact that leadership in the academy is responding to calls for racial justice is a positive step—one driven in part by a new generation of students expecting more. But it remains important to acknowledge that there have been programs and individual faculty who have been addressing cultural competence and antiracist work in their curricula and approach for decades, and they deserve and demand more allies. As a number of participants recognized, these imbalances won't be corrected overnight and will take years of embedding social justice and community-based work in these programs in order to truly transform the field, but we can look to committed leadership and students emerging from these programs to continue to move the dial toward progress.

2020 AMPED EVERYTHING UP

The impact of the events in 2020 on the museum sector have been significant and for many museums and many museum workers, catastrophic. The sector on the whole has constricted, by some estimates during the pandemic to as much as 30 percent,[4] though time will tell what the actual impact on museum closing or reductions in the number of preexisting jobs, contracts, and partnerships will be. With much uncertainty around the professional prospects for emerging museum professionals, it is no surprise that faculty at museum studies programs around the country have been reflecting on (and trying to plan for) the potential impacts. Although at other times in history when the economy has suffered globally, admissions to graduate schools has increased. During our discussions, the museum studies faculty members and administrators identified a number of key challenges that have, like many fissures in our social fabric, been exacerbated by the pandemic, though, they admit, are not emergent problems but have been ones long facing higher education more broadly.

One challenge mentioned by a number of the people we spoke with is the preponderance of museum studies programs across the country. As referenced in the introduction, there are over one hundred active programs currently of various sizes, and as one program director said, perhaps presciently, "all of them will not survive." Part of the challenge is that museums themselves are struggling to add back positions lost or furloughed during the pandemic, and with so many graduates of these programs emerging from their programs each year, there may not be enough museum jobs to make the cost and time spent worth it. Coupled with the systemic challenges facing higher education in general, including more competition, the student loan crisis, and decreases in enrollment. Many museum studies programs have been largely on-line or hybrid programs that include on-line and in-person learning, so the shift from the pandemic had minimal impact in terms of format for those programs. Perhaps the pandemic will have the effect of pushing more people into graduate programs in museum studies, but some programs are already seeing a decrease in numbers of applicants and in class sizes as a result of the pandemic. Others, according to the faculty we spoke with, are purposefully limiting the number of students because of what appears to be a rather bleak outlook for museum employment prospects. And the impact has befallen the structural aspects of the programs as well, which include paid internships, seasonal employment, and field experiences that had to be sidelined because of museum closures and budget restrictions for many museums.

But the challenges faced by museum studies programs as a result of 2020 weren't limited to the shrinking of the sector related to employment. Social distancing mandates also posed challenges for programs that are accustomed to in-person teaching and to the modicum of museum partnerships and field experiences that are regular features of these programs. "Placements," said one director, "are seen as closely tied to the academic process and provide the hands-on components for students." Without these placements, the programs struggled, though, and exacerbated an ongoing problem of support by museums themselves to provide field-based training opportunities accompanied by the appropriate infrastructure located at the museum so students receive true learning and skill-building experiences. "Museum staff need to support museum studies students, but '. . . many museums aren't structured to support the staff working with students' and many of these field opportunities were discontinued during the pandemic because of closures and social distancing, setting the structure building—economic, staffing, and otherwise—necessary to support them back even further." It is un-

Jason Porter and Mary Kay Cunningham

clear how much of these museum-based program elements will return to museum studies programs after the pandemic subsides.

The other challenge mentioned by the museum studies faculty members was the heightened partisanship during the election year and the challenge of working with students in settings where everything took on a political tone. "By January 6th, the faculty recognized the fact that museums will have participants (from across the political spectrum). How do we embrace all participants? We don't provide answers. We provide opportunities for dialogue. How do we live up to our beliefs and deal in a civil, loving way with people who do not feel the same way? Civility brings civility but it's very hard to do." Pivoting to conversations about how students can engage in dialogue with visitors became a higher priority based on the demands of the moment. The year "2020 just amped everything up. We realized we needed to go deeper with our antiracist teaching, with exercises where we examine our own practice and sets of beliefs. We focused on how to help students have hard conversations with visitors, and this resulted in more meetings with students and discussions about the incidents that were happening in the culture, not just museum work." This need to participate in conversations with students seems to be another aspect of the pandemic that may remain long-term as museums, as trusted public institutions and loci of learning, move away from positions of neutrality about social issues toward articulating points of view on everything from police violence to hate crimes to attacks on science and the media.

THE FUTURE AND THE NEED TO INNOVATE

As we mentioned in the introduction to this chapter, these conversations with museum studies faculty were not meant to prognosticate or read tea leaves to determine the future of these academic programs. Rather they illuminated a degree of consensus around the need for change in these programs in response to the needs and realities of the field, and there was some agreement as to what that change might look like.

For those museum practitioners who partner with museum studies programs and their students regularly, we are accustomed to creating internship projects or practica, guest lecturing at classes, providing "problems" for student groups to address through research projects, or hosting visits to our museums by classes of students. These are typically low stakes and low investment opportunities for the museum and the academy to intersect, though only occasionally are these relationships established as close, meaningful, interconnected partnerships. Yet, for museum studies departments to continue to be relevant for students and to maintain their own viability, the panel felt strongly that such partnerships were one avenue to furthering student development while simultaneously deepening museum experiences for visitors.

Our panelists had different ideas for how these partnerships might work, but all agreed that they involved working closely with museums and other organizations to tap into the transferable skills taught that could better serve the current needs of the field. Some of the participants mentioned partnerships with non-museum entities such as hospitals, libraries, and government agencies to bring cultural experiences like exhibitions and programs to the public. Museum studies programs that are teaching students curatorial, educational, or interpretive practice could be utilized in these alternative but also public-facing spaces. One of the panelists said that, "in order to survive, we have to pair up with libraries and other cultural organizations. The European heritage and cultural sector has been increasing emphasis on human rights, well-being, and they are beginning to recognize that the public has a much broader definition of arts and culture than the one defined by our leading arts organizations. So training institutions like ours could realign our courses to address a larger sphere of related career possibilities."

Another impact mentioned in our conversation was the impact of technology in museum practice and certainly in the learning and teaching happening during the pandemic. The rise of digital technology, both in the tools used by museums to work with visitors (who, as discussed in other chapters of this book) who have come to expect additional layers of interactivity and content available in multiple forms, and in the way educational organizations have adapted to almost exclusively use technology tools to teach and learn, may also have long-term impacts on museum studies. The change in the workplace during the pandemic has caused a situation in which "students and faculty were learning together how to learn online." It is unclear at the time of this writing how long-lasting these adaptations to technology will have on how these programs are taught and how technology overall will change museum practice. To many of the faculty members' programs represented by this group, technology has increasingly become integrated into the ways that students are learning and in the interpretive tools they are encountering out in the field. Further development of coursework and practical experience in the field with technology at the center will likely become even more of a core aspect of preparing for the museum education work of the future.

Other ideas to evolve museum studies included placements of students in paid positions as interpreters in historic sites, interpretive centers, nature parks, or other venues where they can get experience interacting with the public and "work with people in the trenches" to better understand community engagement. Some participants saw these types of partnerships in settings adjacent to the museum world as a way to expand students' notions of education as a didactic, traditional endeavor and one that is limited to classrooms and galleries as opposed to thinking about educational work occurring in a variety of locations across the broader learning ecosystem. This expansion of partnerships may help to expand the options that museum studies programs provide for a professional path after graduation. One panelist described a potential partnership in which the museum studies program would partner with state education departments to allow the degree to count toward a teaching certificate. Others discussed creating partner networks with their alumni and enlisting graduates in fields in and outside of museum work to support students in museum studies programs. Perhaps these partnerships could expand what we typically think of as the pipeline to museum work. It remains to be seen whether these types of partnerships could be offered to scale to make an impact on the job prospects of participants, but the fact that many of our panel participants had similar thoughts about them, suggests this might be one avenue to address the challenges of a constricting museum field amid burgeoning museum studies programs.

Regardless of whether these specific ideas would expand the reach of museum studies into other fields, what emerged as common ideas were that these faculty members and directors feel like the museum studies programs of the last thirty years face a number of inflection points—some economic, some related to content and coursework, and some related to professional training—that means the impact of 2020 will likely force this particular area of the academy to change significantly in the future. But the onus for these changes does not, in their opinions, rest solely with the programs themselves, but also with museums and their practitioners. If tackling equity and diversifying the field are truly important to museums, then museums must make investments in the preparation and nurturing of future museum workers. Systemic inequity continues to plague the field, and they include the reliance of many museums on the free or low-paid labor of museum studies students. "These systems need to be fixed. Museums need to start paying," and contribute to "the structures that are required to train the students and support the staff that are working with students."

CONCLUSION

The reason we wanted to include this chapter in this book was because we observed firsthand as practitioners that year after year, many students graduate from museum studies programs without ample prospects for employment in the field. Especially for museum educators, the question of the value of such a degree given its inherent challenges of expense, time, and perhaps yet-to-be-proven necessity of an advanced degree for procuring a position, seems an important one. When we gathered this group of faculty members and directors together for this conversation, we didn't want to approach it from a place of skepticism, challenging them to articulate why their work and their programs matter. Instead, we wanted to hear directly from program staff about what they perceive as the benefits and struggles and how the events of 2020 will impact their work long-term.

We did not include the voices of museum studies students and former students in this discussion. But we acknowledge that their voices are a critical component to any conversation about the future of these programs and of preparation of whatever kind for museum work. A number of the faculty members we did speak to noted that their programs were partnering with and responding to students on the direction of curriculum and pedagogy and program structure. Since the field of museum education has yet to agree universally that museum studies or related degrees will be required for procuring positions at museums, questions about the degrees' value and necessity will continue to be debated.[5] It is certainly true that degrees and certificates in fields across the humanities and other disciplines will always have to prove their worth when they do not, as our panelists mentioned, define themselves as preparatory training for employment. And it seems clear from our conversations that this type of program for job training is not desired by the faculty or the students; the desire to be readied for the field is only one benefit that students see for their time in museum studies programs. So prospective students face a complex decision in whether to pursue these programs if they aspire to work in museums.[6] More thorough reviews that include longitudinal analysis of students' experiences during and after their museum studies programs will provide additional information for the field and for museum studies faculty as well as for students.

What we heard during these conversations was largely inspiring and ultimately hopeful for how museum studies programs can evolve and meet an uncertain future. Most of the discussion was about innovation, about ideas that would break norms for academic programs, and about ways these programs are trying to meet the calls for bringing equity and inclusion to fore in their programs and at the same time enticing a more diverse student body.[7] As a number of participants admitted, it's likely that not all of the hundreds of museum studies programs that currently operate in the United States will survive long-term, but with the support of the field, the move toward generalized studies and field-base preparation, and an increase in options for using the degree in settings beyond just traditional museums, appears that these programs will be preparing the next generation of museum educators long into the future.

The challenges, however, are both very real and rooted in systemic problems, some of which overlap with museum work overall. The museum studies programs of the future must respond not only to the needs of twenty-first-century visitors but also to the needs of students and communities. To do so will require big ideas and persistent work toward change. And they will, in fact, require the participation of museums and their practitioners as well as academics. Whether there is a willingness for this level of systemic change is up to all of us.

PARTICIPANTS

Brian Hogarth, Director of the Leadership in Museum Education Program, Bank Street College

Gretchen Sorin, Director, Distinguished Service Professor, Cooperstown Graduate Program

Lotte I. Lent, Assistant Director Museum Education Program, George Washington University

Jessica Luke, Director, Museology Graduate Program, University of Washington

Susan B. Spero, PhD, John F. Kennedy University, Museum Studies.

Gregory Stevens, Director, Master of Arts in Museum Professions; Director, Institute of Museum Ethics, Seton Hall University

DISCUSSION QUESTIONS

1. How does your museum work with any museum studies programs? How could you expand your relationship to represent the types of partnerships mentioned by the panelists in this chapter?
2. The panelists spoke a lot about skill development across museum disciplines. How do your institution's hiring practices focus on deep expertise vs. a broad swath of skills and experience?
3. The reevaluation of curriculum and pedagogy that occurred in 2020 brought the inclusion of antiracist and social justice focus into these museum studies programs. What structures need to shift in the field to correspond to the types of learning experiences students are having in these programs?

NOTES

1. Wilkinson Consulting. 2020. "National Snapshot of COVID-19 Impact on United States Museums." AAM Research and Reports, https://www.aam-us.org/2020/11/17/national-snapshot-of-covid-19/.
2. Bryant, Janeen, Barbara Cohen-Stratyner, Stacey Mann, and Levon Williams. 2021. "The White Supremacy Elephant in the Room." American Alliance of Museums, https://www.aam-us.org/2021/01/01/the-white-supremacy-elephant-in-the-room/.
3. American Alliance of Museums. 2018. "Facing Change." Facing Change, https://www.aam-us.org/wp-content/uploads/2018/04/AAM-DEAI-Working-Group-Full-Report-2018.pdf.
4. Wilkinson Consulting. 2020. "National Snapshot of COVID-19 Impact on United States Museums." AAM Research and Reports, https://www.aam-us.org/2020/11/17/national-snapshot-of-covid-19/.
5. Carnall, Mark. 2013. "Will a Museums Studies Degree Help You Get a Job in a Museum?" UCL Culture Blog, www.blogs.ucl.ac.uk.
6. Simon, Nina. 2007. "Warning: Museum Studies Degrees Spawn Legions of Zombies." *Museum 2.0*, http://museumtwo.blogspot.com/2007/04/warning-museum-graduate-programs-spawn.html.
7. Wright-Greene, Jada. 2017. "Tools for Recruitment and Engagement in Museum Studies." AAM Diversity, Equity, Accessibility, and inclusion, https://www.aam-us.org/2017/01/08/tools-for-recruitment-and-engagement-in-museum-studies/.

BIBLIOGRAPHY

American Alliance of Museums. 2018. "Facing Change." Facing Change, https://www.aam-us.org/wp-content/uploads/2018/04/AAM-DEAI-Working-Group-Full-Report-2018.pdf.

Bryant, Janeen, Barbara Cohen-Stratyner, Stacey Mann, and Levon Williams. 2021. "The White Supremacy Elephant in the Room." American Alliance of Museums, https://www.aam-us.org/2021/01/01/the-white-supremacy-elephant-in-the-room/.

Carnall, Mark. 2013. "Will a Museums Studies Degree Help You Get a Job in a Museum?" UCL Culture Blog, www.blogs.ucl.ac.uk.

Simon, Nina. 2007. "Warning: Museum Studies Degrees Spawn Legions of Zombies." *Museum 2.0*, http://museumtwo.blogspot.com/2007/04/warning-museum-graduate-programs-spawn.html.

Wilkinson Consulting. 2020. "National Snapshot of COVID-19 Impact on United States Museums." AAM Research and Reports, https://www.aam-us.org/2020/11/17/national-snapshot-of-covid-19/.

Wright-Greene, Jada. 2017. "Tools for Recruitment and Engagement in Museum Studies." AAM Diversity, Equity, Accessibility, and inclusion, https://www.aam-us.org/2017/01/08/tools-for-recruitment-and-engagement-in-museum-studies/.

9

Creating Empowered Educators

Lorie Millward

ABSTRACT

Empowered educators can be the secret sauce in developing meaningful programming and opportunities for museum visitors that are authentic to the organization, relevant, and responsive to important issues and emerging paradigms. In this chapter, we will explore how hierarchical structures influence empowerment, the importance of strong, but flexible systems, team cultivation, and the inherent challenges of developing educators as coleaders and coauthors of their own work experience. Then, we will present a case study from my work at Thanksgiving Point and explore how educators reimagined an education department to become a provocative learning environment that fosters personal and professional growth among its team.

THE CONUNDRUM OF CHANGE

Change is constant. Everything changes, we change, our ideas change, our desires change, our families change, our communities and the issues that impact our work change. So why is it always so difficult to make real and important changes to the ways in which we operate? Since the world constantly shifts and moves beneath our feet, one would think we'd be accustomed to adapting what we do and how.

As museums strive to stay relevant as these changes occur, educators look for new ways to engage and expand their audiences. Often, we do this by experimenting with types of programming, modes of delivery, and by cultivating external partnerships that help us create new experiences for diverse community groups.

However, it can be difficult to sustain some of these efforts or even get them off the ground because our attempts and new approaches may not fit into our existing systems and structures or have the foundational support necessary for innovation or change to occur. Similarly, when important societal issues and shifting paradigms ask us to reflect upon our biases and practices and respond in ways that may be outside our comfort zones, do our ideas about leadership and authority get in the way of our ability to change in response? And in what ways do the boots-on-the-ground educators contribute to or drive those changes? As community aspirations shift, it's those frontline, in-it-all-the-time staffers who are likely the ones to know first. But do they feel empowered to influence and implement important changes or to realign our structures? Too often, we don't make educators feel safe and supported enough to devise solutions and take risks to change our practices.

Typically, we coach teams to have a growth mindset, try new things, and evaluate our progress. We train them on the content, how to write lesson plans, how to deliver programs and facilitate visitor experiences. But do we recognize and cultivate educators as leaders, regardless of the positions they hold? As directors and managers, are we willing to relax our grip on oversight and administration and, as we do with our community partners, co-create an environment that is reflective of and provides meaningful learning opportunities for the audience (in this sense, our own educators)?

In this chapter, I will share how, at Thanksgiving Point, we grappled with these questions and ultimately endeavored to create an environment wherein educators were empowered to lead in real ways, take risks, and ultimately, elevate the nature of facilitated interactions and museum programs.

THE OPPORTUNITY TO EVOLVE

When I arrived at Thanksgiving Point in early 2013 it was on the heels of a radical institutional restructure (which I detail later in the chapter), which left folks a little unsettled. Recruited to be part of the core design team responsible for building the Museum of Natural Curiosity, it was my responsibility as curator of Curiosity to inform the educational aspects of architectural, exhibit, and program design for this new museum. It was conceived of as a fully interactive family experience in science and art exploration (for Thanksgiving Point, "family" is defined as any group of humans who want to hang out together). Each gallery was populated with intuitive and playful exhibits that would allow guests to encounter scientific phenomena and interpret their experiences, questions, and new understandings through artful expression and play. It would be the institute's first facilitated venue and, as such, would rely on skilled educators to engage guests in challenges, explorations, and inquiry-based discovery.

This highly experiential model was new for Thanksgiving Point, and I was tasked with implementing staff training on the science of how people learn, to assist in the development of inquiry-based programs, and to refine the programs that existed before. The challenge to evolve and deepen the guest experience was exciting to me, and I was full of enthusiasm and lots of ideas about how I could help the team I joined to accomplish this. But first, some background to set the scene.

AN INSTITUTIONAL REORGANIZATION CLEARS THE WAY

Thanksgiving Point Institute is a multi-museum, farm, and garden complex in Lehi, Utah, dedicated to cultivating transformative family learning through shared experiences in the natural world. Its venues include the Museum of Ancient Life—focused on natural history; Ashton Gardens—a large interpretive estate garden; Farm Country—a small interpretive working farm, the Museum of Natural Curiosity—an interactive family STEAM experience, and Butterfly Biosphere—a life science museum and butterfly conservatory. Before I arrived, the existing venues were structured in a traditional way and, while part of a larger organization, essentially operated as individual attractions, with oversight from a large senior management team made up of the executive directors who often competed with one another for audiences, memberships, and gate revenues. Interestingly, though, none of the venues had an education department, and as visitorship increased and guests sought out educational experiences, the institute found a creative way to provide activities by expanding an important partnership.

Early in its history, Thanksgiving Point partnered with the state land grant institution, Utah State University (USU), to inform and guide horticultural and agricultural practices. Building on this, the institute and USU expanded this partnership to host 4-H Extension educators who delivered programs at all venues. This arrangement proved mutually beneficial as Thanksgiving Point gained access to content specialists, researchers, and educators, and USU gained access to Thanksgiving Point's venues and burgeoning audience, using its sites as labs to work out programming ideas and to engage a broader audience with its research efforts.

In the closing months of 2012, while designing the Museum of Natural Curiosity, and contemplating the prospect of adding yet another senior manager, venue executive team, departments, and staff, we realized we had an opportunity to create a more efficient and effective organizational model. This new model would allow Thanksgiving Point to grow, adding additional venues and services over time without becoming administratively top heavy and unwieldy in the process. It would allow individuals on staff to play to their strengths and require full collaboration from a once-siloed group of people. This resulted in a radical rethinking of how to manage and evolve this expanding nonprofit.

Over the next few months, the institute dissolved venue organizational structures and eliminated siloed teams. The senior management team was pared down to a few individuals, each responsible for a discrete aspect of the operations and a new strategic plan was written. Former executive directors were challenged to focus on their core strengths and repositioned to apply their specific skill sets in ways that would benefit the entire organization. To illustrate, one such executive director with keen knowledge of repair and maintenance became the director of facilities for the institute as a whole and accepted responsibility for all facilities work across Thanksgiving Point's sprawling two campuses. Similarly, another director took on the goal of improving guest services across venues by ensuring consistency of training and developing team members who—now that we had established shared standards and expectations—could greet guests and conduct transactions at any venue.

This immediately improved efficiencies, reduced duplication of work, and produced significant cost savings. The new system also favored a flattened hierarchy that depended on the collaborative efforts of a joint management team to guide the institute's affairs and day-to-day activities. No more siloed departments, directors, teams, or competition between venues.

In addition to three 4-H Extension staff who were responsible for all programs, there were a few part-time education assistants hired by Thanksgiving Point to help with program delivery. This small, decentralized team, worked out of a tiny make-shift office in the institute's Show Barn and was the only team at that time whose members were not employed by a specific venue or directed by Thanksgiving Point managers. With Extension leading the educational charge, this team of six to eight individuals implemented many of the wonderful youth programs developed by 4-H and used the "Do, Reflect, Apply" experiential model[1] adopted in the 1970's from David Kolb's learning cycles theory.[2] This method of teaching is simple to follow and is supported with easy-to-access resources and existing curricula. In this way, USU filled the educational niche with expertise and people that the institute did not yet have on its own staff. However, the mandate to employ a different kind of inquiry-based approach at the forthcoming Museum of Natural Curiosity challenged these educators to expand their knowledge of other pedagogical models and questioned our structure for education.

Although the educators were not structurally affected by the recent reorganization, a challenge to approach programming differently was unsettling and not particularly welcomed by some staff. It was in this environment of upheaval where I began inciting yet another big change.

ENVISIONING A DIFFERENT KIND OF EDUCATION DEPARTMENT

Everything was new. A new museum with new visitors and a new department which required new programs and new staff. However, with no existing framework or formal department in place across the different sites, it was a once-in-a-career opportunity to dream big and think about how to position educators in the place of most potential and to empower them, not only to deal with newness and change, but to drive these processes themselves.

Senior management tasked me with building and leading an education department, and along with a creative phenom named Heather Paulsen as cultivator of curiosity (the Thanksgiving Point equivalent of assistant director) and the 4-H Extension leader, Dave Francis, we decided to use this rare moment in time to create a framework that would anticipate and embrace change and empower educators.

With a vision to develop opportunities for guests to have connective and personally meaningful experiences in our museums, we needed to create an environment where our educators had similar experiences. We wanted to create a workplace driven by curiosity, with opportunities for playful learning, where questioning and wondering would be explored as a function of our day-to-day work. Trying to figure out how to split up programs or areas of responsibility to create tiers of ascending management authority seemed inauthentic in an organization that had just dissolved similar hierarchies on an institutional level. With an entirely clean slate and a goal to empower our educators, why would we adopt the usual org chart structure and traditional hierarchical roles?

In her article, "From the Margins to the Center,"[3] education and organizational consultant, Tina Nolan, asked three questions about crafting one's personal identity as a leader.

1. What are your core values?
2. What do you stand for?
3. If you could run your department and/or your institution any way you wanted to, what would it look like? How would it look for your colleagues and for the visitor?

It helped that my own educational values matched the core values in Thanksgiving Point's new strategic plan, which included perpetual prototyping/continual improvement, the value of play, process over content acquisition, cross-departmental collaboration, and shared experiences. Also, what I stood for as a leader—shared responsibility and individual empowerment—mirrored the recent structural changes of the institute.

The trust placed in me from the senior management team made it possible to think about how these values and ideals could inform the design of a flattened hierarchy reflective of the organization's mission and our values, and nimble enough to adapt and change over time. Working in close collaboration with Heather, Dave, and the small group of team members we had at the time, we sketched out a system that would allow a measured transition beyond dependence on 4-H Extension programs and staff and give our fledgling department a foundation upon which to build capacity, establish its own unique voice, and grow into a fully realized, new model of an education department.

NATURE PROVIDES INSPIRATION

The successful outcome of the reorganization provided a model for how to decentralize power to share responsibility and decision making among a team. As a biologist and former zoo keeper, I looked at how other large groups of creatures lead in a collective fashion. From Canada Geese taking turns as the flight leader to the egalitarian structure of bonobo society to the decentralized power structure of bees, I saw examples that required all members of a group to take the lead at times and at other times to step back and let others, more fit for particular challenges, step forward. This biomimicry thinking is called "scoping"[4] and it begins with asking questions about how nature works and how those workings may apply to specific human challenges. In my case, the question was, "How do animals and plants determine leadership and self-organize?"

Recent research conducted to identify the leadership paradigms in moving animal groups provides interesting evidence of the impacts of shared authority within a dynamic group. Scientists learned that individual-to-individual influences within a population were powerful and ultimately led to group-level impacts and collective decision making that benefited the whole.[5]

The findings also shine a light on the levels of influence individuals have and the need for a strong but flexible leadership structure in a shared authority paradigm. As an example, one individual with a high level of influence (meaning its individual-to-individual actions resulted in positive changes within the group) may be given sole authority to make a decision that impacts everyone; for instance, in which direction the group will go, while another individual may contribute to decisions that require less influence.[6] Basically, one must earn the right to lead. If biomimicry gave me insights into how other creatures successfully share leadership, how could we apply those insights to our group of mammals?

The idea was this—what if, instead of the director and a tiered team of managers dictating the framework and systems needed to guide the people and work of the new department, we engaged all of its team members as co-creators and as coleaders in this effort? We envisioned an organizational chart that shifted from tiers to gears. Ergo, the organizational chart was not strictly hierarchical and was visualized as cogs working in tandem, with different, but equally important roles.

At this point we shed the moniker "Educator" and adopted the title and ethos of "Explorer." Believing that titles should be aspirational, Explorer felt more consistent with the new mission of cultivating transformative family learning, and set the expectation that, instead of educating our guests, we would explore alongside them as co-creators and coauthors of *their* experiences. Each Explorer was part of a "Cog" and shared responsibility for direction and leadership of the programs governed by that cog. Cogs were comprised of salaried, full, and part-time Explorers (including our USU partners, me, and the former vice president of design and Programming) to ensure that each person had the opportunity for input, professional growth, and leadership.

Next, we identified areas of responsibility. The director would provide oversight of the entire machine and support a cadre of program specialists and explorers. Over the next few months, we interviewed and added to our small team, growing the original group of eight to seventy-five people in order to broaden our offerings and to facilitate in each of the Museum of Natural Curiosity's five galleries. This staff growth spurt was anticipated in the new museum's pro forma, and funds to establish a larger team were raised during the capital campaign. At the same time, we were developing statewide outreach programs which, after a provisional phase, garnered $750,000 in ongoing state funding. These funding sources combined, allowed us to build the team quickly.

We wrote job descriptions with inclusive language and in a fun, conversational tone, and rethought the usual qualifications, removing barriers like level of educational attainment and length of experience in the field. We sought out people who were creative, empathetic, and eager to play. The idea was that if we populated the department with individuals who reflected diverse aspects of our community, the programs developed by this team would be guest-centric, responsive to changing needs, and interesting to a wide spectrum of visitors. We were quickly building a superteam of humans from a variety of backgrounds, with different points of view, lived experiences, and from a range of ages. It was, however, necessary to do a little housecleaning at this point to remove negative and corrosive individuals who were impeding growth and making changes unnecessarily difficult for everyone.

LAYING THE FOUNDATION

In the first year, our focus was to develop common goals and a shared purpose. At this early stage it was important to create the initial methods and systems needed to get the team started with supportive structures and tools. The most immediate need was to clarify our philosophy and expectations and get everyone singing from the same sheet music. Adapting Wiggins and McTighe's Understanding by Design model[7] of creating a prioritizing framework required clearly defining a long-term goal—for us this was the institute's mission, the Big Idea—what our part was in achieving that goal,[8] Enduring

Understandings—the philosophies that would guide our work,[9] and Essential Questions—thought-provoking queries that led to the essence of our goal.[10] Heather and I found value in our work, prior to joining Thanksgiving Point, in combining this model with elements of differentiated instruction and added in measurable objectives—Know, Understand, and Do[11] for activity planning. These objectives and tasks were supported by assessment rubrics we created to ensure we were progressing toward our goals.

In this way, we developed a strong guiding document for the new department. This framework also served as the model for each Cog to follow in outlining the philosophies and expectations specific to their areas of work.

A PARADIGM SHIFT

Next, we needed a game plan for building and inspiring our new team. In the quest to promote independent, critical thinking and keep the diversity of ideas and viewpoints in play, we laid out a strategy that would promote a culture of dynamic, communal learning that included a shared vocabulary and was centered in playful learning. Further, we wanted to build a stable foundation for our new learning ecosystem, design opportunities for personal and professional growth and development, and establish a solid yet flexible platform for our budding community of practice.

The first challenge was breaking down the idea of education as a didactic effort dependent on a knowledge holder (teacher) imparting wisdom to empty vessels (students). With each of Thanksgiving Point's museums focused on different content areas, it wasn't realistic to expect Explorers to have a deep understanding of every concept in order to facilitate programs and interactions with visitors. Our directive to change the nature of the guest experience also pushed Explorers to reevaluate their ideas about teaching and about who holds the power in learning environments. It seems like it would be a relief to relax one's grip on the need to have all the information and, instead, discover and honor guest motivations, background knowledge, and interests, but it was upsetting to many. It took a significant reframing of dogmatic mindsets to deconstruct and rebuild new understandings and to gain comfort with pure curiosity. We, like many of our guests, needed permission to play, to wonder, and to not know.

Museums are not school. But museum educators often try to replicate the formal education environment by holding programs in the same types of classrooms or using similar curricula and resources, and by employing didactic teaching methods.[12] Why? Taking into account the theory of situated cognition,[13] learning is heavily influenced by the environment and its physical and social elements. As described by Rogoff et al.,[14] the formal classroom does not allow for learner choice or control over the content one must learn, nor the methodology by which one will be taught.

There is a kind of comfort and certainty with the familiar classroom setting for educators and learners alike. However, knowing that up to 95 percent of a person's learning over their lifetime happens outside of formal settings,[15] through informal investigations, conversations around the dinner table, pursuing hobbies, and visits to interesting places like museums, zoos, parks, gardens, and other wonderful informal learning settings, it was, yet another opportunity to realize the great responsibility we had as part of our guests' lifelong learning journey. As a result, the Basic Training series was born and focused on informal education principles and the science of how people learn.

BUILDING CAPACITY

The Basic Training series was divided into three sessions that took place over a three-month period of time, which allowed Explorers ample time to process, develop, and practice with one another and with guests between sessions. Each session had a similar format: playful learning, discussions about a research-focused reading assignment, written reflections, introduction to supportive tools, and on-the-job homework.

Part 1, "Introduction to Inquiry and Facilitation," threw Explorers into a design challenge right off the bat. They were asked to build a catapult capable of sending a marshmallow across a specified distance. Supplies were scattered around the room and Explorers could choose from wire hangers, tape, straws, rubber bands, utensils, and other household items for construction. As we explained the challenge, we worked on launchers of our own, modeling how to help participants understand the task without giving explicit directions. After this round of playful learning, we unpacked the activity and discussed the process, frustrations, and epiphanies, and the curiosity sparked by the activity. Explorers came to this session prepared to discuss readings from *Surrounded by Science*[16] that described the characteristics of informal learning environments. Having experienced an inquiry-based activity and discussing some fundamental research, we assigned on-the-job homework and presented them with tools to further their new knowledge.

The tools included The Inquiry Think Sheet, an at-a-glance comparison of behaviors that were or were not consistent with inquiry and a Personal Inquiry and Facilitation Rubric and Reflection (table 9.1). Each section of the rubric was one part of the learning process we employed: Inquiry Mindset, Observations, Wondering, Inferring, and Discourse. Explorers used these tools during each shift to self-assess understandings, progress, and challenges. They were supported by "Leads" who were more experienced teammates and who acted as mentors, talking through the rubric and reflection with the team each day, and helping everyone set goals. Explorers worked in this way for a month, gaining experience and developing skills using inquiry on the floor.

The written reflections completed and turned in at the end of each session created the opportunity and platform for voicing concerns, questions, disagreements, and frustrations. The feedback they shared helped us understand where to focus additional cultivation experiences and content for upcoming training sessions.

One example of this feedback, pointed to the disconnect between our inquiry-based approach and the formal teaching in the classroom.

> You asked for reservations or confusion we might have. My main concerns are about user expectations and conflicts with curriculum. Teachers still follow an answer-based curriculum. They want us to address certain "right answers." As staff we feel stress not knowing how to include the old curriculum with the new science standards AND making things student-directed.

Understanding concerns such as this one, gave us glimpses into misunderstandings that we could address in training as well as in conversations, meetings, and observations.

Part 2, "Evaluating Our Understanding and Practice," explored how to expand application of new knowledge and covered topics such as behavioral indicators of engagement, body language and non-verbal communication, John Falk's visitor identities,[17] and how to approach guests. The reading assignment, "A Thirst for Learning,"[18] sparked discussion about the motivations to learn and the kind of learning experiences we wanted for ourselves and our guests. The tools provided at this stage included facilitation cards that were laminated and worn on lanyards and acted as cheat sheets to use when Explorers got hung up or overwhelmed.

Each card focused on one of the Personal Facilitation and Inquiry Rubric areas to further support development of a common vocabulary. They were also a useful tool in reframing the ubiquitous table-top activity. Those activities were hard to give up. After all, a nice rectangle upon which to place cool things is a comfortable barrier which captures the attention of guests. But they also keep guests at arm's length. It was safe (and you got to sit down). We didn't intend to kill this classic program type

Table 9.1 Thanksgiving Point Education Department Personal Inquiry and Facilitation Rubric

	Consistent		Inconsistent	
Inquiry Mindset	I created an environment in which multiple ideas were valued and explored.	I created an environment in which others' ideas were valued.	I created an environment in which others' ideas were accepted.	I created an environment in line with my own ideas and agenda.
Observations	Modeled, encouraged, and allowed time for observations.	Provided opportunities for observation.	I pointed out what to observe or notice.	I explained what learners were seeing.
	Learners noticed new or unexpected things.	Learners made comparisons and used descriptive language.	Learners spend little time engaging.	Learners don't engage at all.
Wondering	Provided a safe environment in which questions and explorations were encouraged.	Provided an environment where some questions and explorations were allowed.	I listened to questions and provided answers.	I asked questions that required a "right" answer.
	Learners ask many questions and explore possibilities.	Learners ask questions but don't explore.	Learners ask questions in order to elicit a definitive answer.	Learners don't feel comfortable asking questions.
Inferring	I encouraged and modeled guessing.	I provided opportunities for guessing.	I provided limited opportunities for guessing or limited the outcomes.	I provided something with a predetermined outcome or answer.
	Learners feel comfortable making and sharing their guesses.	Learners make guesses.	Learners feel uncomfortable making guesses.	Learners do not make guesses.
Discourse	I provided opportunities for and encouraged dialogue.	I directed the conversation.	I provided opportunities for learners to respond in specific ways or times.	I immediately explained content or phenomena.
	Learners engage in sustained relevant discussion with others.	Learners contribute to relevant discussion.	Learners talk briefly about what they noticed.	Learners only listen to Explorer/facilitator.

What did you do well? List specific examples.	What were some challenges?	What one thing do you want to work on?	What are some strategies you can use to improve in this area? (Leads have great suggestions too!)

After completing a shift, evaluate your facilitation using the rubric. Talk with your Lead to discuss and record what you did well, what was challenging, and ways you might improve your practice.

Focus
Staff-led projects

Good to Know
Allow staff-led projects to be an inquiry filled, playful experience.

You can and should limit the number of participants to seats at the table(s) dedicated to the project. If you are full, invite visitors to come back later.

PLAYING
Help visitors get interested.

- Invite visitors to join in and create
- Create and tinker with your own item(s)
- Keep the table full of interesting/unexpected items to use

EXPLORING
Ask questions to help visitors create and engage in inquiry.

Don't explain step by step how to do a project, if it can be avoided.

- What do you notice about these...?
- What do you need to get started?
- How do you think you could get it to...?
- Why do you think it did that?
- What I noticed was...what do you think?
- How could you change things to get the outcome you want?
- What if you tried...?

CONNECTING
Help visitors make connections to their own understanding.

Example questions

- Is it different than you expected? Tell me how/why.
- Does that remind you of anything?
- How do you know that?
- Have you seen or done anything like that before?
- You can explore this same idea with...

Figure 9.1 *Lorie Millward*

(just yet), so we developed a facilitation card specifically for staff-led tabletop activities (figure 9.1) to ensure that any that the team developed fit into our new facilitation schema.

Other tools such as Tips for Engaging Adults and Pick Up Lines addressed specific concerns that Explorers shared via reflections and which gave us insight into some of the habits of mind that continued to trip them up.

> One thing I am still not sure about is using an inquiry approach across several ages, particularly for older individuals. I am worried about using this approach with adults, I'm afraid adults will be uncomfortable and feel like I don't think they understand or that they are dumb.

Providing ample opportunity for team members to share their thoughts without fear of reprisal and where all viewpoints and perspectives were welcomed, made possible a more trusting community as time went on. Skeptical Explorers began to share their efforts to overcome fears about change and provided us the opportunity to model for them the openness we desired to see in their growth as leaders.

> I was told in training to "embrace the ambiguity." It was hard for me, but now I think this ambiguity can be the educational sweet spot. I also agree that inquiry fits right along with Thanksgiving Point's mission of "transformative family learning." The fact is, our goal is not merely to entertain, but to transform guests through their experience here. To me this means our goal is not to teach about a certain dinosaur but, rather, to instill the desire and capacity to learn about it for them-

selves here and after they leave. We are not feeding people fish; we're teaching fishing lessons, or better yet, instilling a lifelong love of fishing.

Part 3, "Supporting Learners," built on the progress the team was making in employing inquiry and gaining comfort with the new structure. After the usual round of playful learning, and discussion of the reading assignment, "Learning Together: Families in Museums Staff Training Curriculum," produced by the Boston Children's Museum and Chicago Children's Museum,[19] a new tool was introduced to assist Explorers with developing inquiry-based activity plans that were grounded in the, then new, Next Generation Science Standards and aligned appropriately to grade levels. This session also served as an introduction to leadership characteristics, supporting the growth of skills important for our shared-governance structure. With a framework in place along with shared understandings developed in Basic Training and tools to support growth, it was time to relinquish even more control and empower the Explorers to take the next step—shared leadership and authority.

The next series of sessions, Advanced Training happened over another three-month period and focused on leadership while we continued to provide pedagogical support. To model our shared-governance ideal, we co-created these trainings along with the Explorers. They came up with interesting topics and activities that addressed questions they had and issues they were facing. Part 1, "Learning New Strategies" focused on leadership challenges and how to apply leadership in different scenarios.

Explorers shared personal experiences that had challenged them and turned those into a tool called Leadership Scenarios. This document posed questions that they worked together to answer, sharing with one another their own ideas, struggles, and feedback questions. These scenarios reflected everyday situations and opportunities to lead. One such scenario asked, "You are helping with a cooking class (although not teaching) and the instructor keeps getting off topic and you see some of the guests are becoming frustrated. How do you handle the situation?" Another highlighted expectations about responsibilities as a coleader and stated, "You are changing galleries at Curiosity. While walking through the hub, you notice two Explorers talking. When walking through the hub to take a lost item to the front desk ten minutes later, the same Explorers are still talking. What do you do?"

For my part, I sought out and vetted resources about different styles of leadership that we read, discussed, and used to inform what our collective leadership style would be. The next two sessions, "Making Connections" and "Applying New Understandings" allowed Explorers to deepen their leadership acumen.

For example, the team connected with the idea of using coaching techniques as leadership tools[20] and this approach fit well with King's[21] "guide on the side" model that our 4-H Extension partners employed. For this distributed leadership structure to work, it was essential that Explorers felt comfortable enough to coach, support, and lead one another. To that end, another session focused on how to engage in peer-to-peer observation and evaluations.

We created a tool that standardized this process to remove, as much as possible, the personal, subjective factors that can often cause people to take offense at or shy away from feedback. The Observation Protocol was a tool that supported the rubric and self-reflection, creating even more consistency with common vocabulary. An intensive six-month training program may seem adequate, but it was important to us that Explorers were challenged on a daily basis. For this purpose, Heather and some of the Explorers came up with an idea to engage everyone in short sessions before and after each shift. This daily practice became crucial to sustaining shared leadership, collaboration, and vision.

We provided time on the clock for this important work, which was NOT easy to get through the budgeting process, at least at first. However, adding thirty minutes before a shift for warm-ups, led by Explorers, to set goals and engage in an activity or discussion to ignite their own curiosity, and thirty minutes after each shift for wrap-ups, also Explorer-led, to reflect, plan, and transfer information to the incoming shift, was vital to team cultivation. It prepared them to facilitate with thousands of guests—

sometimes six thousand people—over the course of a day. It also provided time and space to transition and have some quiet time after an enormous number of high-energy interactions.

CLARIFYING ROLES AND RESPONSIBILITIES

Our newly minted structure and extended trainings created fiscal and programmatic efficiencies, while reducing (though not eliminating) the need for intensive personnel management and remediation. It was also necessary to establish a decision-making process for our coleaders. The first question everyone asks when I mention shared leadership is, "Who makes the big decisions?" It's a valid question and one, among others, that we had to wrestle with in sustaining a flattened hierarchy.

Be advised, though, that flat didn't mean non-existent, nor did it mean that key administrative functions and high-level decisions were left to the group. Think back to the time you were reading about groups of moving animals and how individuals earned their turn at making important decisions for the group.

Our approach was not "we-decide-everything-as-a-group"; rather, it was about empowering the individuals in the group to distribute authority and identify who, within their group, was best suited for a given challenge. For us, that meant clearly defining roles and detailing what someone in that role would be expected to do and how it was as important as every other role to keeping the wheels turning. As curator of Curiosity, there were director-specific functions and expectations which required my particular skill set—budget oversight, liaising with policy makers and donors, buck-stopping, and so on. I had a specific and important role, but so did everyone else. The Explorer Role Statement provided clarity about the expectations for individuals serving in that capacity. For example, this excerpt from that statement codified the shared leadership requirement:

> Explorers share responsibility for leadership and governance of the Education Department and work collaboratively to develop and refine programs, assist with program and facilitation training, mentor fellow team members, and provide peer-to-peer leadership. To this end, each Explorer is part of at least one Cog to ensure that all have the opportunity to share their insight, experience, strengths, and concerns or opposing viewpoints.
>
> Each Cog must govern itself, set and achieve specific and mission-driven goals and share responsibility and accountability for program successes and/or challenges. This requires Explorers to demonstrate leadership skills such as integrity, collaboration, open communication, innovative thinking, and courage to fail.

The role statement also explained our system of shared accountability and how performance was measured.

STANDARDIZED SYSTEMS

Just as the role statement standardized personal and cog performance expectations, a work outline template explained what cog meetings needed to accomplish. With so many different cogs and the expectation that everyone moves between them based on the needs of a project, program, or for the purpose of building acumen in an area of weakness, a Cog Work Outline provided a structure for group work. Using this tool, Explorers were supported yet challenged and, as they shifted in and out of other cogs, the format for group work and decision making was familiar and didn't require renegotiation or learning a new cog's methods. This simple tool was the oil that kept our gears turning as it eliminated purposeless meetings and promoted accountability. A reminder of the purpose of cog work was always included on the tool to ensure it was top of mind going into a jam session. It stated, "We recognize that through shared responsibility we cultivate transformative learning experiences for our team and our guests in order to meet our programming and fiscal goals." Additionally, we provided examples during training on how to effectively co-create and use time together effectively and efficiently.

Even when things are running smoothly, when everyone is singing "Kumbaya," and the team is producing next-level work, it's important to remain in a state of vigilance about process and systems. A successful shared leadership structure doesn't mean that no oversight or management is required or that things will always be great if everyone is invested. When humans get comfortable, they get complacent and those groovy flexible systems can become rigid and calcified in no time, turning cogs into siloed teams. It was necessary to think about how to create some discomfort every once in a while and to shake up individuals' responsibilities regularly to encourage blood flow to different muscles.

Curiosity can be a powerful weapon against complacency as the discomfort of ambiguity can lead to a desire to explore, learn, and discover. Continually experiencing some discomfort is like having a pebble in one's shoe. It is not really painful, but the irritation it causes makes us sensitive, and over time it can build up from discomfort to disquiet to a desire to change. This is vital, not only to avoiding complacency, but, more importantly, to feeling empathy for others.

Disquiet teamed with shared vision, flexible systems, and nimble people can and should provoke a deeper reflection on your department's work and continual reexamination of department and individual biases that may create barriers to equity and inclusion and limit creative potential. Each one of us has a personal and professional circle of influence and, when we commit to using the powerful platform of museum education to bring our individual-to-individual influences to bear as a collective force, we have the opportunity and responsibility to drive fundamental changes that forward a more inclusive organization that won't shy away from important issues.

There have been, are, and will always be key moments in time in which museum people can make a mighty difference through exhibits, programming, and in spaces that encourage dialogue, deepen understanding and empathy, and allow us to think critically and creatively, together. For Thanksgiving Point, practicing shared leadership, building flexible systems, and cultivating empowerment positioned our team to act quickly and courageously in the face of a global health crisis (new), a social injustice crisis (not new), earthquakes, and even hurricane-force storms that rocked our state. We didn't get it right every time, but our collaborative mindset allowed us to think on our feet and respond quickly.

IMPACT ON THE EMPLOYEE EXPERIENCE

Ultimately, the test of any style of leadership is if it prepares individuals to take on bigger challenges—within or without the organization. We saw rapid growth and increased leadership acumen in many of our team members, which allowed us to evolve and deepen our programming and to continue to attract interesting people to our organization. The flattened cog system was developed to empower our team, involve them in playful learning, and provide authentic leadership opportunities. Rather than share my own perspective about how Explorers experienced the new environment, I asked one former Explorer, now the institute's volunteer director, Ashley Clouse, to talk about what it was like to make the leap from building skills and comfort-level to taking on the shared leadership of a vital area of programming—facilitation at the new Museum of Natural Curiosity. Ashley now works with five hundred or so volunteers in various areas of the institute's operations and has employed a similar shared governance framework with the Volunteer Advisory Board to organize, empower, and cultivate our dedicated non-paid team members.

> When I started, the cog system was being born. It was exciting and a little scary. It quickly became clear that this wasn't a "show up, do your thing, and go home kind of job." There were some pretty hefty expectations. The cog system made me feel the importance of the work we were doing, as well as how essential my and my fellow team members' role was in achieving our mission. Everyone needed to participate to make it happen. It was empowering.

Because of the high expectations and shared responsibility for department leadership, I had to push myself to grow into that role. We were provided with in-depth trainings on inquiry, facilitation, visitor identities, and leadership. I felt invested in and believed in, which, in turn, made me want to support the organization to the best of my ability. I also felt like I had a seat at the table. In conversations with the Director, I felt that, not only could I share my perspective, but that it would be heard and valued. I didn't feel like I had to go along with whatever suggestions the Director or others made because the department structure made it so that I could push back and not feel like I would be punished for it.

If the structure of the Education Department hadn't been what it was, I wouldn't have stuck around. I also know that the growth I had during that time, both professionally and personally, readied me for new roles at Thanksgiving Point but also set me up for success wherever my career path may take me.

As I described earlier in this chapter, I believed that a challenging and rewarding work experience would translate into the kind of free-choice, playful guest experiences that we had been mandated to deliver when opening the Museum of Natural Curiosity. But I didn't know how to prove that. Luckily, the organization was also wondering how visiting Thanksgiving Point impacted our guests' lives. Hence, my colleague, Dr. Stephen Ashton, the director of Audience Research and Evaluation, undertook a study to learn more.

IMPACT ON THE GUEST EXPERIENCE

In 2016, three years after the education department's formation, Dr. Ashton partnered with Brigham Young University Master of Public Administration faculty and students to conduct research to learn if we were truly delivering on our mission of cultivating transformative family learning.[22] We invited community members unfamiliar with Thanksgiving Point to bring their families to each of our (at the time) four museums and provide data about their visits via a retrospective post-then-pre survey.

As a result of their museum visits, these guests reported gaining increased understanding of the natural world and the learning process, improved scientific questioning and exploration, greater self-confidence, and a more positive outlook.[23] We were thrilled to learn about the immediate benefits our guests experienced, and we were excited (to say the least) about the long-term social impacts of museum visitation.

Extensive research shows that the short-term effects reported by study participants lead to stronger family relationships, reduced drug use,[24] increased educational attainment,[25] and a greater sense of health and well-being.[26] We shared our findings with the entire Thanksgiving Point team to help them understand the magnitude and importance of the work they were doing to facilitate opportunities for free-choice learning. Eager to help other museums understand their own community impact, we partnered with the Utah Division of Arts and Museums to conduct an expanded statewide study in 2018. The research team identified other indicators that were added to the research questions to address intercultural competency and attitude changes toward specific content areas. Of the 104 total number of indicators measured, 100 of them, or 96 percent, showed statistically significant positive change.[27]

Some of these reported changes included an increased understanding that exploration leads to learning, heightened confidence to challenge how things are usually done, seeing value in learning from people different from oneself, and an increased appreciation for arts, sciences, and conservation.[28] These findings highlighted just how essential museums and their people are, which further validated our team members' feeling that the work they were doing was indeed important.

LESSONS LEARNED

A dear friend and Museum Studies "shero," Susan Spero, asked me once to jot down some of the lessons I learned as a result of undertaking this process. Nearly a decade later, they still ring true for me, and I share them here in hopes that some of them might benefit you as well.

LORIE'S EPIPHANIES REGARDING KICKING THE BEEHIVE, CREATING A FLATTENED HIERARCHICAL STRUCTURE, AND INSTITUTING A SHARED GOVERNANCE PARADIGM

- There will always be resistance. Don't be surprised by it. It will come from all directions and even from those who are supportive of the concept and see the potential for great outcomes.
- Only move forward with radical change if it puts the organization as a whole in the position of the most potential. Organizational structure must mirror and support the institutional mission and foster what you articulate as the desired guest experience.
- Everyone who will be affected by changes must be involved in making those changes and have buy-in, or, at least, every opportunity for buy-in. Help folks see the mission-centric reasons for the change and the new opportunities it presents.
- Don't initiate deep collaborative work or shared governance if you are squeamish. More collaboration = more drama, especially at first as people try to find their place in the new schema.
- Have empathy for those struggling with or outright fighting change, but don't let it hobble your progress. Continue to challenge the status quo and move forward with an attitude of kindness and support. Remember, not everyone will go with you.
- Prepare to enter uncharted territory. Anticipate issues and prepare to help people through them by providing the initial tools, systems, and strategies they will need to get through the bumpy beginnings of doing things in a new way.
- Demonstrate your own accountability by being transparent about your decision making, sharing challenges you face, asking for help, and delivering on your word. This will help them to understand what is expected of them as a coleader.
- Make time for your team to practice balancing collective decision making and retaining autonomy in a shared-authority system. Be cautious that autonomy is not confused with authority. Authority is earned as we demonstrate accountability to ourselves, our team, and our organization. Ensure that retaining autonomy doesn't equate to disengaging in leadership or shirking accountability when conflicts arise.
- As your team builds capacity and comfort, loosen up on the reins and begin sharing control. Empower your team in authentic ways and have high expectations. Celebrate mistakes and successes equally, always recognize effort, and be genuinely thankful for the team that you have.

HOW CAN THIS APPLY TO MY ORGANIZATION?

You may not be in a position to blow up your department's structure (or maybe you are!). In any case, empowering educators in whatever ways work for you could be helpful as you consider shifting focus from the "way we do things" to envisioning how things *could* be done. Reimagining the education department as a dynamic learning environment in its own right can help you cultivate and empower your team to co-create programming and experience opportunities that are organizationally authentic and responsive to the changing aspirations and new challenges of the community of which your museum can—and must—be a vital part. As Ashley stated, there were key elements of the shared governance system that made her feel empowered. I suggest investigating these key elements as part of any strategic change plan.

APPLYING HUMAN-CENTERED DESIGN TO TEAM STRUCTURE

No matter what type of organization you work in, and what your current hierarchical structure is, if your interest is to change the nature of power distribution with a goal to better serve and grow with your community, these elements can support your efforts. It can be useful to think of these through the lens of human-centered design. We often apply design thinking to exhibit and program development, but the processes involved can be just as effective for empowering educators.

The process begins with empathy. What are your educators seeing, hearing, or feeling in the workplace? What do they hope to experience? What are their professional aspirations and personal values? How do you capture that information? You might use a simple empathy map to gather observations or conduct a values survey, then follow up with individuals to discuss your inferences and learn more about their aspirations and challenges. The next stage of the design process is ideation.

With an empathetic understanding of your team's professional aspirations and challenges, involve them in discussions about how the work environment could foster growth, collaboration, and deepen their own and the guests' experiences. Generate a lot of ideas, draw out potential hazards, and encourage everyone to provide input. Ashley described this as having a seat at the table.

Empowerment begins, in my opinion, with understanding one's value and a willingness to explore how that value can be applied to better the group and its work. This is where training comes in. Beyond pedagogical approaches and leadership cultivation, educators must know that the work they do is an essential part of the larger learning ecosystem and that the results of their work can and will have lifelong impacts for those with whom we interact during the course of the day. When they truly know the importance of informal education and their role in it, the high expectations and measures of accountability you put in place will be expected and understood as part of an effort to support their growth and ability to create opportunities for rich, meaningful guest-led learning. Now, the prototyping phase of the process can begin in earnest.

Armed with training and a shared vision and purpose, put ideas into action. Don't expect perfection, and keep in mind that everything we do is a prototype in some form, and the more time we have to play with and refine a new idea, the better the final prototype will be. I say final prototype because if we think of the work we produce or the systems we create as responses to the needs of a particular moment in time, we set the expectation for ourselves to continually evaluate what we do and how we do it with an aim toward continuously adapting and evolving, which brings us to another part of the design process: reflection and refinement.

Develop a system and supportive tools to evaluate each element of your new efforts. In what ways are educators responding to changes? Is the employee experience reflective of the team's aspirations? How has the guest experience changed? What weaknesses have been exposed in the system or "product" that need to be addressed? Does the new idea still work when a different challenge presents itself? In what ways and on what schedule will refinements be made? Thinking through these questions and others with your team, valuing their insights and input will only strengthen their empowerment. Going back to Ashley's comments, she felt like she could disagree with me or pushback without fear of reprisal, and it highlights the importance of sharing authority, especially when further changes need to happen. Remember, shared leadership is only authentic if it is honored when things are going in directions that differ from where you would have taken them.

Distributing leadership can be terrifying. What if it fails miserably? What if everyone leaves? But what if it offers opportunities and growth that you wouldn't have had otherwise? In my experience, entering uncharted waters with a crew of dedicated educators was worth it. Not just for our team's improved and empowered work experience, but for the quality of programs and guest interactions that resulted from the sometimes-turbulent sea change. After all, museums exist to make humans better and museum people exist to make museums better. Better able to weave into the fabric of their communities and better able to welcome anyone who chooses to explore alongside us. Kumbaya!

DISCUSSION QUESTIONS

This chapter is all about creating a department culture that fosters desired educator and guest experience outcomes.

1. What is the culture of your education department and how often do you assess its strengths, challenges, and outcomes? Who is included in making those assessments?
2. Which aspects of your current culture would you like to change? How would changing these aspects affect the team and guest experience? In what ways do educators influence those changes?
3. What are the benefits and challenges of your current organizational structure and hierarchy, and, in what ways could empowering educators address some of those challenges?
4. In what ways and to what degree do you currently empower your educators? How do you measure the effects of this empowerment? What are the challenges of empowerment that you/they experience and how are they addressed?

NOTES

1. 4-H Extension, "Experiential Learning Model."
2. McLeod, "Kolb-Learning Styles and Experiential Learning Cycle," 45.
3. Nolan, "From the Margins to the Center," 117.
4. Beynus, *Biomimicry: Innovation Inspired by Nature*.
5. Strandburg-Peshkin et al., "Inferrering Influence and Leadership," vol. 373.
6. Smith, et al., "Leadership in Mammalian Societies," 54.
7. Wiggins and McTighe, *Understanding by Design*, 70.
8. Ibid., 56–81.
9 Ibid., 82–104.
10 Ibid., 105–25.
11. Tomlinson, *The Differentiated Classroom*, 45.
12. Rogoff, "Models of Teaching and Learning," 329.
13. Bane, "Museums and Education."
14. Rogoff, "Models of Teaching and Learning," 329.
15. Falk and Dierking, "The 95 Percent Solution."
16. National Research Council, "How People Learn," 1–17.
17. Falk, "Identity and the Museum Visitor Experience."
18. Falk and Dierking, *Lessons without Limit*, 1–18.
19. Porter and Cohen, *Learning Together*.
20. Sabatine, "Coaching as a Leadership Tool," 44.
21. King, "From Sage on the Stage to Guide on the Side," 33.
22. Parkin et al., "Thanksgiving Point Social Impact Study Evaluation Plan."
23. Ashton and Nelson, "Thanksgiving Point Social Impact Study."
24. Willis, Vaccaro, and McNamara, "The Role of Life Events," 349–74.
25. Flouri and Buchanan, "Early Father's and Mother's Involvement," 141–53.
26. Packer and Bond, "Museums as Restorative Environments," 421–36.
27. Ashton et al., "Brace for Impact," 26–31.
28. Ibid., 26–31.

BIBLIOGRAPHY

4-H Extension. "Experiential Learning Model." *Wisconsin 4-H*, 2021, 4h.extension.wisc.edu/resources /volunteer-resources/4-h-foundations/experiential-learning-model.
Ashton, Stephen, Johnson, Emily, Nelson, Kari Ross, Ortiz, Jennifer, and Wicai, David. "Brace for Impact." *Museum*, May 2019, pp. 26–31.

Ashton, Stephen and Nelson, Kari Ross. "Thanksgiving Point Social Impact Study Evaluation Plan." Unpublished Manuscript, 2016, pp. 1–4.

Bane, S. "Museums and Education: Connecting the Elements of Education to Science and Children's Museums." *Engineering*, 2008.

Benyus, Janine. *Biomimicry: Innovation Inspired by Nature*. Harper Perennial, 1997.

Falk, John. *Identity and the Museum Visitor Experience*. 1st ed., Routledge, 2009.

Falk, John and Dierking, Lynn. *Lessons without Limit: How Free-Choice Learning Is Transforming Education*. Illustrated, AltaMira Press, 2002.

Falk, John and Dierking, Lynn. "The 95 Percent Solution." *American Scientist*, vol. 98, no. 6, 2010, p. 486.

Flouri, Eirini and Buchanan, Ann. "Early Father's and Mother's Involvement and Child's Later Educational Outcomes." *British Journal of Educational Psychology*, vol. 74, no. 2, 2004, pp. 141–53.

King, Alison. "From Sage on the Stage to Guide on the Side." *College Teaching*, vol. 41, no. 1, 1993, pp. 30–35.

McLeod, S. A. "Kolb-Learning Styles and Experiential Learning Cycle," Simply Psychology, 24 Oct. 2017, www.simplypsychology.org/learning-kolb.html.

National Research Council. *How People Learn: Brain, Mind, Experience, and School: Expanded Edition*. National Academies Press, 2000. https://doi.org/10.17226/9853.

National Research Council. *Surrounded by Science: Learning Science in Informal Environments*. Illustrated, National Academies Press, 2010.

Nolan, Tina R. "From the Margins to the Center." *Journal of Museum Education*, vol. 34, no. 2, 2009, pp. 171–82. *Crossref*, doi:10.1080/10598650.2009.11510633.

Packer, Jan and Bond, Nigel. "Museums as Restorative Environments." *Curator: The Museum Journal*, vol. 53, no. 4, 2010, pp. 421–36. *Crossref*, doi:10.1111/j.2151-6952.2010.00044.x.

Parkin, E., Omerza, J., Tanner, E., Zhao, J. "Thanksgiving Point Social Impact Study Evaluation Plan." Unpublished Manuscript, 2016.

Porter, Tim and Cohen, Tsivia. *Learning Together: Families in Museums Staff Training Curriculum*. Boston Children's Museum and Chicago Children's Museum, 2012.

Rogoff, Barbara. "Models of Teaching and Learning: Participation in a Community of Learners." *Handbook of Education and Human Development*, edited by Eugene Matusov and Cynthia White, Blackwell, UK, Oxford, 1996, pp. 388–412.

Sabatine, Janice Manzi. "Coaching as a Leadership Tool." *The Analytical Scientist*, no. 3, March 2013, pp. 44–46.

Smith, Jennifer E., Gavrilets, Sergay, Borgerhoff Mulder, Monique, Hooper, Paul L., El Mouden, Claire, Nettle, Daniel, Hauert, Christoph, Hill, Kim, Perry, Susan, Pusey, Anne E., van Vugt, Mark, Alden Smith, Eric. "Leadership in Mammalian Societies: Emergence, Distribution, Power, and Payoff." *Trends in Ecology and Evolution*, vol. 31, no. 1, 2016, pp. 54–66. *Crossref*, doi:10.1016/j.tree.2015.09.013.

Strandburg-Peshkin, Ariana, Papageorgiou, Danai, Crofoot, Margaret C., Farine, Damien R. "Inferring Influence and Leadership in Moving Animal Groups." *Philosophical Transactions of the Royal Society B: Biological Sciences*, vol. 373, no. 1746, 2018. *Crossref*, doi:10.1098/rstb.2017.0006.

Tomlinson, Carol Ann. *The Differentiated Classroom: Responding to the Needs of All Learners,* 2nd edition (2014-05-20). Association for Supervision & Curriculum Development, 2021.

Wiggins, Grant and McTighe, Jay. *Understanding by Design*. 2nd Expanded, Assn. for Supervision & Curriculum Development, 2005.

Willis, Thomas Ashby, Vaccaro, Donato, McNamara, Grace. "The Role of Life Events, Family Support, and Competence in Adolescent Substance Use: A Test of Vulnerability and Protective Factors." *American Journal of Community Psychology*, vol. 20, no. 3, 1992, pp. 349–74. *Crossref*, doi:10.1007/bf00937914.

10

Cultivating a New Mindset for Professional Development

Beth Maloney

ABSTRACT

Museum education professional development relies heavily on field-specific books, journals, media, conferences, case studies, and training. While this methodology offers important insights for our practice, it can feel narrow and even prescriptive, given the increasingly connected, shifting, and multidisciplinary world in which we live, work, and teach. Professional development for the twenty-first century must look to a wider catchment of resources and content; it should focus not only on demonstrating and testifying to successful techniques, but also, and perhaps more importantly, on the cultivation of a mindset that is open to learning, reflection, exchange, and growth. This chapter argues that the field should build activities, resources, and skills that position professional growth as the active and engaged process of life-long learning in service to our work as museum educators.

WHAT COUNTS AS PROFESSIONAL DEVELOPMENT?

I love conferences. I love gathering in a city far from my own, with hundreds of colleagues, to embark on a series of scheduled panels and conversations. More specifically, I love the casual and unplanned chats, encounters, and connections; meeting new friends, reconnecting with former colleagues, hearing from people working in our field (or adjacent ones), and following along on social media. I like to notice and reflect on what is highlighted and what is missing. Truthfully (when funding makes it possible), I simply love traveling to other places, seeing the ways others are working, finding synergies or dissonance, and thinking, grappling, and learning in this context. Though at the moment, it seems hard to imagine when we will be able to physically gather again, I am hopeful, and I can't wait.

While working on a session for the 2020 American Association of State and Local History (AASLH) conference with fellow panelists Kate Gruber, Evelyn Orantes, and Rahul Gupta, I came to a realization. As much as I love attending sessions, I was finding the work of *planning* this session, in and of itself, educational. The four of us met over the course of several months, listened to each other, reflected on our own work, and gained new insights in the examples we shared; we were actively working with and learning from each other.

Why share this story? Because, the *process* of preparing for this session was a rich and important experience and a reminder that professional learning can occur in unexpected places. One might only imagine continuing education as a specific training, online workshop or webinar, conference session, academic course, or lecture. Yet, for me, the preparation for this panel was professional development; and if professional development can be found in unexpected places, perhaps it's just a matter of actively seeking it out, looking for it, and creating it for ourselves.

DEFINING PROFESSIONAL DEVELOPMENT

Historically, professional development for those working in museum education has relied heavily on field-specific books, journals, media, conferences, and training. This model takes its cue from the world of academia, with a focus on foundational theory, publication, analysis, and scholarly critique. Scholarship is an essential part of our field; it serves both as a mechanism for sharing and exploring insights into our practice and also as a record of work for reference (in the field and beyond), inspiration, and reflection. But many of these established professional development channels have barriers to participation built into their structures. Conference registration, journal subscriptions, and workshop fees must be budgeted for and can limit staff participation or interest. Many people may not be able to take advantage of opportunities.

Moreover, relying solely on this model of professional development elevates a particularly narrow approach to learning. In their article, "Redefining Professional Learning for Museum Education," Lynn Uyen Tran, Preeti Gupta, and David Bader argue that professional development experiences like the ones outlined above are essentially "stand alone experiences: once you finish, you're trained up." They argue that this approach embodies "a deficit perspective of the participants" where the focus is on one-way transmission of information or skill with the goal of emparting discrete units of information. Experiencing professional development in this way means that we, as educators, tend to default to this model when we teach and work with learners.[1] Tran, Gupta, and Bader propose that what is needed is a model of professional learning that focuses on learning about one's own practice and one's own approach, which they feel is fundamental, not just for personal but also for field-wide growth.

So, what could this new model of professional development look like? Are there fundamental elements that promote both the individual and growth across the field of museum education? In her blog, educator and historian Leslie Madsen-Brooks states that "professional development is not about training." She proposes that professional development should help an individual become an "experienced and open-minded learner" who is a "generous collaborator" engaged in active conversations and the stimulation of creative and critical thinking.[2] Professional learning can be expansive, beyond daily job responsibilities, and generative of a wider view of our work.

For me, a working definition of professional development that might foster this kind of growth includes opportunities for conversation and networking within our field; exposure to new ideas and skill-building moments; reflection and analysis of one's own practice, agency, and intention in determining the focus for learning; and the opportunity to apply "lessons learned" to future work.

THE CASE FOR CULTIVATING A MINDSET

As working practitioners in the field of museum education, we recognize the value of learning through doing, applying techniques and ideas to practice. Given the increasingly connected, shifting, and muti-disciplinary world in which we work, we need adaptive and creative strategies for professional learning and development. In addition to looking to field experts, established practices, association published books, museum media, museum conferences, museum blogs, social media, I believe we can find professional development in other places and in other formats. Professional development for the twenty-first century must look to a wider catchment of resources, content, and approaches.

As museum educators, we preach lifelong learning. Our professional associations pledge to "advance the purpose of museums as places of lifelong learning"[3] and are built on the premise that there is value in exploring art, history, nature, and scientific concepts throughout one's life. The National Art Education Association hosts a "committee on lifelong learning." The Association of Science and Technology Centers' annual meeting has an "informal education and lifelong learning session track" focusing on the role that science centers play in the educational lives of audiences. Again and again, in history education, we argue that practicing historic inquiry leads to skills applicable throughout one's life. And, regardless of our disciplinary focus, the premise of so much of our work as museum educators—leading object-based discussions, field trips, adult programs, intergenerational learning—relies on the idea that people learn at all ages and that lifelong learning has intrinsic value.

So, let's apply the concept of lifelong learning to our own careers and professional growth as museum educators. Professional development opportunities should be less a cannon of established truths to learn and more an active cultivation of an ongoing learning mindset that seeks education and skill-building opportunities, and centers proactive, self-motivated, and ongoing growth over time. A mindset for professional growth that allows us to "learn as we go" means that conversations with peers and community members, reflective practice, experimentation, and applying techniques from other fields can be opportunities for professional development.

This shift in thinking keeps us nimble, adaptive, and resourceful. Indeed, it may even inspire policy changes in museums with respect to what counts and what gets funding among opportunities for professional learning. For example, instead of setting aside funding for conference registration, there might be different kinds of learning goals for each staff member, established in an individual's learning plan during a given fiscal year. Applying a learning mindset means professional development opportunities become more active, applied, customized, and even democratic. It widens possibilities and, at least in my experience, provides greater job satisfaction and growth.

What follows in this chapter are four areas—each with its own identifying aphorism—where we might focus and create professional development opportunities that cultivate a learning mindset. Each will be discussed at greater length later in the chapter.

1. Outside of the museum bubble: What can we learn from adjacent organizations and partners? Are there new or different ways of working that can inform and stretch our own practice? What can we learn from contemporary context and current events occurring beyond the museum?
2. Same but different: What can we learn from other museums and cultural organizations? What work is happening in museums of different disciplines or who serve different constituents? What can we learn from peer organizations of varying size and geographic location?
3. Mentors and Friend-tors: What do our mentors, peers, friends, colleagues and one another have to teach us about our own practice? Could establishing regular check-ins with colleagues help us integrate new ideas and work through challenges and issues? How can we make new friends and get out of our regular circles of professional interaction?
4. Check yourself: What can we learn from taking a close look at our own practice? Are we actively looking for blind spots and asking for feedback in accountable ways—from audiences, teachers, colleagues? Are we mindful in applying lessons learned through reflective practice to improve our own work?

In each of these areas, I will identify how focusing on growing a mindset is beneficial, offer an example and outline some activities to consider or key questions you might ask yourself to expand your notion of professional development.

OUTSIDE OF THE MUSEUM BUBBLE, AND IN THE HERE AND NOW

During 2020, rising calls for social and racial justice, economic pressures, and public health emergencies changed our lives—in small and large ways. In ways beneficial and deleterious, the field of museum education experienced changes as well. Many people lost jobs, found their hours cut, or their responsibilities shifted. Conversely, our field also experienced a massive wave of resource sharing, program reshaping, and new ways of working.

Free webinars, conferences, accessible online conversations, and connections between organizations and colleagues led to a groundswell of discussions on new approaches to address the moment. As museums closed their doors, reduced hours, and adjusted programming, many practitioners leaned on each other for mutual support, collaboration, and information sharing. Museum educators shared practical tips on what kinds of online platforms to use and how, insights on what was working, and pricing models and pedagogical approaches. We didn't have time to pull together a conference session (most of those were cancelled or postponed anyway) or publish an article, and we reached out beyond our field to peers in formal education, technology, libraries, and nonprofits. We got creative in finding resources to help us adjust to the new normal.

During this year, I was working with colleagues at the Baltimore Museum of Industry (BMI) on the development of an exhibition about the experience of women who worked at the Bethlehem Steel Mill at Sparrows Point, near Baltimore. Our exhibition was slated to open in a small temporary gallery in the museum building. But given the constraints of COVID-19, it became increasingly clear that an indoor installation might not be safe or accessible for our audience. As we tossed around ideas for how we might move forward, we looked outside of the BMI to see what others were doing.

Several examples of simple, outside installations kept popping up on my social media feed: the Minnesota Historical Society's *History at Heart* exhibition,[4] an exhibition called *Swedish Dads* installed on the fence around the American Swedish Institute,[5] and a newspaper article describing the New York Historical Society's pop-up exhibition, *Hope Wanted; New York City Under Quarantine*.[6] Referencing these examples from peer organizations, we talked through what might be possible for our exhibition. Could we reformat and reconfigure our own exhibition plans? What would we give up and what could we gain from making such a shift?

Seeing the work of colleagues who were experimenting with new approaches and needing to work within the constraints of the pandemic ourselves, we decided that taking a risk would be worth it. As a group we made the decision to rework our plans and install a series of panels outside along our campus's perimeter fence. This became the museum's first outdoor exhibition, highlighting personal quotes and photographs and paired with an audio companion piece. What felt like a risky decision has brought unexpected positive results. Our *Women of Steel*[7] exhibition generated engagement from a wide range of visitors, including neighbors passing by who were unfamiliar with the exhibit's story, funders intrigued by the increased visibility of our storytelling, and women who appeared in the exhibition or who shared similar work experiences in mills and factories who marveled at the museum representing their life experience so visibly.

But how was this experience professional development? The decision to make a shift in our plans was an incredibly important reminder for staff—across the organization—to center audience members. Moving the exhibition outside required a lot of reworking our original ideas, but in the end, it made our project more accessible to audience members. Additionally, because counting views and attendance is a challenge given the outdoor location of this exhibition, we're looking at other methods for measuring and understanding the impact of this project. Comments and engagement from community partners, museum supporters, neighbors, colleagues, and people connected to this story speak volumes to the emotional chord this project strikes. Because of this exhibition, we have seen an uptick in interest to donate artifacts, contribute to our fundraising efforts, participate in public programming, and share community stories through our blog or the *Sparrows Point: An American Steel Story* podcast[8] we created in association with this project. This ripple effect has reminded us of the kinds of energy that can be generated when we position resources in ways that are accessible and meaningful. Indeed, the experience with *Women of Steel* has been a good preview for what benefits future projects might yield and how we might ascertain their impact and success. We had never considered using our outdoor space in this way but will do so going forward in an effort to make exhibitions more accessible to the broader community.

How can you apply these ideas to your own professional development work?

- Consider actively looking for new approaches to your regular ways of working. What different steps might help you achieve the same goals? As a thought exercise, imagine delivering a program or product in a new or different format; how might you meet your goals through an alternate approach?
- Share your work via informal conversations, on social media or blog posts. Ask for feedback. Be honest about insights, practical tips, challenges, and lessons learned. We all benefit from participating in field-wide dialogues.
- Take twenty minutes to think about the sources you currently turn to for professional development and do an audit. Are you getting the information you need? Do you feel like you are engaged in productive growth? If so, in what ways? And if not, where else might you turn for the information and inspiration you need?

SAME BUT DIFFERENT; WHAT ARE OTHERS DOING?

In the rush of our working lives, it's easy to get tunnel vision. Schedules are busy, deadlines loom, and our lenses can narrow as we focus only on the work at hand. But luckily there are some simple and easy ways to take a break, get perspective and even have fun. In the same way we work to engage visitors to come and visit our museums, attend our programs, and engage with our community work. I invite you to consider visiting a museum. Yes, that's right. Field trips to other institutions can be incredibly insightful if we position the experience as professional development.

Looking at work happening in other museums, learning settings, libraries, schools, and community-based spaces can be a way not only to learn from existing models but look and reflect upon your own work. How are these organizations and spaces approaching teaching and interpretation? What models seem to be challenging? What seems to be gaining traction? Can you experience them yourself (or with a few colleagues) and consider the elements that add to their success?

During the Fall of 2019, the entire staff of the BMI took a day away from work. We closed the museum and everyone on staff went on a field trip to Eastern State Penitentiary (ESP) in Philadelphia. Our goal was to have a shared experience visiting a historic site together, meet with colleagues and learn about their approaches and vision, and take some time to reflect on what we might be able to apply to our own work. Specifically, the question we asked ourselves was "How do museums effectively address contemporary issues?"[9] We structured the visit with a tour, lunch with ESP staff, and then free time to explore the site. And we also made a point of reflecting on the experience afterward through conversation and writing. This wasn't an over-programmed experience; there was no pre-test or assessment of what was learned, but the outcomes continued to resonate long after the date of the excursion. Having a shared experience was not only fun but helped us get to know each other in new ways, laying a foundation for our work together, moving forward. Additionally, we were able to experience, as visitors, the methods used by a peer historical organization to keep audiences and a commitment to contemporary issues at the center of their work. And all of us, regardless of our roles at the museum, were reminded of the importance of other museum practices such as customer service, design, wayfinding, and the power of well-designed and intentional interpretation.

How was this experience professional development? It was an opportunity for networking within our field and exposure to different approaches. But it was also a prompt for reflective and analytical work. Visiting ESP helped deepen an awareness of the power of public history tied to current issues; the teaching staff at ESP made direct connections between the history of their site, the legacy of criminal justice reform, and contemporary corrections. We were inspired to look at our own practice in comparison with that of our colleagues at ESP. Based on that reflection, we took action to experiment with our own approaches. By the time we launched our Zoom programming in the Fall of 2020, we made the decision to focus on issues in contemporary work—inviting panelists to explore the role of unions in the time of COVID, the impact of the pandemic on migrant crab-pickers, and the role and legacy of systemic racism on the workplace.

It is always useful to visit other museums—to experience the museum setting as a visitor and also as a practitioner. In order to make these types of visits professional development, we need to apply a specific mindset to the experience. Not every space is a perfect match but working to find a lesson that you might learn is part of growing that mindset—remember, there are ways to learn from different museum types, from exhibits as well as programs, and from ideas worth adapting, and those that would never work in your setting.

How can you apply these ideas to your own professional development work?

- Identify three interpretive venues in your community that you might visit on a field trip and then set a date and visit, on your own or with colleagues. You might attend a program, ask for a tour, meet for a coffee with individuals working at these organizations, or attend a virtual exhibit or program. Before you go, consider three questions you can ask yourself or individuals working there. Then, after your field trips, spend a little time writing or talking about insights, questions, or reflections on the experience.
- Working with a colleague at your museum, share an example of a time you gained insight or professional development from an unexpected source. What did you learn? Were you able to apply anything from this experience to your work?
- Make a list of "adjacent" organizations—places that might not be museums, per se, but might function in a similar way such as monuments, public libraries, maker spaces, social service providers, performance venues, or even retail locations. Choose one or two and visit on your own or with colleagues (or participate in their virtual offerings). As you experience this space, consider commonalities and differences from your own workplace. Is there anything that you can modify, scale, or experiment with in some way?
- After you've visited other places, invite colleagues from other museums or cultural organizations to come and take a critical look at your own institution. Try to listen to feedback with an open mind. Afterward, be sure to debrief, in writing or conversation. Look for these conversations to shine light on your blind spots.

Friend-tors: friend + mentor

Many in our profession attest to the value of mentorships. The mentor/mentee relationship can be truly transformative. Particularly for museum educators and others in the nonprofit sector, mentorships can fill an important gap, as there may not be as many structured career development opportunities as exist in the for-profit field.[10] Our professional organizations have established mentorship programs like the EdMEM[11] program through the education committee at AAM, which matches emerging museum education professionals with those who have been in the profession for years. Mike Madeja, head of education at the American Philosophical Society, has been instrumental in helping to structure and run this program. In a conversation with me this past winter, he shared some common

Beth Maloney

themes that have emerged from evaluations over the past five years. Specifically, both mentors and mentees were grateful for the space for reflective practice that this more structured program creates; by establishing protected time to check in, connect and engage, this program makes space for thinking about career and professional growth—space that might have otherwise been consumed by day-to-day work activities. Participants in the program also shared that the relationship provided both a sounding board for immediate issues and also expanded the view of field and career possibilities. And, finally, program participants indicated that they felt there were mental health benefits associated with having a reliable, accountable colleague with whom to speak on a regular basis.

Like a mentoring experience, peer mentoring, or connecting with colleagues who are "at your level" or at a similar stage of professional life, can provide helpful and productive benefits. These relationships might feel more informal and less hierarchical. Proving grounds for museum education peer mentorship include museum education roundtable groups like NYCMER,[12] emerging museum professional meetups,[13] twitter conversations like #museumedchat,[14] or the Facebook group Museum Mingle.[15] Regardless of the structure of the relationship, mentoring or peer mentoring, connecting with colleagues is best when it's symbiotic and collaborative, with partners learning from each other and providing support around common challenges or field-wide issues.

Personally, I've experienced mentorship in many different ways—as a mentee, as a mentor, and, most recently as a "friend-tor." By this term, I mean colleagues working at a similar stage in our professional lives, whom I admire and who have become *friends* and also peer mentors. When I was growing my consultant practice, I made a point of reaching out to get to know people who were also consulting; my aim was to learn from them, share experiences, insights, and connections. Especially when working as an independent consultant, a community of peers and friends can feel like some-thing you have to create for yourself—to problem-solve issues related to clients, share tips on the business side of things, or come together on larger contracts. I've also built friend-torships through shared projects like serving on boards or designing conference panels. For example, when I worked with fellow board members at the Museum Education Roundtable, we came together around common goals, learning from and with each other through our work. And sometimes, friend-tors can be found when simply connecting around a topic or project, grounding conversations in book club discussions, lunch-and-learns, or in other experiences that provide structure but extend beyond the formality of the conference or meeting setting.

For me, friend-torships may differ from more traditional mentorships in that there is a particular kind of self-efficacy that can come from this kind of relationship. Self-efficacy, meaning one's belief about our ability to perform, helps determine what we do with knowledge and skills we possess. In her article "Raising Docent Confidence in Engaging Students on School Tours," Teri Evans-Palmer posits that when we observe individuals with whom we identify as they accomplish goals and tasks, we feel more prepared and able to take on similar goals and tasks. This, in addition to "verbal persuasion," literally helps us achieve more.[16] For me, witnessing and assisting friend-tors with work and career issues, being a sounding board and a source of advice, has absolutely raised my own sense of career self-efficacy. Mentor or friend-tor relationships cost time and energy but in the end, they are worth it—for support, resource sharing, advice, networking, and partnership.

How are these relationships a part of one's professional development? They provide a framework to help us teach each other, build a support network, work through challenges and issues, gain feed-back, practice listening skills, get a wider perspective and a broader array of examples, expertise, and resources. Additionally, these relationships offer a set time for reflection, encouragement to apply new ideas, and the opportunity to hold ourselves accountable. Whether you start with a close group of people you know and interact with professionally or reach out to new colleagues—those perhaps you've heard present or whose work you are familiar with—the intention of establishing a community of practice can be a powerful guiding principal. This intention setting around an issue, a problem, or professional growth is key and helps position the mentor or friend-tor relationship as professional development.

How can you apply these ideas to your own professional development work?

- Is there someone in your existing network of peers—in your community or even outside your community—who might be a good friend-tor? Working with a colleague or friend, consider ways you might reach out to this person and establish a friend-tor relationship (or just go ahead and do it!) Your first step is simply making contact.
- Once you've connected with a mentor or friend-tor, consider coming up with a goal or set time and agenda (i.e., a lunch date, a meeting to address a particular issue you're working through). If it helps, start off with a discussion of confidentiality. Don't be afraid to state what you need in order to have a productive and authentic conversation.
- Whether you're hoping to be a mentee or a mentor, be proactive and look for opportunities for both via established organizations or informal channels. Sometimes a mentor relationship can come naturally from an informational interview. Other times, it may not pick up speed, but don't be discouraged. The key is to build your network of support more than it is to forge a formal partnership.
- Engage in conversation with peers—those with similar roles at different organizations—on a regular basis like a scheduled monthly meeting. You might consider discussing a museum-field related issue, an article (or even a book chapter!), or just use the time for a general checking in. Whether you have a set agenda or not, focus less on transaction and more on relationship building and trust.

CHECK YOURSELF

One of the most challenging things we can do as professionals is critically look at our own work and try to identify our blind spots. There are many methods we can use to check ourselves, but they all require making the choice to do so. As Elisabeth Nevins writes in the introduction to the *Journal of Museum Education* issue, "Expanding Our Community of Practice; Professional Development in Museums," we need "new models of professional development which foster 'communities of practice' and 'give agency to participants to shape the experience to meet their own needs.'"[17] The intention of actively shaping your own experience and having agency in your own professional growth is key to a learning mindset.

One way to examine one's own practice is simply to ask for and be open to feedback from supervisors, from peers, and from those we manage. This kind of "360 review" is a tool to gather feedback from all directions with a focus on actionable steps. Feedback may not always be positive; acknowledging that we all have areas where we need or choose to grow is an important step to allowing that growth to happen. Purposefully establishing a framework or approach for asking for feedback can help keep you accountable.

Borrowing from the field of educational learning and teacher training, consider establishing regular meetings or conversations with critical friends. Professional development in the teaching field defines critical (meaning essential, important) friends as a regular group of colleagues who use a series of questions to provide feedback to teachers who want to improve their classroom teaching. A critical friend is "a trusted person who asks provocative questions, provides data to be examined through another lens, offers critiques of a person's work as a friend . . . an advocate for the success of that work."[18] This model posits that actively seeking out assistance, through critique, analysis, and group thinking around a particular issue, is a key component to professional growth.

Another way to examine your own practice is to engage in regular, individual reflective work. Establish a time and space for thinking back on projects that have been completed. Perhaps this comes with the opportunity to write a summary report for a grant or as part of your own record keeping or review of program evaluations. After taking some time to digest the impact and work of the program,

Beth Maloney

ask yourself if there were any lessons to be learned? What would you have done differently? Did the essential outcomes of this work have the desired impact? There may be new insights about your own approach or strategies that come with shifts and changes in your job, or new projects. If you are on the lookout for them, you can use these moments to inform your professional growth. Journaling or establishing a process with colleagues or peers to share thoughts can help codify your reflective practice. Goal-setting around reflection, with a mechanism for tracking, can help result in regular self-accountability and a change in practice.

With peers either at your organization or within your community of practice, you might be able to work collaboratively to create a broader network for reflective practice. In their article, "Creating and Sustaining a Culture of Reflective Practice: Professional Development by and for Museum-Based Maker Educators," Rebecca Grabman, Talia Stol, Annie McNamara, and Lisa Brahms describe the way they structured in-house professional development for their museum education staff. Their approach was based on two components. The first was establishing the primacy of learning through making—meaning the active, hands-on experience of creating your own learning, specifically around problem-solving experiences. The second was the idea that learning in communities of practice helps all participants—those with more experience as well as those new to a subject—to find deeper engagement and shared experience.[19] They found that this approach provided opportunities for museum educators to cultivate and sustain a culture of reflective practice that made their work more relevant and responsive to the communities they served.

Events of 2020 upended my work at the BMI in a way that offered sometimes uncomfortable moments when I had to examine and reflect on our role as a cultural organization and also my work as a museum educator. With the profound ways the pandemic laid bare social and racial inequities in Baltimore, it quickly became clear that our resources could make a difference and offer a service, specifically to teachers and students in Baltimore City public schools. What did this mean for me and my own reflective practice? I had been considering my own practice during this incredibly challenging time and trying to ascertain the lessons I could take personally and for the museum where I work. As part of this process, I tried to identify what felt most gratifying and essential—where it was clear that we were doing work that meant something. I kept coming back to key moments when I felt like our work mattered; a Zoom room full of laughing students and teachers, a thank-you note from an instructor from the Citizenship Preparation Program at Baltimore City Community College, a voicemail from a former steel worker who brought four carloads of people to see our outdoor exhibition. I'm in this work for the emotional resonance with visitors. That is what keeps me going.

How was this process of personal reflection professional development? Over the past few years, I have been struggling to define "community" with my work at the museum. Who is our audience? What are we offering in terms of a service? How can we be a community and cultural anchor? Acknowledging that we absolutely have more work to do, my reflections on the unique challenges of our work in 2020 have reminded me what it feels like to move, as Stephen Weil wrote more than twenty years ago, from "being about something to being for somebody."[20] I'm continuing to actively look to resources like the Empathetic Museum,[21] "critical friends" like those I met at the 2019 MASS Action convening,[22] and communities of practice like the International Coalition of Sites of Conscience[23] to help me and my museum examine our role as a partner with and in service to our communities.

How can you apply these ideas to your own professional development work?

- Are there mechanisms in your own work life that lend themselves to the active cultivation of reflective practice (i.e., reporting to supervisors, reviewing evaluation results, submitting or sharing a grant report)? How might you take advantage of these existing checks and balances to help you engage in regular reflective practice (and move beyond annual performance reviews)?

- In what ways are you diversifying and enriching your own media sources? Look for scholarship regarding practices where you may not have familiarity or fluency. Track articles, deepen your library, create a reading group or even write to authors to establish a relationship around content that challenges you.
- Are you asking for feedback on your projects—from peers, those you supervise, and from visitors? And when you ask and receive that feedback are you actively listening and prepared to take action? You can take this feedback query as an opportunity to cultivate transparency and acknowledge that you are growing as an organization and an individual.

CONCLUSION—A MANIFESTO

Now is the time for an active reimagining of professional development for the field of museum education. And the responsibility lies with us. Relying exclusively on a set of practices limits the learning we can and must do to create relevant, responsive, and meaningful work in our field and substantive professional growth for ourselves. If we reform our stance and look to activate moments of learning in multiple places and spaces, we are better positioned to grow as museum professionals and to further the evolution of the field. Our professional organizations are starting to make these changes. The American Association for State and Local History has begun to look critically at their continuing education programs.[24] But we can begin this work immediately, individually, and collectively.

The cultivation of a mindset open to learning, adaptation, response, reflection, exchange, and growth is applicable across varying museum types, content areas, and at every level. The secret lies within your own perceptions, your own frameworks, and your ability to consider how and in what ways you *can* learn. Working on our own professional growth is a dynamic and intentional process. If we believe that one can learn throughout life, from various places and in multiple ways, then we can develop an awareness and a mindset for ourselves—by looking to colleagues in different fields, roles, or regions, by actively cultivating sustained conversations and relationships with peers, or by looking critically at our own practice. Besides simply benefiting us as individuals, a more expansive view of professional development de-silos our museum education practices and asks what we can learn from other fields like informal education, communications, equity practice, and customer and user experience.

We must expand the notion of professional development—looking to the contemporary context within which we are working, to adjacent and peer organizations, to friends and mentors, and to our own reflective practice. If we structure experiences for ourselves in all realms of our work, if we cultivate that mindset and develop additional and rich channels for professional growth, we can become agents of our own change. Our field, as Elisabeth Nevins writes, was "once called an 'uncertain profession,'[25] (but is now) embracing its expertise and actively advocating for the powerful and personal learning that only museum-based pedagogy can inspire."[26]

Whether you are collaborating on developing a new program or a session for a conference, accepting feedback from peers or supervisors, reaching out to find mentors and friend-tors, field tripping to a park, cultural site, or museum with colleagues, ask yourself, what can I learn from this? To borrow from the field of physics, and Newton's first law of motion, a body in motion stays in motion. A person open to learning, with a professional development mindset, continues to learn and grow.

DISCUSSION QUESTIONS

1. This chapter outlines four categories where you might create professional development opportunities that cultivate a learning mindset. Working with a critical friend, take a close look at your own current professional development practice. Conduct an audit and consider the four categories outlined in this chapter. Are there blind spots or any opportunities for diversification? Track your conversation and see if it inspires additional explorations.

2. Read this chapter with a team of coworkers. Together, take the time to work through the questions and prompts that follow each of the four categories. Does anything resonate? What is missing? Consider the different insights each of you brings to a discussion of these ideas. What can you learn from each other?

3. Establish a time and space for your own professional reflective practice either through journaling, conversation, or even a mechanism already in place at your work. Consider setting a time on your calendar each week. Task yourself with identifying moments in your work when there might be a lesson learned. What would you have done differently or better? What resources might help you?

4. Looking ahead at your professional development practice, use the four categories outlined here to help establish an individual learning plan. Consider each category, come up with one or two related activities, and put these on a timeline. Can you formalize sharing opportunities so that when you have accomplished something, you can reflect and share that experience?

NOTES

1. Lynn Uyen Tran, Preeti Gupta, and David Bader "Redefining Professional Learning for Museum Education," *Journal of Museum Education*, 44, no. 2 (2019) 135.
2. Leslie Madsen-Brooks, "Professional Development in Museums." May 4, 2009, accessed February 2021, https://museumblogging.com/2009/05/04/professional-development-in-museums.
3. "Mission Statement," Education Committee of the American Alliance of Museums, accessed December 2020, http://ww2.aam-us.org/resources/professional-networks/edcom.
4. "History at Heart; Helping Minnesotans Find Affirmation, Support, Comfort and Connection." Minnesota Historical Society, accessed March 2021, https://www.mnhs.org/historyisnow/history-at-heart.
5. *Swedish Dads*, Jun 20, 2020–Oct 04, 2020. American Swedish Institute, accessed March 2021, https://www.asimn.org/exhibitions-collections/exhibitions/swedish-dads.
6. Tess Thackara, "Takes of Hope and Resilience as a Museum Reopens," *New York Times*, August 13, 2020, https://www.nytimes.com/2020/08/13/arts/design/New-York-Historical-covid-reopen.html.
7. "Outdoor Exhibitions," *Women of Steel*, Baltimore Museum of Industry, accessed March 2021, https://www.thebmi.org/exhibitions-2/.
8. Aaron Henkin, *Sparrows Point: An American Steel Story*, podcast audio, January–March 2021, https://www.npr.org/podcasts/941175499/sparrows-point-an-american-steel-story.
9. Beth Maloney, "Museums + Contemporary Issues." *Point to Point* Blog. Baltimore Museum of Industry. September 2019, accessed March 2021, https://www.thebmi.org/esptrip/.
10. "Finding a Guide: The Value of Having a Professional Mentor." *Philanthropy News Digest*, August 4, 2009. Accessed March 2021, https://philanthropynewsdigest.org/columns/mycareer-pnd/finding-a-guide-the-value-of-having-a-professional-mentor.
11. Education Committee of the American Alliance of Museums. Museum Education Mentor Program (EdMEM) description, accessed March 2021, https://www.aam-us.org/professional-networks/education-committee/initiatives/.
12. New York City Museum Educators Roundtable, accessed March 2021, https://nycmer.org/.
13. Baltimore Emerging Museum Professionals. Facebook group, accessed March 2021, https://www.facebook.com/groups/BaltimoreEMPs/.
14. MuseumEdChat (#MuseumEdChat), accessed March 2021, https://twitter.com/museumedchat?lang=en.
15. Museum Mingle; Education and Programming. Facebook Group, accessed March 2021, https://www.facebook.com/groups/297517578317594/.
16. Teri Evans-Palmer, "Raising Docent Confidence in Engaging Students on School Tours," *Journal of Museum Education*, 38, no.3 (2013): 357.
17. Elisabeth Nevins, "Expanding Our Community of Practice: Professional Development in Museums," *Journal of Museum Education*, 44, no. 2 (2019): 131.
18. A. L. Costa and Kallick, B., "Through the Lens of a Critical Friend," *Educational Leadership*, 51, no. 2 (1993, October): 50.

19. Rebecca Grabman, Talia Stol, Annie McNamara, and Lisa Brahms, "Creating and Sustaining a Culture of Reflective Practice: Professional Development by and for Museum-Based Maker Educators," *Journal of Museum Education*, 44, no. 2 (2019): 157.
20. Stephen E. Weil, "From Being about Something to Being for Somebody: The Ongoing Transformation of the American Museum," *Daedalus*, vol. 128, no. 3 (1999): 229.
21. The Empathetic Museum, accessed March 2021, http://empatheticmuseum.weebly.com/.
22. MASS Action, accessed March 2021, https://www.museumaction.org/resources.
23. International Coalition of Sites of Conscience, https://www.sitesofconscience.org/en/home/.
24. "AASLH Announces IMLS Grant to Improve Our Continuing Education Program." American Association of State and Local History, accessed March 2021, https://aaslh.org/aaslh-announces-imls-grant-improve-continuing-education-program/.
25. Stephen M. Dobbs and Elliot W. Eisner. "The Uncertain Profession: Educators in American Art Museums," *Journal of Aesthetic Education*, vol. 21, no. 4 (1987): 78.
26. Elisabeth Nevins, "Expanding Our Community of Practice: Professional Development in Museums," *Journal of Museum Education*, 44, no. 2 (2019): 133.

BIBLIOGRAPHY

American Association of State and Local History. "AASLH Announces IMLS Grant to Improve Our Continuing Education Program." Accessed March 2021, https://aaslh.org/aaslh-announces-imls-grant-improve-continuing-education-program/.

American Swedish Institute. *Swedish Dads*, June 20, 2020–Oct 04, 2020. Accessed March 2021, https://www.asimn.org/exhibitions-collections/exhibitions/swedish-dads.

Baltimore Emerging Museum Professionals Facebook Group. Created February 8, 2016. Accessed March 2021, https://www.facebook.com/groups/BaltimoreEMPs/.

Baltimore Museum of Industry. "Outdoor Exhibitions." *Women of Steel*. Accessed March 2021, https://www.thebmi.org/exhibitions-2/.

Costa, A. L., and Kallick, B. "Through the Lens of a Critical Friend." *Educational Leadership*, 51, no 2 (1993, October), 49–51.

Dobbs, Stephen M., and Elliot W. Eisner. "The Uncertain Profession: Educators in American Art Museums." *Journal of Aesthetic Education*, 21, no. 4 (1987), 77–86. JSTOR, www.jstor.org/stable/3332832.

Education Committee of the American Alliance of Museums. Mission statement. Accessed December 2020, http://ww2.aam-us.org/resources/professional-networks/edcom.

Education Committee of the American Alliance of Museums. Museum Education Mentor Program (EdMEM). Accessed March 2021, https://www.aam-us.org/professional-networks/education-committee/initiatives/.

The Empathetic Museum. Collaborative collective of museum professionals since 2014. Accessed March 2021, http://empatheticmuseum.weebly.com/.

Evans-Palmer, Teri. "Raising Docent Confidence in Engaging Students on School Tours." *Journal of Museum Education*, 38, no. 3 (2013), 364–78, DOI: 10.1080/10598650.2013.11510787.

Grabman, Rebecca, Talia Stol, Annie McNamara and Lisa Brahms. "Creating and Sustaining a Culture of Reflective Practice: Professional Development by and for Museum-Based Maker Educators." *Journal of Museum Education*, 44, no. 2 (2019), 155–67, DOI: 10.1080/10598650.2019.1596735.

Henkin, Aaron. *Sparrows Point: An American Steel Story*. Podcast audio. January–March 2021, https://www.npr.org/podcasts/941175499/sparrows-point-an-american-steel-story.

International Coalition of Sites of Conscience. Founded in 1999, https://www.sitesofconscience.org/en/home/.

Madsen-Brooks, Leslie. "Professional Development in Museums." Museum Blogging. May 4, 2009. Accessed February 2021, https://museumblogging.com/2009/05/04/professional-development-in-museums.

Maloney, Beth. "Museums + Contemporary Issues." *Point to Point* Blog. Baltimore Museum of Industry. September 2019. Accessed March 2021, https://www.thebmi.org/esptrip/.

Minnesota Historical Society. "History at Heart; Helping Minnesotans Find Affirmation, Support, Comfort and Connection." Accessed March 2021, https://www.mnhs.org/historyisnow/history -at-heart.

Museum as a Site for Social Action. Accessed March 2021, https://www.museumaction.org/re sources.

MuseumEdChat twitter hashtag and weekly chat. Joined 2017. Accessed March 2021, https://twitter .com/museumedchat?lang=en.

Museum Mingle; Education and Programming. Facebook Group. Created June 11, 2020. Accessed March 2021, https://www.facebook.com/groups/297517578317594/.

Nevins, Elisabeth. "Expanding Our Community of Practice: Professional Development in Museums," *Journal of Museum Education*, 44. no. 2 (2019), 131–34, DOI: 10.1080/10598650.2019.1602815.

New York City Museum Educators Roundtable. Accessed March 2021, https://nycmer.org/.

Philanthropy News Digest. "Finding a Guide: The Value of Having a Professional Mentor." August 4, 2009. Accessed March 2021, https://philanthropynewsdigest.org/columns/mycareer-pnd/find ing-a-guide-the-value-of-having-a-professional-mentor.

Thackara, Tess. "Takes of Hope and Resilience as a Museum Reopens" *New York Times*. August 13, 2020, https://www.nytimes.com/2020/08/13/arts/design/New-York-Historical-covid-reopen .html.

Tran, Lynn Uyen, Preeti Gupta and David Bader. "Redefining Professional Learning for Museum Educa-tion." *Journal of Museum Education*, 44, no. 2 (2019), 135–46, DOI: 10.1080/10598650.2019.1586192.

Weil, Stephen E. "From Being about Something to Being for Somebody: The Ongoing Transformation of the American Museum." *Daedalus*, 128, no. 3 (1999), 229–58, *JSTOR*, www.jstor.org/stable/ 20027573.

Part III

New Models, Anticipating the Future

11

Building Bridges

THE NEED FOR CULTURAL COMPETENCE IN THE MUSEUM FIELD

Teresa Williams Valencia

As a resident of Ohio, I recognize that I am a guest in the original homeland of the living nations of: The Miami Tribe, the Shawnee Tribe, the Eastern Shawnee Tribe, the Absentee Shawnee Tribe, the Delaware Nation, the Delaware Tribe, the Wyandotte Nation, the Seneca-Cayuga Tribe, the Seneca Nation, the Ottawa Tribe, Peoria Tribe, Pokagon Band Potawatomi, Forest County Potawatomi, Tonawanda Seneca, and others. I extend my respect and gratitude to the many Indigenous people who call these lands home.

ABSTRACT

Museums have a long legacy as colonial institutions. For generations, museums interpreted cultures from an ethno-centric viewpoint and collected cultural resources without permission from their makers. Our hurtful legacy and lack of cultural competence as a field is detrimental to our aim to be welcoming spaces to all communities. We must address these facts if we are to move forward and build bridges between our institutions and our communities. This chapter explores the need for cultural competence in the museum field and how we, as museum professionals, volunteers, and board members, can be better allies to the communities whose history we interpret, cultural resources we steward, and people we aim to serve.

A NECESSARY SKILL

Recent events have brought to the surface the increasing need for museum professionals, as well as volunteers and board members, to be culturally competent. This skill is imperative for the future of our field if we are to remain relevant and trusted organizations.

During my professional experience, I've worked for a museum where a lack of cultural competence caused staff to view the ancestors within their halls as scientific specimens and not the loved ones of indigenous community members that must return home. I've also worked for museums that actively seek to improve their cultural competence in both their business practices and mindset by empowering the communities that they serve to tell their own stories and training their staff to value cultural differences. These vastly different viewpoints on the role of communities in the interpretation and care of their cultures and cultural materials prompted my research into how increasing museum professionals' cultural competence can help museums become better allies and supporters of the communities which they aim to serve, the history and stories they wish to tell, and the cultural resources which they steward.

In 2017, I graduated with my Museum Studies MA and MBA from John F Kennedy University, which was located in the Bay Area. As part of my studies, I explored the need for the critical skill of cultural competence in the museum field through my master's thesis.[1] In 2018, I participated in a panel discussion called *Seeding Authority: A Symposium on Decolonizing Museum*s where I presented my viewpoints as a non-Native Hawaiian curator working at Iolani Palace, a sacred and important site for Native Hawaiian people. I discussed how cultural competence played a role in my understanding and my positionality as someone outside the culture that was entrusted by this Native Hawaiian organization to steward cultural resources and interpret history at this site. Essentially, I saw my role as an administrative one that facilitated Native Hawaiians sharing their own histories and training our education staff, both paid as well as volunteers, in cultural competence and respectful interpretation. In 2019 at the Western Museums Association, I participated in the panel discussion *Seeding Authority: A Roundtable Discussion on Decolonizing Initiatives at Four Institutions* in which I had the honor to co-present with amazing folks actively working on decolonizing their museums and increasing the cultural competence of both the museum professionals and the organizational policies for the institution they represent.

This chapter is based on my research and personal experiences with cultural competence in the museum field. Although my research and experience working with communities is focused on how museums engage with indigenous communities, I believe that many of the key findings and conclusions of my research in cultural competence are applicable across museums and their community engagement work. In sharing my research and experience, I hope to inspire others to actively build their own cultural competence and that of their institutions so that museums may build authentic, respectful, and deep connections to the communities they serve.

WHAT IS CULTURAL COMPETENCE?

Cultural competence, as defined by the National Center for Cultural Competence, is "a set of congruent behaviors, attitudes, and policies that come together in a system, agency, or among professionals and enable that system, agency or those professions to work effectively in cross-cultural situations."[2] The American Association for Health Education defines cultural competence as "the ability of an individual to understand and respect values, attitudes, beliefs and more that differ across cultures, and to consider and respond appropriately to these differences in planning, implementing and evaluating."[3] According to the National Center for Cultural Competence, there are five essential elements of a system or institution's ability to possess cultural competence. They are, as follows:

1. Valuing diversity
2. Having the capacity for cultural self-assessment
3. Being conscious of the dynamics inherent when cultures interact
4. Having institutionalized cultural knowledge
5. Having developed adaptations to service delivery reflecting an understanding of cultural diversity[4]

WHY IS CULTURAL COMPETENCE IMPORTANT TO THE MUSEUM FIELD?

The social justice movements around Black Lives Matter, Missing and Murdered Indigenous Women (MMIW), and Stop Asian American and Pacific Islander Hate (Stop AAPI Hate), and as well as others, are rooted in the desire to address the deeply entrenched racism in America. Smithsonian secretary, Lonnie G. Bunch, recently wrote an article in which he said that the constant violent acts against Black people have caused us to "confront the reality that, despite gains made in the past 50 years, we are still a nation riven by inequality and racial division."[5] Our country's very foundation is rooted in inequality. These roots of racism are apparent in the foundation of museums as well. If we, as institutions, are to continue to hold a trusted place in society, we must be willing to address our field's racist past, actively work to better ourselves, and continue to work with communities to empower them to tell their own stories in museum spaces.

For most of the time that museums have existed, they blocked entrance to visitors of color and, if they did allow access to diverse visitors, often limited access to basic amenities like restrooms.[6] Museums in the 1890s held strong beliefs about how museum visitors should act and behave. Schwarzer states that, "as if in church, visitors should be properly attired and reverent. As if in a stranger's house, they should be exceedingly polite and not handle anything not belonging to them."[7] The Metropolitan Museum of Art's director in the 1890s has been quoted as saying that,

> We do not want, nor will we permit, a person who has been digging in a filthy sewer or working among grease and oil to come in here, and by offensive odors emitted from the dirt on their apparel, make the surroundings uncomfortable for others.[8]

To put it bluntly, visitors that were not middle or upper class and white were unwelcome in museums. Museums, by barring access to their institutions, actively reinforced the racism and ethnocentric views of the time. Racism, as defined by Haunani-Kay Trask in her book *From a Native Daughter: Colonialism and Sovereignty in Hawai'i*, is a "system of power in which one racial/ethnic group dominates another racial/ethnic group for the benefit of the dominating group; economic and cultural domination as well as political power are included in the systemic dominance of the exploiting group" where ethnocentrism is "preference for and belief in the centrality of one's own ethnic/racial group in one's everyday life."[9]

In recent years there has been progress by museums, albeit slow and with many missteps, toward rebuilding relationships with diverse communities. However, the fact remains that the colonial perspectives of culture still exist in museums today.

CREATING MEANINGFUL AND SINCERE CONNECTIONS BETWEEN MUSEUMS AND COMMUNITIES

Cultural competence is a skill that will assist museums and their staff, volunteers, and board members to engage in a meaningful and sincere level with communities. The goal for all museums should be to evolve to be "a center where people gather to meet and converse, a place that celebrates the richness of individual and collective experience, and a participant in collaborative problem solving. It is an active, visible player in civic life, a safe haven, and a trusted incubator of change."[10]

Interpretation is an important part of a museum's public service and touches everything that it does, from developing exhibitions to creating educational materials. For museum professionals who interpret or tell the story of a culture other than their own, community engagement with that culture is of utmost importance. This means that the community must participate in all aspects of the entire interpretive experience.

One way museums can demonstrate that their staff and institutions possess cultural competence is through shared authority. Through my review of the literature and following my research, I believe that a simple definition of shared authority is embracing the expertise and knowledge of both those within and outside of the museum. As Elizabeth Duclos-Orsello states in her *Journal of Museum Education* article "Shared Authority: The Key to Museum Education as Social Change," despite the general conversation in the scholarship and the increased support for museums as civic/social spaces, there remain many questions about why and how museum education initiatives (broadly defined) might address the most critical social needs or concerns of their communities. The *Journal of Museum Education* takes up these questions directly and works at providing some answers by way of employing the concept of "a shared authority" as a frame. The idea is simple: sharing authority with both the public and/or colleagues at non-museum entities can be a powerful and accessible tool for museums of all stripes to effectively educate others about or engage in pressing social concerns and social change efforts.[11] Furthermore, museums "must divest ourselves of the special authority sometimes granted to us. . . . And we must enter democratic partnerships with other members of our communities."[12] By sharing authority, museums can begin to acknowledge community expertise in representing their own culture and in contributing cultural resources. However, the question arises of whether shared authority is enough? Shouldn't museums move beyond the idea of sharing authority and toward empowering communities if we are truly to become culturally competent?

Taking the concept of shared authority one step further is the concept of seeding authority. During my time as director of curation and education at 'Iolani Palace in Honolulu, Hawai'i, I had the privilege and honor to work with Noelle Kahanu, Dr. Karen Kosasa, and Halena Kapuni-Reynolds, who referred to the practice of seeding authority as a foundational practice. Seeding authority means that in order to build our cultural competence as a field we must both "cede" the authority of the museum professional and "seed" trust and authority in the communities we work with.[13] An excellent article, "Ceding Authority and Seeding Trust" (2019), discusses the way that the San Diego Museum of Man (now the Museum of Us), conducted this process to address both their past institutional lack of cultural competence as well as the steps they took to move their museum toward cultural competence, decolonization, respectful interpretation, and repatriation of ancestors. This museum's perspective is that they must "recognize that [their mission] can only authentically occur in a context of truthfulness and transparency about the ways that our museum participated in the colonial enterprise. For the greater part of our history, we harmed indigenous communities by participating in the extraction of their belongings, cultural practices, and bodies in service to the museum's goals of preservation and education."[14]

So, how do we start this process of sharing authority or, better yet, seeding authority? Margaret Kadoyama, author of *Museums Involving Communities: Authentic Connections*, provides a framework to help establish these relationships. The benefits to establishing these relationships are plentiful and include building your organizational and individual cultural competence, creating more respectful interpretation, and creating opportunities for community driven content and cultural resource stewardship. However, all this starts with understanding the community itself through interviews and conversations, not assumptions. Through listening and learning from the community with which the museum hopes to engage, it can create a community action plan. This document will outline what the community's wants, needs, and desires are of the museum as well as creating a detailed plan of what action will be taken, who will do it, and how it will be done in the interest of partnership and communication.

Some examples of questions museum professionals need to ask to create a community action plan and involve the community in cultural resource stewardship, interpretation, and exhibitions are:

1. Who are their stakeholders and leaders?
2. What are their wants, needs, desires, and assets of that community?
3. What are the goals of engaging with the community? Why does the museum seek deeper involvement from the community?
4. What are the resources needed to accomplish this, and where do we get them?

5. How will we measure our results (How do we know we reached our goals)?
6. What do community members think about our programs and our museum?[15]

INTERVIEWS WITH MUSEUM PROFESSIONALS

In the course of my research on cultural competence in the museum field, I spoke with museum professionals and indigenous cultural practitioners. A detailed list of the interviewees and the questions asked can be found in the appendix to this chapter. Through these interviews, the participants gave me key insights into the current views toward cultural competence, the relationship between indigenous community members and museums, as well as recommendations for how museums can build and repair relationships with communities. Based on my research and interviews, the following key conclusions were drawn: (1) Cultural competence means listening and respecting another culture; (2) Museum professionals need to acknowledge the expertise of community members and cultural practitioners; (3) Cultural competence is important to every museum staff person and at every level of the organization; (4) Colonial culture feeds into the lack of cultural competence; and (5) Institutions implementing cultural competence practices need to support the process not only conceptually, but also by providing financial support. We will explore each of these key conclusions in the following sections of this chapter.

IMPORTANCE OF LISTENING AND RESPECT

In the interviews for this project, when asked the question "What does cultural competence mean to you?" the participants responded most often with two common concepts: (a) respect for another culture and (b) engaged listening. Participant B stated that, "cultural competence at its heart is the ability to listen." It was the opinion of the participants that without a willingness to communicate, reach out, and give respect to the process of learning about another culture, one cannot become culturally competent. As Participant D stated, "If you want to know about a culture, you have to go spend time with them." Participant F went into further detail about the listening process, stating that cultural competence includes "knowing how to ask and knowing how to listen . . . [it is about] being responsive to the answers that you get and the guidance that you're given."

Overall, these interviews highlighted the fact that museum professionals need to become engaged and respectful listeners to community members. This means taking the time and creating the space to host conversations about what the community wants from the museum and the museum's staff. Being responsive to the desires of community members in setting the terms for what the museum can (and cannot) share about their culture and how it is interpreted and for the ways the museum cares for its cultural resources must be a high priority to a museum aspiring to cultural competence. In addition to listening, museums also need to take to heart these conversations, act on what is shared, and be transparent about the process of listening and planning. It is important, as well, that the museum share in a transparent way how it may have failed the community in its past and own colonial practices, assumption-based interpretation, or exclusive (vs. inclusive) programming.

RECOGNIZING COMMUNITY EXPERTISE

There is a ʻōlelo noʻeau [Hawaiian proverb] that says "ʻaʻohe pau ka ʻike i ka hālau hoʻokahi [all knowledge is not taught in the same school]."[16] We, as museum professionals, tend to hold academic degrees in high esteem, sometimes higher than lived experiences. As a field, we must shift this way of thinking if we are to truly serve our communities in the best way possible. During the course of my interviews, the participants agreed that although museum professionals may have a field of expertise, they are not the expert when interpreting a culture they do not belong to, nor are they the authority for deciding what traditional care methods to employ in collections care. As Participant F stated, when museum professionals work with communities, they need to be "putting authority behind [community knowledge] and not thinking unilaterally and doing what they think is best, but really being inclusive and ceding the authority." Participant H stated that, "there are people from our communities that are the experts. When I think about a museum professional, it is an ongoing learning process. You're not ever going to know everything about something. You may know a lot, but you're never going to be a full expert. We look to our community as being the entity to present that knowledge the way they see fit." The importance of acknowledging that museum professionals are not the experts and allowing for communities to interpret their own history was highlighted through the interview with Participant I, who stated that "narratives [about indigenous people] shape how the public interfaces with us, and they are foundational. Museums, because they are so widely used by public schools for the hands-on piece of the curriculum on indigenous people, if they don't get it right they are laying false, misleading, and stereotypical information about Native people, which is almost impossible to unsettle. . . . It is almost as if once that foundation is laid in the 3rd and 4th grade it becomes very difficult [for people] to see Native people as living, dynamic individuals."

CULTURAL COMPETENCE THROUGHOUT THE ORGANIZATION

It is of utmost importance that everyone within the organization (staff, volunteers, and board members) increase their cultural competence. Throughout the organization, an environment of cultural openness, understanding, and empathy must be built if museums are to grasp the full power of cultural competence. This was highlighted in my interviews. Participant I spoke about how museums that don't engage with communities in the interpretation of their culture often have stereotypical and racist content in their education programs and exhibits. Another interviewee offered that frequently, if a museum incorporates any type of training about indigenous culture, they will only bring in one Native person to do a training for docents, but they do not provide a similar training for the board of trustees or executive staff; the people who are doing everything behind the scenes often have no idea about the legacy of genocide or the history of the collection that they steward.

There remains a need for a field-wide standard or set of expectations for cultural competence training in our field. This is an essential component that is still missing. Although at the time of this interview, Participant I expressed that there were a handful of institutions starting to make cultural competence training central to the functions of their specific museum. To name two examples, the San Diego Museum of Man, now the San Diego Museum of Us, hosts a decolonization in-house training for their staff and board of directors, and the San Jose Children's Museum has begun conducting cultural competence research to implement at their institution. Although at the time of my research there was a very small sample of museums implementing cultural competence training, these two institutions mark a start in establishing this type of training as essential. Now, five years after my initial research, I'm happy to report that more museums are developing and implementing cultural competence training. This shows not only how important cultural competence is to our field, but how museums are embracing the need for it. I'm happy to share that the organization I currently work for (Ohio History Connection), is conducting cultural competence training for their American Indian policy. It is a mandatory training for all the organization's staff throughout different departments. This type of adoption of training and education programs related to cultural competence demonstrates to the organization, and to some extent to the field at large, that the relationships with communities, especially indigenous communities, is important to do effectively.

IMPACTS OF COLONIAL CULTURE

Museums are colonial institutions. Our field's history is rooted in this legacy. We must acknowledge this if we are to move forward. Participant B summed this up in the statement that "cultural competence means recognizing that we live in a colonial culture and that we've been conditioned that way. . . . It means examining how our thinking and our institutions are affected by [colonialism] and looking at ways that we and our institutions can become informed about that history, how it manifests today and how we can make decisions to change that [thinking] for the betterment of society as a whole." Ways that museums can address their colonial histories is to follow examples of other institutions, such as the Museum of Us, who have developed and implemented a number of policies addressing their colonial history.

The first policy addressing the curating of ancestral remains states that the Museum of Us will "only accession and/or curate human remains when express written permission is given to do so by the deceased individual, their next of kin, or an authorized designee of the descendant community."[17] Through this policy, the museum aims to repatriate ancestors to their home communities or, when deemed appropriate by these communities, care for the ancestors at the museum.

The second policy they enacted is called the Colonial Pathways Policy. It highlights the museum's commitment, beyond following applicable state and federal laws, to decolonizing and improving the cultural competence of their organization by analyzing the ways that cultural resources came to be at the museum. It states that the Museum of Us will

> accession and/or curate Indigenous cultural resources only in instances where it has documented consent to do so from the Indigenous community, or when it can demonstrate that the cultural resource left an Indigenous community through a decolonized pathway. . . . SDMoM will establish a process for reviewing all the Indigenous cultural resources currently held at the Museum in consultation with descendant communities to determine their preference for disposition. Disposition might include ongoing stewardship at the Museum, return to the community [repatriation], or any other mutually determined outcome consistent with applicable law.[18]

In addition to the example set for by the Museum of Us, the Ohio History Connection passed in 2019 an American Indian policy which provides employees, board committees, and volunteers of the organization a framework for best practices to establish and maintain successful and meaningful relationships with federally-recognized Indian tribes. The policy acknowledges that this shift in organizational mindset is "an important step towards bridging the divide and healing through education and partnership."[19]

These policies are excellent examples of a museum holding themselves accountable and working to become increasingly culturally competent through decolonization and community engagement practices.

FUNDING MATTERS

In order to implement cultural competence practices in a museum, there must be funding to support the initiative. Without putting funding behind implementing cultural competence training for museum staff, the initiatives are bound to fail because they do not have the support from throughout the institution, nor the support to pay the necessary expenses related to cultural competence training. The museum where Participant B works does an excellent job of putting resources into professional development. They highlighted this through the following statement: "We have provided ongoing professional development to the full staff and to the board on decolonization ideas and initiatives. As we move the institution forward and develop policies, we [will continue to] provide those policies and training to the full staff and board so that they can be approved and adopted. We also encourage staff to look at outside opportunities. We sent a number of staff up to two day training in Seattle and Portland about undoing institutional racism."[20] In addition to placing funding emphasis on cultural competence training, the museum must also be willing to put funding into implementing these policies. For example, setting aside funding for community consultation meetings and for paying cultural practitioners for their time and knowledge. Unfortunately, it seems to be a standard practice that museums do not value the time and knowledge imparted by cultural practitioners in the same way that they value, for example, a museum educational consultant or conservator's time and knowledge. This sentiment was expressed by several of the participants interviewed. In order to implement cultural competence practices, funding must be set aside so that the meaningful work is viewed as an investment made for the betterment of the organization and for attitudinal change.

RECOMMENDATIONS FOR MOVING FORWARD TOGETHER

Based upon my research, I recommend the following to museums interested in implementing cultural competence moving forward. These recommendations are discussed at length in the subsequent sections.

1. Cultural competence training must be required for all museum professionals.
2. Cultural competence must be embraced in the organizational mindset and business practices.
3. Acknowledge that cultural competence is an ongoing process.
4. Museums must stop waiting and reach out to communities.
5. Adopt an institutional mindset that community knowledge is essential and commit to spending the time and money necessary to do this work effectively.

MANDATORY CULTURAL COMPETENCE TRAINING

In order for museums to be successful in building and repairing relationships with communities, they must start by having ongoing and required training for all museum staff. This must be part of the onboarding process and continuing professional development for everyone that works for the institution—from the board of directors to the visitor services staff selling tickets. I believe that museum educators, as professionals that develop and implement learning opportunities, are in an excellent position to help create these trainings.

I recommend an in-depth at focuses on:

1. The history of the community that the museum is seeking to build a relationship with and engagement with local members of the community.
2. The history of the museum field and its relationship with the specific community that the museum wishes to work with.
3. The specific history of the institution and its relationship with the community it wishes to engage with.
4. The museums' collection, including elements in the collection that fall under Native American Graves Protection and Repatriation Act (NAGPRA) and represent its colonial legacy.
5. Basics of cultural competence.
6. Steps to implement cultural competence practices in the museum.

Guest speakers at this workshop would include respected representatives chosen by the community members and museum professionals from other institutions where cultural competence practices are already being implemented. Measuring the success of cultural competence training will be an ongoing process and will most likely be a qualitative, rather than quantitative, measure. Museums can see if their trainings are successful by assessing any difference in mindset their staff demonstrates through their work and their interpersonal relationships. A change in mindset is extraordinarily hard to measure and impossible to change without the individual acknowledging its importance, but it can be reflected in the way that individuals approach their work.

One way to begin to measure this change in mindset toward becoming more culturally competent is to start with an evaluation survey both before and at the end of the training to see if a change in mindset has begun as well as following up the training with check-ins with the staff's supervisor around issues of cultural competence. The initial evaluation survey could ask questions such as the following and be used as a tool to drive future conversations.

1. Was this training helpful to you?
2. How has this cultural competence training changed the way that you view your work?
3. How do you see yourself implementing cultural competence in your work?
4. What further resources can be provided to you to help you increase your level of cultural competence?

CULTURAL COMPETENCE MUST BE EMBRACED IN THE ORGANIZATIONAL MINDSET AND BUSINESS PRACTICES

Museums need to start implementing cultural competence practices from the beginning of the staffing process, starting with recruiting and hiring. This means that cultural competence must be embraced and incorporated into the organizational mindset and moved to the forefront of its business practices, including the aforementioned onboarding procedures and ongoing professional development opportunities. Not only will this allow the museum to hire individuals who either are, or committed to be, culturally competent individuals, but it will also show external partners and community members that the museum is committed to these practices. In terms of hiring, interview teams can center their conversations with prospective candidates around cultural competence questions. Examples of these types of questions are:

1. What value do you see in incorporating multiple viewpoints, both academic and traditional knowledge, into your work?
2. Can you tell me of a time when it was more important for you to listen than to talk?
3.   How do you see your worldview as shaped by the culture in which you were raised?
4. Has there ever been a time in which your values were challenged by someone with a different perspective? How did you handle the situation?

In addition to requiring culturally competent business practices, working with communities in the interpretation of their culture and care of their objects must be a required job duty for museum professionals, especially those designing or administering programs for the public.

ACKNOWLEDGE THAT CULTURAL COMPETENCE IS AN ONGOING PROCESS

Cultural competence is a process. It takes time, effort, and an open mind. I believe that cultural competence is a skill that museum professionals must constantly improve upon while acknowledging that it is not possible for any one person or organization to ever truly become completely culturally competent. We will always have more to learn and biases that we must overcome. Part of the process of becoming increasingly culturally competent is acknowledging this fact and yet constantly striving to improve. As museum educators, you will see this firsthand as you develop, evaluate, and change your programs to becoming increasingly culturally competent and welcoming.

MUSEUMS MUST STOP WAITING AND REACH OUT TO COMMUNITIES

The famous phrase "if you built it, they will come" does not serve museums well. Oftentimes we believe that if we create a program, install an exhibit, or host an event that community members will find their way to us. We just need them to walk through the door. But often this approach simply does not work. Why? It is due to many factors, but when it comes to cultural competence we must acknowledge that museums haven't always been welcoming places, especially for communities who have been victimized or erased by museum curators, educators, and other staff. In fact, your museum still may not be a welcoming place. We, as a field, must stop waiting for communities to walk through our doors and reach out to us. Museums must take the first step in reaching out; we must go outside the four walls of our institutions and into the community. We must respectfully ask how we can become more welcoming and culturally competent places. Don't go with expectations. Go to listen and learn. One of the people that I interview, Participant H, eloquently stated, "[cultural competence] is a matter of respect and being open minded to what the community has to say about the cultural material . . . [museum professionals need to] put that ego aside and listen to what our communities say about the collections that they are stewards of and allow [the community] to provide more insight into the collection as well as providing insight into exhibition content and overall input into the museum."

COMMUNITY KNOWLEDGE IS A GIFT AND BUILDING TRUST TAKES TIME

Realize that when community members share knowledge with the museum that it is a gift. Museum professionals must respect that they have no right to knowledge and should not feel entitled to receive it. Respect that any knowledge being imparted to you is a gift. Also, be sure to understand what knowledge is being shared with you that is for your ears only and not meant to be shared in a museum program. Asking questions is OK but be respectful and be open to the idea that community members may not want certain knowledge to be shared with the general public. Based on what I was taught by different elders that mentored me in some indigenous communities, certain knowledge and activities are only conducted by a specific gender (male or female) and other knowledge or activities are conducted by a specific age group (youth or elders).

When this knowledge is gifted to you, I believe that you must respectfully act upon it in an appropriate manner. Or, if knowledge is not shared with you that must be respected. I'll give personal examples of what I mean. The first is an example of a cultural practice around handling cultural resources and the second an example of respecting knowledge that is not yours to know.

The first example is something I learned firsthand while working for the California State Indian Museum. During the course of my work there, I had the opportunity to care for and clean the basketry collection. The staff worked as a team looking to remove any damaging materials from the baskets and safely clean them. I had finished a very large burden basket and next on the rotation was a jump dance basket. Having been previously taught by an elder that regalia for men and women should not be touched by the opposite gender, I politely asked to switch with a male colleague the baskets that we would be working on in order to show my respect to this cultural practice.

The second example is from my time working at Iolani Palace. During my tenure, I had the honor to organize two separate evenings to welcome new kahili (feather standards) into the Palace under cultural protocol conducted by a respected cultural practitioner. These kahili were created by a master feather worker in honor of King Kalakaua and Queen Kapiolani. Throughout the process of planning these evenings, I was very careful to ask enough questions to make sure that the Palace was ready to welcome the kahili (such as what doors needed to be opened) without prying into the exact protocol that was conducted. It was my way of showing respect to the cultural practitioner and the process. Essentially, I didn't want to ask for knowledge that was not mine to keep, such as what every part of the

Teresa Williams Valencia

protocol meant or why and how it was done. I simply wanted to create a welcoming and open space where the cultural practitioner could conduct the protocol in a way that they saw fit without inserting myself as an outsider to the culture into the process.

FINAL THOUGHTS

By recognizing that museums operated from an ethnocentric paradigm for centuries, museum professionals are now taking the first steps toward cultural competence. In order to be successful in implementing cultural competence in a museum, it has to be made important to every staff person. This means that everyone from the board of directors to the visitor services staff selling tickets to frontline educators need to understand the basic concepts of cultural competence and uphold the institution's desire to practice it. In order to reflect cultural competence's importance to the institution, it must be listed on job descriptions, written into the institution's values and, most importantly, made part of the everyday dialogues within the institution.

Through sharing my research, I hope that our field will continue to acknowledge the need for cultural competence in their institutions. I also hope that museums will find concrete reasons why they should implement cultural competence training in their institutions and consult with communities on the interpretation of their culture and the care of their cultural resources.

This research, however, is just the beginning to understanding the need for cultural competence in building and repairing relationships between museums and communities. More research and interviews need to be done into individual communities' experiences with museums because although the information included in this chapter can help museums begin the process of cultural competence, individual communities have their own unique backgrounds, experiences, and desires from their engagement with museums that must be recognized.

My research and experience is just one voice among many that is contributing to the conversation about the need for cultural competence in the museum field moving forward. We must work together in this process. Working face-to-face with communities and visitors to your institution puts you in a unique position to witness the effects of cultural competence firsthand. I challenge you to look for ways to increase your own cultural competence and to challenge your museum to do the same. Start researching, listening, and learning from the communities you serve and whose histories you share. Help plan a cultural competence workshop for your museum. Research and write a land acknowledgment recognizing the indigenous peoples whose land you call home.[21] As museum educators, feel empowered to take these first steps toward the goal of creating meaningful and authentic relationships with communities.

DISCUSSION QUESTIONS

1. How can cultural competence help improve your practice as a museum professional?
2. How would increasing the cultural competence of your museum's staff, volunteers, and board members help your organization address contemporary social justice movements and conversations around diversity, equity, and inclusion?
3. How has a lack of cultural competence impacted your museum? What was learned from this situation? How did the museum move forward?
4. How do you believe that respecting community knowledge and input in interpretation at your museum would benefit both the community and your organization?
5. What commitments can you make to increasing your own cultural competence? What commitments can you make to helping your organization increase its cultural competence?

NOTES

1. Teresa Williams Valencia, "Building Bridges: Cultural Competency in Museums," Master's thesis. John F. Kennedy University, 2016.
2. National Center for Cultural Competence, Definitions of Cultural Competence, https://nccc.george town.edu/curricula/culturalcompetence.html.
3. National Center for Cultural Competence, Definitions of Cultural Competence, https://nccc.george town.edu/curricula/culturalcompetence.html.
4. National Center for Cultural Competence, Definitions of Cultural Competence, https://nccc.george town.edu/curricula/culturalcompetence.html.
5. Lonnie Bunch, "It Is Time for America to Confront Its Tortured Racial Past," Last modified on May 31, 2020, https://www.smithsonianmag.com/smithsonian-institution/it-time-america-confront-its-tor tured-racial-past-180975012/.
6. Marjorie Schwarzer, *Riches, Radicals and Rivals: 100 Years of Museums in America* (American Association of Museums, 2006), p.10.
7. Marjorie Schwarzer, *Riches, Radicals and Rivals: 100 Years of Museums in America* (American Association of Museums, 2006), p.11.
8. Marjorie Schwarzer, *Riches, Radicals and Rivals: 100 Years of Museums in America* (American Association of Museums, 2006), p.11.
9. Haunani-Kay Trask, *From a Native Daughter: Colonialism and Sovereignty in Hawaii* (University of Hawaii Press, 1993), p. 252.
10. American Association of Museums, *Mastering Civic Engagement: A Challenge to Museums* (American Association of Museums Press, 2002), p. 9.
11. Elizabeth Duclos-Orsello, "Shared Authority: The Key to Museum Education as Social Change" (*Journal of Museum Education*, 2013), p. 122.
12. Karen Halttunen, "Groundwork: American Studies in Place," *American Quarterly* 58, no. 1 (March 2006): p. 12.
13. Noelle Kahanu, "Seeding Authority: A Symposium on Decolonizing Museums," University of Hawaii at Manoa. November 9–10, 2018.
14. Ben Garcia, et al., "Ceding Authority and Seeding Trust" (American Alliance of Museums, 2019), https://www.aam-us.org/2019/07/01/ceding-authority-and-seeding-trust/.
15. Margaret Kadoyama, *Museums Involving Communities* (American Alliance of Museums, 2018).
16. Mary Kawena Pukui, *ʻŌlelo Noʻeau: Hawaiian Proverbs & Poetical Sayings* (Bishop Museum Press, 1997).
17. Ben Garcia, Kelly Hyberger, Brandie Macdonald, and Jaclyn Roessel, "Ceding Authority and Seeding Trust" (American Alliance of Museums, 2019), https://www.aam-us.org/2019/07/01/ceding-authori ty-and-seeding-trust/.
18. Garcia et al., "Ceding Authority and Seeding Trust."
19. The Ohio History Connection, American Indian Policy, 2019.
20. Participant B, personal communication, October 13, 2016.
21. "Land Acknowledgement: You're on California Indian Land, Now What? Acknowledge Relationships to Space & Place Toolkit," California Indian Culture and Sovereignty Center and California State University San Marcos American Indian Studies. Accessed on April 29,2021, https://www.csusm.edu/cicsc/land .pdf.

BIBLIOGRAPHY

American Association of Museums. *Mastering Civic Engagement: A Challenge to Museums*. American Association of Museums Press. 2002.

"American Indian Policy." The Ohio History Connection. Accessed April 29, 2021, https://www.ohio history.org/OHC/media/OHC-Media/Documents/OHC-American-Indian-Policy-Board-Ap proved-2019-09-19.pdf.

Bunch, Lonnie. "It Is Time for America to Confront Its Tortured Racial Past," *Smithsonian Magazine.* Last modified on May 31, 2020.

"Definitions of Cultural Competence." National Center for Cultural Competence. Accessed April 29, 2021, https://nccc.georgetown.edu/curricula/culturalcompetence.html.

Duclos-Orsello, Elizabeth. "Shared Authority: The Key to Museum Education as Social Change." *Journal of Museum Education*. 2013.

Garcia, Ben, Kelly Hyberger, Brandie Macdonald, and Jaclyn Roessel, "Ceding Authority and Seeding Trust." American Alliance of Museums. July 1, 2019.

Halttunen, Karen. "Groundwork: American Studies in Place." *American Quarterly* 58, no. 1 (March 2006): p. 12.

Kadoyama, Margaret. *Museums Involving Communities*. American Alliance of Museums. 2018.

Kahanu, Noelle. "Seeding Authority: A Symposium on Decolonizing Museums." University of Hawaii at Manoa. Presentation on November 9–10, 2018.

"Land Acknowledgement: You're on California Indian Land, Now What? Acknowledge Relationships to Space & Place Toolkit," California Indian Culture and Sovereignty Center and California State University San Marcos American Indian Studies. Accessed on April 29, 2021, https://www.csusm.edu/cicsc/land.pdf.

Pukui, Mary Kawena. *ʻŌlelo Noʻeau: Hawaiian Proverbs & Poetical Sayings*. Bishop Museum Press. 1997.

Schwarzer, Marjorie. *Riches, Radicals and Rivals: 100 Years of Museums in America*. American Association of Museums. 2006.

Trask, Haunani-Kay, *From a Native Daughter: Colonialism and Sovereignty in Hawaii*. University of Hawaii Press. 1993

Valencia, Teresa Williams. "Building Bridges: Cultural Competency in Museum." Master's thesis, John F. Kennedy University. 2016.

APPENDIX A—RESEARCH METHODOLOGY FOR MASTER'S THESIS PROJECT

As part of my research, I conducted a literature review and interviews as well as examined job announcements for museum curators and collections managers. Both the literature and the interviews were in alignment and called for the need for cultural competency. Most of the literature specifically illuminated how other fields, such as medical and education fields, already place an importance on cultural competency while the literature about museum-specific cultural competency practices was lacking. However, the interviews conducted highlighted the cultural competency work being done presently in museums based on these foundations. Unfortunately, although the interviews showed work was being done around cultural competency in museums, it was mainly inward facing, hence the reason why the terms cultural competency, cultural sensitivity, and cultural awareness were not openly listed on job descriptions. This shows that the theory is being discussed, but that the practice of cultural competency in museums is still lacking. Throughout the research process, I spoke with nine participants from three main groups: museum curators/collections managers, museum executive directors, and indigenous community members. Through these interviews, the participants provided key insights into the current views toward cultural competency, the relationship between indigenous community members and museums as well as recommendations for how museums can build and repair relationships with indigenous communities.

Each participant was asked different questions, ranging from 9–11 questions, depending upon the role that they played in the museum field. A full list of interviewees can be found in this document as appendix B, and interview questions can be found at the end of this document as appendix C. In addition to interviewing participants, I also examined twenty-six job announcements for museum curators and collections managers. These job announcements were pulled from job search engines as well as positions listed directly on individual museum websites. They came from a range of different types of museums, such as history, science, and art, but all jobs worked in some way with interpreting indigenous culture or stewarding objects from indigenous communities. Unfortunately, I did not find any mention of the words cultural competency, cultural sensitivity, or cultural awareness. Only two of the jobs listed working with indigenous community members as a key component to the position.

APPENDIX B—LIST OF INTERVIEW PARTICIPANTS

Due to the sensitive nature of these communications and out of respect to the individuals that participated, the names and locations where these individuals work have been kept private.

1. Participant A: A native Hawaiian museum curator who actively works with the Native Hawaiian community to interpret Hawaiian culture, both from a historic and contemporary perspective.
2. Participant B: A deputy director of a museum actively seeking to decolonize their institution by training their staff in decolonization techniques and working with indigenous community members to write and design exhibitions.
3. Participant C: A Chumash assistant museum director and registrar who cares for indigenous collections and is also a cultural practitioner.
4. Participant D: A Chumash cultural practitioner who actively works with museums so that they may accurately and respectfully interpret indigenous culture.
5. Participant E: A collections and education director who works at one of the largest museums in the United States that interprets indigenous cultures and has been in the museum field for over twenty years.
6. Participant F: A director of collections at a large California museum that houses indigenous collections and works with the indigenous communities in the area to ensure objects are cared for using traditional care methods.
7. Participant G: A director of an indigenous institution who has worked with museums regarding the Native American Graves Protection and Repatriation Act (NAGPRA) since the start of the law and continues to build training programs to help museums engage with indigenous communities.
8. Participant H: A Paiute community outreach specialist who helps build bridges between indigenous communities and the museum so that they may work together to develop exhibitions and education programs.
9. Participant I: A Chumash curator and museum studies professor who worked at an art museum and collaborated with indigenous community members to develop exhibitions which tell the story of indigenous people both historically and contemporarily.

DATES AND TYPES OF COMMUNICATION WITH INTERVIEWEES

Anonymous, personal communication, October 4, 2016, in person
Anonymous, personal communication, October 13, 2016, phone
Anonymous, personal communication, October 27, 2016, phone
Anonymous, personal communication, November 1, 2016, phone
Anonymous, personal communication, November 8, 2016, phone
Anonymous, personal communication, November 15, 2016, phone
Anonymous, personal communication, November 17, 2016, phone
Anonymous, personal communication, November 18, 2016, phone

APPENDIX C—LIST OF INTERVIEW QUESTIONS

Each participant was asked different questions, ranging from 9–11 questions, depending upon the role that they played in the museum field.

Interview Questions for Museum Professionals:

1. What does cultural competency mean to you?
2. Do you think cultural competency is an important part of a curator's work? If so, why?
3. What does cultural competency look like in your museum?
4. What cultural competency training is available to you through your institution or professional development resources and how often is this training offered?
5. Has a lack of cultural competency impacted your museum? If so, how?
6. What are examples of curatorial policies at your institution related to cultural competency?
7. What is the process your institution goes through to incorporate indigenous voices in its curatorial practices?
8. How do you ensure that indigenous communities are accurately represented in your museum?
9. Does your museum actively engage with cultural practitioners of the indigenous communities which your museum interprets? If so, how were these individuals selected?
10. Will you please share with me your collections management policy, cultural competency training materials, and procedures for consulting indigenous communities?

Interview Questions for Museum Executive Directors:

1. What does cultural competency mean to you?
2. Do you think cultural competency is an important part of your organization's work? If so, why?
3. What does cultural competency look like in your museum?
4. What cultural competency training is available to you and your staff through your institution or professional development resources? If so, how often is this training offered?
5. Has a lack of cultural competency impacted your museum and its business practices? If so, how?
6. What part of your business practices highlights the importance on your staff being culturally competent?
7. Is cultural competency a trait that you look for in new hires or look to develop in your current staff?
8. What relationship exists between your museum and the indigenous communities in your area?
9. What is the process your institution goes through to incorporate indigenous voices in its museum practices?
10. Does your museum actively engage with cultural practitioners of the indigenous communities which your museum interprets? If so, how were these individuals selected?
11. Will you please share with me your organization's collections management policy, cultural competency training materials, and procedures for consulting indigenous communities as well as hiring notices you've posted for museum curators?

Interview Questions for Indigenous Community Stakeholders / Cultural Practitioners:

1. What does cultural competency mean to you?
2. Do you think cultural competency is an important part of a museum's work? If so, why?
3. What relationship(s) exists between your community stakeholders and museums that interpret your culture?
4. How were these relationships established? Who initiated the relationship and what was the motivation for starting the conversation between your community and the museum that interprets your culture?
5. To your knowledge, are indigenous voices incorporated into collections care, exhibitions, and interpretive materials at museums that house objects and represent your community?

6. Has a lack of cultural competency impacted your community's relationship with museums that interpret or house objects from your culture? If so, how?
7. What are your recommendations for building and improving relationships between your community and museums that interpret your culture?
8. What are some of the most important things that you want curators interpreting and caring for objects from your culture to know?
9. Will you please share with me any materials that you have developed for working with museums? Examples of these materials may include museum-indigenous community consultation policies, cultural knowledge guidelines for museum curators and recommended or required traditional care policies for curators taking care of sacred objects and objects of cultural patrimony for your culture.

12

The New Children's Museum

INNOVATING WAYS TO SUPPORT TODAY'S CHILDREN

Tomoko Kuta

ABSTRACT

Appropriating practices from the arts and from methodologies of play can provide rich, engaging ways to connect with visitors of all ages in children's museums. Thoughtfully-designed, creative art installations and hands-on art-making provide ways for children to develop a variety of skills and have fun! Integral to successful engagement with children and families is a well-trained frontline staff who can facilitate immersive, hands-on experiences that foster participation and learning.

> Art has the role in education of helping children become like themselves instead of more like everyone else.
>
> —Sydney Gurewitz Clemens

INTRODUCTION: EARLY CHILDHOOD EXPERIENCES

I was born in Japan in the late 1960s and spent my childhood years in three different countries. From a very young age, wherever I lived, I had the freedom to roam and play outdoors with friends of different ages often unaccompanied by adults. In Japan in the suburbs of Tokyo, at an early age, I walked to friends' houses. Living in Tuckahoe, New York, I played in the woods behind our apartment building. In Ealing, London, I found adult attitudes toward children to be more strict, but I still rode my bicycle to the park on my own to meet friends. These experiences taught me to navigate new languages, different accents, customs and norms, and schools, and to initiate relationships with new friends and teachers.

In contrast to my 1970s childhood, today's children rarely have the opportunity to step outside their homes without an adult nearby. Today's norms are different; most caregivers do not feel comfortable letting young children go out alone. In addition, compared to childhood just a few decades ago, adults today play a very active role in organizing and directing their children's lives, including extracurricular activities such as organized sports and academic preparation.

Parents actively seek enriching experiences for their children and visiting children's museums is a rite of passage for many young families. Knowing this, many children's museums strive to deliver opportunities for free play that are largely missing from childhood today. Replicating an urban backyard experience is the goal of the New Children's Museum, the organization where I worked for almost ten years. Providing this enriching visitor experience takes the coordination of many moving parts that include the exhibitions, hands-on activities, and of course, the staff who work on the front lines.

The New Children's Museum is a nonprofit organization devoted to nurturing children and supporting families. The museum conducts its work by championing art and play. To execute its unique focus on the arts, the museum commissions artists to co-create exhibitions and programs alongside its creative team. Museum staff works with artists to build large-scale immersive art installations for children to play in. Additionally, the museum focuses on the art-making process that helps children build skills. The museum believes that children need the open-ended experiences of both play and art-making to develop as well-rounded human beings, and they need trained staff to support their activities. Over the years, colleagues from a variety of organizations have visited the museum to learn more about its practices. This chapter highlights key strategic activities—the art commissions and installations, hands-on activities, and the role of staff, in particular the playworkers at the New Children's Museum—that have helped it engage audiences in this unique art- and play-focused way.

THE NEW CHILDREN'S MUSEUM: HISTORY, MISSION, AND VISION

The New Children's Museum was founded in 1983 by six women—all mothers—who were motivated by personal and community needs. (See figure 12.1.) In its early years, the museum was located in a small unoccupied space in a shopping mall in La Jolla. In 1989, the museum moved to a warehouse

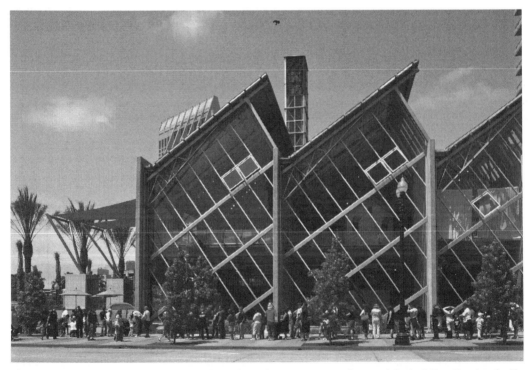

Figure 12.1 On opening day, May 4, 2008, the line of visitors wrapped around the building. *Reprinted with permission from the New Children's Museum.*

Tomoko Kuta

at its present location in downtown San Diego. After a planned closure of almost six years, in 2008, the museum reopened in a brand new building specifically designed by renowned architect Rob Wellington Quigley as a children's museum. At that time, the museum changed its name to the New Children's Museum and solidified its focus on the arts. Today, the museum is highly regarded as an arts-based children's museum that invests staff, time, and financial resources toward commissioning contemporary artists to build unique and playful large-scale art installations and offers diverse programs for children and families.

The New Children's Museum is part of the larger history of the nonprofit children's museum field that has been experiencing tremendous growth since 1990 across the United States.[1] The children's museum movement parallels the ever-deepening understanding and evolving attitudes toward raising children. Where once children were valued for their economic contributions to the family, today, childhood is accepted as a defined and delineated stage of life sacrosanct with the unique activities of education and play. Providing opportunities for children that lead to happy, healthy, and successful lives is one of society's most important goals.

Children's museums posit an interesting case study for understanding the evolving needs of families in America and how these needs are met. The first two children's museums in the United States which opened in 1899 and 1913 were located in large urban cities. These children's museums and others that followed in the early decades of the 1900s were partly the result of millions of families moving from rural to urban areas as well as immigrants settling in large American cities at the turn of the twentieth century. Families living in urban areas needed places for their children to play.

The late 1800s through the early twentieth century was also a period in which children's rights gained momentum. Major milestones included protective child labor laws and the rise of universal public education. These changes and others that followed are evidence of changing attitudes toward children and child rearing.

Economic growth in the years 1945 to 1960 helped expand America's middle class, leading to lives that for many included leisure. The nuclear family also became the household norm. Traditionally, multiple generations living under one roof allowed older, experienced family members to help raise children. Without grandparents nearby, families looked externally for support and resources. These demographic changes were accompanied by parallel surgencies in child psychology which focused on the emerging understanding that childhood is characterized by distinct stages of development and that these require certain stimuli in order to fully manifest. The concept of children as miniature versions of adults thus further waned in the twentieth century and childhood as a distinct stage of life with unique characteristics and needs led to further study and increased interest in child-rearing practices.

The proliferation of children's museums began in the 1970s, around the same time that the word "parenting" came into being.[2] Previously, focusing on child rearing had been the privilege of those with the economic means and time to do so. Today, that scenario is very different. While it is still a privilege to spend time and money on providing children access to different activities, there is greater awareness of the critical first years of a child's life and thus a strong desire and push by caregivers and professionals of diverse economic backgrounds to provide their children with opportunities to stimulate their growth in positive ways. The evolution of family life, universal public education, and the emergence of child development and psychology gave rise to new fields and industries that focus on children. Children's museums are one outcome of this.

The large and growing number of children's museums also signals shifts in families' expectations for childhood. The emphasis on childhood and its counterpart, parenting, have given rise to new areas of study and have influenced the proliferation of businesses related to psychology and education that capitalize on the needs of parents and children. Different parenting styles promote specific child-rearing practices and most of the businesses and activities appear helpful. However, some practices and parenting styles with nicknames such as "helicopter parent" and "tiger mom" also reveal trends that take controlling children's upbringing to an extreme and thus have become the focus of much recent debate.

Children's museums serve young children, typically ages two to five,[3] the period before most attend school full time and thus when many parents are looking for ways to entertain and educate their children. All children's museums aim to engage through a combination of play and learning. Staff at children's museums work hard to meet the expectation that their spaces are fun and safe while at the same time, they focus on providing activities that contribute to the development of fine and gross motor, sensory, cognitive, and social skills. Because of the need to serve large numbers of children, children's museums provide activities and build interactives that can structurally withstand the "love" of thousands of little touches, kicks, pulls, and pushes. Many children's museums include mini versions of adult worlds: grocery stores, fire trucks, and so forth, a nod to the learning that can be activated through mimicry. This type of engagement is also the result of children's museums being run by those who are at least one generation older and their norms and expectations. As is true with many facets of life, one's own experiences bear a strong influence over what is seen as important and valuable for others, especially our children.

VISITOR EXPERIENCE STUDY

Since the Brooklyn Children's Museum first opened in 1899, the field of children's museums has greatly matured. Today, there are over four hundred children's museums in the United States. As significant informal educational institutions, the drive to serve families and make real community impact have grown. As a result, research in the field about the benefits of children's museums has also blossomed. From October to December 2018, the New Children's Museum undertook its own visitor experience study with the firm Deloitte.[4] In this study, Deloitte sought to illuminate the visitor journey and make recommendations to improve visitor engagement. Employing a design thinking approach[5] to better understand visitors, Deloitte helped to uncover current visitors' journey maps to the museum, identifying the experiences of visitors as they prepared for their visit, the time spent in the museum as well as their post visit experiences. This approach shed light on the impacts of our marketing, including the museum's website and amenities such as parking and greetings from staff upon arrival. Surveys with member and nonmember families uncovered five key themes as top priority for visitors: (1) cleanliness, (2) navigation and signage, (3) safety, (4) space and layout, and (5) mixed-age areas (which pointed to the need for many families to be able to have siblings of different ages play together). What was missing from the feedback was the top priority the team and I had been emphasizing: what art installations children engage with and the different hands-on art-making activities we offered.

To understand our visitors' priorities and develop new practices to better serve them, Deloitte identified five clusters of users who exhibit specific behavior patterns in the museum setting. Calling them guardian personas, they represent the diverse behaviors, attitudes, and motivations of adults toward their museum visit. The five personas identified in the Deloitte study for the museum are: the go-with-the flow guardian, the guarded guardian, the invested member, the first-timer, and the explorer.[6] These personas helped highlight different needs of adult caregivers gathered from surveys and helped motivate the museum staff to ideate new opportunities for visitors at the museum. This study also made it very clear that depending on one's outlook as a parent or adult guardian, expectations for the museum experience vary greatly. Children's museums are sites of social intersections where diverse families with their unique norms engage and play with other families. Different parenting styles lead to different opinions about what is appropriate for children. It also leads to different outcomes in children's behaviors.[7]

WHY ART?

To understand the various ways in which the New Children's Museum engages its audience, it is important to see why and how the museum harnesses the arts to fulfill its mission. The museum focuses on the arts because it believes that exposure and engagement with the arts lead to life skills such as creativity, confidence, problem solving, interpersonal skills, critical thinking, collaboration, resilience, and optimism. These skills build character and help one to appreciate differences in respectful ways. At the museum, the emphasis on the arts translates into two broad categories of activities: exhibitions and programs.

ART INSTALLATIONS PRESENTED AS URBAN BACKYARD EXPERIENCES

Rather than present miniaturized facsimiles of the adult world like grocery stores or fire stations, the New Children's Museum turns to contemporary artists whose practices explore relevant societal themes. We capitalize on the inventiveness of artists to design large-scale immersive art installations for children and their families to explore and enjoy. The New Children's Museum partners with artists to create unique environments for children to have the kinds of experiences that running around freely once provided to earlier generations. The open-endedness of art is the critical key ingredient. The installations in the museum do not dictate any one particular way to play: children can apply their own play motivations as they enjoy the museum. To provide these opportunities, the museum team is in constant search of artists who possess the skills and interest to build interactive art installations—sculptures and environments—that engage the senses, provoke exploration, and invite physical play. Over the years, the museum has commissioned hundreds of artists and created dozens of temporary installations to fill the galleries. The team selects artists who demonstrate the potential to give children a different way to look at the world through their art. The most successful projects are led by artists who understand, love, and accept all children without condition, including their lack of adult orderliness and logic, noisiness, ability to be messy, unpredictability, and inclination to break things as they play and explore.

HANGING TOGETHER IN A GIANT HAMMOCK

One example of how the New Children's Museum works with artists is our installation, *Whammock!* completed in 2019. A longtime museum board member first introduced me to the work of artist Toshiko Horiuchi MacAdam.[8] I visited her largest installation located in Hakone, Japan, and a few years later, in 2017, I called her studio and began a two-year conversation which eventually led to a new art commission for the museum. MacAdam, an internationally-acclaimed Japanese fiber artist now living in Nova Scotia with her Canadian husband and collaborator, began her career like many other artists—with exhibitions in galleries and museums. However, at an early point in her career a shift occurred. During a gallery opening, some curious children climbed onto (and into) her hanging fiber art. Rather than chastise the children, she took this experience as a moment to reflect and pivot her work. The children were having fun and using her artwork in ways she hadn't imagined. She saw potential in how the children activated her work with their bodies. Now, many decades later, MacAdam produces elaborate, large scale hanging textiles as site-specific installations around the world for children and adults to climb into.

Whammock! was developed over two years and required many conversations and several trips by the artist and her husband to San Diego. Finally, in June 2019, the museum opened the hand-crocheted net made from forty miles of dyed and braided nylon rope. Colored in rich hues inspired by San Diego's deep blue skies, bright orange fields of California poppies, and culturally rich Mexican folk art the installation is a highlight at the museum. Measuring 18' x 60' x 25', the installation cheerfully welcomes visitors to explore and enjoy. This signature art installation provides visual pleasure, a sense of wonder about its structure and a challenge for play. Titled *Whammock!* by the artist, this large-scale climbable net is a giant communal hammock where children work together as they climb and sway together inside the net. (See figure 12.2.)

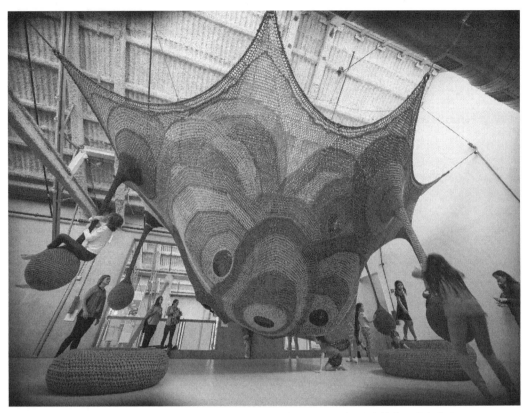

Figure 12.2 *Whammock!* by artist Toshiko Horiuchi MacAdam, 2019. © *2019 Phillipp Scholz Rittermann*

The artist created several openings in the lowest layer of the net for children to enter and begin their journey up through the installation. As children pull and wriggle their bodies up, they find successive openings in the layers above them eventually leading to an expansive open top layer carefully enclosed by a bright rainbow-colored safety net. Each child's movement in, on, and through the net causes the entire installation to move, so that everyone in the net (the net can hold two tons of weight) is also jostled. The net is gorgeous and offers a challenging climb. Most adults do not enter and are left looking up as their children ascend away from them. In this way, the artist created an adult-free zone where children from different family groups mix and play together. Sometimes a younger child may get stuck or become frightened inside the net. When this happens, I've often heard the voices of slightly older children helping them out. These kinds of encounters are exactly the intent of this artwork.

Whammock!, like the other installations in the museum, provides opportunities for children to explore on their own and decide for themselves what and how they will play. Some children climb all the way up, some are satisfied with swinging on the pendulums that hang on the outer and lower layers of the net. I once passed a young boy of about five years old excitedly telling his mother, "that was the scariest thing!" He was flush in the face and sweaty from the exertion of climbing, but you could hear and feel the sense of accomplishment and pride in his voice. Bravo young boy for stretching beyond your limits!

Art installations provide unique opportunities for kids (and adults!) to explore and exercise their curiosity. Throughout the museum, children overlay their play inclinations with what and who they come into contact with. The museum's role is to provide interactive material via the commissioned art installations, physical challenges, and "loose parts"[9] to engage children's inquisitiveness and their drive to achieve.

THE CASE FOR OPEN PLAY

The various playscapes and interactives offered at the New Children's Museum underscore the museum's open-ended approach to play—infinite play versus finite play.[10] While an open-ended approach is technically defined as not having rules, building into a space still requires careful planning. Open-ended play is also best when supported by trained staff who understand why this type of play is important and know how to encourage it. Open play gets at one of humankind's most important tenets: self-determination. Everyone, children and adults alike, needs to feel in control over their lives.

CHILDREN'S PLAY AND THE PRACTICE OF PLAYWORK

The main reason families visit the museum is to play, and boy, do children come ready to play![11] To support our visitors, we hire and train staff to interact with visitors. While the staff's first and most important priority is safety, their next focus is engagement. Staff assigned to different art installation galleries practice playwork, a practice originally founded in the United Kingdom. The idea behind playwork is simple yet profound. Playwork is the practice of supporting children that nurtures their natural inclinations, it is not about coming up with a specific activity and getting the kids to participate in it. The most important skills for playworkers to master are observation and decision making. Playwork engagement with children takes many forms. For example, sometimes a group of children may be playing in an area but something doesn't quite work or something might be missing. The exceptionally observant playworker will notice this and provide the necessary support without calling attention to themselves or insinuating a specific way of playing into the situation. This helps maintain the momentum of the playing children and allows them to further their play and even learn how to take care of similar situations in the future. (See figure 12.3.)

I once noticed a small group of children playing in a very popular art installation called *The Wonder Sound* (2016–current) by artist Wes Bruce.[12] In the space is a large fifteen-foot-tall pulley system operated by hand turning a wooden crank. When working smoothly, turning the crank activates a pulley that can carry small plush objects to the second level of the fort-like structure. But the pulley had gotten stuck and was no longer spinning. A group of children had been trying to unjam the pulley by pushing and pulling on the crank, but to no avail. There was initially a lot of chatter about what to do, but as time wore on, some kids started to walk away and the chatter began to fade. Just then, a playworker walked into the area and noticed what was going on. They approached the remaining kids at the pulley without saying anything. They noticed that something had gotten stuck in the crank's turning mechanism. They stood alongside the kids and acted just as frustrated as them. Then, they said a few words similar to the chatter of the kids, "It's not working! It's not turning!" Then, they said, "There might be something stuck in the crank. Let's take a look." The kids and playworker found a plush toy that had gotten caught in the gears. Realizing that it would take an adult to safely pull the toy out, the playworker announced, "Since I've fixed this before, I'm going to pull it out." And they did, and it fixed the problem. As soon as the crank could be spun again, the pulley was able to be loaded with plush items and sent to the kids waiting on the second level. Play resumed. The playworker joined for a few seconds in the play with the children, mimicking their actions and words and then stepped away. The group kept on playing—the play process had regained momentum. In this scenario, what didn't happen was the staff person entering the area took charge to fix the problem. The staff person shared with the children how to evaluate the situation and find the source of the problem rather than intervene in a traditional sense. Also, there was no discussion about who may have been to blame for the pulley to get stuck, so emotions remained at an even level.

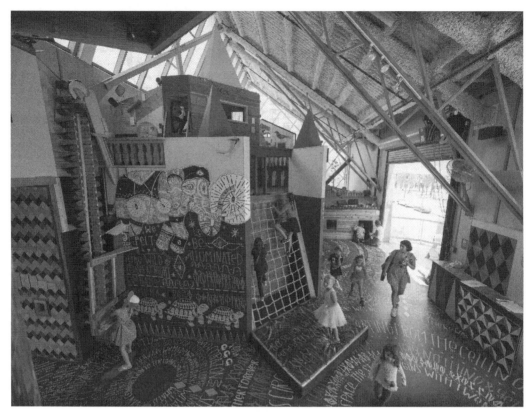

Figure 12.3 *The Wonder Sound* by artist Wes Bruce, 2016. © *2019 Phillipp Scholz Rittermann.*

Playworkers carefully observe what's going on and encourage play without leading or altering the intent of the children. They make quick decisions about if, when and how to intervene to support children in their play. They also reach out to parents and other adult caregivers to talk and learn more about them. In these ways, playworkers build relationships with the visitors to the museum. Because playworkers are at the service of children, the children begin to see these adult carers as supportive and empowering. The adults notice how they work with their children and also form their own relationships with them, thus building respect and trust that extends to how the visitors feel about the museum. In all of these ways, playwork is like a powerful multitool that adjusts to the situation at hand and helps staff interact with visitors as needed.

The intentions behind playwork are: support children in their play so that they can follow their motivations, test out their ideas, and exercise their skills. And while these seem basic, playwork requires training and practice because it is very different from the ways in which adults traditionally engage with children. For example, playworkers are not like teachers who overtly maintain their status as the more capable adult, and who know the correct answers. Playworkers do not have any agenda for the children. There may be a climbing net nearby, but playworkers do not expect all children to climb. If a child finds a different way to play with the climbing net than typical climbing, for example by weaving their hands in and out of the net, that's great. Play needs to be directed by the children to be the most effective for learning and development. Playworkers do not lead, they unobtrusively encourage play. They act in and among the children. They have no particular agenda or lesson to teach, but they remain flexible and observant in order to go with the flow the children create.

Tomoko Kuta

Unlike security guards or more conventional museum floor staff, playworkers go beyond safety and security oversight, beyond walking through spaces and picking up after children. They do not stand in areas as the overseeing "adult"; they are typically in an inconspicuous location, watching all around them but not taking an authoritarian stance. This approach is extremely important in order to let children play on their own terms without feeling watched or directed. This approach has occasionally been the source of debate and consternation among other staff at the museum. Adults are comfortable with "teacher" and "adult supervisor" but not necessarily with a fully grown adult on payroll who does not patrol areas or loudly reprimand rule breakers but rather, seemingly just watches kids and plays with them. But there is so much to playwork. It is complicated work that brings many benefits. For example, playworkers are actively aiding and teaching in ways that strongly connect with children's needs. Playwork is also empowering to the staff as they get trained on how to respond to individual situations based on their ability to make assessments and to read the natural patterns of play of children. Playwork is the antithesis of authoritative teaching, and it works best in settings where open-ended play is possible.

Another wildly popular area in the museum contained the art installation, *No rules . . . except* (2018–2021)[13] by artist Brian Dick. Based on his mentor Allan Kaprow and the series of happenings Kaprow created in the 1960s and 1970s,[14] the installation was a large room filled with mattresses covering the entire floor and walls. Other features like tires made from foam cushions completed the installation. *No rules . . . except* was a fun and high energy area of the museum where children could run, jump, and literally bounce off of the walls! Sometimes the play got rough and kids knocked into each other. Sometimes there were children who had a difficult time self-regulating and acted in ways that caused others concern. Sometimes kids started throwing the large tire cushions around, inadvertently hitting others and knocking young children over. *No rules . . . except* always had a playworker on site to support the play process of the children and to ensure that no one got seriously hurt.

While the children play, parents are often nearby, especially if their child is young. Playworkers make careful note of this. Some situations require their intervention and some do not. If adults jump in to protect their children, playworkers support that by letting it happen. For example, if an area where a young child is playing is suddenly taken over by older children whose actions may potentially hurt the young child, the adult may move the young child to a new area. That's a good response. If, also, the adults of the older children intervene by reminding their children that there are little ones around and to be more careful, that's great too. It is not the role of playworkers to shout out rules while kids play. They will intervene for safety only when it looks like a situation will escalate into a serious problem.

If some children begin to fight, playworkers first observe to see if the children can resolve the problem themselves. This hands-off approach may make many caregivers anxious, but once upon a time children of mixed ages played together far away from the eyes of adults and they had to figure out how to resolve challenges. The museum believes that problem-solving and resiliency are critical skills that all children need to develop and exercise. If the fight escalates to the point where physical harm may occur, the playworker will jump in to diffuse the situation, often by creating distractions and requiring another playworker from an adjacent area to help. However, in most cases, children resolve the fight by themselves. Allowing for self-determination is a critical component of playwork.

Why is it so important for children to regulate themselves? The answer can be found in a quote from *The Playwork Primer* by Penny Wilson, "the processes of playing . . . allow(s) the internal world of the child to come out and discover how to experience and assimilate the external world."[15] When most people think of play, they don't think about the play that has existed for millennia and that helps develop us as human beings. Most people appreciate play today for the photo ops they capture on their phones—their child playing in a field of bright orange Halloween pumpkins, kids playing in the sand at the beach or park. But play is more than a fun moment captured as an image: it impacts our development as human beings and nurtures our emotional capacities. For this to occur, children need to be allowed to act on their natural inclinations and practice self-regulation.[16]

While at times questioned, the practice of playwork has yielded many beneficial outcomes at the New Children's Museum: children are supported in their play and strong bonds have been formed among children, staff, and adult caregivers. Staff receive training about engaging with children that can transfer to all aspects of life involving interacting with others. The museum often hears about families becoming museum members and coming to the museum asking after specific staff, playworkers in particular, to see if they are working on the day of their visit.

THE NEED FOR EXPERIENTIAL LEARNING: HANDS-ON ARTMAKING

The art installations provide one way for children and their adult caregivers to engage with each other and with the museum. Through installations like *Whammock!* the museum's many art playscapes offer ways for children to use their bodies and minds to explore, promoting gross and fine motor skills as well as critical thinking. Another way in which the museum responds to the needs of children is through our daily Studios Program that includes diverse hands-on art-making activities. In this category exist our many arts education studios. The museum building comprises three floors and each floor has art installation galleries as well as studios where children can immerse themselves in hands-on art-making. These experiences give children the chance to work with different materials, tools, and concepts to facilitate curiosity to explore the world and learn new skills.

One of the main areas for creative expression is the outdoor painted object studio. Like all of the museum's endeavors, this studio is all about pushing boundaries and letting children test their assumptions. Currently, there is a 1954 Dodge truck available for children to paint on with oversized brushes and tempera paint. In this studio, kids learn how to handle wet, gooey paint on a large three-dimensional object that's outdoors where the sun, wind, and rain bear its effects. Painting on a large object alongside others makes negotiating space and movement critical. This is a particular favorite for young children where they are free to paint on a car! (See figure 12.4.)

INNOVATORS LAB

Another important area for slightly older children is the maker space. In 2016, the New Children's Museum opened a STEAM maker space now called the Rosso Family Foundation Innovators LAB. This STEAM-focused maker space promotes activities that touch on science, technology, engineering, and mathematics alongside the arts.

One of the first Innovators LAB projects engaged three contemporary artists to investigate STEAM-related concepts and develop three individual and successive workshops. Once the artists came up with their initial concepts, they worked closely with museum educators to refine the workshop, tools, and materials. Ultimately, the museum teaching artist team received training on how to facilitate the workshops with children. Teaching artists at the museum are trained artists who specialize in engaging young audiences in art-making activities and promote material exploration. The underlying philosophy of the Innovators LAB workshops parallels the playwork model: focus on the children and provide information and resources they need, encourage children's creativity and independence by allowing for flexibility in the outcome of the projects, and engage children by asking questions and also provoke them to ask questions.

The series kicked off with artist Marisol Rendón who explored buoyancy by helping young innovators design and make their own mylar balloons in a project called *Fly Together*. In her workshop, children learned about buoyancy, the properties of the gases helium and oxygen and how propellers help lift and carry objects (like airplanes) through the air. When the children completed their mylar balloon, they attached a remote controlled micro blimp motor to it. Through a software application on a tablet, the children got to test how weight, size, and shape affect lift, stability, and steering. Teaching artists encouraged participating children to design the shape of their mylar balloon after sharing im-

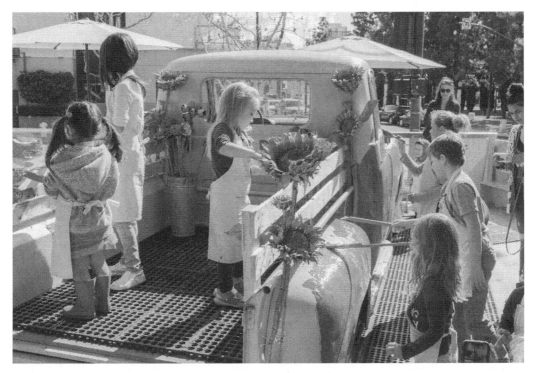

Figure 12.4 Flower Truck, 2018. *Reprinted with permission from the New Children's Museum.*

portant information about buoyancy. They helped the children through the steps of the workshop and showed multiple examples so that the children understood the activity but didn't end up adhering to any one way to complete the project. (See figure 12.5.)

The second artist in the series was Scott Shoemate, and he created a workshop called *Balance This*, which let children learn about how gravity, balance, and motion work together to keep objects like tops spinning without falling. Shoemate also demonstrated balance through weight and created beautiful wooden sculptures with adjustable parts so that children could experiment with weight and balance. For his workshop, the museum purchased a lathe which staff had to learn how to use. Teaching artists taught children, ages seven and up, how to carve a two-inch diameter candle into a symmetrical wax top based on their own designs.

Miki Iwasaki was the third artist partner in the series. As an architect, he explores the experience of manmade space and what influences our perception of the environment. For the museum, he experimented with ways for children to explore color, light, and shape. He designed a large, clear acrylic, walk-through tunnel onto which flat, translucent, colored plastic shapes could be attached. A large light mounted onto wheels could be moved around the outside of the tunnel to shine light through it and any attached colored plastic shapes. This allowed children to layer different colored flat shapes on top of each other and see how a red square on top of a blue circle could produce a ray of purple light as light passed through these two shapes. Mixing colors with light produces different results from mixing paint pigment and this activity delighted children because it gave immediate results. Museum teaching artists explained the color wheel and how primary and secondary colors are made and encouraged participants to guess outcomes as they experimented.

As programming has continued in the Innovators LAB, the museum has offered hands-on workshops for children ages seven and up that have been designed by other subject matter experts such as

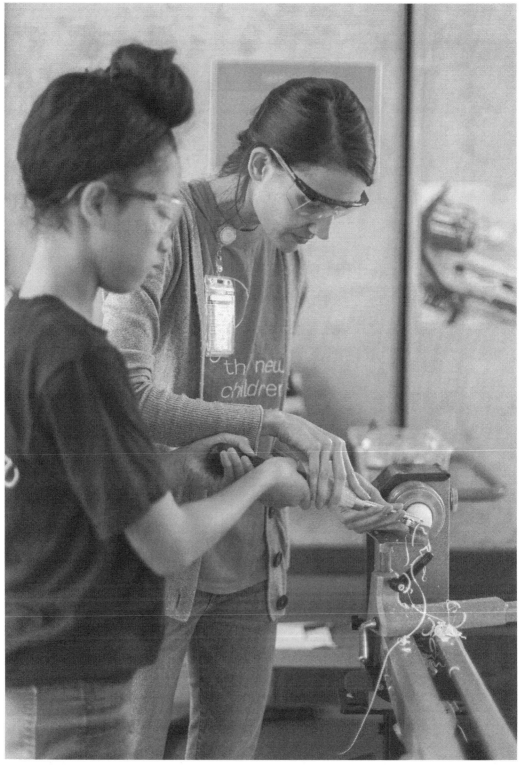

Figure 12.5 Innovators Lab, 2017. *Reprinted with permission from the New Children's Museum.*

engineers. These activities included creating a wind turbine with blades of different sizes and shapes to understand the transfer of power and best ways to harness wind for energy. Led by teaching artists, the Innovators LAB continues to champion creativity, inventive design, aesthetics and innovative uses of different materials and modes of expression through a range of creative, hands-on processes.

THE FUTURE OF CHILDREN'S MUSEUMS

On March 16, 2020, the New Children's Museum closed its doors to the public due to the rise in cases of COVID-19 in San Diego County and the need to heed health advisories against group gatherings. Immediately, the organization shifted all in-person programs to online content (regular weekly virtual offerings via the website and on social media) and then added the distribution of physical learning kits to complement the activity videos.

Regardless of the pandemic, the New Children's Museum has always been aware that there are many families who will never be able to visit the museum without support. Reasons such as economics, transportation, and even cultural differences can serve as barriers. To truly serve the community and be fully accessible and inclusive, the museum allocates resources to reach out to underserved areas in San Diego. The museum has focused on community programs such as school visits, outreach workshops, partnerships with social service agencies as well as fundraising efforts in order to offer these programs for free or heavily discounted. While being a major challenge, the closure due to the pandemic gave the museum unexpected opportunities like expanding reach to more organizations and individuals during the closure via virtual programming.

As the museum's closure continued into the beginning of the academic year in the fall of 2020, the museum converted its school visit program into a virtual school tour, which includes a prerecorded video that can be viewed on demand by the teacher at a time convenient to them and is accompanied by an activity workbook for students pre-Kindergarten through grade 6. With this pivot, the museum is serving more students than through its previous in-person field trip program because the virtual program is not bound by capacity limitations of the building. With most public schools closed to on-site learning, supporting teachers with resources is a critical mandate for the museum. It has diverted funds to offer the virtual school visit program for free to Title I schools.

The major negative result of the pandemic on the museum was the furlough and subsequent layoff of all of its frontline staff, including those who worked at the welcome desk and the playworkers and teaching artists. As the museum prepares to reopen in spring 2021, the museum is examining how to welcome back guests so that they feel safe. This involves bringing back staff who are still available from the original team and hiring new employees as needed. The goal of safety will always remain number one for the museum, but its role to engage, so that children and families find creative ways to explore and play, remains paramount. In the new post-pandemic world, the museum will devise new strategies to engage with children and develop installations and programs that reinforce the world's new post COVID-19 safety protocols. Nonprofit cultural organizations will play an important role in the massive healing that will take place as society reopens from over a year of closure. The invaluable frontline teams who directly interface with the public will serve as role models in this effort.

In addition to COVID-19, 2020 was also the year in which social justice movements calling for racial equity gained irreversible momentum. Children's museums across the United States connected through the Association of Children's Museums and made strong statements in support of Black Lives Matter, committing themselves to diversity, equity, access, and inclusion. For the New Children's Museum's next chapter, staff and board are pledging actions that will lead to a more just future. This will be expressed in how all families are welcomed, the commitment to continue to provide access to those who need support to visit, hiring a more diverse team, providing training that fights racism, building a board that reflects the community, and continuing to commission artists who share in the focus to stand up for racial equity and social justice to build community. This work is already underway.

While the circumstances in which the New Children's Museum functions has changed, the focus on the arts and experiential opportunities remain key to the organization' ability to connect with children and families. For reopening and moving forward into the future, the museum is planning new artist commissions and hands-on educational activities that will ensure its continued growth and success. The various engagement activities will be showcased by a new and restructured visitor experience team. In another year, the New Children's Museum will have new practices to share with the museum and education fields that uplift children and continue to serve and support diverse families.

DISCUSSION QUESTIONS

1. Working with artists has helped the New Children's Museum provide unique educational and play opportunities. The approach has also helped distinguish it from other children's museums. How might the creative perspectives from an artist help enrich your work while supporting your educational goals?
2. The chapter describes how playworkers approach their work, especially how they keep their focus on the child. How might this user-centric method help you expand your work with diverse audiences even in different subject areas and settings?
3. Hands-on workshops informed by subject matter experts can help increase the sophistication of educational programming. The key to success is pairing external partners with an organization's internal team so that any new proposed activities meet the needs of visitors. What unexpected subject matter experts might you connect with to amplify your programming?

NOTES

1. The Brooklyn Children's Museum, founded in 1899 was the world's first children's museum. The second was the Boston Children's Museum, opened in 1913. By 1975, there were approximately thirty-eight children's museums in the United States and an additional eighty museums opened between 1976 and 1990. Another 130 opened between 1990 and 2007. As of 2021, the Association of Children's Museums estimates that there are over 400 children's museums in the United States.
2. The verb parenting is only about forty-five years old—it came about in the 1970s. From *Act Natural: A Cultural History of Misadventures in Parenting* by Jennifer Traig.
3. Although children up to the age of twelve and sometimes older also visit and enjoy children's museums. Children's museums have also recently been offering adults-only programming.
4. Deloitte is a global provider of audit and assurance, consulting, financial advisory, risk advisory, tax, and related services, https://www2.deloitte.com/us/en.html. Findings and suggestions were captured in a final report titled, *Voice of the Visitor.*
5. Design thinking is a human-centered approach to finding solutions that include five stages of action: empathize, define, ideate, prototype, and test.
6. Deloitte study for the New Children's Museum, *Voice of the Visitor*, January 2019.
7. Research in the field of child development is rich with content about parenting styles and their impact on children.
8. Artist Toshiko Horiuchi MacAdam: https://netplayworks.com/NetPlayWorks/Home.html.
9. Loose parts, as an educational approach, is defined as providing small objects that can be manipulated into use in a variety of open-ended ways.
10. From *Finite and Infinite Game: A Vision of Life as Play and Possibility* by James P. Carse.
11. Play is recognized today as critical to healthy childhood development. The opposite of play is not work, it's depression. From *The Play Ethic* by Pat Kane.
12. Artist Wes Bruce: http://www.livethecuriouslife.com.
13. The installation *No rules . . . except* was permanently deinstalled in 2020 during the museum's closure due to COVID-19 because there was no easy way to keep the installation safely sanitized.
14. From *Childsplay: The Art of Allan Kaprow* by Jeff Kelley.

15. *Playwork Primer* by Penny Wilson, 28.
16. *Mind in the Making* by Ellen Galinsky, 12–66.

BIBLIOGRAPHY

Bateson, Patrick and Paul Martin. *Play, Playfulness, Creativity and Innovation*. Cambridge, United Kingdom: Cambridge University Press, 2013.

Brown, Stuart with Christopher Vaughan. *Play: How It Shapes the Brain, Opens the Imagination, and Invigorates the Soul*. New York: Avery, 2009.

Carse, James P. *Finite and Infinite Games: A Vision of Life as Play and Possibility*. New York: Free Press, 1986.

Dickerson, Megan and Diana Weisbrot. *Playworking the Children's Museum: A Not-Quite-How-To Guide*. Volume 1, May 2017.

Eliot, Lise. *What's Going On in There? How the Brain and Mind Develop in the First Five Years of Life*. New York: Bantam Books, 2000.

Galinsky, Ellen. *Mind in the Making: The Seven Essential Life Skills Every Child Needs*. New York: Harper Studio, 2010.

Gopnik, Alison. *The Gardener and the Carpenter: What the New Science of Child Development Tells Us about the Relationship between Parents and Children*. New York: Picador, 2016.

Kane, Pat. *The Play Ethic: A Manifesto for a Different Way of Living*. London: Macmillan, 2004.

Kelley, Jeff, *Childsplay: The Art of Allan Kaprow*. Berkeley and Los Angeles: University of California Press, 2004.

Kendi, Ibram X. *How to Be an Antiracist*. New York: Random House, 2019.

Oldenburg, Ray. *The Great Good Place: Cafes, Coffee Shops, Bookstores, Bars, Hair Salons and Other Hangouts at the Heart of a Community*. Cambridge, MA: Da Capo Press, 1989.

Simon, Nina. *The Participatory Museum*. Santa Cruz: Museum 2.0, 2010.

Traig, Jennifer. *Act Natural: A Cultural History of Misadventures in Parenting*. New York: Harper Collins, 2019.

Wilson, Penny. *Playwork Primer*. Alliance for Childhood, 2009.

Yenawine, Philip. *Visual Thinking Strategies: Using Art to Deepen Learning across School Disciplines*. Cambridge, MA: Harvard Education Press, 2013.

13

Human-Centered Improvement in Learning Institutions

Julie Smith

ABSTRACT

Centering the lived experience of those your museum aims to serve in your improvement efforts will ensure that your solutions match your problems. This chapter will share examples of how improvement efforts and systemic change designed for schools can be applied to solving problems facing museum educators. Practicing the mindsets and utilizing tools that help you see your system from the user's perspective is the first step toward making lasting change while building relationships with your community. In this chapter, we will utilize a common problem facing museum education departments (e.g., a volunteer cadre that does not reflect the diverse community they serve) to explore the process and importance of focusing on systemic change by being problem specific and centering and listening deeply to the stories of your desired audiences' experiences.

SEE THE SYSTEM

> *Every system is perfectly designed to get the outcome it is getting.*
>
> —Paul Batalden

In order to remain relevant, museums, schools, and the like, must do better at meeting the needs of today's diverse audiences. Siloed decision making, hierarchical department structures, and staff and volunteer programs that don't reflect the communities they serve are just a few of the pressing issues faced by museums. Improvement requires change. Unfortunately, in many mission-driven organizations, change often fails to bring about the desired improvement. Even when smart people are working on the right problems, they will face blind spots. However, a museum, in this case, is able to become human-centered in its improvement approaches, and begin to see the system from the lived experiences of those it aims to serve, and to engage solutions that can be built with their communities rather than for them.

Libertory Design and Improvement Science are two improvement processes used in education that are also starting to gain traction when designing educational experiences in the museum sector.[1] A critical principle of both these processes is to see the system that produces the current outcomes. This seeing is not a one-time event—especially when it comes to solving large-scale problems that are preventing departments from evolving. Seeing the system is a way of thinking, visualizing, and understanding the system you are trying to improve. Formal and informal educational settings alike are learning the importance of understanding the complexity of systemic change and centering community in the design of solutions. This chapter aims to share examples of how systemic change was designed in schools and how this approach might apply in museum settings with solving problems facing museum educators.

Community Design Partners (CDP), a team of facilitators, coaches, and advisors, has worked with formal education settings to be successful at seeing their systems through the lens of their end users—the students and families that have been disproportionately served by the current system. CDP has learned from their partners that successful improvement initiatives require challenging historically held beliefs about who has the power to make change, examining the role that data and research play in making change, and understanding how empathy becomes essential to ensure that change is sustainable over time. We believe that these mindsets, tools, and processes to "see your system" translate to any mission-driven organization, including museums. Specifically, we will explore:

- The need to **be problem-specific**
- **Two tools for seeing the system** through the lived experience of the user
- **Apply** lived experience learnings to reach your own goal

BE PROBLEM-SPECIFIC—DEVELOPING YOUR PROBLEM STATEMENT

If I had an hour to solve a problem I'd spend 55 minutes thinking about the problem and 5 minutes thinking about solutions.

—Einstein

Solving problems from a systems perspective starts with understanding the problem you are trying to solve in as deep and comprehensive a way as possible. A problem is roughly defined as an issue or outcome that is not aligned with the mission, the goals, or the organization's values. Creating a good problem statement (a description of the issue and how it's rooted in the system), is critical to guide and focus the work and to create a shared understanding of what a museum hopes to improve.

There is not a single "right way" to identify and study problems. Sometimes, groups are already charged with a specific problem to solve (e.g., diversifying the museum's programming content and format to welcome more of the community it serves) but need to understand the causes of the problem more deeply. Other times, groups come together to address a more general issue (e.g., decreasing visitation) but have not truly identified the specific problem they want to tackle. It is critical to understand that identifying and understanding a problem won't always require the same number of tools or follow a linear path. Rather, a team must embrace a systems perspective—examining how every aspect of the museum's operations may play a role in the problem—and use the tools best matched to its context and need.

To illustrate this point we will explore a problem from formal education environments that we believe is also prevalent in informal education environments. School systems across the nation struggle to create racially affirming spaces for all students. Evidence of this problem is found in the disproportionality of data from student discipline records, to attendance, to grade point averages, to post-secondary enrollment. While there are many root causes that need to be addressed that are rooted

Julie Smith

in historical context, oppression, and white supremacy, one root cause is lack of educator diversity. Research shows that having a racially diverse workforce improves outcomes for all students/learners and specifically students of color.[2] In the context of the museum, a parallel concern could be stated as: *Museum educators and frontline volunteers do not racially reflect the visitors they want to engage in their communities.* In much the same way that diverse teachers in schools help students, we can extrapolate that a more diverse team of educators in museums would help to better welcome and connect with the diverse communities they serve.

In the publication *Demographic Transformation and the Future of Museums,*[3] The Center for the Future of Museums reported:

> The U.S. population is shifting rapidly and within four decades, the group that has historically constituted the core audience for museums—non-Hispanic whites—will be a minority of the population. This analysis paints a troubling picture of the "probable future"—a future in which, if trends continue in the current grooves, museum audiences are radically less diverse than the American public, and museums serve an ever-shrinking fragment of society. (Farrell et al. 2010)

Culture + Community in a Time of Crisis: A Special Edition of Culture Track's new collaboration between LaPlaca Cohen and Slover Linett Audience Research, survey results "not only confirms but further illustrates the huge racial disparity in cultural audience composition, and [forecasts] the work ahead for the sector."[4]

These reports highlight the disparities of our systems in building racially affirming spaces to attract, engage, and support BIPOC visitors to museums. And while the problem is as complex as the identities of everyone involved, we believe that the lack of diversity among museum frontline personnel, including many of whom are volunteers, is a contributing factor.

If we are being problem-specific about this issue, we need to state the problem clearly and concisely to understand it. For the sake of this chapter, we will focus on volunteers and ask, Why is there a lack of diversity among museum volunteers? To dismantle the systems that perpetuate a predominantly white, middle-class museum volunteer cadre and imagine something new, we must first approach the problem with honesty and without starting to attach blame or solutions.

Problem statements should be:

- A statement, not a question
- A simple and short statement that captures where change is needed
- Written as a negative that could be backed up with data
- Free of acronyms and jargon

Additionally, some principles to remember in order to develop momentum and accuracy around understanding the problem include:

- Placing your organization's values and those you aim to serve in the center.
- Building an inclusive and diverse team. Ask yourself, who is included in the creation of the problem statement? Who isn't? Why or why not?
- Do not blame the people. People themselves are not the problem. Focus on systems.
- Put aside solutions until later.
- Give permission for errors and incompleteness.

Given our focus on lack of diversity in museum volunteers, some examples of problem statements, depending on the data you have available, might include:

- Our visitors' racial identities don't match our community's racial identities.
- Our museum staff, board, and volunteers aren't racially diverse.
- There is a 11 percent Latinx representation gap among our visitors.
- Racially diverse community members do not feel welcomed or represented in our museum.

Returning to our principles, when the team is considering problem statements, it should ask the following questions:

- **Is the problem blame-free?** A problem such as, "This neighborhood doesn't care about art," assumes that the community is at fault. The museum needs to employ strategies, norms, or discussions that can help keep the discussion focused on the system and not on individuals.
- **Is the problem solution-free?** A problem statement of, "We don't have enough resources," assumes that the solution is more resources, which might be true; however, ask your team what *problem* more resources would solve.
- **Who is experiencing the problem?** It is rare that a problem affects everyone in the same way.
- **Who is being considered in the problem statement and why?** Are the groups being considered in the problem statement represented on the team? Their perspective throughout the improvement process is key. Change needs to happen with them, not to them.
- **Are we actively seeking to understand the problems of historically underrepresented groups?** If yes, what is the evidence?
- **Is the problem a reasonable size and level of complexity for the team to tackle?** A problem that is too broad might sound compelling, but in reality, it may be overwhelming to tackle without narrowing it down. On the other hand, a problem that is too narrow may limit the ability to see the larger system that surrounds the problem.
- **How do we know if the problem it has identified is of reasonable size and level of complexity?** It might not know right away. It might only be through an analysis of the root cause of that problem that it sees where it needs to begin its work.

Let's apply these principles and considerations and elevate the problem statement:

Our volunteer cadre does not reflect the diverse community we serve.

Once the team has identified and clarified the problem statement utilizing the questions above, it is time to begin exploring the possible root causes of the problem.

TOOLS FOR SEEING THE SYSTEM THROUGH THE LIVED EXPERIENCE OF THE USER

After we have created our problem statement, we seek to understand the big picture and resist the urge for quick solutions at scale. We examine our own role in the current system and remain open to how we might be part of the power structures that perpetuate the status quo or outcomes of harm and disengagement. It is imperative that we include diverse perspectives from the community because they have had different, and important, experiences within the system. The goal is to create change *with* community and not *for* community. There are many useful tools that can be adapted to use for your unique and complex context. We are going to share two that have been successful with our partners.

Before utilizing any tools, it is important to start the process of systems analysis by grounding and unpacking the Liberatory Design mindset "Focus on Human Values"[5] (see figure 13.1) that reminds us that in order to create change that empowers communities from the inside out, we must place users at the center of all our work.

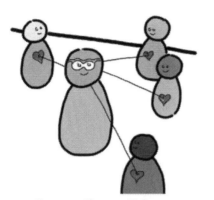

Focus on Human Values

Get to know the community we are designing with in as many different ways as possible. Anchor all of our decision-making in human values.

- Listen from a place of love. Be humble and acknowledge that you are not the expert.

- Honor the stories, experiences, and emotions people share with you.

- Stay connected to the community in all phases of the project.

- Be a participant in collective sense-making.

Focus on Human Values

Figure 13.1 Focus on Human Values. Anaissie, T. Cary, V. Clifford, D., Malarkey, T., and Wise, S. (2021). *Liberatory Design, http://www.liberatorydesign.com.*

Root Cause Analysis

A key aspect to seeing the system is identifying where the problem derives and how it impacts the organization at its core. This requires gaining a deep understanding of the problem the museum wants to solve and the reasons why that problem exists. The process is most effective when the community is represented—at a very minimum those named in the problem statement—to help identify the root causes.

There are several tools that can be used to conduct a root cause analysis. It's not the tool that matters, but the team chooses and applies the tool to most deeply understand the problem. Two root cause analysis tools are (1) the fishbone diagram and (2) empathy interviews.

Fishbone (Cause and Effect) Diagram

The cause-and-effect diagram was developed by Kaoru Ishikawa in 1943 to address quality control issues in steel manufacturing plants. Originally called the "Ishikawa Diagram" as its use spread around the world, it became better known as the Fishbone Diagram because when complete it looks like a fish skeleton. The purpose of a Fishbone Diagram is to identify the root causes of a problem. It is also a helpful way for an improvement team to visualize, discuss, and prioritize the causes they want to address. It helps illustrate a problem by visually representing the details to show how they fit together.

Facilitating the creation of a Fishbone Diagram is simple but ensuring that your museum has diverse and inclusive participants to contribute to that process can be more challenging. The more the museum is able to give voice to various parts of its system and various experiences, the more complete your insight into the system (and the problem) will be.

To begin, draw a fish with bones on chart paper (see figure 13.2). Fishbone diagram templates are readily available online, although many organizations just use post-it notes and poster boards.

1. Make sure everyone has a shared understanding of the problem statement. Then, write the problem statement in the head of the fish.

2. Individually brainstorm as many causes as you can that might contribute to the problem. The facilitator should model some examples and remind participants to:
   a. Avoid placing blame on individuals.
   b. List one reason per post-it.
   c. See the system from different points of view.
   d. For big causes, ask "why" to get more specific.
   e. Embrace "Yes and" the goal is to generate lots of ideas and not fixate on one.
3. Share and categorize the post-it notes in small groups. The facilitator should give participants the following instructions to support their process:
   a. One person shares one cause and others cluster their similar ideas until the category is exhausted.
   b. Move to the next cause and repeat the process until all ideas have been posted.
   c. As a group, examine the "bones" that have been created on the first draft of the fishbone: What can be collapsed? Are there causes that aren't really causes? What needs to be broken apart? Is there anything missing?
   d. Give each bone a short, negative description (e.g., "Volunteer training is insufficient" or "Readings are antiquated"). Labels should be descriptive enough that people outside the group can understand what they mean.
4. Examine importance and relevance by voting with *hearts* and *stars* (optional).
   a. High Leverage: Put a heart by the factor, that if addressed, you think would have a significant impact on the problem.
   b. Practical: Put a star by the factor that is within your control, that your team could address with little effort.

Document, save, and return to the fishbone. It is a type of system map and, as such, can change over time as your understanding of the system deepens. For example, you might read some research or talk to more people in the museum community or beyond who provide new information about the causes of the problem and can update your fishbone as needed.

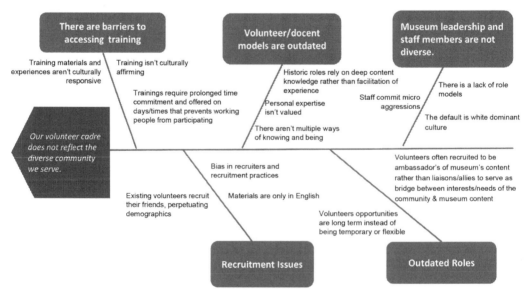

Figure 13.2 Lack of Diversity in Volunteers' Fishbone. Anaissie, T., Cary, V., Clifford, D., Malarkey, T., and Wise, S. (2021). *Liberatory Design, http://www.liberatorydesign.com*

The good news is that a fishbone diagram lets you *see* the complexity of your system and the many root causes to your problem of practice. The not so good news is that you won't be able to fully solve your problem until all of the "bones" are attended too. However, since you can only start where your team and community members have access, understanding, resources, and/or momentum you can continually return to your fishbone and design changes in a single area that will ultimately impact others. Change may be gradual, but you would not be able to do this if you didn't have a thorough picture from the beginning. Another tool to provide your team with a more thorough picture is through conversation with stakeholders and users that we structure as Empathy Interviews.

EMPATHY INTERVIEWS

Empathy means *trying* to understand the experiences and feelings of other people. It is both a mindset to embrace and a skill to practice. While one can never fully understand the experiences of another person, one can listen deeply to their stories and perspectives to uncover unacknowledged needs. The listener must simultaneously examine how their own identities, biases, values, and experiences influence how they make meaning of what others share. While many may already practice empathy, this one practice—the empathy interview—can expose the root causes of the problem and create more human-centered improvement practices.

Empathy interviews usually are one-on-one conversations that use two to four open-ended questions and follow-up probes to elicit stories about specific experiences that help uncover unacknowledged needs and root causes from a system user's perspective. Although there is well-founded attention to data and research-based strategies in museum education, it is critical to include lived experience to more accurately and directly represent the lives of communities often marginalized and excluded from traditional data and research methods (see figure 13.3). For this reason, a museum should conduct empathy interviews with humility and awareness of the potential power dynamics at play.

Since the museum will be engaging under-represented visitors, it is important to this work to build in routines for noticing and reflecting on biases that may be present in relation to the problem statement and to be mindful of how power dynamics might influence what the interviewee shares. Let

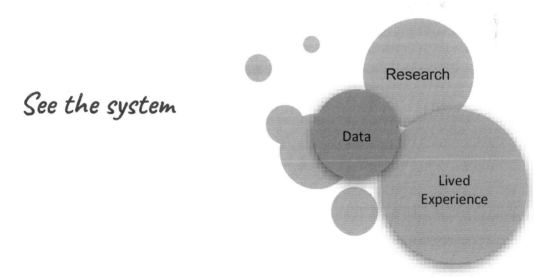

See the system

Figure 13.3 What Is Needed to See the System? Anaissie, T. Cary, V. Clifford, D., Malarkey, T., and Wise, S. (2021). *Liberatory Design, http://www.liberatorydesign.com.*

the interviewees know that the interview is optional, and they can skip any question they don't wish to answer. Let them know that the idea is for them to share stories, rather than just answer questions.

To get the person being interviewed comfortable with sharing stories, have the interviewer start with a simple introductory question. For example, "Tell me about something in your life that has brought you joy recently." Then have the interviewer move on to the 2–4 critical questions that will help unearth themes or critical attributes of a system that could help the museum identify places where it might test changes or adjustments to solve its problem.

Using our problem statement: *Our volunteer cadre does not reflect the diverse community we serve,* we might choose from the following critical questions:

- Question prompt: Tell me about a time you felt welcomed and included in a community space (such as a museum, a library, a store, a park, etc.).
- Suggested probes: What was it like? Why? How did it make you feel?
- Question prompt: Tell me about a time that you didn't feel welcomed or included in a community space.
- Suggested probes: What is it like? Why? How does it make you feel?
- Question prompt: Tell me about a place, anywhere, that you can show up as your authentic self.
- Suggested probes: What is it like? Why? How does it feel?
- Question prompt: Tell me about an experience you have had where you felt you weren't able to show up as your authentic self?
- Suggested probes: What is it like? Why? How does it feel?

Empathy interviews can provide organizations with a lot of qualitative data when protocols are in place for planning and preparation for the interview. Take notes during the interview and capture direct quotes and elevate themes across stories afterward. Note-taking ensures that we document the interview completely, rather than rely on faulty memory or our own biases of what stood out in the responses. In other words, note-taking is one way to protect against implicit bias.

PREPARING FOR THE INTERVIEW

Empathy interviews might seem straightforward but they actually require specific mindsets and technical skills that can be improved through practice. Training interviewers is an important part of preparation. Norming on the purpose of the interview will support the interviewer in what to listen for and where to probe for more details and deeper understanding. Choosing who will be on the interview team is also important, but the most important consideration, even more so than which questions will be asked, is who will be interviewed. Choosing to listen deeply to volunteers and community members who have been historically underrepresented in the organization is a way to operationalize equity. It is important to intentionally target the ideal people to interview and to be aware of who you are leaving out of the process. If only people with typical experiences are interviewed, empathy interviews will only confirm what the museum already knows.

In addition, the following checklist can help ensure that your museum's interviewer training focuses on important aspects of the process.

- **Give space.** Pay attention to how the interviewee is feeling and responding. Never force a story. Be aware that your questions may trigger past trauma. Give space and stop the interview at any time.
- **Stay neutral.** Be careful not to imply that any question has a right answer nor suggest an answer.
- **Be aware of your own bias.** Everyone has biases. The first step is to acknowledge the possible biases you have based on cultural, linguistic, and racial identities. Practice self-awareness and

Practice Self-Awareness

- Acknowledge and challenge our assumptions.
- To surface what we don't know, ask: "What is unfamiliar to me in this situation? Why?"
- Ask: "How does my identity- myrace, class, gender, or another identifier- position me in society relative to privilege and oppression?"
- Ask: "How might my identity impact people and process?"
- Seek out new knowledge about privilege and understanding of equity.

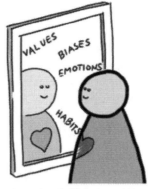

Practice Self-Awareness

Who we are determines how we design. Looking in the "mirror" reveals what we see, how we relate, and how our perspectives impact our practice.

Figure 13.4 Practice Self-Awareness. Anaissie, T. Cary, V. Clifford, D., Malarkey, T., and Wise, S. (2021). *Liberatory Design, http://www.liberatorydesign.com.*

get curious about what your biases may be and how they may influence how others engage with you (see figure 13.4).

- "How does my identity affect how and what people share with me?"
- "How do I maintain awareness of my biases and challenge them?"
- **Take notes.** It may feel like note-taking is rude or impacts the rapport, but actually it is an important safeguard against bias and inference.
- **Follow up if necessary.** Asking questions can sometimes bring up intense emotions or memories. Follow up with the person you interviewed—or find someone else who can—if you think the person needs follow-up care.
- **Practice.** Ask each other the questions genuinely and give each other feedback on how it felt to be the interviewer and interviewee and the quality of the probing.

AFTER THE INTERVIEW: ANALYZING THE DATA

After we hear stories of personal experience related to our organization's work, we will be moved to act. And while it is important to act, we should also go back to our purpose for conducting empathy interviews to make sure our actions are potential improvements and not just responses to our own feelings.

What was the problem of practice you were hoping to learn more about? Or what was the system, policy, or practice you were seeking to see through the lived experience of your users? You will need to code your data to find themes and trends across the stories you heard. It is once again important that themes are elevated by an inclusive and diverse team to ensure that you check for bias.

Themes or needs collected from the empathy interview for our problem statement, *Our volunteer cadre does not reflect the diverse community we serve,* might sound like:

- The museum is not a racially affirming space.
- There is a lack of racial diversity in the museum staff and volunteer training personnel.
- Lack of flexible volunteer times.
- Non-native English speakers do not feel comfortable in the museum.

- The training materials are not culturally responsive or allow for adaptations (language, uniform expectations, etc.).
- People do not know how to find out or apply for volunteer opportunities.

Whichever tool you use to help you understand your system from the lived experience of the users, you will learn invaluable information that you can use to move the change process forward. More important than the tool itself is the belief that the answers and solutions already exist in the wisdom of the community. If we can attend to our own beliefs about who holds the power to make change, we can become curious. This curiosity will make our imperfect attempts at root cause analysis perfect.

WHAT'S NEXT? APPLY LIVED EXPERIENCE LEARNINGS TO REACH YOUR GOAL

Historically, problems are solved because leaders are empowered to make decisions about what to change and how to change it. When we choose to involve the users of our systems in the decision making process, we can share the power and get better solutions and outcomes.

Whatever tool(s) you use to help you see your system, you will inevitably learn things that confirm or challenge your ideas about why a problem exists or ideas about the nature of the problem itself. It is important to get clear about what you want to do next and how to prioritize your first steps. As always, engaging community members in this process is essential so that your decisions don't default to the status quo, or to the way that your organization historically operates. Seeing all the root causes may feel overwhelming. Starting small may feel unrealistic. However, when we start to build solutions within a prioritized area, we do so in a way that touches the other causes because, as Maya Angelou said, "When we know better, we do better."

We suggest you balance improvement initiatives with building a theory of change, or strategic plan, and have a bias toward action approach. "Take Action to Learn" Liberatory Design mindsets (see figure 13.5) remind us that oppression thrives on risk averse behavior. It is important to fail fast and remember that small changes can have huge impacts.

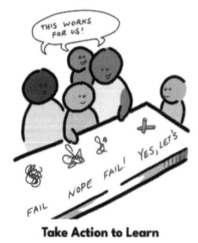

Take Action to Learn

- Co-design safe-to-fail experiments to learn more.

- Build trust through experiments increasing in scale or risk over time.

- Build agency and capacity in the community through co-designed and implemented experiments.

- Balance quick action with thoughtful reflection.

- Choose a direction, not a single or final solution.

Take Action to Learn

The complexity of oppression must be addressed with courageous ongoing action. Experiment as a way to think and learn – without attachment to outcome.

Figure 13.5 Take Action. Anaissie, T. Cary, V. Clifford, D., Malarkey, T., and Wise, S. (2021). *Liberatory Design, http://www.liberatorydesign.com.*

Bring your data to the community and to those you interviewed and allow them to affirm or challenge the themes and root causes based on their lived experiences. Give time for members of your community and the organization to notice and reflect on what they are learning. Anchor back into the improvement mantra "Every system is perfectly designed to get the outcome it is getting." This reflection may raise additional questions that are appropriate to ask yourself as you begin to respond to your data. Does what you're learning move you to act in the parts of the system you historically gravitate toward? Or are there new policies and practices you need to further understand before you act? Do you need more learning? Do you need more collaboration with the community in order to design changes to the systems where needs have gone unacknowledged or unnoticed?

For our example: *Our volunteer cadre does not reflect the diverse community we serve,* there is clear alignment between the root causes on the fishbone diagram and the empathy interview themes. Those charged with designing improvements might consider bringing the following questions to the community and co-designing solutions:

- How might we make volunteering more flexible and desirable?
- How might we make the volunteer training or on-ramping experience more inclusive?
- How might we make a museum visit more about the experience of connecting with visitors and their experience than simply conveying content?

Remember, seeing the system is a way of thinking, visualizing, and understanding. It takes practice. The tools outlined in this chapter are designed to be used—imperfectly—to support the mindsets it takes to make meaningful changes to your organization to better benefit your community, working from the inside.

Museums, like schools and other calcified institutions, struggle to effectively analyze and respond to their systemic challenges. Part of these challenges is a lack of understanding of the root causes and appropriate inclusive decision making in planning to address these challenges and affect change. Given their typically close relationships with community groups and audience segments, museum educators are uniquely poised to lead this work. The example discussed throughout this chapter about volunteers represents the type of systemic problem—and the inclusive responses—that museum educators can address given these relationships. Most museum educators desire substantive and long-term change to address the pressing issues of inequity, access, and representation in their institutions, but in order to ensure the efficacy of these changes, they must take a closer look at their systemic issues, see the totality of the problem, and implement community-based solutions.

DISCUSSION QUESTIONS

1. **What is a problem** that you are trying to solve? How can you articulate it to be rooted in the system?
2. **Whose lived experience** do you need to listen to in order to better understand the (system that is producing the) problem?
   a. What questions would you ask in an empathy interview?
   b. What do you need to do to recruit participants and prepare for the interview?
3. **Who is working on this problem with you**? Who isn't and why? How can you add more voices and perspectives? What might the benefit of a more inclusive and diverse team be?
4. **What biases might you have** in thinking about this problem? Are you already attached to a solution? Why? What happens when you consider other root causes or solutions?

NOTES

1. Design Thinking for Museums. n.d., https://designthinkingformuseums.net/; Mitroff Silvers, "Evolving the Design Thinking Framework towards Greater Equity"; Nasta and Pirolo, "A Design Thinking Approach for Museums."
2. Villegas, Anna Maria, and Jacqueline Jordan Irvine. 2010. "Diversifying the Teaching Force: An Examination of Major Arguments." WACTE, http://www.wacte.org/sites/default/files/files/villegas_irvine-1.pdf.
3. Farrell, Betty, Maria Medvedeva, Cultural Policy Center, and NORC and the Harris School of Public Policy at the University of Chicago. 2010. *Demographic Transformation and the Future of Museums.* American Alliance of Museums, https://www.aam-us.org/wp-content/uploads/2017/12/Demographic-Change-and-the-Future-of-Museums.pdf.
4. LaPlaca Cohen and Slover Linett Audience Research. 2020. *Culture + Community in a Time of Crisis.* Culture Track, https://s28475.pcdn.co/wp-content/uploads/2020/09/CCTC-Key-Findings-from-Wave-1_9.29.pdf.
5. Anaissie, T., V. Cary, D. Clifford, T. Malarkey, and S. Wise. n.d. 2021 "Liberatory Design." Liberatory Design, http://www.liberatorydesign.com.

BIBLIOGRAPHY

Anaissie, T., V. Cary, D. Clifford, T. Malarkey, and S. Wise. n.d. "Liberatory Design." Liberatory Design, http://www.liberatorydesign.com.

Design Thinking for Museums. n.d., https://designthinkingformuseums.net/.

Farrell, Betty, Maria Medvedeva, Cultural Policy Center, and NORC and the Harris School of Public Policy at the University of Chicago. 2010. *Demographic Transformation and the Future of Museums.* American Alliance of Museums, https://www.aam-us.org/wp-content/uploads/2017/12/Demographic-Change-and-the-Future-of-Museums.pdf.

LaPlaca Cohen and Slover Linett Audience Research. 2020. *Culture + Community in a Time of Crisis.* Culture Track. https://s28475.pcdn.co/wp-content/uploads/2020/09/CCTC-Key-Findings-from-Wave-1_9.29.pdf.

Mitroff Silvers, Dana. 2020. "Evolving the Design Thinking Framework towards Greater Equity: An Interview with Tania Anaissie of Beytna Design." Design Thinking for Museums, https://designthinkingformuseums.net/2020/01/22/bringing-equity-into-design-thinking/.

Nasta, Luigi, and Luca Pirolo. 2020. "A Design Thinking Approach for Museums." InTechOpen, https://www.intechopen.com/books/creativity-a-force-to-innovation/a-design-thinking-approach-for-museum-institutions.

Villegas, Anna Maria, and Jacqueline Jordan Irvine. 2010. "Diversifying the Teaching Force: An Examination of Major Arguments." WACTE, http://www.wacte.org/sites/default/files/files/villegas_irvine-1.pdf.

Williams, Adrienne. 2021. "Affirming Spaces Matter for Teachers Too." National Council on Teacher Quality, https://www.nctq.org/blog/Affirming-spaces-matter-for-teachers-too.

14

The Brain Science of Museum Learning

Jayatri Das and Mickey Maley

ABSTRACT

Museum interpretation has long blended tenets of classical educational theory with elements of social psychology and interaction design to engage museum visitors. However, a growing body of research into the neuroscience of learning and cognition that has emerged in recent decades offers new perspectives on the processes by which humans acquire knowledge, find meaning, and make decisions. We now have models for how the human brain works on different time scales, whether focusing attention and integrating sensory information in the short term or rewiring connections and consolidating memories in the long term. In this chapter, we examine how this emerging science influences different approaches to museum interpretation. How does brain science challenge our assumptions, validate existing practices, and inspire new methods of engagement?

INTRODUCTION

In 2015, there was a picture that broke the Internet. Maybe you remember it: a slightly blurry, close-cropped photo of a dress lit from behind in a store, taken by British shopper Cecilia Bleasdale who was considering wearing the dress to her daughter's wedding. The photo ignited a fierce debate about the actual color of the dress. Some people perceived it as blue and black, while others saw it as white and gold. Those in each camp were so certain that their own perception was the truth that they could not imagine how someone else could see anything different.

While the actual dress was blue and black, the viral phenomenon revealed a deeper truth about our experience with the world around us. Our brains create what we perceive to be reality. What many had thought to be an objective, hard-wired process—the pathway by which visual information is encoded and translated by the cells in the eyes and brain—turns out to be more than a little subjective. Our cognitive processing is a hybrid of predictable signaling networks that have developed over evolutionary time and malleable interpretation of those signals shaped by individual experience.

In some ways, museum experiences are not so different from the photo of the dress. Whenever we venture to a museum and experience the collections, exhibitions, programs, and interactive elements on display, our brains continue to construct their meaning based upon our previously processed experiences in the subject matter. Museum professionals have used their understanding of this process when developing their interpretation of subject material. Distilling the values articulated by the Association of Art Museum Interpretation,[1] interpretation—simply put—is how a museum creates an entrypoint for their audience to engage in their content. However, as museums aim to diversify their audiences, it is especially important that interpretation centers the visitor to allow for multiple entry points, welcome the diversity of learners passing through the galleries, and provide culturally responsive learning opportunities to construct upon or shift previously held knowledge.

When we think about engaging visitors, we don't necessarily think about their brains. How, then, is it useful to apply new insights in brain science to informal learning in museums? By understanding predictable brain pathways and functions, museum educators can design experiences with intention, taking advantage of how the human brain has evolved to process our surroundings. At the same time, it is important to appreciate the dynamic nature of the individual brain and make space for unique perceptions and experiences that shape each of us.

THE NEUROSCIENCE OF LEARNING: MYTH VS. FACT

Over the last few decades, new tools and technologies have transformed our understanding of neuroscience and the human brain and rapid discovery continues.[2] A variety of imaging techniques can show us the structure of the brain, how and when different areas are working, how those areas are connected to each other, and how those connections change over time. We can stimulate specific regions of the brain, with increasing accuracy, to treat illness or injury and perhaps even enhance typical functions. These emerging discoveries hold implications for many aspects of our lives, from business to criminal justice to the arts and education.

However, the recent and accelerated advance of neuroscience has meant that these intersecting fields have not always kept up with accurate science. Moreover, the brain is a topic of such public interest that a number of popular myths have arisen about what goes on inside our heads, absent accurate facts. Let's start by looking at a few of these misconceptions, or "neuromyths," that are particularly relevant to education. Our own experience in leading professional development for teachers and educators is supported by research across countries and cultures demonstrating that these neuromyths are widespread among educators.[3]

Myth: We only use 10 percent of our brain. The fact is that we use 100 percent of our brain. Different regions located all around the brain are broadly responsible for carrying out different functions, like core body regulation, our five senses, language processing, memory, emotion, and decision making. Put all of these functions together, take a look with brain imaging technology, and you see that the entire brain is active.

Myth: We are either "right-brained" or "left-brained," and that determines how we think. The brain is divided into two hemispheres, right and left. Contrary to a popular neuromyth suggesting an anatomical division of creative and analytical thinking, the two hemispheres work together to perform most tasks. There is redundancy in both structure and function between the two halves, with a wide band of nerve fibers called the corpus callosum carrying information back and forth to facilitate collaboration. There are a few real differences between the two hemispheres. The right side of the brain, for instance, controls many of the sensory and motor functions of the left side of the body, and vice versa. The right and left hemispheres have also been shown to process different aspects of language. But this division of labor for specific functions occurs independently of any personality traits such as creativity or logical thinking.

Myth: We learn best through a preferred learning style. The concept of learning styles—that an individual consistently learns best through a preferred modality such as visual, auditory, or kinetic—is one that has gained significant traction within the field of education. We have even worked with schools that were evaluating teacher performance based on their perceived ability to tailor instruction to the learning style of each student. Yet there is little scientific evidence supporting the efficacy of this practice.[4] While individuals may have preferences for one modality over another, in practice *everyone* learns better when presented with the same material in multiple modalities, allowing for repetition and engagement of different sensory processes.

Why do these myths persist? Perhaps, as science fiction films like *Limitless* (2011) or *Lucy* (2014) suggest, the idea that we only use 10 percent of our brain opens up the appealing notion of vast, untapped potential. Perhaps being able to categorize people as right-brained or left-brained, or as a certain type of learner, suggests that we can find shortcuts to success. Science has revealed that the brain is much more complicated, but the good news is that the complexity of the brain can inspire new ideas to nurture individuality, affect learning, and foster long-term growth.

Fact: Your brain is always changing. The ability of the brain to rewire its connections, termed *neuroplasticity*, was one of the most fundamental scientific discoveries of the twentieth century. This rewiring takes place on different time scales. There are important long-term changes that take place at key developmental milestones. In infancy, the brain explodes with building connections between cells—more than you will ever need. After that, you "use it or lose it." Throughout childhood, there are a series of sensitive periods during which different brain functions such as face recognition, language, and motor control undergo rapid development.[5] Adolescence is another active period of brain maturation and reorganization, especially for emotional processing, decision making, and other executive functions. During these critical periods, excess connections are pruned away, leaving the most-used pathways to strengthen through experience. While the general architecture of the brain typically matures by age twenty-five, your brain continues to change at a cellular level on a minute-by-minute basis. What we think of as learning and memory involves the capacity of the brain to remodel its wiring constantly. As you form a new memory, your brain alters the number and shape of the connections between cells and the strength of the chemical signals passed between them.[6] This dynamic map of connections in an individual's brain can change at a rate of approximately 13 percent every one hundred days.[7]

Fact: Attention is your brain's information filter. There is so much sensory information in the world around you that your brain cannot process it all. It has to decide what is important through a process called selective attention. Scientists have often compared attention to a spotlight or a zoom lens, where your focus is drawn to a particular location or a feature. What attracts attention? We tend to notice things that have new or changing physical properties, like a contrast in motion or color. We have a specific region of our brains that recognizes faces. We also prioritize attending to information that has been useful in past experience or relevant to a task at hand. Selective attention is an efficient way of directing your limited cognitive resources to the most salient information, but it comes at the expense of noticing information that you might not be looking for.

Fact: Memory is an active process. If only our memories could work like a camera recording everything around us, ready to recall at the push of a button. In fact, memory is an active sequence of encoding, storage, and retrieval, influenced by individual experience at each step (figure 14.1).[8] What are the factors that influence this process? One key aspect is that we encode memories in context, and those context cues enhance later recall. For example, if you learn something new in a distinctive setting, your memory of that fact will be embedded in a more complex experience. A strong emotional association—either positive or negative—can also sharpen a memory. We can consciously leverage

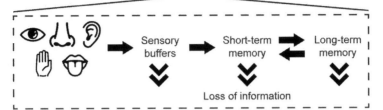

Attention, perception, emotion

Loss of information

Figure 14.1 Summary of information processing in the brain. Environmental input is briefly stored in sensory buffers, then encoded into short-term memory, lasting up to a few minutes. The information is then transferred to long-term memory and available for later recall. These functions and the accuracy of storage and recall are influenced by individual factors such as attention, perception, and emotion. Adapted from Watson & Breedlove (2012). *Photo courtesy of the Franklin Institute.*

these factors to enhance encoding by linking new information to existing knowledge or by creating images and other unique associations in our minds. However, because memory is such a selective, associative process, two people may receive identical information but encode it differently.[9]

Fact: Curiosity is built into our biology. We often think about curiosity as a personality trait. Scientists have more recently begun to define it as an intrinsic information-seeking behavior, with different types of curiosity states, to investigate its underlying biological mechanisms. Consider the thirst for new factual or conceptual knowledge, the desire for more sensory information, or the interest in how other people think, act, and feel. All of us can experience these different types of curiosity at different points in time with different intensities.[10] Neurological evidence suggests that curiosity begins with the brain's emotional arousal when faced with a novel or ambiguous stimulus.[11] Motivational arousal occurs at an optimum level of novelty and complexity—too familiar and the stimulus is insufficient, too complex and arousal can progress into fear. Importantly for learning, this optimum is unique to each of us based on our past experience. Once information is obtained, the brain's reward centers are activated, which subsequently enhances the encoding of the information into long-term memory.

CONNECTIONS AND IMPLICATIONS FOR MUSEUM EDUCATION

Understanding how the brain learns is an essential component of culturally responsive education in the twenty-first century.[12] Society is rich in people of different races, ethnicities, abilities, gender identities, and ages, and changes to traditional museum interpretation are necessary to embrace this diversity. Aging populations, whose influence has dominated museums, are beginning to decline, and the professional populations of Millennials and members of Generation Z do not show the same desire for a museum experience as the older generation once did.[13] Much of this population is seeking agency in their experiences, to have their voices heard and included, and to not have a didactic or rote learning experience that feels manufactured and handed to them.

Along with this generational shift, museums that have long been visited predominantly by affluent, white audiences are striving to relate to the changing racial demographics of their regions. However, there is a pressing urgency for museums to do more to rise to the moment. After protests against racial violence led by Black Lives Matter and sparked by the murder of George Floyd, Ahmaud

Arbery, Breonna Taylor, and others in 2020, many organizations stepped forward to voice their solidarity and support for those hurt by the tragedy. Recognizing a responsibility to create more welcoming and inclusive spaces for all, many museums are looking to shift narratives that have been shaped by the dominant culture. Museums aim to support audiences seeking to reflect and understand trauma, from racial injustice to the collective grief of the COVID-19 pandemic. We desire to facilitate dialogue about how to bring equity and justice to our society and celebrate the diverse communities outside in which our museums are situated and whom we serve. To do so, however, we must understand the museum experience from a visitor's point of view.

A museum visitor brings their whole self to the museum—their memories and experiences, content knowledge, skills, and so forth—and activates any number of these attributes during and after their time at the museum.[14] From neuroscience, we know that an individual person's attention is wired to prioritize novelty, relevance, and emotion, but these are filters which are inseparable from culture. Even beyond the inclusion of content relevant to diverse identities and communities, culture affects the brain in multiple ways.[15] For instance, the nature of social relationships in different cultures influences how individuals learn from each other. Diverse traditions of communication, such as storytelling or music, create familiar patterns for transforming knowledge into memories. Environments welcoming of different cultures and backgrounds create a sense of emotional safety, allowing the brain to relax and tackle the challenges of higher order thinking.

To appreciate how these biological and cultural filters connect to shape a visitor's museum experience, it is important to establish the context of museum learning. Museum learning is voluntary and informal. Visiting a museum is driven by several motivations, and the potential for cognitive and behavioral change increases when those motivations are intrinsically beneficial to the learner.[16] The work done by leading educational and developmental psychology theorists in the early part of the twentieth century—Dewey, Piaget, Vygotsky—and then carried on through the end of the century by others, including Csikszentmihalyi and Hein, opens the door for further development and understanding aided by neuroscience research. Here we look at three examples of connections between brain science and these foundational theories of informal learning.

Neuroplasticity and Cognitive Development

As we grow, so too does our capacity for learning. Previously, we discussed how our brains are always changing; what we think of as learning and memory is really the change in the number of connections and shape of our brain cells. For children, Piaget famously described these progressions as Stages of Cognitive Development.[17] As modern researchers have shown the changes in structural development of the brain from infancy through adolescence, this has strengthened the behavioral observations of Piaget's work.

Briefly, the stages are defined through their relative age and accompanying skill set. Sensorimotor stage is typically observed in learners in the first eighteen months of life who are experiencing learning through their senses, reflexes, and some limited manipulation of materials. In the preoperational stage, observed ages eighteen months to six years, learners construct knowledge based on their perception, and overgeneralize due to their limited experiences. Concrete operational stage covers the early adolescent years to the cusp of pubescence (six to twelve years old), and here we see the growth of the ability to reason in learners while connecting their thinking to previously observed experiences. Finally, the formal operational stage occurs throughout adulthood as we continue to develop our ability to think conceptually and hypothetically, while applying new experiences with our previously understood information to construct new knowledge.[18] The understanding of the simultaneous physical pruning of the neural network and the growth in skills of learners as they advance through these cognitive stages provides a holistic view of the transformation taking place within the brain.

Piaget's work focuses heavily on the growth in the minds of young learners, but the brain continues to alter its connections throughout adolescence and into adulthood. Here the learning theory of andragogy, researched by Malcolm Knowles, picks up to confirm the growth and development of learners throughout adulthood. Knowles's research culminated in an understanding that exceptional adult learning takes place when providing agency to adult learners and creating learning environments that are problem focused, not content focused. He provided six assumptions to adults' learning:[19]

1. The Need to Know—an adult must decide they need to know about something before learning about it.
2. Self-Concept—an adult is aware and recognized by others as being responsible for their own direction, and free from the imposition of others' direction.
3. Adult Learning Experience—adults bring their life experiences, both in quantity and quality, to any educational opportunity providing avenues for deeper, meaningfully constructed knowledge to previous experiences.
4. Readiness to Learn—much like in the growth of young learners through developmental stages, this has connections to real-life applications in adults, and through demonstration of what was in need of being known and its application to real life, an adult would show a readiness to learn further.
5. Orientation to Learning—the application of new knowledge is most effective when it can be used to aid adults in real life situations.
6. Motivation to Learn—adults are responsive to learning through both intrinsic and extrinsic motivators.

These assumptions reflect the "use it or lose it" nature of neuroplasticity; throughout the lifespan, new neural connections must be applied and practiced in order to survive.

Learning Modalities and Constructivist Thinking

As George Hein defines in his seminal 1998 book *Learning in the Museum*, constructivism states that the learner constructs knowledge through personal and social experiences. This theory requires the active participation of the learner and allows the learner to be hands-on and minds-on with information.[20] When a learner encounters a constructivist educational experience in a museum, it will encourage the learner to engage with the world around them and to draw their own conclusions. This requires the learner to connect the new information to existing knowledge previously constructed, thus resulting in a rewiring of connections in the brain. As new knowledge is constructed, so too is the network of connections.

A true constructivist learning experience will allow for multiple learning modalities to be engaged and for deeper understanding to take place in learners. As previously mentioned, we learn best when presented with information through various sensory inputs. Museum learning takes many forms: interpretive labels, demonstrations, electronic media, tours, lectures, interactive stations, maker activities and lessons, and so forth. Presenting information through these multiple means engages and challenges the learner in making these connections. In addition, this same constructivist experience will take place within a social context, as most museum visits do. As Hein states, "the interaction between individual visitors and the rich resource of the exhibition leads to unique outcomes for each visitor. By sharing these experiences with other members of their groups, visitors can enrich the experience for each group member."[21] By engaging visitors through sensory modalities and creating space for people to interact with each other, this experiential learning has a profound impact on the knowledge created within the mind.

Curiosity and Productive Struggle

When it comes to the brain and learning, we have discussed how process is as important as outcome. Curiosity plays an important role in this process by facilitating productive struggle: experiences that challenge visitors at an optimum level of novelty and complexity. These experiences enhance both learning and the ability to learn, by encouraging repeated effort and thereby strengthening connections between and improving the efficiency of brain cells.[22] However, it is important for museum educators to maintain an understanding of the visitor in order to ensure that they have the scaffolding and tools to tackle the challenge while avoiding boredom, disinterest, or fear.

Taking this a step further, Csikszentmihalyi wrote, "complexity . . . involves a second dimension—the integration of autonomous parts";[23] autonomous in this case meaning the individual and their connected group. In museums, productive struggle allows for the visitor to succeed as an individual, overcoming a challenge, while integrating to the larger social nature of museum experience by sharing what they learned, aiding in the learning of others, and so forth. The metacognitive element of this process has a two-fold impact: (1) learners' reward centers in the brain are activated by the accomplishment of new knowledge gained, and (2) the achievement's positive association reinforces the learners' intrinsic motivations that led them to the museum.

These practices can have a profound impact on visitors' memory making. Falk and Dierking[24] discuss this phenomenon of symbolic interactionism, where they describe the recollection of visitors as an appropriation of the museum voice and how learning is directly connected to a personal, prior experience. What is learned is dependent on the setting in which the learning takes place and how the individual interprets the world around them. Continuing to evolve on this practice will allow for visitors to share in the experience and responsibility of reordering and constructing knowledge. As educators, we must reconsider how we encourage productive struggle as facilitators and allow visitors the agency to personalize experiences for themselves.

As illustrated by the three examples in this section, museums have always had the inherent potential for activating long-term memory development, even without explicitly invoking underlying neural mechanisms. Today, visitors still attend museums in groups and share the experience together as a source of entertainment and connection. Younger generations of visitors have taken this a step further to pursue experiences that allow them to personalize their learning and get more involved by seeking engagement to take action in support of a cause.[25] It is no longer enough to simply present the information; we all have the tools to explore content via our own personal devices. Learning in the museum needs to provide a way to engage with content personally and deeply, construct its meaning, and connect to others sharing in the experience. As we are curious and social creatures by nature, learning in such environments will allow for younger generations and more diverse audiences to seek out new connections in the increasingly digital life. Museums have an opportunity to capitalize on this.

APPLICATIONS TO MUSEUM INTERPRETATION AND DESIGN

The reflections and connections we describe in the previous section help us bring into perspective how emerging neuroscience aligns with concepts of educational theory and cognitive science that have formed the foundation of informal learning. However, it's a fair question to ask, then: "So what?" What does an understanding of learning and the brain bring to our work in museums?

While recognizing the importance of neuroscience in identifying the causes of and clinical treatments for neurological disorders, we do not see it as a prescriptive answer to the challenges of formal or informal education. In fact, for many neuroscientists we have worked with, any promise of "brain-based" educational strategies immediately raises the red flag of commercial hype. What brain science can do, however, is to help us think about the *why* behind the *how* of the best practices established in our field through implementation, evaluation, and research. Neuroscience builds a richer appreciation of the complexity of the human brain and the intertwined relationships between brain, behavior, and environment, which in turn can help us develop a more culturally responsive mindset. Here we will share a few examples from our own experience in exhibit development and museum interpretation, as well as work at other institutions, to illustrate the value of these perspectives.

Your Brain is an exhibition at the Franklin Institute about the neuroscience and psychology of the human brain. In tackling this exhibition, we faced the challenge of making accessible a topic that was highly complex, not yet fully understood, largely intangible—and still very personal. As we developed the narrative for the exhibition, we embraced curiosity as the driving emotion for the visitor. We worked with neuroscientists to find examples of new, surprising, or ambiguous phenomena from scientific research. Based on findings from front-end evaluation, we divided the exhibition footprint into smaller galleries to scaffold unfamiliar content. Our design team brainstormed social, multisensory experiences to provoke different types of curiosity (figure 14.2). We iteratively tested explanatory content and device interfaces with visitors through formative evaluation to determine the optimum level of novelty and complexity for different learners. Ultimately, our goal was to give the visitor agency in their learning by inviting them to use *their* brain to learn about *the* brain. Our understanding of curiosity as a dynamic, individual process in the brain allowed us to be intentional in creating an exhibition that encourages visitors to connect with an exciting, emerging field of science through a personal lens. The success of this approach was evidenced by summative evaluation results, with an average visitor experience rating of 4.4 (out of 5) and an average dwell time of forty-five minutes, along with national recognition of the exhibit by the American Alliance of Museums based on "its ability to successfully take a very dense subject matter and make it relatable to the visitor."[26]

Learner-driven interpretation is a second example of how the science of learning has come to be reflected in our practice at the Franklin Institute. Our "Core Four" facilitation strategies were initially developed for *Leap into Science*, a National Science Foundation–funded program that integrates open-ended science activities with children's books in community settings for young children and their caregivers. The "Core Four" strategies for facilitators focus on the process of exploration over content

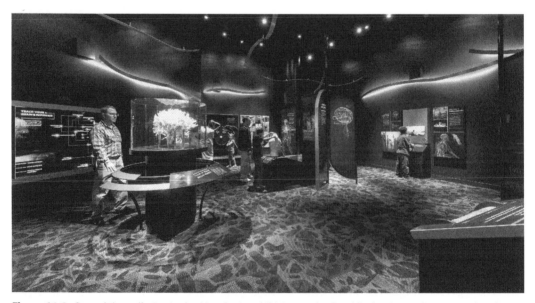

Figure 14.2 One of the galleries in the *Your Brain* exhibition at the Franklin Institute, demonstrating the use of visual icons, environmental design, digital technology, and multisensory interactive devices to engage visitors in learning about the science of their own brain. *Photo courtesy of the Franklin Institute.*

Jayatri Das and Mickey Maley

mastery: (1) ask questions, (2) encourage scientific thinking, (3) cultivate rich dialogue, and (4) make connections. This approach encourages learners to engage with science concepts through a process of observation, exploration, and discovery. We have now expanded this approach to interpreting science concepts for audiences of all ages through museum floor programs, out-of-school programs for older youth, and professional development for educators.

By aligning these techniques with evidence from cognitive neuroscience about what makes for memorable and engaging learning, we find that informal educators and museum volunteers are better able to shift their mindset from a role of a content expert to that of a guide helping visitors explore and understand ideas for themselves. Evaluation results show that educators see the benefits for themselves and their audiences.[27] As one educator shared, "The introduction of the Core Four and other pedagogy has expanded my ability to teach, develop programs, and train my staff to do the same." Another stated, "I learned that when students remain engaged, empowered, and not frustrated, they take in WAY more complex scientific ideas than I could have imagined."

Taking a broader view to invite learners into the active construction of new knowledge, we see the inclusion of design thinking in curriculum, problem solving, and project work as a beneficial application of neuroscientific learning principles. Design thinking utilizes the design process to create, test, and iterate solutions to challenges within learning environments. Usually, this is optimized in a collaborative setting, with social interactions allowing for prior experiences, knowledge, ideas, and learning to be shared and constructed in real time.[28] This process puts people through five stages: empathize, define, ideate, experiment/prototype/test, evolve. At the end, the process leads back to empathy for the intended audience.

With this focus on empathy, design thinking is making its way into the museum field to aid in creating solutions to the unique problems facing visitor learning experiences. Centering the audience explicitly encourages each learner to take an active role in the construction of their knowledge through the experience. Design thinking is embedded in the process of exhibit development at San Francisco's Exploratorium, where each exhibit experience immediately engages visitors with a question: "What do you notice?"[29] This element allows visitors to participate in the museum's process of prototyping different exhibit ideas. For example, as biologists collaborated with the Visitor Research and Evaluation Department to develop new life sciences exhibits, the scientists were opened to the world of talking with visitors to find out what they experienced and the ideas they formed, address any misconceptions, and observe visitors' interactions with their prototypes to inform further iterations of their design.[30] Invitations for exchange like the one described above opens opportunities for the visitor to share how they have immediately personalized the experience, connects them with others directly, and makes them co-collaborators with staff.

Other institutions have investigated more explicit connections between brain science and the museum experience, taking advantage of technology to assess visitor behavior and inform museum design. In an exploratory study at the Museum of Science and Industry in Chicago, visitors were equipped with mobile eye-tracking glasses as they toured the museum in order to investigate how visual attention may correlate with self-reported experiences of awe.[31] This combination of methods allowed the team to identify elements of the designed environment that are associated with evoking awe, as expressed as a feeling of connection or a diminished sense of self. Similarly, at the Peabody Essex Museum in Salem, Massachusetts, researchers use eye-tracking and galvanic skin response to complement traditional survey methodologies in studying the relationship between attention, emotion, and memory.[32] These insights have led the museum to develop exhibit elements that move visitors from passive to active engagement through multiple cognitive modes, such as tactile materials, problem-solving tasks, or judgment tasks that allow them to connect their personal associations and experiences to the art. However, these examples of museums exploring the connections between brain science and museum experiences use technologies that are proxies for brain function. As noninvasive neurotechnologies for measuring direct brain activity—such as electroencephalography

(EEG)—have advanced in recent years, their potential for nonmedical applications such as education has been recognized. Thus far, the practical limitations (e.g., cost, size, usability) of high-accuracy, research-grade equipment have made it difficult to integrate them in real-world settings. Current consumer-grade devices, on the other hand, have lower measurement quality that constrains the types of signals that can be accurately measured.

The relationship between neuroscience and museums can also go in the other direction. As naturalistic environments of learning and visual experience, museums are contributing to the growing field of neuroaesthetics. What happens in the brain when someone interacts with art? Early studies at the Walters Museum of Art in Baltimore, Maryland, asked visitors to rate the aesthetic value of sculptural curves, generating hypotheses for subsequent laboratory experiments that could identify responsive brain regions.[33] At the Menil Collection in Houston, Texas, scientists using mobile EEG systems to record brain activity in visitors have been able to detect signal activation "in context and in action" in response to perception of aesthetically pleasing art.[34] It's important to note that the goal of neuroaesthetics is not to reduce art to a biological mechanism—nor is that possible, given the complexity of the brain. But again, linking brain science to sensory learning experiences in different ways can help us appreciate the multifaceted functions of our brain that make us human.

As we consider the different ways in which concepts of brain science can influence the physical museum experience, we must now expand those to virtual experiences as well. Due to the forced closures in 2020 during the COVID-19 pandemic, many museums moved their experiences online and created new avenues for engagement. For many learners, this digital opportunity was an introduction or reconnection to the museum. In a survey of participants of virtual programs, 57 percent of people who engaged with a natural history museum had not visited one in the past year or more.[35] This trend held for other museum types as well: 51 percent for science museums, 40 percent for art museums, and 37 percent for zoos/aquariums. When their favorite cultural institutions were unavailable in-person, audiences could connect with the museum in a low or no-cost format to relax and recoup, seek resources when transitioning to virtual school, and find ways to distract from the ongoing crisis. The shift to virtual formats brought advantages and disadvantages for accessibility. Many museums were able to expand their reach beyond a geographical region or the usual audience served by in-person learning experiences, and the audience was free to engage as their schedule allowed. However, the forced pivot meant that many museums did not have the capacity to provide these services or the expertise to implement best practices of user experience and interface design for optimal online learning.[36] It's also important to note that many audiences—especially in marginalized communities disproportionately affected by the pandemic—did not have access to the technology necessary to engage. As we look to lessons learned from this time to design virtual environments that support continued, meaningful connections with museums, we will need to refocus with a lens of equity and empathy that places the learner at the center.

CONCLUSION

Emerging neuroscience helps us appreciate what happens inside our heads during a museum experience. What stimuli catch our attention? How do we perceive this information? What do we remember? What makes us want to explore further? How do these factors change over time? Research into the signaling pathways of attention and memory shows how these patterns are encoded in the brain yet are subject to differences in perception between individuals and are changeable over an individual's lifespan. By understanding these mechanisms, we can correct misconceptions that have become ubiquitous in conversations about the brain in popular culture and better apply the best practices of interpretation and design that are foundational to informal learning. We also strengthen our practice of culturally responsive education by appreciating and integrating the experiences of diverse learners.

In reflecting on our own work at a science museum and projects at other institutions, we suggest three key takeaways for museum interpretation, education, and design. First, consider collaborating with neuroscientists, cognitive scientists, or social scientists for cross-disciplinary insights. From identifying design elements that attract attention to constructing emotionally compelling narratives, from analyzing the aesthetics of art to developing strategies for multisensory engagement, museum experiences overlap with questions that are on the cutting edge of science. Science can give us insight into why some things work and others don't, while museums can be unique sites of experimentation that reveal new discoveries about how our brains create our reality.

Second, design intentionally, reflecting on how a visitor's brain might perceive an experience in addition to the content or the narrative you want to communicate. Consider how to reinforce ideas through open-ended multisensory activities. Explore and integrate different cultural traditions of communication and learning. Invite visitors to make personal connections with relevant social cues. Aim for novelty and emotional arousal to create welcoming and memorable settings and tap into different modes of curiosity to encourage questions and further engagement.

Finally, align your practices with evidence. Test your narrative, design, and content with your audience by inviting them to share in the process. As brain science makes clear, we each carry our own cognitive biases based on individual experiences. What seems intuitive, relevant, or common knowledge to one person may not be so to others. While measuring visual attention or emotional response can provide an additional layer of information, even low-tech methodologies of collecting visitor input can successfully build a responsive, data-driven process. Implementing design thinking in your education programs can establish working norms when inviting the visitor to participate. Find learning opportunities to encourage visitors to connect with others and construct knowledge, while providing you the opportunity to collect feedback and iterate on your experiences. Inviting your audience to be part of the process yields a stronger outcome at the end. After all, you'll never know if someone else sees your blue and black dress as white and gold unless you ask.

DISCUSSION QUESTIONS

1. We shared how myths around the structure and operation of the brain have been perpetuated, and the facts uncovered through neuroscience research into the mechanisms at work. What is one piece of information you cannot wait to share with a peer? How will these change your approach when working with different types of audiences?

2. In this chapter, we advocated for the inclusion of visitors taking an active role in the construction of their knowledge and memories. Working with a peer, discuss some ways you can invite visitors to participate further in the learning experiences you've created. What aspirations do you have for the increased participation? How will you learn about the impact this has?

3. Socialization within learning experiences has shown to be effective among learners, as we have discussed in this chapter. So, too, can be said of professionals when designing learning experiences, as shown in the design thinking process. In this chapter, we suggest including experts in neuroscience and cognitive science. Discuss with a museum peer how and where collaborating with people outside your department and museum can positively impact your learning experiences.

4. Did you see the dress as blue and black or white and gold?

5. As we covered in this chapter, and you have likely experienced yourself, we connect information to categories of personal importance. What were some of the prior experiences that you reflected on when processing this information? How will these reflections encourage your next iteration of your facilitated learning experiences?

6. In design thinking, empathy for the audience is strongly encouraged, and kicks off the next iteration of the designed solution. As the audience always changes, and we advocate for them to be

placed at the center of the learning, work with a colleague to create a regular collaborative group to solve future learning challenges in your museum. Who will be the voice of the audience? How will you go about understanding their needs? Who will be around the table to collaborate?

7. A key myth we covered was that we do not have individual learning styles, but in fact people are able to learn through multiple modalities and in fact *everyone* learns better when presented with the same material in multiple modalities. What are the most memorable learning moments in your museum? Through which style is the content shared? Working with a peer, how might you engage visitors with this content through a different learning style?

8. Perception is the attention experience of the brain, and as we discussed earlier, attention is the brain's filter. How will you empathize with the attention needs of your audience? How might you structure your future exhibition development and interpretation to optimize for the perception of your visitors?

NOTES

1. Association for Art Museum Interpretation, "What Is Art Museum Interpretation?" 2019.
2. Rafael Yuste and Cori Bargmann, "Toward a Global BRAIN Initiative." *Cell* 168 (6), 2017, 956-59.
3. Kelly Macdonald et al., "Dispelling the Myth: Training in Education or Neuroscience Decreases but Does Not Eliminate Beliefs in Neuromyths," *Front. Psychol,* 8, 2017, 1314.
4. B. A. Rogowsky et al., "Matching Learning Style to Instructional Method: Effects on Comprehension." *Journal of Educational Psychology,* 107(1), 2015, 64-78; Daniel T. Willingham et al., "The Scientific Status of Learning Styles Theories," *Teaching of Psychology* 42(3), 2015, 266-71; A. R. Knoll et al., "Learning Style, Judgements of Learning, and Learning of Verbal and Visual Information," *Br J Psychol.* 108(3), 2017, 544-63; P. R. Husmann and V. D. O'Loughlin, "Another Nail in the Coffin for Learning Styles? Disparities among Undergraduate Anatomy Students' Study Strategies, Class Performance, and Reported VARK Learning Styles," *American Association of Anatomists,* 12: 2019, 6-19.
5. Takao K. Hensch and Parizad Bilimoria, "Re-opening Windows: Manipulating Critical Periods for Brain Development," *Cerebrum: the Dana Forum on Brain Science*, vol. 11, 2012.
6. Alejandra Ramirez and Melissa Arbuckle, "Synaptic Plasticity: The Role of Learning and Unlearning in Addiction and Beyond." *Biol Psychiatry* 80(9), 2016, 73-75.
7. F-C Yeh et al., "Quantifying Differences and Similarities in Whole-Brain White Matter Architecture Using Local Connectome Fingerprints," *PLoS Comput Biol* 12(11): e1005203, 2016.
8. Kathleen B. McDermott and Henry L. Roediger, "Memory (Encoding, Storage, Retrieval)," In *Noba Text-book Series: Psychology*, edited by R. Biswas-Diener and E. Diener, Champaign, IL: DEF Publishers, 2018.
9. N. V. Watson and S. M. Breedlove, *The Mind's Machine: Foundations of Brain and Behavior*, Sunderland, MA: Sinauer Associates, 2012, 366.
10. M. Gruber, A Valji, and C. Ranganath, "Curiosity and Learning: A Neuroscientific Perspective," edited by K. Renninger and S. Hidi, *The Cambridge Handbook of Motivation and Learning* (Cambridge Handbooks in Psychology), Cambridge: Cambridge University Press, 2019, 397-417.
11. C. Kidd and B. Y. Hayden, "The Psychology and Neuroscience of Curiosity." *Neuron* 88, 2015, 449-60.
12. Zaretta Hammond, *Culturally Responsive Teaching and the Brain.* Thousand Oaks, CA: Corwin, 2015, 3-5.
13. Graham Black, ed. *Museums and the Challenge of Change: Old Institutions in a New World.* Abingdon, Oxon; New York: Routledge, 2021, 5.
14. John H. Falk and Lynn D. Dierking, *The Museum Experience Revisited.* Left Coast Press, 2013, 49.
15. Hammond, 2015, 46-51.
16. M. Csikszentmihalyi and K. Hermanson, "Intrinsic Motivation in Museums: Why Does One Want to Learn?" In J. H. Falk and L. D. Dierking (Eds.), *Public Institutions for Personal Learning*, Washington, D.C.: American Association of Museums, 1995, 69.
17. B. Stein, "Piaget in the Art Museum: Constructing Knowledge through Active Engagement" In *12 Museum Theorists at Play*, edited by Lauren Appel, Kat Harris, Nicole Keller, and David Vining, 2012, 40.
18. Stein, 2012, 40.

19. Malcolm Knowles et al., *The Adult Learner: The Definitive Classic in Adult Education and Human Resource Development*, Routledge, 2014, 47–50.
20. George E. Hein, *Learning in the Museum*, London: Routledge, 1998, 2.
21. Hein, 1998, 174.
22. R. D. Fields, "The Brain Learns in Unexpected Ways," *Scientific American* 322, 2020, 74–79.
23. M. Csikszentmihalyi, *Flow: The Psychology of Optimal Experience*, Harper Perennial Modern Classics, 1990, 41.
24. Falk and Dierking, 2013, 215.
25. Black, 2021, 5.
26. R. M. Hoffstadt, "Winners of the 27th Annual Excellence in Exhibition Competition," *Exhibitionist*, Fall 2015, 8–13.
27. A. Allen and C. Sanford-Dolly, *GSK Science in the Summer™ 2020 Impacts and Programmatic Report*. San Francisco: Rockman et al. Research & Evaluation, 2020.
28. IDEO, LLC. *Design Thinking for Educators,* 2012, 11.
29. Chris Flink, "This Is How a Museum Uses Creativity and Collaboration to Reach 200M Annually." *IDEO U*, 2019.
30. D. King et al., "Developing Interactive Exhibits with Scientists: Three Example Collaborations from the Life Sciences Collection at the Exploratorium," *Integrative and Comparative Biology*, Volume 58, Issue 1, 2018, 94–102.
31. S Krogh-Jesperson et al., "Exploring the Awe-some: Mobile Eye-Tracking Insights into Awe in a Science Museum," *PLoS ONE* 15(9): e0239204, 2020.
32. Tedi Asher, "The Neuroscience of Art Museum Design: Interview with Roger Dooley," *The Brainfluence Podcast*, 2019.
33. Michael Anft, "This is Your Brain on Art," *Johns Hopkins Magazine,* 2010.
34. K. L. Kontson et al., "Your Brain on Art: Emergent Cortical Dynamics during Aesthetic Experiences," *Front. Hum. Neurosci.* 9:626, 2015.
35. LaPlaca Cohen, *Culture + Community in a Time of Crisis: Key Findings from Wave 1*, 2020, 19.
36. M. C. Ciaccheri, "Do Virtual Tours in Museums Meet the Real Needs of the Public? Observations and Tips from a Visitor Studies Perspective," *MuseumNext*, 2020.

BIBLIOGRAPHY

Allen, A. and Sanford-Dolly, C. 2020. *GSK Science in the Summer™ 2020 Impacts and Programmatic Report*. San Francisco: Rockman et al. Research & Evaluation.

Anft, Michael. "This Is Your Brain on Art." *Johns Hopkins Magazine,* March 6, 2010, https://magazine.jhu.edu/2010/03/06/this-is-your-brain-on-art/.

Asher, Tedi. The Neuroscience of Art Museum Design. Interview with Roger Dooley. *The Brainfluence Podcast*. Podcast audio. April 11, 2019, https://hwcdn.libsyn.com/p/a/2/f/a2fc33c5cbda360b/BRAINFLUENCE262.mp3.

Association for Art Museum Interpretation. (2019). "What Is Art Museum Interpretation?" *Association for Art Museum Interpretation,* March 17, 2019, https://artmuseuminterp.org/what-is-art-museum-interpretation/.

Black, Graham, ed. (2021). Museums and the Challenge of Change: Old Institutions in a New World. Abingdon, Oxon; New York: Routledge.

Ciaccheri, M. C. (2020). "Do Virtual Tours in Museums Meet the Real Needs of the Public? Observations and Tips from a Visitor Studies Perspective." *MuseumNext*, June 1, 2020, www.museumnext.com/article/do-virtual-tours-in-museums-meet-the-real-needs-of-the-public-observations-and-tips-from-a-visitor-studies-perspective/.

Cohen, LaPlaca. (2020). *Culture + Community in a Time of Crisis*, posted and accessed on 07/07/2020 at: https://culturetrack.com/research/reports/.

Csikszentmihalyi, M. (1990). *Flow, the Psychology of Optimal Experience.* Harper Perennial Modern Classics.

Csikszentmihalyi, M., and Hermanson, K. "Intrinsic Motivation in Museums: Why Does One Want to Learn?" In J. H. Falk and L. D. Dierking (Eds.), *Public Institutions for Personal Learning.* 1995. Washington, D.C.: American Association of Museums, http://edweb.sdsu.edu/courses/edtec296 /assignments/csik.pdf.

Falk, John H. and Dierking, Lynn D. (2013). *The Museum Experience Revisited.* Left Coast Press.

Fields, R. D. (2020). "The Brain Learns in Unexpected Ways." *Scientific American* 322. doi:10.1038 /scientificamerican0320-74.

Flink, Chris. "This Is How a Museum Uses Creativity and Collaboration to Reach 200M Annually." IDEO U, February 15, 2019, https://www.ideou.com/blogs/inspiration/this-is-how-a-museum-uses-cre ativity-collaboration-to-reach-200m-annually/.

Gruber, M., Valji, A., and Ranganath, C. (2019). "Curiosity and Learning: A Neuroscientific Perspective." In K. Renninger and S. Hidi (Editors), *The Cambridge Handbook of Motivation and Learning* (Cambridge Handbooks in Psychology, pp. 397–417), Cambridge: Cambridge University Press. doi:10.1017/9781316823279.018.

Hammond, Z. (2015). *Culturally Responsive Teaching and the Brain.* Thousand Oaks, CA: Corwin.

Hein, George E. 1998. *Learning in the Museum.* London: Routledge.

Hensch, Takao K., and Bilimoria, Parizad M. (2012). "Re-opening Windows: Manipulating Critical Periods for Brain Development." *Cerebrum: the Dana Forum on Brain Science* vol. 11, 2012.

Hoffstadt, R. M. 2015. "Winners of the 27th Annual Excellence in Exhibition Competition." *Exhibitionist,* Fall 2015 issue: 8–13.

Husmann, P. R. and O'Loughlin, V. D. (2019). "Another Nail in the Coffin for Learning Styles? Disparities among Undergraduate Anatomy Students' Study Strategies, Class Performance, and Reported VARK Learning Styles." *American Association of Anatomists,* 12: 6–19, https://doi.org/10.1002/ase.1777.

IDEO, LLC. 2012. "Design Thinking for Educators," http://designthinkingforeducators.com/.

Kidd, C. and Hayden, B. Y. (2015). "The Psychology and Neuroscience of Curiosity." *Neuron* 88: 449–60.

King, D., Ma, J., Armendariz, A., Yu, K. "Developing Interactive Exhibits with Scientists: Three Example Collaborations from the Life Sciences Collection at the Exploratorium," *Integrative and Comparative Biology,* Volume 58, Issue 1, July 2018, https://doi.org/10.1093/icb/icy010.

Knoll, A. R., Otani, H., Skeel, R. L., Van Horn, K. R. (2017). "Learning Style, Judgements of Learning, and Learning of Verbal and Visual Information." *Br J Psychol.* 108(3):544–63. doi: 10.1111/bjop.12214. Epub 2016 Sep 13. PMID: 27620075.

Knowles, Malcolm S., Holton III, Elwood F., and Swanson, Richard A. *The Adult Learner: The Definitive Classic in Adult Education and Human Resource Development.* Routledge, 2015.

Kontson, K. L., Megjhani, M., Brantley, J. A., Cruz-Garza, J. G., Nakagome, S., Robleto, D., White, M., Civillico, E., and Contreras-Vidal, J. L. (2015). "Your Brain on Art: Emergent Cortical Dynamics during Aesthetic Experiences." *Front. Hum. Neurosci.* 9:626. doi: 10.3389/fnhum.2015.00626.

Krogh-Jespersen, S., Quinn, K. A., Krenzer, W. L. D., Nguyen, C., Greenslit, J., Price, C. A. (2020). "Exploring the Awe-some: Mobile Eye-Tracking Insights into Awe in a Science Museum." PLoS ONE 15(9): e0239204, https://doi.org/10.1371/journal.Pone.0239204.

Macdonald, Kelly, Germine, Laura, Anderson, Alida, Christodoulou, Joanna, and McGrath, Lauren. 2017. "Dispelling the Myth: Training in Education or Neuroscience Decreases but Does Not Eliminate Beliefs in Neuromyths." *Front. Psychol.* 8: 1314, https://doi.org/10.3389/fpsyg.2017.01314.

Mansky, Jackie. "The Neuroscientist in the Art Museum." Smithsonian.com. Smithsonian Institution, June 19, 2018, https://www.smithsonianmag.com/arts-culture/neuroscientist-art-mu seum-180969388/.

McDermott, Kathleen B. and Roediger, Henry L. 2018. "Memory (Encoding, Storage, Retrieval)." In *Noba Textbook Series: Psychology*, edited by R. Biswas-Diener and E. Diener (Eds). Champaign, IL: DEF Publishers, https://nobaproject.com/modules/memory-encoding-storage-retrieval.

Penn Nursing. "Case Studies." Design Thinking for Health, 2021. https://designthinkingforhealth.org/case-studies/.

Ramirez, Alejandro and Arbuckle, Melissa R. 2016. "Synaptic Plasticity: The Role of Learning and Unlearning in Addiction and Beyond." *Biol Psychiatry* 80(9): e73–e75, https://doi.org/10.1016/j.biopsych.2016.09.002.

Rogowsky, B. A., Calhoun, B. M., and Tallal, P. (2015). "Matching Learning Style to Instructional Method: Effects on Comprehension." *Journal of Educational Psychology*, 107 (1), 64–78, https://doi.org/10.1037/a0037478.

Stein, B., "Piaget in the Art Museum: Constructing Knowledge through Active Engagement." In Appel, L., Vining, D., Corwin, M., Keller, N., Harris, K. E. (Eds.) (2012). *12 Museum Theorists at Play*. Retrieved from https://educate.bankstreet.edu/faculty-staff/9.

Watson, N. V. and Breedlove, S. M. 2012. *The Mind's Machine: Foundations of Brain and Behavior*. Sunderland, MA: Sinauer Associates.

Willingham, Daniel T., Hughes, Elizabeth M., and Dobolyi, David G. 2015. "The Scientific Status of Learning Styles Theories." *Teaching of Psychology* 42(3): 266–71, https://doi.org/10.1177/0098628315589505.

Yeh, F.-C., Vettel, J. M., Singh, A., Poczos, B., Grafton, S. T., Erickson, K. I., et al. 2016. "Quantifying Differences and Similarities in Whole-Brain White Matter Architecture Using Local Connectome Fingerprints." *PLoS Comput Biol* 12(11): e1005203, https://doi.org/10.1371/journal.pcbi.1005203.

Yuste, Rafael, and Bargmann, Cori. 2017. "Toward a Global BRAIN Initiative." *Cell* 168 (6): 956–59. https://doi.org/10.1016/j.cell.2017.02.023.

15

No Longer Business as Usual

RECONSTRUCTING RELEVANCY THROUGH CRITICAL RACE THEORY

Melanie Adams and Kayleigh Bryant-Greenwell

ABSTRACT

For museums to be relevant in the twenty-first century, they must not only tell engaging and impactful stories but also help visitors comprehend how those stories continue to play out today. Critical Race Theory (CRT) is one analytical tool to help foster an understanding of the country's racial history and its influence on modern-day decision making. Through the lens of the five-year initiative—Transforming America—Addressing Racial Inequality, from the Anacostia Community Museum, this chapter examines how museum practitioners develop experiences, grounded in Critical Race Theory, that address current racial inequalities and lead toward measurable actions that create a more equitable future.

   For the readers, we intend this chapter to challenge your perspective. Critical Race Theory is a powerful eye-opening, world-expanding force. We hope that you will not only see experiences of America in a new light, but also that this chapter will catalyze different thinking about museum work. This book is intended for an audience of museum educators, though certainly all museum practitioners can find use in the lessons throughout. Our specific use of CRT, as a theory that challenges preconceived notions and breaks barriers, gave us latitude in exploring the roles of museum practitioners. As a project, Transforming America is rooted in educational practice but has museum-wide impacts and implementation. The traditionally strict lines between educator, curator, community manager, and director are intentionally blurred throughout. We see CRT not only as a tool to hold museums accountable to people-centric values, but also as a way to process museum work holistically, breaking free of the limitations of silos and formulaic norms. With this intention in mind, we encourage you to utilize our sharing of experiences broadly in your own evolving practice.

INTRODUCTION

In March 2020, the United States shut down. Gone were the casual trips to the mall. Gone were the Saturdays spent at the barbershop or hair salon. Gone were the spring breaks and graduations. And gone were trips to museums and other cultural institutions. Unfortunately, what was not gone, was the inequality that undergirds this country in a way that makes it seem invisible until a crisis forces it to come crashing to the forefront.

Our nightly news broadcasts and social media feeds are flooded with inequalities that have been compounded by the COVID-19 pandemic. The inadequate technology in many urban and rural areas will only exacerbate educational inequalities. The lack of access to affordable, healthy food in communities of color will continue to put these populations at risk due to preexisting conditions. Many of the people deemed essential workers are people of color who must risk contracting the virus or lose their jobs, and thus their livelihoods. The inequalities brought to light by COVID-19 are not new and should no longer be accepted in our society.

In the middle of this worldwide pandemic, Minneapolis erupted in flames as protestors expressed outrage at yet another Black man killed while being taken into police custody. These protests against police violence, an ongoing narrative in our nation's history, spread beyond the Twin Cities to include communities around the country as citizens took to the streets to make their voices heard. These protests, in conjunction with the impact of COVID-19, clearly illustrate the country's unresolved issues related to race and provide a compelling rationale for museums, in particular, to use their resources to help people not only recognize the racial divide but find ways to eliminate it.

While museums are not social service agencies, they do have the resources to help people recognize inequality, its foundational history in this country, and its continued legacy. But because museums themselves have historically contributed to racialized harm in the exclusion of marginalized populations and focused on the most privileged and elite, it is even more urgent that twenty-first century museums center equality now and for a better future.

Museums should not stand in a place of neutrality but should instead seek ways to bring forth the stories hidden deep in their collections that don't support the myths of America's founding and the dreams it promised to only a select few. Instead of framing the past with our long-accepted facts and figures, we should focus on the community stories that don't shy away from our difficult histories but encourage a type of reckoning and truth telling that has yet to be seen when it comes to issues of race in this country.

Museums, and specifically museum educators, are uniquely qualified to lead museums toward becoming places that help the public confront our country's racial inequalities. The COVID-19 pandemic and the continued violence against communities of color are just a few examples of how communities of color are disproportionately impacted, but there are many more throughout history that illustrate racial inequality's lasting legacy. Museum educators are trained to engage with the public and deliver content in ways that allow them to create avenues of understanding while challenging perceived ideas of the truth.

Using the Anacostia Community Museum as a model, this chapter explores how museum educators can develop and implement programs intended to confront racial inequality. Using Critical Race Theory, educators can reshape their relationship with their audiences by decentering whiteness and expanding their narrative lens. This essential reimaging enables museums to cultivate public discussion, shared understanding, and positive action on racial inequality by using its content to elevate community voices and interrogate long-held historical facts.

HISTORY OF ACM

Any institutions that call themselves museums and do not note with great care the overwhelming possibilities for service to the community should rethink their position so that there can be no undue criticism of these respected institutions and their traditions. Museums must be sensitive to the cries of modern man for a more perfect way to live and to know the truth. (Kinard, ICOM conference in 1971)

Melanie Adams and Kayleigh Bryant-Greenwell

Founded in 1967, the Anacostia Community Museum served as a model for community-based museums around the world. From its humble beginnings in a former segregated movie theater located on a major thoroughfare in Southeast D.C. to its current location less than a mile away on National Park Service land, the museum continues to find ways to "put life in context" to help people understand and participate in our ever-changing world.

The Anacostia Community Museum was founded during a time of great growth within the Smithsonian network. Proposed by then secretary, S. Dillion Ripley, the original purpose of the museum was to serve as a conduit for the museums on the National Mall by displaying artifacts from those museums that would entice people, specifically, African Americans, to cross the river and visit the museums. The leadership of the new museum, led by John Kinard and the community, had other ideas for the Smithsonian's first neighborhood museum.

Instead of being seen as a space to promote the museums on the National Mall, the Anacostia Neighborhood Museum would focus on the insights, perspectives, history, and culture of the people residing east of the river. The programs and exhibits developed in the early years of the museum were driven by community interests in validating African American history, examining contemporary urban life, and reinforcing the growing interest in the diverse cultures of the African diaspora. This focus on the people that are usually left out of the traditional museum narrative would help to define the museum's mission in the coming decades.

THE ANACOSTIA COMMUNITY MUSEUM TODAY

Together with local communities, the Anacostia Community Museum illuminates and amplifies our collective power.

(Anacostia Community Museum mission and statement, 2019)

Relocated in 1987, today the Anacostia Community Museum sits on National Park Service land in Fort Stanton and welcomes about thirty-eight thousand visitors a year to its exhibits and programs. The museum was closed for seven months in 2019 to undergo some capital projects, which included the creation of a more welcoming entry area and a newly designed plaza that can accommodate outdoor programs during the warmer months of the year. This refreshed building follows a newly adopted mission and vision for the museum that reaffirms our commitment to the community and centers its voice in programs and exhibits.

The work of ACM, both in its exhibits and programs, is defined as shared authority because we seek out the voices of people who experienced the events in order to move beyond the facts and figures. The 2018 exhibit, *A Right to the City*, utilizes the tradition of using oral histories to examine the past and to help understand our present and future. *A Right to the City* was developed from more than two hundred oral histories and focused on the stories of citizen advocacy in six D.C. neighborhoods around the central question of "Who has a right to a city?"

In addition to the exhibits, the museum continues to develop and implement programs that reflect the needs of the community. From lecture series about current issues to community gardening to family programs, the museum tries to find an entry point for everyone to feel welcome. Speaking about experiences at other museums, former director of education Zora Martin Felton explained, "I have looked about and have seen no one who looks like me. I have listened and not heard my name called." For the past fifty-two years, the Anacostia Community museum has been a space where people who identified with African and African American culture could see themselves and their stories shared and celebrated with respect and reverence for the struggle from which they came.

CRITICAL RACE THEORY

Founded in the writings of legal scholars, Critical Race Theory serves as a way of uncovering the hidden consequences of race in a society that believes it has solved its race problems. By definition, racism is not an individual performing a singular act, but a system of white privilege that is tied to the distribution of social, political, and economic resources. Critical Race Theory builds upon this definition using tenets that explain how racism remains a characteristic of American life. While museums are educational institutions, we believe the educational applications of CRT used in higher education do not fit the needs of the museum field. Instead, CRT must be used to examine practices and programs throughout the museum, from facilities to human resources to curatorial, in order to shape racially inclusive policies and procedures.

The tenets of Critical Race Theory as explained in the chart below, underpin the founding mission of the Anacostia Community Museum and its role in telling the stories of the African American community. Over the past fifty years, the mission has shifted away from primarily focusing on the African American community to include all communities that have been sidelined in historical narratives. With a new mission to amplify the power of community voices, ACM's programs could easily utilize a CRT framework to illustrate the role race continues to play in society's stories of struggle against inequality. (See table 15.1.)[1]

CRITICAL RACE THEORY FOR MUSEUM WORK

CRT as Educational Framework

> The truth is, however, that the oppressed are not "marginals," are not men living "outside" society. They have always been "inside"—inside of the structure which made them "beings for others." The solution is not to "integrate" them into the structure of oppression, but to transform that structure so that they can become "beings for themselves."[2]
>
> —Paulo Freire, *Pedagogy of the Oppressed*

Even in educational structures intended for inclusion such as museums, when dominant power dynamics are upheld, equity cannot take root. Paulo Freire's pedagogy—long upheld and referenced in museum education philosophy—commands dismantling oppressive structures, creating more equitable structures in their place, and asserting that only through an effort of co-creation, shared knowledge, dialogue, and shared authority can we effect transformative progress.[3] As the foundational critical pedagogy, Freire's influential text squarely relates to the tenets of CRT. Where critical pedagogy claims that the act of teaching is political, CRT tells us that America is an inherently racialized nation. Utilizing CRT as a means to achieve Freire's pedagogical principles of equity through shared authority and co-creation, museums can find new ways to express content, as ACM intended with Transforming America. CRT proves a useful tool in not only actualizing shared authority, but as the necessary driving force to connect racialized experiences and events, intersectional identities, and museum engagement to community responses to injustice.

CRT AS GROUNDWORK FOR A NEW INTERPRETATIVE PLAN

Looking to its next five years and leading up to the country's 250th anniversary in 2026, ACM needed to develop a new interpretive plan. ACM has always utilized the tenets of CRT throughout its decades of exhibitions and programming, though it may not have formally been referred to by name as

Melanie Adams and Kayleigh Bryant-Greenwell

Table 15.1

Tenet	Explanation	Application
Permanence of racism	Racism is a foundational element of American society, making the white experience the norm by which all things are judged as good, right, true, and just.	The purpose of CRT in this instance is not only to recognize racism but to bring it to light for others to see, whether they do something about it or not. Further, CRT displaces the notion of "neutrality" or "color blindness" or more recently, "post racial" as illegitimate falsehoods that distort the work of authentic equity.
Whiteness as the basis for all rights	Historically whiteness was the basis for the right to have property, even the owning of other human beings, the right to safe work, the right to education, and so on. This is evident in the colonization and creation of the United States and all policy making thereafter.	The purpose of CRT in this instance is to challenge the systems, norms, behaviors, and policies that disproportionately favors Whiteness still today.
Civil Rights legislation benefits whites through "interest conversion"	The concept of interest convergence demonstrates that Black people achieve civil rights victories only when white and Black interests converge.[1] Few policies are designed intentionally to solely benefit or separate harm for Blacks. The powerful maintain power and only relinquish portions of it when they have nothing to lose.	The purpose of CRT in this instance is to reveal how Black people are rarely centered in policy making. Further, this tenet demonstrates how the concept of "reverse racism" is a fallacy.
Counter-storytelling as a tool against oppressive norms	Whereas dominant narratives position privileged identities as the norm or a neutral baseline, counter-stories employ the lived experiences and ideas of non-Whites to contradict racist frameworks.	CRT recognizes that counter-storytelling is a liberatory practice to amplify narratives of peoples whose stories are not often told.
Lived experience is an integral component in challenging racism	Narratives of lived experience emphasize the sharing of personal experiences and stories of people of color. These counter-narratives serve as experiential knowledge that only people of color could have because of their lived experiences dealing with racism on a daily basis.	The purpose of CRT is to advance equity for people of color by illustrating the lived experience of systemic racism. Still, the use of such oral tradition as an analytical strategy has been criticized by elitist historians and scholars who devalue the role of storytelling in marginalized societies and, in turn, cite this tenet to discredit critical race theory as a legitimate field of study.

1 Interest convergence is a theory coined by CRT and law scholar Derrick Bell.

its pedagogy. Instead, museum educators reflected on the tenets of CRT in program planning, with questions like:

- How can the museum create experiences that dismantle racism instead of putting it on display?
- How can the museum encourage diverse narratives that benefit people of color without having to submit to the interests of whites?
- How can the museum move away from narratives as told through the eyes of the oppressor?
- How can we bring in artists of color to question the dominant narrative and be seen as a credible voice in their own experiences?

In this line of questioning, educators looked to CRT as the driving force for the holistic interpretative approach to the museum. In typical interpretative planning processes ideas formulate around questions like *What messages are essential to convey?* and *Who is this for?* When CRT is applied as the foundation, it shapes the museum's work around the realities of the unresolved issue of racism in America. As Austin Channing Brown expresses in her memoir, "Ultimately, the reason we have not yet told the truth about this history of Black and White America is that telling an ordered history of this nation would mean finally naming America's commitment to violent, abusive, exploitative, immoral White supremacy, which seeks the absolute control of Black bodies. It would mean doing something about it" (Channing Brown, p. 116). CRT gives museums the means to start doing something about the ongoing lived experiences of racism troubling communities. As a methodology that penetrates personal, community, national, and historical stories and exposes those connections to structures and policies, CRT prepares museum educators to interpret relevant and timely social actions.

CRT AS FOUNDATION FOR TRANSFORMING AMERICA INITIATIVE

Considering that CRT demands a reckoning with power and inequity, it provides a framework for Transforming America emphasizing an urgency to act. CRT is a means for rapid responsiveness to ongoing racial traumas experienced at the personal, community, and national levels. Scholar Michael Eric Dyson summons the national call obliging urgency in abolishing racism. "In his epic, 'I Have a Dream' address in Washington, DC, he [Martin Luther King, Jr.] would warn that this was 'no time to engage in the luxury of cooling off or to take the tranquilizing drug of gradualism.' He trumpeted instead, 'the fierce urgency of now.'"[4] If museums are to address systemic racism, it is not enough to reflect on movements past. Grounded in CRT, Transforming America was developed as a tool to, cooperatively with community experts, challenge harmful power structures and develop new ideas for a more equitable future.

TRANSFORMING AMERICA

By spring 2021, the Transforming America initiative was in its early stages of implementation. The following sections of this chapter can serve as a planning guide for educators interested in taking the theoretical tools of CRT and applying them to museum education work. As discussed, Transforming America programs are intentionally grounded in CRT, through both pedagogy and project design. This reflective examination will show how exhibits and programs can address issues of race through community codevelopment and critical consideration of current issues. In each thematic section of the five-year Transforming America plan, we will also provide questions to be used by educators to help visitors engage more deeply with the content and question their racial beliefs and ideologies.

Transforming America is an initiative to look at a different societal issue each year for five years and to explore how race has been used to create and maintain the current system of inequality. The project will conclude with the country's 250th anniversary in 2026 and a series of year-long community developed projects to address each of the five issues. Through an effort of codevelopment with community leaders, scholars, and concerned citizens, this initiative works two-fold: (1) amplifying the museum as an active space for critical thinking and (2) developing racial equity actions for and with engaged audiences. (See table 15.2.)

Transforming America was designed with three objectives:

- Codevelop social action strategies for local and national audiences.
- Codevelop collective ideas for a more equitable future.
- Codevelop sustainable strategies for community-museum relationship growth.

The initiative would span five years, each with a different focus area of racial inequality. Through this initiative ACM will fill a crucial gap in public institutions and provide a necessary service toward a collectively more equitable future.

A PLANNING GUIDE FOR CRT

First and foremost, the relationship of museum and community partners was imperative to the realization of the initiative. We envisioned a structure that would allow for the museum—its staff, collections, and programs—to serve local organizing and community leaders as an essential resource, tool, and partner in their change-making work. Simultaneously, community partners would help educate museum staff about methods, tactics, and connections to improve the museum's mission competencies and relevance. Together, the collaboration would elevate social change efforts across interrelated communities and boost local action-based efforts.

Secondly, as our application of CRT is to move from the *lens* of racial inequality into *actions* to dismantle oppression, each program, exhibit, and activity for Transforming America required an intentional call to action. Program design incorporates learning, critical thinking, and action planning among visitors. Each participant will engage in social action in the act of collective gathering and then have the opportunity to design their own future action plan for further engagement in activism.

These two components: community authority and action engagement create the core foundation for our practical application of CRT.

Creative Structures for Applying CRT

The following sections provide insights into our strategies and design structures for creating Transforming America. Included are our approaches to using the tenets of CRT as a mechanism for engaging in racial equity, both programmatically but also through partnerships—specifically the ways in which Transforming America partners with community leaders.

These tools informed our program design in terms of content, evaluation, and audience engagement structures.

A few of our defining tools in this work are: Urgency, Continuation, and Accountability. We also provide specific examples of the Transforming America program and codevelopment designs and strategies.

TOOLS

Urgency

As previously discussed in Dyson's analysis of Dr. King's teachings, urgency should be the driving force in addressing systemic racism. Entrenched workplace cultures, restrictive ideologies, and the oppressive power of the status quo are blockades to museum capacity for urgent response.

Table 15.2

Theme	CRT Context	Questions for Accountability
Our Food, Our Future	A 2018 article published by the National Institute of Health, confirms that "the need to target structural racism is critical in the fight for achieving equity in food security and improve related outcomes in people of color."[1]	What is your museum's relationship to food, privilege, and power? What is happening around food access in your geographic area?
Our Housing, Our Future	On May 15, 1911, the mayor of Baltimore, J. Barry Mahool, signed into law the country's first racial segregation ordinance. The law prohibited Blacks from buying a house on a block that was majority white. The mayor claimed, "Blacks should be quarantined in isolated slums in order to reduce the incidents of civil disturbance, to prevent the spread of communicable disease into the nearby White neighborhoods, and to protect property values among the White majority."[2]	What is the racial makeup of your museums' neighborhood? What was it a decade ago? Who is responsible for the generational disadvantages of segregation?
Our Environment, Our Future	The Center for American Progress puts it simply, "Environmental racism and failing infrastructure have plagued communities of color for decades."[3]	Where does your museum's trash end up? Adjacent to which communities? You likely have a Disaster Plan in place for the event of extreme weather, now even more likely with climate change. So, you know what will happen to some objects. Do you know what will happen to your surrounding communities?

Our Education, Our Future	Earlier we laid out a brief history of structural education in Anacostia, alluding to issues of race, but does not put the country's racial underpinnings front and center in the narrative. The story of education in America is founded on racial inequality beginning with the laws against teaching enslaved people to learn to read and write. The power of education was not lost on enslavers who recognized that if enslaved people were educated, they would be better prepared to question their situation. Even today, experts note that, "resisting an education built on a White worldview mean[s] constantly having to evaluate the risks of telling the truth or furthering the myth."[4]	In what ways has the promise of education failed people of color? How can museums become spaces that do not traumatize people of color between truth and myth?
Our Mental Health, Our Future	According to Mental Health America, "Racism is a mental health issue because racism causes trauma. And trauma paints a direct line to mental illnesses, which need to be taken seriously."	In recent years museums have benefited from a correlation of museum visits as therapeutic experiences. How has your museum sought ways to emphasize these benefits for communities of color, who may have less access to mental health options? In what ways can museums diminish the harmful effects of racism for the mental health of communities of color?

1 Angela Odoms-Young and Marino A Bruce. "Examining the Impact of Structural Racism on Food Insecurity: Implications for Addressing Racial/Ethnic Disparities." Family & Community Health, 41 no. 2 (2018): S3–S6. doi:10.1097/FCH.0000000000000183.

2 Wayne Shu, "Baltimore's Legacy of Racial Discrimination," The Stanford Review, May 20, 2015, https://stanfordreview.org/baltimores-legacy-of-racial-discrimination/.

3 Jasmine Bell, "5 Things to Know About Communities of Color and Environmental Justice," Center for American Progress, April 25, 2016, https://www.americanprogress.org/issues/race/news/2016/04/25/136361/5-things-to-know-about-communities-of-color-and-environmental-justice/.

4 Austin Channing Brown, I'm Still Here: Black Dignity in a World Made for Whiteness (New York: Convergent Books, 2018).

In recent years we have seen rapid response efforts take the form of collecting initiatives—acquiring ephemera from marches and protests. But the ethos of rapid response can also be applied to programming and education.

Utilizing urgency as a tool, we designed flexible dialogic programs to respond to the energy of the moment. As a program design, dialogic programs offer more flexibility than traditional instructional programs by placing co-creation and authority in the hands of visitors. As a participatory practice, dialogue provides an immediate and intimate engagement with timely events and topics. These program designs are discussed in further detail in the following sections.

Continuation, AKA Not a One-Off

All too often museum social impact projects are one-offs, developed for momentary appeal within unachievable goals. They lose momentum, and ultimately museums backslide to their former priorities. The absence of action plans in the outpouring of museum solidarity statements with the Black Lives Matter movement is a perfect example of this one-off dilemma.

Transforming America differs from other initiatives in that it is a process for integrating community input and social impact strategies into every aspect of the museum with long-range engagement. Lessons learned from codevelopment will be applied to future engagement and content strategies. This project is the catalyst that will transform ACM. This initiative affirms that ongoing community equity work *is* essential museum work.

Codevelopment connects the museum to communities consistently over the course of the year through ongoing engagements that were intentionally built into the design of the program. As theory applied in practice, we looked to a tenet in liberation theory that states that liberation is not a fixed destination but is instead a journey—specifically it is every action, decision, and practice in an ongoing effort toward creating equity. A fundamental function of CRT is the liberation of people of color from oppressive structures of whiteness.

In this light we designed a slate of programs as engagement touchpoints for visitor experience within each year's theme. Moreover, we implemented a codevelopment architecture via an ongoing Community Advisory Council to participate in the continued rollout and design of the entire Transforming America initiative. This is explained in further detail in the "Codevelopment Strategy and Design" section.

Accountability

Broadly speaking, there continues to be a disconnect between what museums espouse as values and the ways in which museums operate. Embracing accountability as a critical tool for program design, we reimagined our evaluation strategy.

As educators in program design, we often ask ourselves, "How will we define success?" But we typically apply this question only to our program designs and not to our actions themselves. Actions like audience cultivation, challenging perspectives, developing outreach and partnerships, advancing public discourse are all ways we can assess our accountability beyond "we tried."

While metrics like program attendance and visitor feedback remain pertinent in evaluation, accountability of *what* and *how* we took action paints a clearer picture of our efforts to engage in the tenets of Critical Race Theory. We asked ourselves, "*How* are our efforts creating CRT *impacts*?"

In the Transforming America Programs chart we go into further detail about how we linked accountability to the goals of the initiative.

TRANSFORMING AMERICA PROGRAM DESIGN AND STRATEGY

Codevelopment Strategy

In enlisting a strategy of codevelopment as the principle organizing methodology of the project we had to determine what codevelopment meant for us as an institution. Designating community action as the driving force of the project, it was critical that our strategy for codevelopment also reflect activist conventions, including liberation theory, as previously discussed. For this project, codevelopment radicalizes power structures in museum education. Though co-creation of knowledge has become a widely popular approach since Freire, the scale, duration, and process of this strategy was a new experience for us.

Community Advisory Council

Amplifying voices of community leaders with long-standing commitments to racial equity work locally, the Transforming America initiative is guided by an engaged group of community advisors, through the formation of an official council. The Transforming America Community Advisory Committee consists of eight total participants: four permanent spots and four rotating. The four permanent spots will consist of local community activists and scholars. Two of the rotating spots will consist of scholars and activists specific to each year's theme, who may not reside within the local area but have made great contributions to national rhetoric and studies pertaining to the year's theme. The remaining two spots will consist of selected applicants from participating programs and partnerships. Program participants will have the opportunity to apply to the council. Community advisors will convene at least twice a year to strategize in partnership with the museum for generative workshops focused on future-thinking, coping post-pandemic, and community building. Using collective brainstorming and decision making, the council will guide the path for the multiyear initiative. Community advisors will be compensated for their time, labor, and commitment to the museum.

Codeveloped Experiences, Engagements, and Programs

We set a goal to codevelop measurable and actionable ideas for change with our community partners. We wanted to leverage codevelopment to not only change museum experiences but also to change problematic forces within our community. In this sense, codevelopment is a goal itself, to successfully enact a process of shared authority, but also as a means to disrupt museum norms. Therefore, our codevelopment strategy itself was a catalyst for change.

In addition to the council's codevelopment and shared authority, we created programs for the distinct purpose of critical thinking, ideation, and action planning through dialogue with community participants. Our participants are then codevelopers of equity and change.

Program Strategy

Often in museum collaborations, undue burden is placed on communities to educate museums who are under qualified to lead community efforts. With this awareness we prepared a catalog of public program designs that can be flexible and adaptive to different content choices, centered in dialogue so that community participants can thrive in purposeful critical thinking and shared exchange settings, rather than be put in a position to educate the museum on social justice topics. See table 15.3 for such included programs.

Table 15.3

Program	Description	Call to Action	CRT Tenets and Impacts
Community Supper	an evening of action-planning and dialogue over a family-style meal	Connect with leaders in the community who are engaged in equity to broaden the community alliance, build action-driven networks, and enhance your Community Power against racial inequality.	Alliance and collective building strategies promote lived experiences as a means to challenge systemic racism.
Community Action Fair	a daytime table-top fair featuring community leaders and organizations each with a featured take-home action	Various actions provided by participating partners, amplifying one's Personal Power and growing our collective Community Power.	Community leaders and organizations dedicated to creating equity actively engage with and challenge the reality of the permanence of racism.
Community Creativity Day	a day-long all-ages festival featuring activist-artists and makers demonstrations, performances, and workshops	Make and experience art, enhancing one's Personal Power. Support local artist-activists, enhancing our Community Power.	Amplifying community voices is a way to enhance counter-storytelling.
Futurist Lab	a guided workshop for imaging a more equitable future	Envision a better future and begin actions toward it, enhancing your Personal Power.	Developing personal action plans to challenge inequity is a way to challenge and begin to restructure oppressive power dynamics.
Community Coping Post-Pandemic	scholarly talks providing insights into policy making and systemic structures that contribute to and attempt to mitigate the equity gap caused by COVID-19, as well as community healing sessions including group art therapy, deep breathing, and other stress-relieving practices	Call out inequality where you witness it, amplifying your Personal Power. Gather together to heal as a community engaging in our Community Power.	Understanding how still today social infrastructure continues to shield whites from the harshest of conditions faced by people of Color is the first step in challenging Whiteness as the basis for all human rights.

Designing Digital Program Experiences

As previously mentioned, we began to construct the project architecture for Transforming America at the height of the first wave of COVID-19 museum closings in the United States. That painful period taught museums the necessity of expanding digital engagement. However, we wanted Transforming America's digital programs to represent a digitally-native experience and not just act as add-ons or Plan B in the event of further closures. We embraced the inherent worldliness of digital programming and developed a Global Perspectives digital strategy. Global Perspectives programs connect local activists to other activists all over the world, thus expanding the community experience of the Transforming America project to beyond just our neighbors. Activism is happening at a global scale, and we sought to utilize our digital programs to provide connections that couldn't happen otherwise.

Designing Calls to Action

As previously mentioned, action-focused engagement was fundamental to the public programs strategy. To anchor the programs in action, each shared a Call to Action with participants. To further connect participants to the tenets of organizing, each Call to Action specified if the action mobilizes personal, community, or national power. For example, Community Supper programs mobilize community power in the Call to Action to connect with strangers in the community who are engaged in equity, to broaden the community alliance, and to build action-driven networks of change agents, whereas Futurist Labs propel personal power in developing personal action and accountability plans.

Evaluation Strategy

Finally, we designed our *evaluation strategy* for long-term feedback. We wanted Transforming America to connect disparate long-standing community leaders and organizers but also to serve as a gateway to activism to new and emerging change agents. With this in mind, we considered that while participants will hopefully feel urgency toward immediate action, in reality, it may take time for action to occur. Thus, we developed a system for ongoing feedback. We would survey participants immediately after and at varying intervals following a program. We would monitor, collect, and analyze social media data for new trends in organizing. We would also continue relationships with community leaders and organizations and follow their trends in giving and volunteering.

A Year of Transformative Ideas

Focusing on Organizing and Liberation, the Year of Transformative Ideas will build on the knowledge base developed over the first five years of topic-specific issues of racial inequality. Thinking more broadly, the Year of Transformative Ideas will prepare participants to take ongoing action wherever they see inequality in their lives. Deeply exploring different roles in organizing will include: Healers, Artists, Storytellers, Bridge-Builders, Frontline Responders, Caregivers, Disrupters, Visionaries, and Reformers. All participants will navigate their engagement in Racial Liberation, finding their voice and developing their action plans. We look to two design questions to guide our programming choices for this year:

- In what ways can museums help visitors explore their personal strengths and skills as agents of change?
- In what ways can museums evoke transformation for a more equitable future?

Transforming America Theme Years

A 2016 Brookings Institute report summarizes the need for certain areas of focus in racial inequality, and the reasoning for the theme years. "Whether it is water quality in Flint, school quality in Ferguson, environmental hazards in Dickson, Tennessee, or the inferior health care that the majority of Black patients receive nationwide, the African-American experience is different, and is allowed to be different, more than would ever be accepted within White communities."[5] This provides further evidence for the necessity of an applied CRT lens because of the variety and regularity of stories of racial injustice in the news.

CONCLUSION

Summarizing Transforming America

We conceived our community work as work within communities, but also as a change-agent for the museum itself. Rather than paint broad strokes about racist structures disadvantaging local communities, we listened to community leaders and responded to their expertise on social issues. Understanding that isolationism is a tactic of white supremacy to diminish coordination between groups, we enlisted year-long partners to support the direction of each theme year. Museum educator Elizabeth Duclos-Orsello acknowledges that, "Equally as important is the fact that a lack of collaboration across sectors hampers every institution's efforts at effecting social change."[6] Moreover, we emphasized equality in collaboration not only for the sake of cooperation and effective codevelopment, but also because community experts have long been left out of traditional historic interventions. Duclos-Orsello affirms that "in collaborative museum work that aims to be responsive to social needs, all parties involved must be understood to be authorities on topics of value to the collaboration, and must be understood to have the power and position to fully co-create?"[7] Transforming America as an initiative is set up to not only advance community social action but as a means to dismantle problematic elitist structures with traditional museum partnerships. The project will activate the change-making potential of the local community toward community-wide goals of racial equity. The Anacostia Community Museum will be known as a space for social action, confronting hard truths, dismantling social inequities, and imaging a better future.

Museums, Relevance, and CRT

> If we . . . do not falter in our duty now, we may be able, handful that we are, to end the racial nightmare, and achieve our country, and change the history of the world.
>
> —James Baldwin[8]

In conclusion, Critical Race Theory is the foundation for which museums can begin to shift away from the passive detachment from the racial unrest that has always been a part of society toward a newfound relevance that addresses current issues and finally begins to resolve the historic harm in which the field is complicit. Museums are late to the unfolding national conversation around racial equity and are hemorrhaging relevance with every passing opportunity to join in. As museum educators, our role is to stop the complacency, hold our institutions accountable, and lead by example in both pedagogy and practice. For decades museum education has undertaken this work through social programs and counter narratives in interpretation. But now, as museums commit to be better in their public statements and actions, it is time for CRT praxis to pervade as a central guiding pedagogy. As institutions of and in communities, museums do have societal impacts, and in order to have positive ones, museum educators must lead with a critical lens, ever pushing museums to do and be better for all.

DISCUSSION QUESTIONS

1. As the country continues to struggle with how to address racial inequality, what role do you see museums playing to close the racial divide?
2. Museum educators are on the front line working with visitors of all ages. What type of training do you believe educators need to receive in order to be effective in helping visitors understand racial issues?
3. Museums are quick to turn outward when addressing difficult topics, always looking to educate the public instead of looking inward to address their own issues of bias and institutional racism. How can educators help their institutions understand the importance of internal reflection and action before public pronouncements and programs?
4. How can we make sure museum educators are at the tables when decisions are made that impact the visitor experience?

NOTES

1. Bell, Derrick, "Brown v. Board of Education and the Interest-Convergence Dilemma," *Harvard Law Review*, 1980, Vol. 1.
2. Paolo Freire, *Pedagogy of the* Oppressed (New York: Continuum, 2000), 74.
3. Freire, *Pedagogy of the Oppressed.*
4. Michael Eric Dyson, *What Truth Sounds Like: Robert F. Kennedy, James Baldwin, and Our Unfinished Conversation about Race in America* (New York: St. Martin's Press, 2018), 40.
5. Dayna Bowen Matthew, Edward Rodrigue, and Richard V. Reeves, "Time for Justice: Tackling Race Inequalities in Health and Housing," Brookings Institute, October 19, 2016, https://www.brookings.edu/research/time-for-justice-tackling-race-inequalities-in-health-and-housing/.
6. Elizabeth Duclos-Orsello, "Shared Authority: The Key to Museum Education as Social Change," *Journal of Museum Education* 38, no. 2 (July 2013): 121.
7. Duclos-Orsello, "Shared Authority," 122.
8. James Baldwin, *The Fire Next Time* (New York: Dial Press, 1963), 105.

BIBLIOGRAPHY

Baldwin, James. *The Fire Next Time.* New York: Dial Press, 1963.

Bell, Jr., Derrick A. "Brown v. Board of Education and the Interest-Convergence Dilemma." *Harvard Law Review*, vol. 1980, no. 1, 1980. https://harvardlawreview.org/1980/01/brown-v-board-of-education-and-the-interest-convergence-dilemma/. Accessed 5 October 2020.

Bell, Jasmine. "5 Things to Know about Communities of Color and Environmental Justice." Center for American Progress. April 25, 2016. https://www.americanprogress.org/issues/race/news/2016/04/25/136361/5-things-to-know-about-communities-of-color-and-environmental-justice/.

Bowen Matthew, Dayna, Edward Rodrigue, and Richard V. Reeves. "Time for Justice: Tackling Race Inequalities in Health and Housing." Brookings Institute. October 19, 2016. https://www.brookings.edu/research/time-for-justice-tackling-race-inequalities-in-health-and-housing/.

Channing Brown, Austin. *I'm Still Here: Black Dignity in a World Made for Whiteness.* Colorado Springs: Convergent Books, 2018.

Douglas Horsford, Sonya. *Learning in a Burning House: Educational Inequality Ideology, and (Dis)Integration.* New York: Teachers College Press, 2011.

Duclos-Orsello, Elizabeth. "Shared Authority: The Key to Museum Education as Social Change." *Journal of Museum Education*, 38, no. 2, July 2013.

Dyson, Michael Eric. *What Truth Sounds Like: Robert F. Kennedy, James Baldwin, and Our Unfinished Conversation about Race in America.* New York: St. Martin's Press, 2018.

Freire, Paolo. *Pedagogy of the Oppressed.* New York: Continuum, 2000.

Mental Health America. "Racism and Mental Health." Accessed September 25, 2020, https://mhanational.org/racism-and-mental-health.

Museum as Site for Social Action. "From Statements of Solidarity to Transformative Action and Accountability." August 31, 2020. https://www.museumaction.org/massaction-blog/2020/8/31/from-statements-of-solidarity-to-transformative-action-amp-accountability.

Odoms-Young, Angela, and Marino A. Bruce. "Examining the Impact of Structural Racism on Food Insecurity: Implications for Addressing Racial/Ethnic Disparities." *Family and Community Health*, 41 no. 2 (2018): S3-S6., doi:10.1097/FCH.0000000000000183.

Runnel, Pille. "Insight: Innovation and Participatory Culture." *Museum Ideas 2: Innovation in Theory and Practice.* Ed. Gregory Chamberlain. London: Museum Identity, 2016.

Rusk, David. "Goodbye to Chocolate City," DC Policy Center, July 20, 2017, https://www.dcpolicycenter.org/publications/goodbye-to-chocolate-city/.

Shu, Wayne. "Baltimore's Legacy of Racial Discrimination." *The Stanford Review.* May 20, 2015. https://stanfordreview.org/baltimores-legacy-of-racial-discrimination/.

16

The Impact of COVID-19 on the Field of Museum Education

Juline Chevalier

ABSTRACT

When U.S. museums closed to the public in March 2020 due to COVID-19, museum educators sprang into action by sharing resources online and developing new virtual programming to keep audiences engaged. Yet many museum leaders still drastically cut museum education budgets and staff during the ensuing economic downturn. This chapter documents and examines the impacts of these cuts on the field of art museum education through results of a survey implemented by the Museum Education Division of the National Art Education Association (NAEA) in partnership with planning, evaluation, and research firm RK&A. This snapshot of the field in fall 2020 is contextualized with personal stories of educators directly impacted by these drastic changes along with results of other museum surveys.

INTRODUCTION

When I left my museum office on Friday, March 13, 2020, I knew I would be doing my job as head of interpretation from home for a little while because of the quickly spreading novel coronavirus, COVID-19. The day before, the museum had cancelled an in-person program for more than one hundred teachers just a few hours before it was scheduled to start.

For a few weeks, it felt like an opportunity for reflection. I started to do some deep thinking on a few big projects, and I thought I might even get to catch up on the always-present backlog of emails. But the longer we worked from home, the more things changed. Or, more accurately, the more things went back to the stressful grind that many museum educators know. The grind had simply shifted focus to producing digital content and engaging audiences virtually.

The meeting pace ramped back up to my usual three or four per day, but now they happened via Zoom. I did not enjoy staring at a computer screen so much, but I did enjoy wearing pajama pants all day, working from my couch, and being able to pet my dachshund Luigi whenever I pleased.

In late April 2020, I began to see a wave of posts on Twitter from museum workers, many of whom were educators, sharing news of their furloughs and layoffs. These grim announcements continued to cascade in the following weeks. Museum educator, Rachel Ropeik, stated it well in a blog post: "Education and Digital departments were somehow being gutted while simultaneously asked to bear primary responsibility for connecting with visitors who could no longer show up in person."[1]

On May 25, 2020, George Floyd, a forty-six-year-old Black man, was murdered by Minneapolis police. Floyd's death was captured on video and shared widely on social media. Massive public protests against police brutality and racial injustice took place all over the world in the days and weeks to follow. George Floyd's death was a catalyst for a more widespread public recognition, reckoning, and conversation about racial injustice in the United States than had happened in recent memory. A blog post from MASS Action (Museum as Site of Social Action) noted, "hundreds of museums felt compelled to comment after the murder of George Floyd in 2020. However . . . very few museums see themselves as part of the problem. Most statements condemn racism in U.S. society or in the museum field, but do not connect the museum's own systems and practices to the issue."[2]

In late April 2020, Stephanie Downey and Amanda Krantz from arts and culture evaluation firm RK&A reached out to me in my role as the 2019–2021 director of the National Art Education Association's (NAEA) Museum Education Division. They offered their services pro bono to help document the impact of the pandemic and economic recession on the museum education field. In April 2020 Stephanie shared her concerns about museums continuing relationships with K–12 teachers and students,[3] and Amanda cautioned that laying off educators could burn bridges that linked museums to communities they serve.[4] We had several goals for the survey: One was to document and quantify the impact of a global pandemic on museum education in the United States. It felt like museum education departments and staff were taking a bigger hit than other departments, but we did not have data to back it up. We also wanted to see if there were trends in the impacts correlated to museum size, museum governance, or racial or ethnic identity of respondents, among other factors. Finally, we sought to document the drastic shift from creating in-person programming to virtual programming that most museum educators were making. Having this kind of data could help us advocate for our profession, our programs, and the audiences we serve.

I knew that layoffs were coming at my own museum, but I thought that as a department head with a national level leadership position, that I was relatively safe. I was not. On June 22, 2020, my position was eliminated, and I lost my job. I became even more motivated to document the havoc being wreaked on museum education departments.

THE SURVEY

Members of the NAEA Museum Education Division Development Committee worked with Stephanie and Amanda at RK&A to develop questions for the survey. The development committee is made up of the division director, the division director-elect, and representatives and representative-elects from each of the four NAEA geographical regions. These individuals are Jaime Thompson, Mieke Fay, Hajnal Eppley, Kylee Crook, Kabir Singh, Stephanie Stern, Celeste Fetta, Jessica Fuentes, and Gwendolyn Fernandez. The digital survey went live on September 4, 2020.

We sent the survey out via NAEA Museum Education Division member email list three times; shared it through NAEA Museum Education's Facebook and Twitter accounts; promoted it during webinar events; and asked related organizations to distribute it via their email lists. These organizations included the Forum for Leadership in Art Museum Education (FLAME), the Association for Art Museum Interpretation (AAMI), Museum Education Roundtable (MER), and the American Alliance of Museum's Education Committee (AAM's EdCom). We also shared it on a popular museum education listserv, talk@museum-ed. We did not limit the respondents to those that work or had worked at art museums, and we did not ask respondents to identify the focus of their museum. Organizations such as MER and AAM's EdCom serve educators from art, history, and science museums among others, so it is likely that respondents were from a variety of types of museums.

In our communications, we encouraged people to share the survey widely with friends and colleagues who had been furloughed or laid off. We also encouraged multiple staff members from the same institution to reply to the survey. We collected responses to the survey from September 4, 2020 to November 4, 2020. Most responses were received during October 2020.

The survey had thirty questions arranged in four sections: INTRO, EFFECTS OF COVID-19 & ECONOMY, BACKGROUND INFORMATION (museum size and type), ABOUT YOU (demographics), and THANK YOU (option to identify their museum). Most questions were multiple choice with the option to select "all that apply" or only one answer. Most multiple-choice questions offered the option of "other," and respondents could write in their own answer.

Questions seeking information on the following allowed for respondents to type their own answer or enter "unsure": full-time or equivalent employees in the education department in 2019 and now, date of museum reopening, how many years you have worked in museum education, age, and gender. Four questions elicited longer open-ended answers: "What are you most proud of when it comes to the work you have been doing during the pandemic? What goals do you have for pivoting your work through the remainder of the year? What is the most pressing concern you face in regard to work right now? In what ways can the NAEA Museum Education Division best support you at this moment?" Gwendolyn Fernandez skillfully helped analyze responses to open-ended questions in the survey. Responses to these four questions along with content from interviews I conducted with thirteen museum educators add context and personal stories to the quantitative information. All comments are shared anonymously.

Four hundred ten individuals responded to the survey. The first question served as a screener and asked if respondents were employed by a museum when museums closed due to the pandemic (March 13, 2020). Those that were not employed by a museum at that time were prevented from answering the rest of the questions. This reduced the number of respondents to between 245 and 289 for most questions. Eighty-one percent of the respondents were full time employees, 10 percent were part-time employees and 4 percent were contract employees.

DEMOGRAPHICS

If we look at the most popular responses from the demographic data, the average survey respondent is a white woman between the ages of twenty-five and forty-four years old. These findings align with the results of a 2019 survey of art museum educators conducted by Dana Carlisle Kletchka, PhD, which found that most of the 242 respondents to her survey were between the ages of 26–40, white, cisgender women.[5] The average survey respondent to the NAEA/RK&A survey has a master's degree and more than ten years of experience in the museum education field. She works on all aspects of museum education or focuses on K–12 audiences. The museum where she works is a small to mid-size museum with an annual museum budget of less than $5 million, and there are two to ten full-time staff in the education department. The museum charges an admission fee, is a private nonprofit (meaning not a municipal, state, or national museum), and is located in the Mid Atlantic or Southeast United States.

The COVID-19 virus disproportionately affected Black people, indigenous people, and people of color (BIPOC) leading to a larger number of deaths in BIPOC populations than in white populations.[6] In addition, Hispanic and Black people in the United States experienced the most negative impact of the economic downturn.[7] Knowing this, we had hoped to be able to examine the impact of furloughs and layoffs on museum educators who identify as Black, Indigenous, or a person of color, but the number of BIPOC respondents was too small to be able to do analysis that would be applicable to the wider field. In the survey 4 percent identified as Hispanic, Latino, or Spanish; 3 percent identified as Black or African American; 2 percent identified as Asian or Asian American; and 3 percent identified as another racial or ethnic group.[8] This in and of itself is indicative of the problem of overwhelming whiteness in the field. I take responsibility for not doing more work to reach out to BIPOC museum educators. I realize I could have connected with organizations like Museum Hue and the Association of African American Museums (AAAM) to share the survey more widely. Clearly more work is necessary to more effectively connect with BIPOC museum educators to understand their experiences during COVID-19.

CHANGE IN EMPLOYMENT STATUS

Sixty-six percent of respondents said their employment status had not changed when they completed this survey in fall 2020. At that point, many museums had reopened to the public over the summer and, if they charged an admission fee, were making a fraction of the admissions revenue that they were accustomed to. In the survey, we asked when respondents' museums reopened, or were scheduled to reopen. Fifty-nine percent had opened in May, June, July, or August. The rest were set to open in September or later. Of the 59 percent that had reopened, many likely closed again when COVID-19 cases and deaths surged in the winter of 2020. With additional closures, there were additional rounds of layoffs and furloughs. The snapshot captured in fall 2020 certainly does not tell the full story of the impact of the pandemic on the museum education field. Further research is necessary.

As of October 2020, 34 percent of respondents were negatively impacted in some way. Eight percent had been furloughed (employment and pay suspended with the possibility of returning to their position); 8 percent had their pay cut but hours stayed the same; 8 percent had their hours (and thus pay) cut; and 6 percent were laid off (their employment terminated); 5 percent responded with "other" and shared impacts including loss of benefits, pay freezes, promotion without pay raise, resigning, and moving to a different position.

Furloughs, pay cuts, and layoffs did not affect everyone within the museum education field equally. Those in the education department who were most likely to experience changes in employment were those working with K–12 programs, family programs, and teen programs. Those who indicated that they worked in docent training were least likely to be affected. Others least likely to be affected were education department/division heads.

A separate question asked about a change in the number of full-time or full-time equivalent positions in the education department between the end of 2019 and fall 2020. Fifty-four percent reported no change, 41 percent reported a reduction, and 5 percent saw an increase.

Those who work for a museum identified as a private/nonprofit experienced greater changes in their employment status than those working in all other types of museums (e.g., government or college/university museums). Those who work for a museum that charges admission (general, for special exhibitions only, etc.) experienced greater changes in employment status than those working for museums that have free admission.

Those who work for a college/university museum or federal museum were most likely to report no change in numbers of education staff for their museums (85 percent and 82 percent, respectively). Those who work for a museum that has free admission were most likely to report no change in education staffing (81 percent).

IMPACT ON JOB STATUS BY NUMBER OF YEARS IN FIELD

Those who have been working in museums between five and fourteen years experienced less changes in employment status than those with fewer and greater years in the field. Furloughs were highest among those who have worked in museums four years or less. Pay cuts were highest among those in the museum field fifteen years or more. Notably age was not a factor, at least when grouping age into the categories 18–34, 35–54, and 55+ years.

Juline Chevalier

IMPACT ON CONTRACT/HOURLY STAFF

On April 3, 2020, a little more than two weeks after museums closed to the public, online arts news outlet Hyperallergic posted an article featuring this information: "The Museum of Modern Art (MoMA) in New York City has terminated all contracts with its freelance educators, according to an email from education department heads sent on Monday afternoon. . . . MoMA's email ends on a disconcerting note: even when the museum does re-open, 'it will be months, if not years, before we anticipate returning to budget and operations levels to require educator services.'"[9]

Many museums pay educators on a contract or hourly basis to lead guided tours or hands-on art-making. Even before COVID-19 these workers had more precarious working situations than most full-time employees. Contract/hourly education staff typically do not receive benefits, and their hours can fluctuate week to week, meaning that they may not be able to rely upon a steady stream of income. In large cities like New York or Los Angeles, museum educators often want full-time employment but cannot find it, so they do contract teaching at three or four museums. I interviewed one of these educators, who describes himself as a middle-aged white guy, with a PhD in art history. Early in 2020, he was teaching at four New York City museums and was laid off from two of these positions due to COVID-19. He talked about how challenging it is to master enormous amounts of information from multiple organizations, and then present it in the unique pedagogical style used by each institution. He deemed the level of content assimilation, recall, and educational flexibility equivalent to that of doing coursework for his doctorate degree.

Respondents to the survey could select more than one option in responding to the question asking about the status of contract/hourly education staff at their institution. Thirty-four percent said that contract workers had their hours or positions completely cut, and 28 percent reported that the museum reduced the hours of contract workers. Twenty-one percent reported that their institution's contract workers were "retained and will support the museum when open." We cannot be certain whether these individuals were paid while they were retained. Twenty-one percent said the number of contract workers was reduced by the museum.

These negative impacts were not distributed evenly across all museum types. Those who work for federal museums were most likely to report no effect on contract/hourly workers (21 percent). Those who work for a museum that has free admission were most likely to report no effect on contract/hourly workers.

IMPACT ON EDUCATION DEPARTMENTS COMPARED TO OTHER DEPARTMENTS

We examined how education departments fared in relation to other departments in the same institution, and we invited respondents to consider multiple factors like "staffing, budget, responsibilities, etc."

Visitor services is one department that respondents felt was affected more negatively than education. Forty-six percent indicated this while 40 percent felt that visitor services was affected about the same as education, and 14 percent felt visitor services was less negatively affected at their museum.

Senior management was the only department that respondents felt fared better than education: 48 percent indicated as such, 43 percent felt that senior management was affected about the same as education, and 9 percent felt that senior management was more negatively affected than education at their institution.

Development (fundraising), curatorial, marketing, and collections management departments were not perceived to be affected more or less than education departments. For example, 48 percent of respondents said curatorial staff was affected about the same as education staff, and 45 percent said curatorial staff was affected less negatively than education.

Data from an October 2020 survey by Wilkening Consulting and AAM addressed this question by asking museums which positions were most affected by layoffs. Sixty-eight percent selected guest services/admissions/frontline/retail as most affected; 40 percent selected education; 29 percent facilities/maintenance/security staff; and 26 percent curatorial/collections/publications. From these results, museum education was more negatively impacted than all departments except visitor services at most museums.[10]

The numbers above are responses in aggregate, and individual stories present examples of instances where layoffs and furloughs were unevenly implemented. One respondent wrote, "The education department is essentially our museum's lowest priority. We don't generate revenue, and at the end of the day that's what our leadership cares about. We were the only department that had furloughs. I am basically concerned about our continued existence, especially in terms of being able to provide free services to schools that receive Title I funding. I am not optimistic that my furlough won't ultimately end with me being laid off."

BUDGET IMPACT

Museums made these staff cuts due to drastic budget shortfalls. According to analysis of 850 responses from U.S. museums to the Wilkening Consulting and AAM survey, "Responding museums lost an average of $850k each due to the pandemic so far this year. On average, respondents anticipated losing approximately 35% of the museum's budgeted operating income in 2020. On average, respondents predicted anticipating losing an additional 28% of normal operating income in 2021." In that same survey, 67 percent responded "Yes" to the question, "Have you had to cut back on education, programming, and other public service due to budget shortfalls and/or staff reductions?"[11]

In our survey, we asked about the impact to education department budgets. Figure 16.1 documents the cuts. Twenty-four percent indicated that education budgets were reduced 16 to 35 percent, and 22 percent said the education budget was cut 36 percent or more. Reductions of 1 to 15 percent were reported by 14 percent of respondents.

One respondent commented that their education budget was completely cut: "[B]udget is a huge issue as education was the only department cut 100%. Our budget cut leads into our racial equity access issues—the students and families we primarily serve (the neighborhoods closest to us geographically) often do not have easy access to basic art supplies. Though virtual outreach is successful, we can't assume the kids will even have paper and pencils, making art making difficult and inherently elitist."

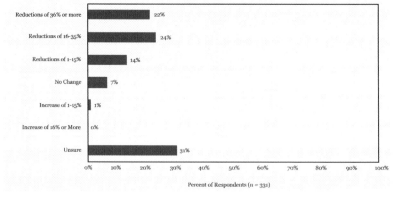

To the best of your knowledge, how has the education department's budget in your current (or former) museum been adjusted for the new fiscal year?

Figure 16.1 Education Budget Impact during the Pandemic. *Source: American Alliance of Museums and Wilkening Consulting, National Snapshot of COVID-19 Impact on United States Museums, November 2020, https://www.aam-us.org/wp -content/uploads/2020/11/AAMCOVID-19SnapshotSurvey-1.pdf, American Alliance of Museums.*

EMPATHY BURNOUT

Museum educators care about others. We asked respondents to rate their concerns on a scale of 1 (low) to 7 (high) about their work at their current or former museum based on policies and protocols. The mean ratings were as follows in order from greatest concern to lowest concern:

5.4	My personal safety
5.3	Safety of docents/volunteers
5.2	Safety of museum visitors
5	Feeling heard within the museum
5	Safety of front-of-house staff
4.8	My mental health and well-being
4.8	Changing responsibilities of my position
4.7	Ability to do Diversity, Equity, Accessibility and Inclusion work
3.8	Increased workload
3.7	Ability to do my work to the quality I desire
3.6	Ability to sustain community relationships

On average, respondents were more concerned for the safety of volunteers, visitors, and front-of-house staff than they were for their own mental health and well-being.

In an open-ended question, we asked, "What are you most proud of regarding work during COVID-19?" One of the top five most popular response types was supporting coworkers. This included pride and admiration for how hard colleagues were working and pride in supporting and caring for one another. This comment was typical of the responses: "I'm proud of how the education staff has created online programming, worked to get the museum open, and has pulled together as a team." Another respondent was proud of, "[t]he support and voice I have created for my staff when top leadership wouldn't." One person shared their goals for the remainder of the year: "Keeping it all together and helping to support my team for their benefit and for that of the museum." It may feel contradictory, but this comment demonstrates that we can champion staff well-being for both humanistic and capitalistic reasons. We can care about staff because they are people with inherent human worth, and also because staff who feel supported can perform their job duties better and better serve their employer.

Caring for others is generally a good thing, but when we do it too much, caring can take a toll on our well-being. Studies of compassion fatigue show that some kinds of empathy can lead to negative effects for the perspective-taker.[12] As educators, we often care for others first before taking care of our own needs, leaving little energy and attention for ourselves. The survey results show that respondents were concerned for many other people in addition to themselves, making it possible that their personal well-being is negatively impacted by this emotional labor.

MOST PRESSING CONCERNS

While this survey revealed museum educators' high level of care for and about others, it also exposed a feeling from some respondents that museum leadership at their institution does not care about staff. Responses to the open-ended question "What is the most pressing concern you face in regard to work right now?" featured these types of responses most frequently:

- Increased workload/not enough time to do work (52 of 245 responses)
- Stress (44 of 245 responses)—included mentions of exhaustion, mental well-being, emotional well-being, burn-out, and uncertainty
- Job security/Future job cuts for self and others (35 of 245 responses)

- Diversity, Equity, Accessibility, and Inclusion (DEAI) (24 of 245 responses)—included doing internal DEAI work with staff, equitable pay practices, and accessibility of museum programs to the public
- Museum management and operations (23 of 245 responses)—included poor communication/transparency from leadership, poor communication across departments, and lack of trust in leadership's decisions

Many of the issues above can be mitigated by leadership that centers workers' well-being and uses clear communication and transparency about how and why impactful decisions are made. Workers who feel stable and supported are likely to be more productive.[13] During a global pandemic, an employer cannot mitigate the stress of lockdowns and a deadly virus, but they can manage expectations in the office or galleries.

The following comments were shared in response to the question, "What is the most pressing concern you face in regard to work right now?"

As a Black woman, I wish my supervisors understood the turmoil of my mental health during the pandemic and uprisings. No one takes into consideration the staff's well-being, it's all about work and constantly pushing/creating events.

The organizational culture. The hierarchical structure & lack of transparency make it difficult to enjoy a job I used to love. Since the murder of George Floyd and the call for social justice, the need for internal DEAI work is pressing and obvious.

I am so angry and frustrated at the leadership and lack of transparency. . . . There is so much lip service around DEI initiatives with little to no actions to back it up. Staff morale, at least in certain departments, is so low. Anger, sadness, confusion, and frustrations are minimized and invalidated from the top. If you speak out and challenge leadership there is fear of retaliation.

We are encouraged to think big and serve, serve, serve our audiences and go all out, more than ever, to support them during COVID—but where do we get our own support? Honestly, while I am glad to be employed . . . we are asked daily to do the impossible.

Overwhelming workload. There is pressure to continue to do core work with students, teachers, volunteers, interns, etc., but we also are fielding increasing requests from other departments (Membership/Development especially) to produce content for their constituencies. Internally, there is a lack of awareness that it takes even more time to adapt/invent and present virtual programs, especially when we do not have exactly the right hardware, software, or training for much of what we're trying to do. This reality, combined with a lack of clear institutional priorities, has created a situation that is really not sustainable and I fear burnout for myself and my team.

The comments above illustrate frustration and disappointment in the inability or unwillingness of museum leadership to care for their staff.

Other comments indicate burnout is a distinct possibility for some: "My hours have been cut in half, but my responsibilities remain largely the same." Another person shared that their goal to the remainder of the year was, "Finding a sustainable level of programs between in-person and virtual, without doubling my already heavy workload. I am afraid that now I'll be expected to constantly have virtual offerings be part of every exhibition/season."

A November 2020 article from *Education Week* describes the demoralization that educators feel and how it differs from burnout:[14]

Teachers' ongoing value conflicts with the work (demoralization) cannot be solved by the more familiar refrain for teachers to practice self-care in order to avoid exhaustion (burnout). Demoralization occurs when teachers cannot reap the moral rewards that they previously were able to access in their work. It happens when teachers are consistently thwarted in their ability to enact the values that brought them to the profession.

Burnout, on the other hand, happens when teachers are pushed to the brink of exhaustion and are entirely depleted. The rhetoric of teacher resilience offers a clear culprit in the scenario of burnout—the teachers themselves who failed to conserve their energy and internal resources.

One reason people are not attracted to teaching, and why some are leaving teaching, is that they do not see it as a place where they can enact their values . . . they do not see teaching as a way to do what psychologist Howard Gardner and his colleagues call "good work." Good work serves a social purpose . . . and upholds the highest ethical standards of the profession.

It is clear from the data that museum educators are suffering from both demoralization and burnout, and there is no easy answer or quick fix for either. Compounding these work challenges are the demands of home life that disproportionately impact women in the best of times but were magnified by the pandemic. Museum education is overwhelmingly female: 93 percent of survey respondents identified as female or cisgender female.

Nahla Valji, senior gender adviser to the secretary general of the United Nations, described the impact of the pandemic on women:

The care work in the home has really grown exponentially with children out of school. We have elder care needs that have increased, we have health systems that are overwhelmed and people who are sick and still require assistance that are now at home. And historically, traditionally, these responsibilities have fallen on the shoulders of women in the home . . . disproportionately, women do more of the work in the home than men—the global average is three times more but that varies. . . . These are hours that could be spent on income generation. It's at the heart of the motherhood penalty, wage inequality, structural biases in recruitment and promotion of women and jobs—and the pandemic is really making it visible.[15]

This response by a forty-five-year-old woman highlights the above challenges: "I am most proud of the fact that I carry on working full-time, entirely from home, with three kids in my house all trying to learn remotely. One of my children I am personally homeschooling, as I feel she is too young to be on Zoom all day for online school. I am OVERWHELMED on a daily basis being pulled in 1,000 directions at once. I am proud that I am able to continue to meet the demands of my job from an environment that is truly terrible for trying to focus and be productive."

Another respondent was proud that, "We had the highest workload output of any department in our institution during our lockdown phase." While I celebrate this person's success, it also concerns me. Are we simply setting the bar so high that museum leadership continues to expect this level of output? This response from another individual sums it up perfectly: "I have created great programs during the pandemic but at what cost to my mental health? I am not proud of anything."

THE SHIFT ONLINE

When museums closed to the public, museum educators shifted their work to digital formats. In a "choose all the apply" question, we asked respondents to identify all the ways their work shifted during COVID-19. Figure 16.2 documents their responses.

These findings align with those from the MER survey implemented in the summer of 2020:[16]

In what ways, if any, have you had to shift or refocus your work/your department's work in your current (or former) museum to support and collaborate with your community? (check all that apply)

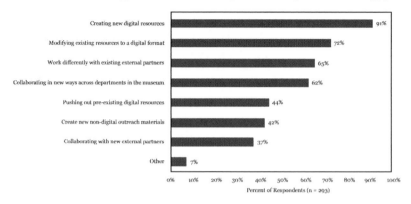

Figure 16.2 Shifts in Work as a Result of the Pandemic. *Source: American Alliance of Museums and Wilkening Consulting, National Snapshot of COVID-19 Impact on United States Museums, November 2020, https://www.aam-us.org/wp-content/uploads/2020/11/AAMCOVID-19SnapshotSurvey-1.pdf, American Alliance of Museums.*

Nearly all respondents have experienced some shift or change in their work, including:

- 94 percent are creating new digital resources
- 62 percent are working to maintain partnerships with schools/communities
- 48 percent are pushing out preexisting digital resources
- 38 percent are working differently with existing partners
- 22 percent are collaborating with new partners

This shift is remarkable for several reasons. For one, it shows the incredible flexibility and adaptability of museum educators. Before COVID-19 museum educators embodied these traits by making changes to a guided tour on the fly or presenting to curators, preschoolers, and senior citizens all in the same day, adjusting vocabulary and tone for each audience.

The shift to virtual learning was exceptionally impressive because it went against what many of us had been taught was the core of our work. For the last thirty years, many museum educators have focused on in-person experiences with real artworks and cultural-belongings to engage people of all ages in hands-on, multisensory experiences.[17] Museum closures demanded museum educators rethink everything and work to connect people and artwork, artifacts, and cultural-belongings using digital reproductions via virtual means. It was a massive shift, but one that so many museum educators did with speed, agility, and tremendous skill.

Responses to the open-ended question, "What are you most proud of when it comes to the work you have been doing during the pandemic?" demonstrated that museum educators were rightfully proud of the work they did to make this digital shift. These are the top five categories of responses:

- Digital/Virtual (110 of 246 respondents)—Transition to virtual formats, creating new digital content
- Navigating Change (78 of 246 responses)—pivoting; doing/learning new things; doing things quickly; being responsive
- Quality and/or Quantity (35 of 246 responses)—we've done so much; we've kept the quality high
- DEAI (24 of 246 responses)—working on diversity, equity, accessibility, and inclusion; paying interns; paying students
- Internal Support (18 of 246 responses)—mentions pride in team, supporting staff, caring for one another

Some representative responses to this question:

> My team has migrated all of our existing curriculum to digital formats and has developed new offerings as well within a short amount of time. I am so proud of them!

> Proud of the quality and quantity of digital assets we produced with minimal support and resources. Daily pre-recorded videos, a 20-minute pre-recorded virtual field trip for schools, member-only live workshops, live Instagram conversations about social justice, 16-session virtual camp (with one month to prepare) . . .

> Our education department has developed numerous ways to continue working virtually with all of our constituents—and we basically started from scratch. Virtual programming was non-existent. We are now provided programming for ALL the audiences we previously served.

> Quickly pivoted from in-person summer camp to all-virtual summer camp when most other organizations in the area just cancelled their programs. We made it happen with little resources, no training, and sheer grit!

An important theme that emerges from the responses above is the fact that some museum education staff did not have the technological resources (whether equipment or training) that would have helped them to make these huge shifts.

LACK OF TECHNOLOGY

We asked if museum educators had the technology (laptops, remote access to shared files, access to video conferencing) they needed to work from home. Thirty-three percent responded that they were using their own technology. Twenty-nine percent said their museum supplied some, but not all, the tech they needed, and only 28 percent said their museum gave them everything they needed.

In a separate question, we asked about access to tools they needed to develop digital programming (computers, cameras, microphones, high speed Internet connections, editing software, people who can edit video or money to pay for training to learn). Thirty-seven percent responded that they had the basics that they needed to do their work, and 18 percent said the museum did not have these tools, but they were using their own equipment to make it happen. Fifteen percent said they had everything they needed, and 8 percent said what they needed was coming to them. Five percent responded that they did not have what they needed and would not be getting it.

One person shared their most pressing concern was "Lack of support staff for digital and videography projects," and another wrote, "It has been difficult figuring out exactly what tech is needed, actually getting it, or having to go through multiple levels of approval (whether successful or otherwise) to purchase."

Some shared that they were most proud of figuring out ways to work around these limitations: "The collections-based video content that I've been developing for K–12 audiences. The videos have been challenging since we don't have adequate camera equipment/expertise to actually film with the objects, so we're . . . create[ing] narrated PowerPoints with close captions to share objects. Poor image quality for a few objects has also led me to think creatively to find substitutions or redesign slides."

One survey respondent wrote that they were most proud of, "Learning how to film and edit videos without any formal instruction." This idea of teaching yourself new skills was common in the interviews I performed as well. One individual shared that she stayed up until midnight over multiple nights learning how to edit video through trial and error. A part-time educator (the only education staff at a very small historic house) taught herself In-Design to create visually appealing resources for family audiences. When she presented three finished documents to her boss, the director, he was very pleased and requested she complete three more to give to him the next day. She informed him that it had taken her a month to complete the three examples he liked so much.

Because museum educators are so good at creative problem-solving, divergent thinking, and adapting to new situations, our museum colleagues, and especially museum leadership, do not always understand how hard we are working and how much effort it takes to do these things. We do it because we love what we do, and many feel we owe it to our audiences to provide them a wonderful experience. But, museum leadership needs to understand that these are herculean efforts and not sustainable work models.

SILVER LININGS

While there have been many obstacles for museum educators to overcome, there have been a few bright spots. Several survey respondents described situations in which they had previously wanted to create digital offerings but had not been able to make it happen. This response is typical of these kinds of comments: "I'm also proud to finally say we can offer distance learning opportunities! I've been wanting to develop distance learning experiences since I started at the museum 15 years ago. It took a pandemic to get it done, but we did it!"

One person shared, "I am most proud of being able to innovate in a way that was not previously possible. The museum (in prior times) had highly emphasized the physical experience of being in the museum . . . so we had no online educational materials. The work that I have done has all been breaking new ground." The part-time educator at a small historic house said that her small museum did not have any digital programming before the pandemic, and she felt enormous pressure to come up with some. She had to figure it all out on her own as she taught herself new technological skills while working to create meaningful programs. Another educator at a museum with fewer than forty full-time staff, found that as the education department shifted their work and programs to digital, they became a resource for other departments. While it was great to have their work and skill-set valued, she added that it was putting stress on the department, and education staff soon realized they could not say yes to all their colleagues' requests.

For those that created asynchronous content (video, activity guides, narrated slide shows), there is the benefit that these materials will continue to be useful for teachers, students, and families well after the pandemic subsides. Virtual programs also have the ability to reach a wider audience than many small or medium museums reach with in-person visitors. One educator who works at a museum in the Midwest said she loves seeing people from California, and even Japan, tune into their live web programs.

Several individuals mentioned new external collaborations that resulted from museum closures. It seems that as museum staff connected with other museums in their area to simply survive an uncertain time, partnerships and collaborations developed that had not existed before. One respondent shared that they, "hope to keep a rich dialogue going with other institutions and educators that was begun under duress but has proven to be an invaluable way to reflect on and hone practice."

Another person described their collaborative effort: "I am most proud of a cross-arts organizations partnership that pushed out quality arts ed throughout the pandemic. This group is now shifting gears and is continuing as a concerted arts education outreach initiative across art forms, disciplines, and organizations to create a collective impact model for after school engagement, arts equity in schools, and family outreach."

At least seven responses to open-ended questions highlighted the fact that their new ways of working improved collaboration across museum departments: "The way that it has forced departments to collectively work together in new ways that have increased communication and built internal capacity."

Juline Chevalier

NOT ALL DIGITAL

While generating digital programming was a core focus of museum education staff, many were also figuring out ways to serve audiences who were not able to access virtual programming. These limitations could be due to lack of access to reliable Internet service or lack of access to tools like laptops or tablets. Additionally, some caregivers were trying to limit the amount of time their children spent using screens, so analog activities were sought after. Many museums worked to distribute art activities and materials to those in need, and at least six respondents described these kinds of efforts in open-ended responses: "We created and distributed 1,200 high quality 'art kits' as part of an access grant that were really well received. We reached communities that we often do not with our in-person programming," and, "We distributed 12,000 free art kits with activity booklets to our local school's meal distribution site and local food pantries."

DEAI

George Floyd's murder and the ensuing global uprisings made it clear that everyone, especially historically white-dominated institutions like museums, needed to do some serious work on equity and inclusion. It was top of mind for many museum educators. The 2020 MER survey found that 71 percent of respondents selected "advancing anti-racism and supporting DEAI" as their biggest area of concern in their museum work.[18]

For some museum educators, this crisis offered an opportunity to do work that their museum had not previously prioritized. One respondent wrote, "I am pleased that I've been able to move forward some DEI initiatives that weren't getting a lot of traction previously." Another was proud of, "the pressure I've put on managers and leadership challenging our lackluster DEAI efforts."

A survey performed in 2019 by the Cultural Competency Learning Institute (CCLC) in a report titled *The State of DEAI Practices in Museums* found, "Museums report that DEAI is an organizational priority but have not taken strategic, consistent action at an organizational level foundational enough to support and achieve enduring equity and inclusion." In addition, "Museums focus less on the internal organizational dimensions of DEAI compared with public facing aspects."[19] Research firm Ithaka S+R completed a survey of art museum directors just as museums closed due to COVID-19 in March 2020. One of their findings was, "in the aggregate, art museum directors support EDI initiatives in the abstract but do not view these efforts as a central part of their own work."[20]

Museum educators are often those tasked with connecting to the community and serving previously underserved audiences, so it makes sense that they have been doing DEAI work for longer than many of their museum colleagues in other departments. As education staff are cut and education department budgets are slashed, the remaining human and financial resources will have to be carefully distributed. It seems inevitable that some or all DEAI work led by museum educators will stop or slow immensely.

WHAT ABOUT DOCENTS?

Art museums have a long history of using volunteer docents and guides to lead guided tours in art museums. As volunteer positions, they are open only to those who can afford to devote time and energy to unpaid work, and since most trainings are offered during business hours, most who work a full-time job are unable to participate. This has led to these volunteer positions being dominated by wealthy, white women over sixty-five years old.

In the conversations I have had with museum educators on their shift from in-person K–12 tours to live facilitated virtual programs, very few have used volunteers to lead live virtual programs. Some have said that their volunteers are not comfortable with the technology used to implement the tours

(Zoom or Google Classroom) and are unsure in their ability to trouble-shoot a technology problem in the middle of a session. If staff need to be present to assist with technology, then staff might as well lead the program.

In the survey, we inquired if volunteers were being asked to do the work of previously employed museum staff and 81 percent of respondents replied "no." This may reflect an understanding that museum education requires specialized training, experience, and expertise, as any established profession, and their work cannot easily be done by volunteers. But it may also mean that there are no staff available to manage, train, and schedule volunteers to do work that staff had been doing. Nine percent were unsure whether volunteers were being used in this way, and 5 percent replied that yes, volunteers were doing some work that staff used to perform.

Since so many volunteer docents and guides have not actively been giving tours for a year or more, this moment of disruption offers museum education staff an opportunity to carefully consider how they want these programs to work in the future. Can we continue to use volunteers to this extent as part of truly equitable and inclusive practice?

CONCLUSION

The Survey Tool

This survey was created to help document the impact of a global pandemic and ensuing economic recession on the field of museum education. Survey data and interviews provide quantitative and qualitative information to document the huge shift in types and amount of work that museum educators have done during COVID-19 and the emotional toll it has taken. We took this snapshot six to seven months into the pandemic, but after the survey stopped accepting responses, the pandemic went on and museum education continued to change. I plan to implement the survey again in the fall of 2021 to capture another snapshot of the field at a time when we expect visitors and staff to have returned to more in-person museum activities and programming. Comparing the data from fall 2020 to fall 2021 will help tell a more complete story of the impact of a global pandemic on museum education in this pivotal moment in world history and in the history of U.S. museums.

Implementing the survey again will also offer an opportunity to improve on some of the survey's shortcomings. This survey was limited due to the lack of a question asking respondents to identify the type of museum where they work (i.e., art, history, archaeology, etc.). Another limitation was the low response rate by BIPOC museum educators.

One of the strengths of this survey was the ability to examine the correlation of museum type (private nonprofit, municipal, etc.) and whether the museum charges an admission fee to the level of impact on museum education staff and budgets. Another strength was the richness of responses to the open-ended questions. They have provided insight into the emotional well-being of respondents and humanized the quantitative data with lived experiences.

Future Research

One of the main aspects of museum education work that I would like the next survey to document is changes to volunteer docent programs. I hope that many museum educators take this moment of disruption to revamp volunteer docent programs and replace them with paid staff. In addition, I want to track whether those who lost their museum education jobs during the pandemic remained in the field. If they left museum work, what kind of jobs did they find? I am also eager to explore the shift back to in-person programming: what kind of balance can be achieved between resuming in-person programs and continuing virtual programs?

An Early Blow to a Young Profession

Museum education is a young profession. The Museum Education Division of NAEA was established in 1981; only forty years before COVID-19. In such a young field, a historic, worldwide health and economic event is bound to have an important impact. We cannot know the long-term effects of current budget and staff cuts to so many museum education departments, but our survey results will provide future museum educators with data to help them look back and understand. In the first forty years of establishing the profession, museum educators have worked to document programs, perform evaluation, create literature, establish best practices, and develop graduate programs, in part, to justify museum education's existence to museum leaders and solidify museum education as a necessary part of any museum. An Ithaka S+R survey from early 2020 shows that nearly 100 percent of art museum director respondents identified providing educational programming as "highly important" now and five years from now.[21] However, our survey documented the huge hit that museum education has taken during COVID-19. Museum leaders' actions of cutting education staff and budgets speaks much louder than their survey responses. I expect that museum educators and museum education as a field will persist, and I hope that the results of our survey can help isolated museum educators understand that they are not alone.

Tool for Advocacy

I hope that these survey results help museum educators understand just how much they accomplish and the deeply negative impact overwork can have on their well-being. Museum educators must find effective ways of communicating to leadership the breadth, depth, and value of their work. I hope they are empowered by this survey to advocate for their work and strategically manage expectations (their own and of others) of their output and workload. I believe museums and the arts are incredibly important, and they offer unique experiences that can be impactful in life-altering ways. However, they are not necessary to sustain life, and museum workers and leaders need to prioritize staff well-being over churning out exhibitions and programs at the cost of museum employees' health.

Pride in Museum Educators

More than anything, the responses to the open-ended questions and the interviews I have conducted with individual museum educators have left me in awe of what museum educators have accomplished in these difficult times. They have created huge amounts of quality programs and resources under incredibly limiting circumstances.

I will end with a survey response that also perfectly sums up my feelings on the matter: "I am most proud of the education team. They have researched, surveyed, benchmarked, and distilled this info to what would be most appropriate for our audiences and collection. We've done this for all age groups and abilities. I mean literally across our entire department. Their output has been simply amazing. I've only felt professional pride like this a few times in my entire career."

DISCUSSION QUESTIONS

1. Reflect on your personal experiences during COVID-19. What of your experiences did you see reflected in this chapter? Which of your experiences seem unique to you? Consider your identities (race, gender, ability, marital status, etc.) and how those affected your experiences.
2. With other education staff (at your museum or another institution), generate a list of what your museum director and other leadership (senior staff and board members) value most at the museum. Look to documents like a strategic plan, but also pay attention to what individuals

talk about most and praise in meetings. Draft short descriptions of your education programs or projects that you think speak directly to those values. Strategize a way to share this information with the director.

3. Museum educators do too much. It is easy to add a new program each year, but it can be difficult to end a program. On your own, or with other museum educators, make a list of all the programs your department presents. Identify the target audience for each program and program goals. Estimate the amount of staff time needed to run the program and compare that to the number of people served and how deeply they are engaged. Identify a program that is not reaching its target audience/goals or one that is taking a lot of staff time for little audience reward. Imagine what it would look like to end this program. Consider who would be most upset and why. Think about how you could manage expectations. Develop a timeline and a series of steps needed to bring the program to a close and end the program.

4. Identify your "why." Reflect on why you got into museum education in the first place. Do you have the same motivation(s) today? What do/did you find rewarding about your current job and previous jobs? What do you find frustrating about your current job? Identify things you can do to increase the number of rewarding things and minimize the frustrations. Can you lead more tours if that makes you happy? If large, lengthy meetings are draining your energy, can you attend some and read the minutes for the rest? Identify where you have control and work to make changes.

NOTES

1. Rachel Ropeik, "Reflections on Tumult and a Year's Worth of Weekly Affirmations," February 11, 2021. https://theartropeik.medium.com/reflections-on-tumult-a-years-worth-of-weekly-affirmations-4bb c7a6887f1.
2. "Museums and Anti-racism: A Deeper Analysis," MASS Action: Museum as Site for Social Action, October 30, 2020, https://www.museumaction.org/massaction-blog/2020/10/30/museums-and-anti -racism-a-deeper-analysis.
3. Stephanie Downey, "How Can Museums and Schools Continue Their Relationship During and After COVID-19?" Art Museum Teaching, April 27, 2020, https://artmuseumteaching.com/2020/04/27 /museums-schools-covid-19/.
4. Amanda Krantz, "Caution: Laying Off Museum Educators May Burn Bridges to the Communities Museums Serve," *RK&A Blog*, June 24, 2020, https://rka-learnwithus.com/caution-laying-off-museum-ed ucators-may-burn-bridges-to-the-communities-museums-serve/.
5. Dana Carlisle Kletchka, "Art Museum Educators: Who Are They *Now*?" *Curator* 64, no. 1 (January 2021): 79–97.
6. Daniel Wood, "As Pandemic Deaths Add Up, Racial Disparities Persist—And in Some Cases Worsen." *NPR*, September 23, 2020, https://www.npr.org/sections/health-shots/2020/09/23/914427907/as -pandemic-deaths-add-up-racial-disparities-persist-and-in-some-cases-worsen.
7. Mark Hugo Lopez, Lee Rainie, and Abby Budiman, "Financial and Health Impacts of COVID-19 Vary Widely by Race and Ethnicity," *Pew Research Center*, May 5, 2020, https://www.pewresearch.org/fact -tank/2020/05/05/financial-and-health-impacts-of-covid-19-vary-widely-by-race-and-ethnicity/.
8. We used the racial and ethnic categories used by the U.S. Census for this multiple-choice question. We recognize that these categories are far from inclusive and disliked by many, but we felt it allowed for the possibility of greater ease of comparison with other data sets.
9. Valentina Di Liscia, "MoMA Terminates All Museum Educator Contracts," *Hyperallergic*, April 3, 2020, https://hyperallergic.com/551571/moma-educator-contracts/.
10. American Alliance of Museums and Wilkening Consulting, *National Snapshot of COVID-19 Impact on United States Museums*, November 2020, https://www.aam-us.org/wp-content/uploads/2020/11 /AAMCOVID-19SnapshotSurvey-1.pdf, American Alliance of Museums.
11. AAM and Wilkening, *National Snapshot of COVID-19 Impact.*

12. Anneke E.K. Buffone, Michael Poulin, Shane DeLury, Lauren Ministero, Carrie Morrisson, and Matt Scalco, "Don't Walk in Her Shoes! Different Forms of Perspective Taking Affect Stress Physiology," *Journal of Experimental Social Psychology* 72 (2017): 161–68.
13. Emma Seppälä and Kim Cameron, "Proof That Positive Work Cultures Are More Productive," *Harvard Business Review*, December 1, 2015, https://hbr.org/2015/12/proof-that-positive-work-cultures-are-more-productive.
14. Doris A. Santoro, "Teacher Demoralization Isn't the Same as Teacher Burnout," *Education Week*, November 11, 2020, https://www.edweek.org/teaching-learning/opinion-teacher-demoralization-isnt-the-same-as-teacher-burnout/2020/11.
15. Francesca Donner, "How Women Are Getting Squeezed by the Pandemic," *New York Times,* May 20, 2020, https://www.nytimes.com/2020/05/20/us/women-economy-jobs-coronavirus-gender.html.
16. Museum Education Roundtable, *Survey of Members and Readers*, December 2020, PDF, http://www.museumedu.org/download/1573/.
17. Jacqueline Terrassa, Olga Hubbard, Emily Holtrop, and Melissa Higgins-Linder, *Impact of Art Museum Programs on Students: Literature Review*, 2016, Literature Review, https://arteducators-prod.s3.amazonaws.com/documents/916/e071a28e-d487-4403-87c5-4221bc8f8cc1.pdf?1488265701, Alexandria, VA: National Art Education Association.
18. Museum Education Roundtable, *Survey of Members and Readers,* 4.
19. Cecilia Garibay and Jeanne Marie Olson, *CCLI National Landscape Study: The State of DEAI Practices in Museums,* 2020, PDF, https://www.informalscience.org/sites/default/files/CCLI_National_Landscape_Study-DEAI_Practices_in_Museums_2020.pdf, Garibay Group.
20. Liam Sweeny and Jennifer K. Frederick, *Ithaka S+R Art Museum Director Survey*, 2020, Research Report, https://doi.org/10.18665/sr.314362, New York: Ithaka S+R.
21. Sweeny and Frederick, *Director Survey*, 13.

BIBLIOGRAPHY

American Alliance of Museums and Wilkening Consulting. *National Snapshot of COVID-19 Impact on United States Museums.* November 2020. https://www.aam-us.org/wp-content/uploads/2020/11/AAMCOVID-19SnapshotSurvey-1.pdf. American Alliance of Museums.

Buffone, Anneke E. K., Michael Poulin, Shane DeLury, Lauren Ministero, Carrie Morrisson, and Matt Scalco. "Don't Walk in Her Shoes! Different Forms of Perspective Taking Affect Stress Physiology." *Journal of Experimental Social Psychology* 72 (2017): 161–68.

Carlisle Kletchka, Dana. "Art Museum Educators: Who Are They *Now*?" *Curator* 64, no. 1 (January 2021): 79–97.

Di Liscia, Valentina. "MoMA Terminates All Museum Educator Contracts." *Hyperallergic.* April 3, 2020. https://hyperallergic.com/551571/moma-educator-contracts/.

Donner, Francesca. "How Women Are Getting Squeezed by the Pandemic." *New York Times.* May 20, 2020. https://www.nytimes.com/2020/05/20/us/women-economy-jobs-coronavirus-gender.html.

Downey, Stephanie. "How Can Museums and Schools Continue Their Relationship During and After COVID-19?" *Art Museum Teaching.* April 27, 2020. https://artmuseumteaching.com/2020/04/27/museums-schools-covid-19/.

Garibay, Cecilia, and Jeanne Marie Olson. *CCLI National Landscape Study: The State of DEAI Practices in Museums.* 2020. PDF. https://www.informalscience.org/sites/default/files/CCLI_National_Landscape_Study-DEAI_Practices_in_Museums_2020.pdf, Garibay Group.

Krantz, Amanda. "Caution: Laying Off Museum Educators May Burn Bridges to the Communities Museums Serve." *RK&A Blog.* June 24, 2020. https://rka-learnwithus.com/caution-laying-off-museum-educators-may-burn-bridges-to-the-communities-museums-serve/.

Lopez, Mark Hugo, Lee Rainie, and Abby Budiman. "Financial and Health Impacts of COVID-19 Vary Widely by Race and Ethnicity." *Pew Research Center.* May 5, 2020. https://www.pewresearch.org

/fact-tank/2020/05/05/financial-and-health-impacts-of-covid-19-vary-widely-by-race-and-eth
nicity/.

MASS Action. "Museums and Anti-racism: A Deeper Analysis." *MASS Action: Museum as Site for Social Action.* October 30, 2020. https://www.museumaction.org/massaction-blog/2020/10/30/muse
ums-and-anti-racism-a-deeper-analysis.

Museum Education Roundtable. *Survey of Members and Readers.* December 2020. PDF. http://www
.museumedu.org/download/1573/.

Ropeik, Rachel. "Reflections on Tumult and a Year's Worth of Weekly Affirmations." *theartropeik.medium
.com.* February 11, 2021. https://theartropeik.medium.com/reflections-on-tumult-a-years-worth-of
-weekly-affirmations-4bbc7a6887f1.

Santoro, Doris A. "Teacher Demoralization Isn't the Same as Teacher Burnout." *Education Week.*
November 11, 2020. https://www.edweek.org/teaching-learning/opinion-teacher-demoraliza
tion-isnt-the-same-as-teacher-burnout/2020/11.

Seppälä, Emma and Kim Cameron. "Proof That Positive Work Cultures Are More Productive." *Harvard
Business Review.* December 1, 2015. https://hbr.org/2015/12/proof-that-positive-work-cultures
-are-more-productive.

Sweeney, Liam, and Jennifer K. Frederick. *Ithaka S+R Art Museum Director Survey 2020.* Research Report. https://doi.org/10.18665/sr.314362, New York, NY: Ithaka S+R.

Terrassa, Jacqueline, Olga Hubbard, Emily Holtrop, and Melissa Higgins-Linder. *Impact of Art Museum
Programs on Students: Literature Review.* 2016. Literature Review. https://arteducators-prod.s3.ama
zonaws.com/documents/916/e071a28e-d487-4403-87c5-4221bc8f8cc1.pdf?1488265701. Alexandria, VA: National Art Education Association.

Wood, Daniel. "As Pandemic Deaths Add Up, Racial Disparities Persist—And in Some Cases Worsen."
NPR. September 23, 2020. https://www.npr.org/sections/health-shots/2020/09/23/914427907
/as-pandemic-deaths-add-up-racial-disparities-persist-and-in-some-cases-worsen.

17

The Power of Proximity

Lauren Zalut and Sean Kelley

ABSTRACT

Over the course of ten years, Eastern State Penitentiary Historic Site, an abandoned prison turned criminal justice museum in Philadelphia, shifted its interpretive practice by centering the voices and perspectives of people personally impacted by incarceration. As a site visited by large numbers of white, middle-class tourists who report feeling personally disconnected to the issue of incarceration, the historic site has positioned itself as the national prison museum; transforming from a site focused exclusively on the past to one that addresses contemporary social justice issues. We have made mistakes, attempted (and sometimes failed) to harness the chaos of institutional change, had countless conflicts as thought partners, and been criticized both internally and externally as we navigated the ethics of working with currently and formerly incarcerated people. Despite these challenges, getting proximate has become essential to our work and changed the way we work. Visitors and coworkers alike (especially us) report transformational experiences around our programs and exhibits. This chapter describes the decade-long process undertaken by the interpretive and exhibition teams to evolve our institution from a historic site to a locus of dialogue about social justice.

INTRODUCTION

> Proximity is important . . . get close to the people and communities affected by mass incarceration.[1]

This quote from civil rights attorney and museum founder Bryan Stevenson has become a touchstone at Eastern State Penitentiary Historic Site (ESPHS). We say it in meetings. We feature it in our mass incarceration exhibit. We believe that its sentiment can apply more broadly, however, to any interpretive work that aims to center the voices of marginalized people.

It's easy to quote a respected civil rights leader in an exhibit. But the real work has been earning internal support and trust from board members and front-facing staff, and, more critically, from currently and formerly incarcerated people we hope will join us as advisors, programming partners, and teachers. But will the resulting tours, events, and exhibits be compelling museum experiences that achieve our vision of deepening the national conversation about criminal justice reform? In our experience, which has included people who are closest to the issue on our staff, on our board, as program partners, and in shaping what we do, we have made the work at Eastern State better and more authentic. Our collaborators with lived experience challenged us to do better work, to fill in our blind spots. They've made ESPHS tours, exhibits, and programs matter more to visitors, too.

Throughout, this work has been, and remains, messy and fraught. The challenges include: getting internal buy-in to change the narrative about mass incarceration; working to design education programming that meets our mostly white audience where they are coming from; and inspiring our audience to want to learn more. We've struggled to effectively support front-facing education staff (especially people of color) as they navigated the power dynamics of dialogues about prison with complete strangers; identifying ways to partner ethically with currently and formerly incarcerated people; and we've learned how to do this as people without firsthand experiences in prison ourselves. We believe that despite the challenges, the engagement with formerly and currently incarcerated people, the programming we created together, the institutional transformation of our mission and values, and the engagement with new and existing historic site audiences on a deeper level demonstrate how essential proximity is to our work.

Since Eastern State Penitentiary opened as a historic site in 1994, we have made attempts to bring marginalized voices into interpretation. People who were incarcerated at Eastern State narrate parts of our audio tour. We restored the historic synagogue that was part of the site and created an exhibit about Jewish life at Eastern State. We interpreted the experience of George Norman, a man incarcerated for freeing his wife from slavery. We uncovered the stories of LGBTQ people, some of whom had been incarcerated for "crimes" related to their sexual identity.

A series of site-specific artist installations, begun in 1995, has often addressed contemporary issues in American criminal justice reform. Nick Cassway installed his *Portraits of Inmates in the Death Row Population Sentenced as Juveniles* outside Eastern State's Death Row in 2006. Michelle Handleman installed *Beware the Lily Law*, highlighting the experiences of transgender people in the American prison system, in 2009. The site has hosted more than 150 art installations to date. But these projects and a similar attempt to change the narrative didn't bring us as close as we wanted to engaging in dialogue about the systemic issues of mass incarceration.

EARLY MISSTEPS

For many years, our interpretation failed to answer what we now believe is an unavoidable and critical question: What can all of this teach us about criminal justice reform today? Most visitors experience the site primarily through an audio tour. As originally recorded in 2003, the tour featured voices of people incarcerated and employed at Eastern State but included no contemporary perspectives or context. It ended with the vague prompt, "We hope your experiences here today will encourage you to reflect on today's criminal justice system." However, there was nothing offered to visitors to spur on this reflection.

During interpretive planning in 2012, we came to recognize that we were doing far too little to address contemporary issues with our museum voice. What followed was a series of expensive and time-consuming failures, most notably the development of an exhibit comparing the lives of people incarcerated at Eastern State with the life of someone incarcerated today. The concept was flawed: we were trying to illustrate the experiences of a generation through the lens of two specific lives, which put unrealistic pressure on those specific stories to illustrate broad societal patterns. And we hadn't engaged deeply with the incarcerated man whose life we planned to feature in the exhibit (although we did secure his permission), eventually learning that his victim's family remained angry and resentful of his refusal to admit guilt in the crime. After months of work, we quietly gave up on the exhibit. We needed another strategy.

EASTERN STATE PENITENTIARY

Eastern State Penitentiary opened as one of the first true penitentiaries in the world—built to inspire true regret (or penitence) in its inhabitants through isolation, or solitary confinement. Many of the troubling patterns and practices we notice in the criminal justice system today existed within the walls of this prison. Today, Eastern State stands as a stabilized ruin turned criminal justice museum visited annually (before COVID-19) by more than 300,000 people from around the world. The historic site centers the stories of the eighty thousand men, women, and children who were incarcerated at Eastern State, many of whom were marginalized by mainstream society. (See figure 17.1.)

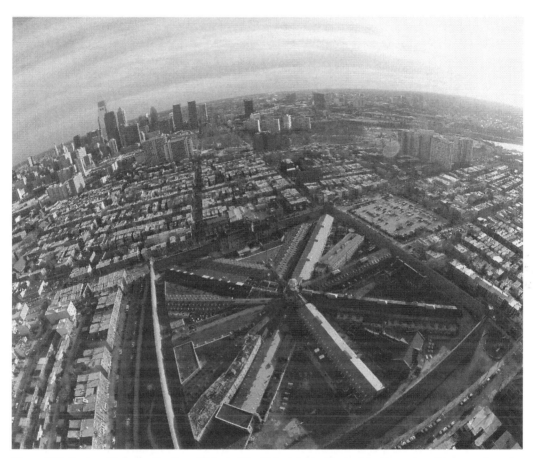

Figure 17.1 Eastern State Penitentiary Historic Site, Philadelphia. Photo: Tim Emgushov. *Photo courtesy of Eastern State Penitentiary Historic Site.*

Most visitors to the historic site are white, middle-class leisure travelers—more than 60 percent identify themselves as never having broken the law, been arrested, or known someone who is or has been incarcerated. This audience, while typical for a museum or historic site, is in stark contrast with people incarcerated in the United States—a majority of whom are poor people of color.[2]

Since June 2020 when our nation endured a coast-to-coast reckoning with racial injustice in the criminal justice system, we have seen (mostly through Zoom) a greater awareness of the reforms our criminal justice system desperately needs. We have also spent the COVID-19 pandemic and reopening(s) of the historic site working to find ways to deepen our work with the people of Philadelphia, a city with the highest incarceration rate of any large jurisdiction in the United States,[3] where approximately 55 percent of residents identify as people of color, 23 percent of people live in poverty,[4] and where violence involving a gun is nearly 40 percent ahead of the previous year.[5] We'll discuss the projects and perspective shifts that have impacted our practice most of the past ten years.

STATISTICS

Following the initial, failed attempt at an exhibit about prisoners from the past and present, we drew the conclusion that individual experiences aren't always the best place to begin discussing mass incarceration with our audience. Any given life is unique. A visitor who is skeptical that the American phenomenon of mass incarceration was brought about by policy changes could say, "This person's life isn't typical," or "This person isn't sympathetic, so I don't see the problem."

We know now that individual experiences have proven to be powerful tools in opening up discussion about criminal justice. But we decided to start conversations with visitors with statistics instead. Regardless of any individual person's experiences in the past two generations, statistics from the 1960s through the 2000s illustrate the massive shift toward increased criminalization, increased policing, more aggressive prosecution and far, far longer jail and prison sentences, all of which has resulted in higher incarceration rates and disproportionate impacts on people of color and people living in poverty.

How would visitors react? In 2012 we began discussing some simple, current statistical context in small focus groups. We had assumed, for many years, that visitors would hear discussions of contemporary issues as partisan and inappropriate. We found that, with a little bit of prototyping with graphic representations and experimental tours, visitors found the discussions compelling. In 2013 we added a simple set of statistics—the massive growth in U.S. incarceration rates in comparison to other nations—to the end of the main audio tour. As a result, visitors began asking our staff more questions about current issues in criminal justice.

We doubled down on the strategy of using statistics. The following year we constructed a sixteen-foot tall, 1.5 ton infographic sculpture in the center of both the audio and guided tour routes. *The Big Graph* can be read from three sides, displaying the skyrocketing rate of U.S. incarceration over time; the growing racial disparities in the U.S. prison population over time; and how this compares to all other nations of the world, none of which come close to the U.S. rate of incarceration. (See figure 17.2.)

We had been deeply focused on how visitors would respond to this major change in interpretive content, evaluating everything from the text to the need to cite our sources directly on exhibit panels. We didn't, however, give enough thought to how the jobs of the education staff were about to change. Several loved the graph, and most embraced the challenge of working it into their tours, but a few were deeply opposed to it. Those that opposed it had a point: they hadn't been hired or trained in a significant way to discuss race and the criminal justice system with strangers. (As one staff member pointed out at the time, the choice not to bring up the subject of race and the criminal justice system had itself been a statement.) We developed a simple set of "non-negotiables": bedrock values that the education staff could use to end conversations that had become unproductive. One non-negotiable, for instance, states that we don't debate the contention that some racial or ethnic groups are prone to criminality. But non-negotiables weren't enough, and in the end two educators from our staff of twelve left.

The Big Graph has fundamentally changed the visitor experience at Eastern State. Its scale and prominence on both the audio and guided tour routes make a statement, telling visitors that the era of mass incarceration, with its racial inequities, is fundamental to any discussion of American prisons. And what better place to have these conversations than in the historic cellblocks of a once-revolutionary, now-abandoned prison?

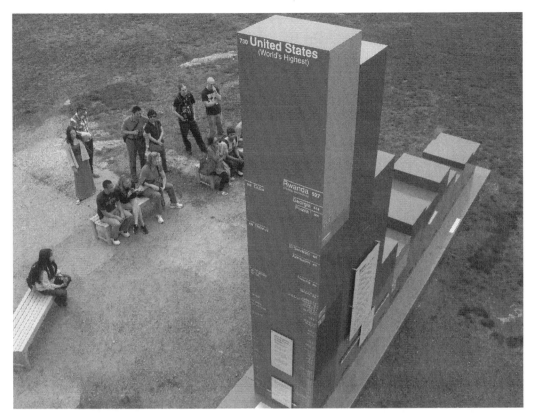

Figure 17.2 The Big Graph illustrates the rate of incarceration in U.S. history, which began to spike to historic levels in the 1970s. It also illustrates the racial disparities in the U.S. prison population growing worse in the era of mass incarceration. The narrow edge, shown here, ranks all the nations of the world by their rate of incarceration. Photo: Rob Hashem. *Photo courtesy of Eastern State Penitentiary Historic Site.*

DIALOGUE

Eastern State Penitentiary Historic Site's educational framework is built on dialogue. Dialogue invites people with varied lived experiences and differing perspectives to engage in open-ended conversation. The goal of dialogue is not resolution, but collective learning.[6] We work to reveal how the story of Eastern State is not over, that we are all connected to the criminal justice system (even if we are not aware of it), and that we can change the future of incarceration if we want to.

For many visitors, this is the first time they've considered prison beyond what they've seen in pop culture or in news headlines. During guided programs, we work to hold nonjudgmental space, meet people where they are while sharing information, and asking questions that we hope will inspire reflection, curiosity, and maybe even action. We plant seeds in visitors that we hope will grow, even if we never see the fruits of that labor ourselves.

The structure of guided tours (and now exhibitions) has been influenced by the arc of dialogue, taught to us by the team at International Coalition of Sites of Conscience. Dialogue through well-crafted questions while provoking curiosity and critical thinking. The educator holds space for collective learning to occur by setting group agreements for discussion and by sharing compelling content and asking questions that they would be comfortable answering themselves.[7] Open-ended questions build on each other; beginning with an icebreaker, then move into prompts that allow participants to share personal experiences so they can find themselves in the issue of incarceration. The dialogue then invites visitors to discuss experiences outside of their own lives, and then finishes with the facilitator synthesizing the conversation with the whole group.

We have found this strategy productive with visitors who are new to the topic of prisons, or feel personally disconnected from incarceration. However, there is tension within the dialogic approach. It is hard to hold nonjudgmental space when a visitor expresses an opinion we personally disagree with or which stands at odds with our own identities and lived experiences. It's hard to not challenge comments that are upsetting to us. Educators take responses personally; and we have all struggled when we are triggered by an opinion a visitor expresses that counters our social justice perspective. It is not always easy to have empathy for visitors with whom we disagree and to navigate what is productive for the group vs. what our end goal is as educators. Letting go of expectations and assumptions is probably one of the most difficult parts of dialogic learning. Realizing that we must take a posture of learning along with and from visitors, and that we don't hold all the knowledge, which can be at odds with traditional approaches to museum education. But when a program builds momentum and visitors say things that surprise us or share that they are inspired to learn more about incarceration because of an exhibit or tour, it solidifies that the dialogic approach is the one that makes the most sense for us.

PRISONS TODAY EXHIBIT

With work on *The Big Graph* underway, we were already planning another major exhibit that would address the root causes of mass incarceration and its impact on individuals and communities. This time, we were determined to work closely with people and communities at the heart of some of the policy issues we endeavored to address. We activated our network of colleagues working in prison reentry services and established a new network of advisors to center the perspectives of lived experience in prison. We hosted a dinner for advocacy groups in the region, telling them what we planned to do and asking for input. We began meeting with a group of incarcerated men in a Pennsylvania state prison. And we started the years-long process of developing what is now *Prisons Today: Questions in the Age of Mass Incarceration*.

Advisor Sarah Pharaon, from the International Coalition of Sites of Conscience, encouraged us to consider the four truths outlined by the South African Truth and Reconciliation Commission: Forensic Truth, Personal Truth, Social Truth, and Reconciliatory Truth.[8] While this framework has become more common in museum interpretation in recent years, it was a revelation to us at the time, and it deeply impacted the exhibit development, tour content, and education staff training moving forward.

Prisons Today was originally structured around the questions "What are prisons for?" and "Do prisons work?" The exhibit would lay out the accepted justifications for incarcerating an individual (*deterrence*, *incapacitation*, *rehabilitation*, and *retribution*) and examine evidence supporting and refuting the effectiveness of American prisons at achieving that goal. We continued our interpretive approach to provide potentially overwhelming evidence in simple ways, using statistics to encourage visitors to form their own perspectives.

Advisor Nazgol Ghandnoosh of The Sentencing Project pushed back. "Are you really going to tell your audience that there's an active debate about some of these outcomes?" She was right. The overall message of the exhibit, in this iteration, could have evoked a sense that mass incarceration policies, such as the War on Drugs, are still being debated among scholars and informed policy makers.

But that would have been a disservice to our audience. There are far too many Americans in prison. The exhibit development team knew that. Our board of directors knew that. In time, we found that our visitors knew that, too. Our instinct to avoid committing to a subjective opinion about incarceration in any concrete way was rooted in a false notion that, as a museum, we should strive for neutrality and that our audiences would reject an exhibit not built on a foundation of objectivity. But, we found that neutrality was neither a realistic nor helpful goal. While we remain committed to

Lauren Zalut and Sean Kelley

a genuine respect for multiple perspectives, we also believe that our audiences deserve to know our institution's most deeply held beliefs: mass incarceration *isn't* working, and we must rethink the future of criminal justice reform together.

We prototyped *Prisons Today* for nearly a year. We were intentional that the exhibit was for our visitors, not for us, and that we should experiment to find tools and language that would engage them. The vast majority of the exhibit interactive prototypes failed, often for simple mechanical or logistical hurdles. But sometimes a small compromise led to big improvements. A game designed to spark conversation about our visitors' privilege faced a fundamental challenge: prototype users often rejected the word *privilege*. We changed the name from "Check Your Privilege" to "Early Experiences Matter," and visitor response improved. *Prisons Today* opened in 2016, and since then, it has remained a central and impactful facet of the visitor experience. (See figure 17.3.)

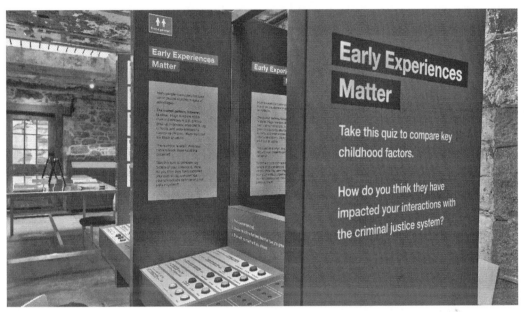

Figure 17.3 Prisons Today: Questions in the Age of Mass Incarceration at Eastern State Penitentiary Historic Site. Prototyping demonstrated that removing the word "Privilege" from the interactive's title increased the number of people wanting to engage with it, even though the content had not changed. Photo: Darryl Moran. *Photo courtesy of Eastern State Penitentiary Historic Site.*

HIDDEN LIVES ILLUMINATED

In 2017 ESPHS took on its most ambitious and proximate project to date, *Hidden Lives Illuminated*. This multi-faceted project included facilitating animation classes led by teaching artists inside active correctional facilities, culminating in a free month-long film festival of the resulting animations and nightly community engagement programming. Films were screened onto ESPHS's thirty-foot facade, literally bringing the stories of people inside prisons into public space.

This project also served the goal of centering the voices of people directly impacted by the criminal justice system: victims of crime, currently and formerly incarcerated people, as well as political figures like the commissioner of the Philadelphia jails, and government agencies like the Pennsylvania Board of Probation and Parole. *Hidden Lives Illuminated* highlighted that we are all connected as humans, despite the prison walls that keep us apart, that people in prison are the best narrators and storytellers to illuminate the realities of incarceration, and that people on all sides of the criminal justice system need a seat at the table if true reform is going to be achieved. This project was also the biggest expression of ESPHS's institutional transformation. The *Hidden Lives Illuminated* project team worked weekly in a men's state correctional facility and a women's county jail, navigating spaces that are living legacies of the abandoned prison we work in. (See figure 17.4.)

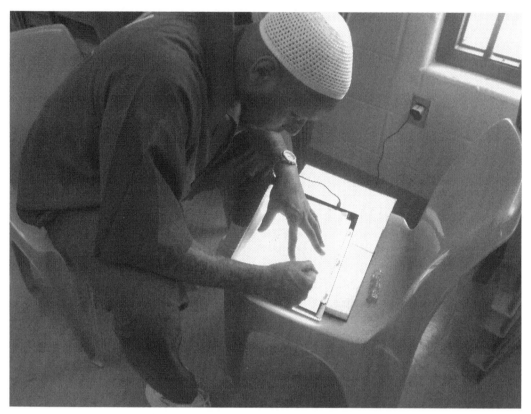

Figure 17.4 Incarcerated filmmaker Quasheam R. (PA Department of Corrections policy will not allow use of last names) works on his animated film, *Lymph Notes*, for Eastern State Penitentiary's *Hidden Lives Illuminated*. Photo: Madeline Quinn, Pennsylvania Department of Corrections. *Photo courtesy of Eastern State Penitentiary Historic Site.*

There were many complex facets of the project:

- Getting permission from the state Department of Corrections and County Jail was no easy task.
- Prisons are not easy spaces to gain access to, let alone to bring filmmaking and sound equipment into.
- We had to set up two education curricula for two different correctional settings: one with the same students from week-to-week for the state prison where residents live for years, and one for students who we might only see once or twice as people can stay in county jail for days, months, or years.
- We recruited incarcerated filmmakers and paid them for their work.

Lauren Zalut and Sean Kelley

- Assembling a team of staff and advisors with experience in animation, filmmaking, teaching in correctional facilities, community engagement/organizing, and the lived experience of incarceration was not an easy task.
- We created an outdoor movie theater with a thirty-foot-high prison wall as a movie screen.
- Partnering with an event space owned by a controversial real estate company criticized for its ties to gentrification.
- Confronting our own personal biases about race, class, and gender.
- Our project team was separated by incarceration.
- Navigating the ethics of working with currently incarcerated people and their families.

Once again, we experienced internal conflict (within ourselves, our own organization, and within the project team). There were moments when we were sure the project would fail, times when we thought the filmmakers wouldn't get paid (they did!), and tense meetings when we realized we had said or done something we thought was adding value to the project, but which ended up impacting a collaborator negatively. We apologized, recalibrated, and kept moving forward.

In the end, the program created twenty short, animated films that surprised us, moved us, and made us laugh; eight hundred postcards of solidarity written by audience members to incarcerated filmmakers; programming created in collaboration with more than twenty criminal justice organizations representing different perspectives; one grand finale for five hundred people, including seventy-five members of the filmmakers' families. The highlight of the finale was when one of the filmmakers, who was released from prison just days before, introduced his own film to the audience. *Hidden Lives Illuminated* films are now available online and are screened for visitors every day we are open.

CHANGING HIRING PRACTICES

In 2013, as part of our goal to connect every program to both past and present states of incarceration, we conceived a new program for family audiences, Pets in Prison. This program, for families with children ages 7–12, highlighted the role of animals at Eastern State, including audience favorite Pep, a retriever who was "incarcerated" at the penitentiary for allegedly harming the Pennsylvania governor's cat in the 1920s.[9] To bring the story of Pep into conversation with those of animals living behind prison walls today, we formed a collaboration with a local recidivism reduction program dedicated to saving at-risk dogs and improving the lives of vulnerable people. New Leash on Life USA pairs dogs from local shelters with people experiencing incarceration who care for and socialize the dogs. The goal is for the dogs to be adopted into loving forever homes, while incarcerated trainers learn skills, get jobs upon release from prison or jail, and stay out of prison.[10]

Little did we know how significantly this collaboration would transform ESPHS. Throughout the years spent collaborating on Pets in Prison, Rob Rosa, the vice president of the dog-training program, who was formerly incarcerated, joined our board of directors. He also mentored us as we learned about reentry from prison. He advised on exhibits and began to recruit returning citizens (formerly incarcerated people) to work for ESPHS.

In 2015, ESPHS hired a formerly incarcerated dog-training alumnus into a Visitor Services position. He approached us about taking on a greater role within a public program focused on food in prisons. He prepared *chi-chi*, comfort food that people in prison prepare from items purchased in the prison's store or commissary. Over a bowl of chi-chi he spoke with visitors about his personal experience with incarceration, a conversation that he initiated, and a conversation that he could choose to have or not have. The success of his role in the program led him to approach us about leading brief tours of Eastern State's dining halls and kitchen where he could share his lived experience in prison. He picked this location because food is a universal concept nearly everyone can relate to, but his tour took visitors beyond just what prison food is like, he revealed how the chow hall was a place one would gain an understanding of a prison's culture, residents, and staff.

His tours were also the first time that the education team noticed visitors asking how they could make an impact and become active in criminal justice reform. This staff member continued to proto-type guided tours that included his lived experience. We began to fund-raise and assemble advisors who could guide us through the questions surrounding hiring people with criminal records to work in museum education and help us consider how we could best support formerly incarcerated staff members. This support included providing assistance as they navigated returning from prison as well as in training them in the complexities around sharing personal, and at times traumatic, stories with complete strangers. We were concerned about the possibility of exploiting returning citizens as well as creating a voyeuristic experience for visitors. We were striving to promote real connection and deeper conversations about incarceration and how it impacts individuals and communities, but we didn't want to retraumatize the new staff members either.

For a year, we conducted research, funded by the International Coalition of Sites of Conscience. We spent time with the Philadelphia reentry community, revised our background check process, and completed trauma-awareness coursework. We attended meetings with currently incarcerated men at State Correctional Institution—Graterford. We assembled advisors with a variety of expertise in-cluding individuals who had lived in prison, had worked in probation and parole, prison reentry social work, and academia. We learned to use people-first language by replacing the outdated term "inmate" with "incarcerated people," and were called-in[11] for paternalistic thinking about the project. After this research and community engagement work, we felt prepared to begin recruiting formerly incarcerated people into front-facing education positions, which we called the Pilot Program, later termed the Re-turning Citizens Tour Guide Project.

From 2016 to 2018, we hired three cohorts of formerly incarcerated seasonal educators who led guided tours that incorporated their lived experience with prison (if they chose to share it). After each cohort, we adjusted the program. We hired tour guide co-facilitators to mentor Returning Citizen Tour Guides and mitigate exclusion that occurred in the workplace. There were initially some staff mem-bers who were concerned about hiring people with criminal records, though the project was designed to challenge the stereotypes of incarceration. Tour guide co-facilitators served as a built-in support system for Returning Citizen Tours Guides as they went through training and gave their first few tours. We provided social workers for mental health support and hosted professional development sessions to build skills and knowledge. Managers provided one-on-one support to the Returning Citizen Tour Guides in looking for new work at the end of season, and in learning how to use computers. We also learned how to navigate internal conflict. We disagreed a lot during the first year of the project, espe-cially about how to promote the program. (See figure 17.5.)

There is an assumption that people who have criminal records struggle in the workplace, but what we noticed is that common struggles of learning content and arriving to work on time were the same as with coworkers who had never experienced incarceration personally. Similarly, there is an assump-tion that people with criminal records cannot work in museum education but are better fits for back-of-house positions within museums. With input from lawyers and human resources professionals, we were able to navigate background screenings that ensured we were not judging a person by their past mistakes but were onboarding people who were truly great fits for the education position.

The most necessary changes to the project came in 2019, when we hired Reem (who had once called us paternalistic at a state prison a number of years before) to work as the supervisor of edu-cation and community engagement on the ESPHS team and take the helm of the Returning Citizens Tour Guide Project, among other job responsibilities. It became clear that this project could not be led by a white woman who had never been incarcerated, but rather required leadership from a per-son with lived experience in prison. And that for ESPHS to be the national prison museum, formerly

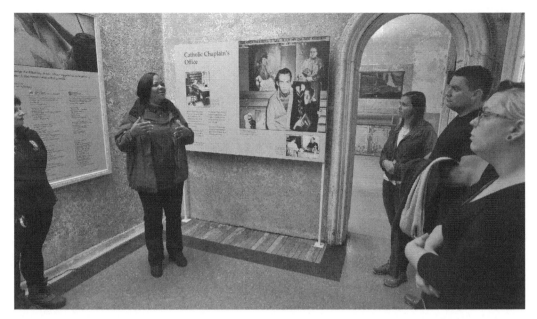

Figure 17.5 Eastern State Penitentiary educator, Sharmaine Thomas, discusses the role of religion for incarcerated people, both historically and today. Photo: Darryl Moran. *Photo courtesy of Eastern State Penitentiary Historic Site.*

incarcerated people had to be on the leadership team; making hiring decisions, shaping education programming, and deciding how resources are used.

Similarly, it became clear that we could not continue to hire for a role explicitly called Returning Citizen Tour Guide. Although unintentional, people working in this role often felt they *had* to share their lived experience in prison during their work, and this put them in a box on the team. Even in the face of these challenges, each person who worked in the role of Returning Citizens Tour Guide or as an advisor to the project transformed the culture of ESPHS. This project led to: the first formerly incarcerated person joining the board of directors; drew new interest from funders committed to social justice; catalyzed new programming with reentry and racial justice collaborators; pushed us to be more trauma-aware and use person-first language; and expanded the way we hire for all positions at ESPHS.

Under the leadership of the supervisor of education and community engagement and with funding from the Institute of Museum and Library Services, we changed the Returning Citizens Tour Guide project and expanded our commitment to fair chance hiring with the creation of a reentry fellowship called LEAD—Lived Experience Activating Dialogue. The vision for this fellowship is to provide a first job for someone when they return from incarceration and to hire them for a role that does not center exclusively on their lived experience in prison. This paid fellowship will expose them to museum work and build skills for other career pathways and put people who have lived experience in prison into critical roles shaping education and public programming at ESPHS.

COVID-19

When the COVID-19 pandemic arrived in Philadelphia, ESPHS was on track to continue building projects and programs rooted in deep commitment to its mission and remaining proximate to people impacted most by incarceration. With the resulting months-long closure, we, like many museums, pivoted to virtual experiences with the goal of keeping as many staff as possible. We offered our free monthly *Searchlight Series* discussions on a weekly basis, inviting criminal justice experts to share their insights. We introduced a new video series called *Prisons and the Pandemic*, a weekly program to educate a general interest audience on the pandemic's devastating impact on people in prison, who live in crowded communal environments where disease spreads rapidly.

As the COVID-19 pandemic kept us working remotely, we began to feel deep grief for the in-person work that is the core of museum education, but we remained hopeful that we'd gain new audiences with the expanded reach of virtual programming. Our grief only deepened as our coworker Reem, supervisor of education and community engagement, passed away from complications related to COVID-19, halting work on the reimagined reentry fellowship formerly known as the Returning Citizens Tour Guide Project. We had hoped he'd write this book chapter with us.

As we continued to navigate working for a historic site during a worldwide pandemic, we were forced to lay off staff across the organization. All this came shortly after the murder of George Floyd, amid a summer of uprisings against police violence, and a nationwide reckoning focused on racial injustice within the criminal justice system; as well as calls for museums to acknowledge their role in systemic racism. We found ourselves navigating internal and external conversations about racial justice. We acknowledged we should have done more to support staff of color in teaching emotionally demanding education programs, reflecting on the role of ESPHS as a museum interpreting criminal justice reform, and figuring out how to continue to do our work with a smaller team who was grieving the passing of a coworker and leader within the organization.

Out of this grief, we found our resilience. We maintained relationships with our currently incarcerated advisors and found ways for their stories to continue to reach ESPHS audiences. We recommitted ourselves to fair chance hiring as we work to rebuild the team and hit our stride with virtual programming. We launched a new education workshop co-taught with staff from PAR-Recycle Works, a reentry organization specializing in electronics recycling. This workshop has the explicit goal of inspiring action on criminal justice reform and shares how people can get involved at a time when it seems so many are ready to move beyond dialogue and into action.

CONCLUSION

The change to the ESPHS organizational culture throughout this journey to center marginalized voices has been striking. Our board of directors rewrote the organization's mission and values statements in 2017. We now attract staff and board members who want to be here because of this work. We have attracted new funders and new members as a result. This change is felt in every aspect of the organization. The team is united about the very real impact our mission can have.

Visitors remark how deeply this new programming moves them and encourages them to reflect. One visitor wrote to say that a conversation with her daughter and a formerly incarcerated educator gave her the confidence to go home and tell her daughter that she had an incarcerated uncle.

Sometimes we tell ourselves that we are the closest thing the United States has to a national prison museum. As the nation with the highest per capita incarceration rate on earth—about 2.2 million people behind bars—we could certainly use one. Often, we feel like we fail to live up to that standard.

But we have learned lessons to carry us forward on this journey, and we encourage other museums to consider this interpretive model knowing where we went wrong so you don't repeat our mistakes Proximity is important, yes, and every step closer to the people and communities that our programming and exhibits will address, is a step closer to impacted people telling their own stories in their own words. At Eastern State this looks like more formerly incarcerated people joining the interpretive team and leadership in key roles, such as educators, directors, and board members. It has been important for us to be space-makers, to include formerly incarcerated collaborators in professional speaking engagements, public programs, and meetings with museum colleagues, government officials, and funders.

As we discussed above, there is, however, very real tension in this work. Some interpretive staff become frustrated that the nature of dialogue at a museum that serves visitors who are new to learning about incarceration allows for many big, broad conversations with visitors. But deep, extended engagements can be rare. The lines between advocacy, activism, and antiracism can be blurry. Internal, honest discussions are critical. It's important for all parties to keep an open mind while acknowledging their biases, and this is difficult work to do among large, disparate groups of strangers. We have found that encouraging a culture of prototyping and risk taking, meeting with coworkers regularly to identify pinch points in the work, observing programming, and providing ongoing professional development and training have been critical to supporting the education team.

There will be critics. Some people will think this programming has gone too far and will attack it as partisan. Others will attack it for not going far enough. Having a thought partner you trust is helpful when you're questioning your decisions. Do the personal work to learn about your own biases, assumptions, and triggers, too.

Some museums have done well with long-term plans for deep interpretive change. Our path has been iterative, experimental, and punctuated by significant mistakes and opportunities for reflection. We encourage our colleagues to make small changes while they plan for something bigger. Take some chances and see what happens as you work toward transformation.

We believe these lessons can apply not just to social justice programming at historic sites but can be broadly applied across museum disciplines. Museums that interpret so-called "vice" of previous generations could learn a lot from organizations that support people in addiction, and perhaps who engage in sex work, today. Museums that interpret the homes of wealthy industrialists might learn from members of trade unions. These relationships may feel dangerously at-risk for exploitation—and they often are—but that cannot become an excuse to simply exclude these voices and these important stories. In short, people who are closest to the problem are the most knowledgeable about how to fix the issue; people who have lived experience are the most qualified to speak convincingly about the experience; sadly in interpretive spaces, these people rarely have a seat at the table. Museums could change this.

Our journey has been marked by a series of intensive collaborations, most notably with formerly and currently incarcerated people. These relationships opened the door to examining our own hiring practices and reflecting on how we tell the stories we tell. We encourage you to do the same in your institution. Even though this work is messy, complicated, and challenging, it just might have the effect of changing your museum and changing the public's understanding of the issue you care about. And as with our experience at ESPHS, it might even change you.

DISCUSSION QUESTIONS

1. This chapter describes how a historic site expanded its hiring practices to recruit people with criminal records. Consider how you can change or adjust your own hiring policies to hire people with barriers to employment. Who on your institution's team could be your ally in a fair chance hiring initiative? Are there people that you could be more inclusive of when you are recruiting for open positions at your workplace?
2. The authors described how getting proximate to the issue of incarceration led them to find new collaborators that deepened their mission and strengthened their education programs. What does getting proximate mean for you at your organization?
3. The chapter reviews how working with one new local grassroots partner organization transformed their work. Working with a colleague at your institution, determine what is one program

where you can work with a local grassroots organization to encourage visitors to take action on a social issue? In what ways could you structure the program to inspire visitors to take action?

4. The authors talk about the role that conflict played in this period of transformation at ESPHS. Think about a recent workplace conflict you had to navigate. What did you learn from it?

NOTES

1. Bryan Stevenson. *Just Mercy* (New York: Spiegel & Grau, 2015).
2. The Sentencing Project. "Trends in U.S. Corrections." Updated May 2021.
3. "Summary." Philadelphia, PA, Safety + Justice Challenge, accessed May 12, 2021, https://www.safety andjusticechallenge.org/challenge-site/philadelphia/.
4. "QuickFacts, Philadelphia City, Pennsylvania." U.S. Census. Updated July 2019, https://www.census .gov/quickfacts/philadelphiacitypennsylvania.
5. The Philadelphia Center for Gun Violence Reporting. "Tracking Gun Violence in Philadelphia: May 5, 2021." Updated May 5, 2021, https://www.pcgvr.org/2021/05/05/tracking-gun-violence-in-philadel phia-may-5-2021/.
6. International Coalition of Sites of Conscience. "Facilitation Toolkit." 2016, https://www.sitesofcon science.org/wp-content/uploads/2019/07/MMP-Toolkit-ENGLISH.pdf.
7. Ibid.
8. Marie Toner and Sarah Pharaon. "Taking Action by Fostering Activism at the Pearl S. Buck House." *Journal of Museum Education*, August 27, 2020, 240–52.
9. Gifford Pinchot, Letter to Col. John C. Groome, Warden, Eastern Penitentiary, July 29, 1924.
10. "Who We Are." New Leash on Life USA, accessed May 12, 2021, https://www.newleashonlife-usa.org.
11. Calling-in is an alternative to calling-out and invites someone into an uncomfortable conversation rooted in learning and growth. Learn more from Professor Loretta J. Ross: https://lorettajross.com.

BIBLIOGRAPHY

"Facilitation Toolkit." International Coalition of Sites of Conscience. 2016, https://www.sitesofconscience .org/wp-content/uploads/2019/07/MMP-Toolkit-ENGLISH.pdf.

New Leash on Live USA. "Who We Are." Accessed May 12, 2021. https://www.newleashonlife-usa.org.

"Philadelphia, PA." Safety and Justice Challenge, October 24, 2018. https://www.safetyandjusticechal lenge.org/challenge-site/philadelphia/.

Pinchot, Gifford. Letter to Col. John C. Groome, Warden, Eastern Penitentiary, July 29, 1924.

Stevenson, Bryan. *Just Mercy*. New York: Speigel & Grau, 2015.

The Sentencing Project. "Trends in US Corrections." Last modified May 2021, https://www.sentenc ingproject.org/publications/trends-in-u-s-corrections/.

Toner, Marie and Sarah Pharaon. "Taking Action by Fostering Activism at the Pearl S. Buck House." *Journal of Museum Education*, August 27, 2020.

"Tracking Gun Violence in Philadelphia: May 5, 2021." The Philadelphia Center for Gun Violence Reporting, May 5, 2021, https://www.pcgvr.org/2021/05/05/tracking-gun-violence-in-philadel phia-may-5-2021/.

U.S. Census. "QuickFacts, Philadelphia City, Pennsylvania." Updated April 2017, https://www.census .gov/quickfacts/philadelphiacitypennsylvania.

Index

Note: Page numbers in italics indicate a figure and page numbers in bold indicate a table on the corresponding page

About the Editors and Contributors

ABOUT THE EDITORS

Jason L. Porter

Jason Porter is the Kayla Skinner Deputy Director for Education and Public Engagement at Seattle Art Museum. Previously, he served as the director of education and programs at MoPOP (Museum of Pop Culture) in Seattle, as director of education and public engagement at the San Diego Museum of Man (now Museum of Us) and associate director of education at the Skirball Cultural Center in Los Angeles. His work focuses on experiential education and public programs that serve community, school, family, and teacher audiences and on using the arts as a vehicle for personal transformation and social change. Prior to entering the museum field, he was a public school teacher. He received a BA in English from Tufts University, an MA in education from Seattle University, and an EdD from UCLA. His dissertation examined charter schools meeting the needs of special education students. Professional development activities have included presentations at conferences including AAM, CAM, and WMA, serving as a mentor to emerging museum professionals and teaching as a guest lecturer in a number of museum studies programs. He has been a board member of AAM's Education Professional Network (EdCom) from 2014 through 2016, a jurist with the Excellence in Exhibitions competition in 2017 and 2018, a grants reviewer for IMLS in 2018, and a member of the peer review board of the *Journal of Museum Education* (JME) since 2016. When he's not working, he's reading, writing, cooking, cycling around town, or visiting other museums. He lives in an apartment that has a view of the Space Needle with his dogs, Penny and Ellie, and his husband, Mark.

Mary Kay Cunningham

In the last twenty-five-plus years, Mary Kay Cunningham has served over thirty-five different cultural institutions or attractions in the diverse roles of consultant, manager, museum educator, volunteer coordinator, and docent. She founded Dialogue Consulting in 2001 to support institutions improving their visitor experience through inclusive and collaborative interpretive planning, programming, and professional development. Her passion for facilitating group learning that brings together staff, volunteers, and communities to navigate institutional change is the hallmark of her work.

Mary Kay is the author of *The Interpreters Training Manual for Museums* (AAM, 2004, and University of Macerata Italy, 2013) that guides frontline staff in facilitating meaningful learning conversations with visitors. As a professed learning addict, she pursues and supports professional development in the field by serving on the editorial board of the *Journal of Museum Education* since 2010, creating and instructing a graduate-level course on Visitor Experience design at the University of Victoria, British Columbia, since 2013, and presenting over forty-five sessions or workshops in the last twenty years for professional meetings including AAM, APGA, ASTC, CAM, NAI, and WMA.

ABOUT THE CONTRIBUTORS

Melanie Adams

Melanie A. Adams, PhD, currently serves as the director of the Smithsonian Anacostia Community Museum. Before joining the Smithsonian, Adams served as the deputy director for learning initiatives at the Minnesota Historical Society overseeing the state's twenty-six historic sites. Prior to Minnesota, she spent twelve years at the Missouri Historical Society as the managing director for community education and events. Adams is an active member of the museum community and served on the board of the American Association for State and Local History and is a former president of the Association of Midwest Museum.

Adams has taught museum studies classes for the University of Missouri–St. Louis and Bank Street College of education. She is the author of numerous articles and blog posts as well as a regular conference presenter on issues related to museum education, community engagement, and race. She holds a bachelor's degree in English/African-American studies from the University of Virginia, a master's degree in education from the University of Vermont and a doctorate from the University of Missouri–St. Louis in educational leadership and policy studies.

Veronica Alvarez

Veronica Alvarez, EdD, is an educator, historian, and arts advocate. She believes access to quality arts instruction is a social justice issue. After twenty years in the museum field, she recently transitioned to the California Institute of the Arts as the director of community arts partnership with a special appointment in the Critical Studies Department.

Dina Bailey

Dina Bailey is the CEO of Mountain Top Vision, a consulting company that works with organizations on trainings and strategic initiatives that support more inclusive communities. She has been the director of methodology and practice for the International Coalition of Sites of Conscience, the inaugural director of educational strategies at the National Center for Civil and Human Rights, and the director of museum experiences at the National Underground Railroad Freedom Center, and a high school English teacher at Pike High School. Dina holds a bachelors in middle and secondary education, a masters in anthropology of development and social transformation, and a graduate certificate in museum studies. She has been an adjunct professor at Johns Hopkins University and at George Washington University; and, she has been published in both the formal education and museum fields. Dina is proud to be the secretary of the American Association for State and Local History, the board chair of Next Generation Men and Women, and the chair of the American Alliance of Museums' Education Committee. Dina may be reached at dina@mountaintopvisionllc.com and www.mountaintopvisionllc.com.

Kayleigh Bryant-Greenwell

Kayleigh Bryant-Greenwell is a Washington, D.C.-based museum equity specialist with over ten years of museum and nonprofit experience at the intersections of social justice and antiracist practice. Currently serving as head of public programs with Smithsonian American Art Museum and the Renwick Gallery, she is responsible for an extensive calendar of programs across two museums, leading new outreach and inclusion initiatives toward developing new audiences and cultivating public engagement. In the wake of COVID-19 she led an internal cross-departmental task force toward reopening strategies. In summer 2020, she served on a six-month part-time detail with the Smithsonian's Anacostia Community Museum to develop a new initiative on race and community. She serves on the board of Washington Project for the Arts, and on the Artist Selection Committee of Halcyon Arts Lab and VisArts in Rockville, Maryland. Additionally, she participates in the Museum As Site for Social Action and Empathetic Museum movements. She received her bachelor of art in art history from the University of Maryland, College Park, and master of art in museum studies from George Washington University.

Mac Buff

Mac Buff (they/them) is the associate director of education for student and teacher programs at Tacoma Art Museum. Mac began their teaching career at age sixteen, giving horseback riding lessons to young children. Since that time, they have nearly two decades of experience in museum education, formal classrooms, and youth development at sites along the West Coast of the United States, as well as Northern Ireland. Mac received a master's degree in elementary education from the University of California–San Diego in 2014. They contributed to the American Alliance of Museums' *Toolkit for Gender Transition and Transgender Inclusion* and have presented on LGBTQ+ inclusion at regional and national conferences. Mac serves on the Washington Art Education Association board as museum representative and interim chair of the Justice, Equity, Diversity, and Inclusion Council. They facilitate workshops on equity and inclusion for museums, nonprofits, and educational organizations of all sizes. Mac lives in the beautiful Pacific Northwest with their wife and very spoiled dog. More information about their work can be found at www.mac-buff.com.

Enrico G. Castillo

Dr. Enrico G. Castillo obtained his undergraduate degree from the University of Virginia and his MD with a concentration in underserved populations from the University of Pittsburgh. He completed his psychiatry residency and public psychiatry clinical fellowship at Columbia University. He spent his public psychiatry fellowship as a medical director on a North Bronx Assertive Community Treatment team and as a staff psychiatrist for a "housing first" outreach team for the chronically street homeless in lower Manhattan with the organization Janian Medical/Project for Psychiatric Outreach to the Homeless. Dr. Castillo was a UCLA Robert Wood Johnson Foundation Clinical Scholar and obtained his MS in health policy and management from the UCLA Fielding School of Public Health.

Dr. Castillo's research has been conducted in close partnership with local, state, and national agencies and community organizations including the Office of the Surgeon General, the New York State Office of Mental Health, the Los Angeles County Departments of Mental Health and Health Services, the RAND Corporation, and Healthy African American Families II. Dr. Castillo's research is focused on community-public-academic partnerships, the integration of mental health and social services, public mental health and homelessness/housing policies, and medical education on structural competency and health equity.

Juline Chevalier

Juline A. Chevalier is passionate about helping people connect to visual art, each other, and themselves in meaningful ways. She has more than twenty years of experience in art museum education and interpretation, and she is dedicated to making museums relevant and accessible to as many people as possible. Two of her favorite questions are "So what?" and "Why are we doing it this way?" She tries to ask them of herself and others in museums as often as possible and as kindly as possible.

Juline holds a bachelor of arts degree in art history from the University of Virginia, and she received a master's degree in education from the Harvard Graduate School of Education. For ten years, Juline was the curator of education at the Nasher Museum of Art at Duke University. She was the head of interpretation and participatory experiences at the Minneapolis Institute of Art for five years and joined the staff of the James A. Michener Art Museum in Doylestown, Pennsylvania, as director of public engagement in 2021. She served as the director of the National Art Education Association Museum Education Division from 2019 to 2021 and is an active member of MASS Action (Museum as Site of Social Action).

Jayatri Das

Jayatri Das, PhD, is director of science content and chief bioscientist at the Franklin Institute and an invited fellow of the Center for Neuroscience and Society at the University of Pennsylvania. She has led development of several exhibitions at the institute—including *Your Brain*, a national award-winning exhibit about the neuroscience and psychology of the human brain, and *SportsZone*—and directs in-person and virtual programming initiatives to advance informal science education about emerging health issues, materials science, synthetic biology, and other areas of current science and their societal impact. She also serves as an advisor to the National Informal STEM Education (NISE) Network.

Das earned undergraduate degrees in biology and biochemistry from Penn State and a PhD in evolutionary biology from Princeton University. Prior to joining the Franklin Institute, she conducted postdoctoral work at both the Koshland Science Museum and the University of Pennsylvania. In 2016, she was honored with the American Alliance of Museums' Nancy Hanks Award for Professional Excellence.

Elizabeth Gerber

Elizabeth Gerber is senior content specialist at the Los Angeles County Museum of Art. From 2005 to 2011 she served as director of school, teacher, and community programs at LACMA. Elizabeth was an integral part of the team that launched the Charles White Elementary partnership.

Sarah Jencks

Sarah Jencks is an educator who, since 2007, has served as director of education and interpretation at Ford's Theatre in Washington, D.C. Her work is at the intersection of history, civics, theater, and education. She was previously a middle school teacher and an arts educator.

Sean Kelley

Sean Kelley is senior vice president and director of interpretation at Eastern State Penitentiary Historic Site in Philadelphia. He produced the site's award-winning audio tour, now heard by more than a million visitors, and has curated more than one hundred site-specific artist installations in the building. He conceived and developed *The Big Graph*, a sixteen-foot infographic sculpture that illustrates the skyrocketing U.S. Rate of Incarceration and curated the companion exhibit *Prisons Today: Questions in the Age of Mass Incarceration* which won the 2017 Overall Award for Excellence from the American Alliance of Museums. From 2017 to 2019 he oversaw *Hidden Lives Illuminated*, a project which resulted in twenty original films made by currently incarcerated individuals and projected them for a month onto Eastern State Penitentiary's façade.

Mr. Kelley visits active prisons and writes critically about prison museums and sites of detention. He speaks widely on the responsibility of museums to address controversial and painful subjects, as well as the ethical and management challenges posed by large-scale fundraising events in sites with complex histories. He has served as adjunct faculty at Rutgers University, teaching museum studies in the graduate program in public history, and at the University of Pennsylvania.

Tomoko Kuta

-Senior Director of Education and Visitor Services, San Diego Botanic Garden, 2021–current
-Former Deputy Museum Director, The New Children's Museum 2011–2021

Working in a museum was not something that I dreamed about as a girl. In my teens I thought about being a creator, specifically a fashion designer. But I discovered a love of showcasing artists when I landed my first museum job. Since that first experience, I've enjoyed over twenty-five years of engaging diverse audiences in the arts in different museums and positions. At the New Children's Museum, I was part of the leadership team when the organization received national recognition from the Institute of Museum and Library Services. For over nine years, I had the distinguished honor of leading a talented team to commission significant art installations, design impactful educational programs, and delivered outreach workshops in communities far from the museum. I know the work was successful because, over the years, attendance and membership, along with the museum's reputation, grew. My drive for excellence in nonprofit work comes from a commitment to serve others. Armed with a BS from Cornell University, an MA from the University of Chicago, and life experiences as an immigrant and having a disabled brother, I have devoted my career to working in arts and cultural nonprofit organizations to ignite new interests and nurture creativity in others. My work also extends to serving on the board of the California Association of Museums.

In the whirlwind of all that took place since March 2020, I went through my own transformation. I realized that I wanted to continue to grow and decided to leave the museum. I am now working in a new sector of the nonprofit field at San Diego Botanic Garden where I will adapt the practices of engagement and education for children to a larger and more diverse audience. I too am continuing to learn.

Mickey Maley

Mickey Maley began serving as program lead for museum education, MA, and teaching courses at University of the Arts in 2019. Mickey has ten years museum education experience serving most recently as assistant director of public programs at the Franklin Institute where he gained experience in facilitating learning on the museum floor through hands-on and live performance experiences, developing visitor-centered programming and training for staff and volunteers, and collaborating on exhibit educational programs.

Mickey has his master of science in education in leadership in museum education from Bank Street College of Education, and his bachelor of science in physics, and is a current member of the Museum Education Trends Committee for the Education Professional Network and a museum assessment program peer reviewer—both with the American Alliance of Museums. Past nonprofit leadership positions include serving as a board member for the Philadelphia chapter of the Emerging Museum Professionals network.

Beth Maloney

Beth Maloney is the director of interpretation at the Baltimore Museum of Industry. She leads the education and programming team and collaborates on exhibition development, interpretation, and institutional planning. In addition, she runs an independent consulting practice, coaching staff at museums and historic sites as they create engaging, interpretive experiences. Beth currently serves as a mentor with the EdMEM program through the American Alliance of Museums Education Committee. She is a past president of the Museum Education Roundtable and a former guest editor of the *Journal of Museum Education*. Beth holds a BA in history and English from Swarthmore College and an MSEd in museum education from Bank Street College of Education.

Lorie Millward

Lorie Millward is an agent of change and has championed free choice learning and mold-breaking throughout her thirty-plus years in the field. She has authored several articles and book chapters related to her work and was the inaugural recipient of the STEM Innovator of the Year award from the Utah governor's Office of Economic Development. She has served the field as president of the Utah Museums Association, the Western Museums Association's vice president of programs and innovation, and as a member of the American Alliance of Museum's diversity committee.

Her range of experience and expertise includes museum design and construction, creation of immersive learning environments, exhibition development, formal and informal education, audience research, evaluation, and the natural sciences. Lorie's greatest academic and professional achievement, however, is the impact her efforts have had in the lives of those with whom she has explored. She is a dancer, naturalist, traveler, and grandma to the world's best boy.

Catherine Awsumb Nelson

Catherine Awsumb Nelson, PhD, is a research and evaluation consultant specializing in pre-K–12 education, with a particular focus on measuring and strengthening the impact of investments in teacher learning and leadership.

Mark Osterman

Mark Osterman is a museum administrator, researcher, technologist, and artist. He has a doctor of education with a research focus in arts, literacy, and technology. Mr. Osterman has taught at Miami Dade College, facilitated specialized workshops in art educational theory and practice for the University of Miami, The Wolfsonian-FIU, and the Lowe Art Museum. He has presented nationally on technology in museums and art educational theory and research studies and has published work in the *Journal of Museum Education* and the *Journal of Educational Multimedia and Hypermedia*, among others.

Mr. Osterman has worked for the Brooklyn Museum of Art, the Museum of Art and Design, the Wolfsonian-FIU, Vizcaya Museum and Gardens, and currently at the Lowe Art Museum–University of Miami. His museum work has focused on strategic thinking, interpretive technology initiatives, curriculum development, and developing evaluation and assessment tools related to museum practice. Mr. Osterman has volunteered professionally by serving on the board of directors for MCN, conference committee chair for AAM EdCom, a member of the Museum Education Division Peers Initiative for NAEA, and as a grant reviewer and panelist for Miami-Dade Department of Cultural Affairs.

Scott Pattison

Scott Pattison, PhD, is a social scientist who has been studying and supporting STEM education and learning since 2003, as an educator, program and exhibit developer, evaluator, and researcher. His current work focuses on engagement, learning, and interest and identity development in free-choice and out-of-school environments, including museums, community-based organizations, and everyday settings. Dr. Pattison specializes in using qualitative and quantitative methods to investigate the processes and mechanisms of learning in naturalistic settings. He has partnered with numerous educational and community organizations across the country to support learning for diverse communities. For more information about his work, visit: https://www.terc.edu/profiles/scott-pattison/.

Smirla Ramos-Montañez

Smirla Ramos-Montañez, PhD, is a bilingual (Spanish/English) and bicultural (Puerto Rican/American) researcher and evaluator focusing on culturally responsive studies related to informal STEM learning. Dr. Ramos-Montañez has led and supported a variety of projects, including program and exhibit evaluation as well as STEM education research to provide accessible, culturally relevant, and engaging experiences for diverse audiences. Currently, she is working with Dr. Scott Pattison to better understand family interest pathways and how to foster long-term interest in the engineering design process. For more information about her work, visit: https://www.terc.edu/profiles/smirla -ramos-montanez/.

Beth Redmond-Jones

Beth Redmond-Jones is the vice president of exhibitions and facilities at the Monterey Bay Aquarium. Prior to her current position, she was the vice president of engagement and education at the San Diego Natural History Museum (TheNat). Beth is an accomplished and award-winning museum professional with extensive experience in exhibitions, master and strategic planning, museum programming, facilities operations, and financial management. Under her leadership, exhibition and digital teams have won numerous awards, including the American Alliance of Museum's (AAM) Excellence in Exhibition Competition, AAM's Sustainability Excellence Award, AAM's Excellence in Label Writing Award, AAM's Media and Technology MUSE Award, and the Balboa Park Sustainability Award.

Beth holds a master's degree in museum studies from John F. Kennedy University and a bachelor's degree in art history from the University of New Hampshire. She served on the board of the National Association for Museum Exhibition, a professional interest group of AAM, and AAM's 2019 and 2020 National Program Committee. In 2006, Beth was recognized by the convergence of Museum Talent Project as a next-generation leader who demonstrates creativity and innovation in leadership, learning, and organizational change. She has been actively exploring how museums can more effectively serve those with hidden disabilities, especially autism and sensory processing challenges.

Anna Schwarz

Anna Schwarz is the head of school and teacher programs at the Skirball Cultural Center in Los Angeles. In this role, she collaborates with an ensemble of full and part-time educators to create, implement, and evaluate in-person and online programming for teachers and students in grades pre-K–12. Programs include gallery tours, in-school residencies, live performances, and a year-long teacher professional development series focused on introducing educators to arts-integration teaching techniques that foster students' critical thinking, creative problem-solving, collaboration, and civic literacy skills. Along with her team, Anna's work focuses on creating experiences that reflect the Skirball's mission, connect our audiences to arts and culture, to history and the world, and most of all, to one another. Anna holds a BA in translation and pedagogy from College of Foreign Language Teachers at John Paul II Catholic University of Lublin, Poland. Prior to her work in museums, Anna was a German language teacher in Poland's public schools.

Hallie Scott

Currently the specialist, university audiences, at the Hammer Museum, Dr. Hallie Scott is committed to facilitating programs that center the goals and ideas of young people and that generate exchange and learning between educators. Her previous experience includes overseeing teen programs as an education specialist at the J. Paul Getty Museum; working as the education director at the Wassaic

Project, a contemporary art center and residency in Dutchess County, New York; and teaching art history courses as a teaching fellow at Brooklyn College. She has a PhD in modern and contemporary art history from City University of New York, Graduate Center, and wrote her dissertation on artists, architects, and dancers who developed experimental education initiatives in the 1960s and 1970s. Hallie presently serves on the editorial board for *Viewfinder: Reflecting on Museum Education* e-journal and is the 2019–2021 Community Engagement Chair for Museum Educators of Southern California.

Julie Smith

Julie Smith is a human-centered continuous improvement specialist and co-founder of Community Design Partners (CDP). Her background as a K–12 teacher and administrator inspired her curiosity and passion for meaningful, community-centered change. She is driven by the desire to disrupt the root causes of inequities caused by white supremacy. Julie founded Community Design Partners as a place to center empathy as a mindset and practice through work with philanthropic organizations, school districts, state and county agencies, and youth development organizations. CDP is currently working on a student-powered improvement project that supports organizations to empathize with those they serve with the end goal of empowering youth and families to lead the change that is needed.

Theresa Sotto

Theresa Sotto is a museum educator, arts education advocate, and writer who is passionate about arts learning initiatives grounded in social justice and inclusive practices. She has worked at the crossroads of education, equity, and the arts for over twenty years. In her current role as associate director of academic programs at the Hammer Museum, Theresa oversees educational programming for university, family, and K–12 school audiences. She also coleads the Hammer's internal diversity and inclusion group, which initiates strategies for embedding inclusive practices in the museum's work. Prior to joining the Hammer, she worked at the Getty Museum, the University of Arizona Poetry Center, and the John F. Kennedy Center for the Performing Arts. Theresa's curricula and programs work have received honors and awards from the American Alliance of Museums, the California Association of Museums, and the Best in Heritage global conference. She frequently leads trainings for museum professionals on implicit bias and privilege awareness, and she has presented across the United States on topics related to inclusive gallery teaching, innovative programming models, and diversity and inclusion initiatives.

Rachel Stark

Rachel Stark is currently the director of education at the Skirball Cultural Center in Los Angeles where she oversees the development and implementation of award-winning cross-generational programs designed to spark imagination, foster empathy, and encourage civic engagement. Prior to her time at the Skirball, she played key roles in the Education Department at the Los Angeles County Museum of Art (LACMA) for more than a decade. Stark has served on the board of the Museum Educators of Southern California and presented at the American Alliance of Museums and the National Art Education Association conferences about dynamic approaches to working with adult learners using co-expertise models. She is a published author who has contributed to the *Journal of Museum Education* and other arts and museum education publications. Stark holds a BA in history/art history from the University of California, Los Angeles, and an MSEd in museum education leadership from Bank Street College of Education.

Teresa Valencia

Teresa Valencia is the virtual field trips coordinator at the Ohio History Connection where she creates virtual experiences for youth focused on cultural inclusivity and social justice. From 2016–2020, she served as the director of curation and education for Iolani Palace. There she managed the restoration efforts of the Palace and its royal collections, developed new exhibits and partnerships, as well as expanded the Palace's educational outreach in the community. Before joining Iolani Palace, Teresa held various education, research, and outreach positions at the Asian Art Museum in San Francisco, Golden Gate National Parks Conservancy, Maidu Museum, and the California State Indian Museum. Teresa received her museum studies MA as well as an MBA from John F Kennedy University. Her thesis work focused on the need for cultural competency in the museum field. She has presented at several local and regional conferences on this subject. She currently lives in Ohio with her husband Joe and two sons, Aiden and Matthew.

Lauren Zalut

Lauren Zalut works as director of education and tour programs at Eastern State Penitentiary Historic Site. In this role she oversees education programs, guided tours, and leads family and school programming. Using the historic site as a catalyst for conversation on contemporary social issues, Lauren has worked with the education team to incorporate dialogue facilitation, lived experience in prison, and content about mass incarceration into guided programs. She has led Eastern State's fair chance hiring initiative, recruiting and hiring formerly incarcerated people in a variety of roles. Throughout her career she has initiated collaborative programs between grass-roots organizations, social service agencies, and museums. This includes her work co-teaching museum studies graduate course *Prototyping for Community Engagement* and as museum educator and communications coordinator at the Wagner Free Institute of Science, where she launched partnerships like the science café, Science on Tap, and the Philadelphia Honey Festival.

Lauren earned a master's degree in museum education from the University of the Arts and a bachelor's degree in art with a concentration in visual studies from Tyler School of Art at Temple University. She is also trained to teach college courses in correctional facilities through the Inside-Out Prison Exchange Program at Temple University. Lauren believes that museums can be spaces that create social change, and she works to design inspiring, accessible, and transformative visitor experiences. She lives with her husband, son, and chickens in Philadelphia.